MAKING HUMANS

NEW RIVERSIDE EDITIONS

Series Editor for the British Volumes
Alan Richardson

For a complete listing of our American and British New Riverside Editions, visit our web site at **http://college.hmco.com.**

NEW RIVERSIDE EDITIONS
Series Editor for the British Volumes
Alan Richardson, Boston College

Making Humans

Complete Texts with Introduction
Historical Contexts   •   Critical Essays

MARY SHELLEY, Frankenstein

H. G. WELLS, The Island of Doctor Moreau

Edited by Judith Wilt

BOSTON COLLEGE

Houghton Mifflin Company
BOSTON   •   NEW YORK

Sponsoring Editor: Michael Gillespie
Editorial Associate: Bruce Cantley
Associate Project Editor: Martha Rogers
Editorial Assistant: Reba Frederics
Cover Design Manager: Diana Coe
Manufacturing Manager: Florence Cadran
Marketing Manager: Cindy Graff Cohen

Cover image: © Bill Lisenby/Corbis

Credits appear on page 360 which is a continuation of the copyright page.

Printed in the U.S.A.

Library of Congress Control Number: 2001133337
ISBN: 0-618-08489-4
1   2   3   4   5   6   7   8   9-FFG-06   05   04   03   02

CONTENTS

ABOUT THIS SERIES
Alan Richardson

The Riverside imprint, stamped on a book's spine or printed on its title page, carries a special aura for anyone who loves and values books. As well it might: by the middle of the nineteenth century, Houghton Mifflin had already established the "Riverside" edition as an important presence in American publishing. The Riverside series of British poets brought trustworthy editions of Milton and Wordsworth, Spenser and Pope, and (then) lesser-known writers like Herbert, Vaughan, and Keats to a growing nation of readers. There was both a Riverside Shakespeare and a Riverside Chaucer by the century's end, titles that would be revived and recreated as the authoritative editions of the late twentieth century. Riverside editions of writers like Emerson, Hawthorne, Longfellow, and Thoreau helped establish the first canon of American literature. Early in the twentieth century, the Cambridge editions published by Houghton Mifflin at the Riverside Press made the complete works of dozens of British and American poets widely available in single-volume editions that can still be found in libraries and homes throughout the United States and beyond.

The Riverside Editions of the 1950s and 1960s brought attractive, affordable, and carefully edited versions of a range of British and American titles into the thriving new market for serious paperback literature. Prepared by leading scholars and critics of the time, the Riversides rapidly became known for their lively introductions, reliable texts, and lucid annotation. Though aimed primarily at the college market, the series was also created (as one editor put it) with the "general reader's private library" in mind. These were paperbacks to hold on to and read again, and many a "private" library was seeded with the colorful spines of Riverside editions kept long after graduation.

Houghton Mifflin's New Riverside Editions now bring the combination of high editorial values and wide popular appeal long associated with the Riverside imprint into line with the changing needs and desires of twenty-first-century students and general readers. Inaugurated in 2000 with the first set of American titles under the general editorship of Paul Lauter, the New Riversides reflect both the changing canons of literature in English and the greater emphases on historical and cultural context that have helped a new generation of critics to extend and reenliven literary studies. The Series is not only concerned with keeping the classic works of British and American literature alive, but grows as well out of the excitement that a broader range of literary texts and cultural reference points has brought to the classroom. Works by formerly marginalized authors, including women writers and writers of color, will find a place in the series along with titles from the traditional canons that a succession of Riverside imprints helped establish beginning a century and a half ago. New Riverside titles will reflect the recent surge of interest in the connections among literary activity, historical change, and social and political issues, including slavery, abolition, and the construction of "race"; gender relations and the history of sexuality; the rise of the British empire and of nationalism on both sides of the Atlantic; and changing conceptions of nature and of the human.

The New Riverside Editions respond to recent changes in literary studies not only in the range of titles but also in the design of individual volumes. Issues and debates crucial to a book's author and original audience find voice in selections from contemporary writings of many kinds as well as in early reactions and reviews. Some volumes will place contemporary writers into dialogue, as with the pairing of Irish national tales by Maria Edgeworth and Sydney Owenson or of vampire stories by Bram Stoker and Sheridan Le Fanu. Other volumes provide alternative ways of constructing literary tradition, for instance juxtaposing Byron's *The Giaour,* an "Eastern Tale" in verse, with Frances Sheridan's *Nourjahad* and William Beckford's *Vathek,* its most important predecessors in Orientalist prose fiction. Chronologies, selections from major criticism, notes on textual history, and bibliographies will allow readers to go beyond the text and explore a given writer or issue in greater depth. Seasoned critics will find fresh new contexts and juxtapositions, and general readers will find intriguing new material to read alongside familiar titles in an attractive format.

Houghton Mifflin's New Riverside Editions maintain the values of reliability and readability that have marked the Riverside name for well over a century. Each volume also provides something new — often unexpected — and each in a distinctive way. Freed from the predictable monotony and rigidity of a set template, editors can build their volumes around the special opportunities presented by a given title or set of related works. We hope that the resulting blend of innovative scholarship, creative format, and high production values will help the Riverside imprint continue to thrive well into the new century.

INTRODUCTION
Judith Wilt

Twentieth-century science crossed the dateline into the third millennium, announcing it now had a blueprint for the human genome and the technology to clone a human. It was a pivotal moment in a desired and dreaded trajectory whose central imaginative focus, in Western thought at least, remains Mary Shelley's 1818 novel *Frankenstein*. H. G. Wells's 1896 novel *The Island of Doctor Moreau* is a lesser-known point in this trajectory. Yet gathering these two texts for the first time into one volume spotlights an important and sometimes overlooked aspect of the more famous story. Both texts belong generally among stories of the rogue intellect self-punished; *Frankenstein*, especially in its later critical and film readings, has a place among stories of invented "mechanical" beings. But the novels together actually emphasize the nineteenth century's deep concern with the entanglement of humanity in the flesh; with philosophical, political, scientific, and medical articulations of the body; with the body's miraculous and tragic making of humans, making of itself human; with the body's uncanny replication of itself in time and extension of itself in space, and its mysterious drives toward transcendence.

Jean Baudrillard's dense and eclectic study of *Simulacra and Simulation* musters a huge spectrum of such replication and extension, charting humanity's progressive alienation from its body. There are, he reminds us, prostheses as well as offspring, doubles and miniatures, shadows and phantoms, models and maps, machines and systems, not to mention all the vast phenomena of "representation," from two-dimensional words and images, talking cartoons and moving pictures, to the three-dimensional bad-faith resemblances of the clone, and the hologram, and every cultural critic's favorite scarecrow, Disneyland. In such a world, what becomes of the concept of reality, and that concept's handmaids of "value" and "meaning"? And why do we pursue this trajectory away from the real body? The most menacing answer comes from the former Disneyland animatronics expert who is the villain of Brian Forbes's 1975 film version of Ira Levin's Gothic novel *The Stepford Wives*: "Because we *can*."

Frankenstein and *The Island of Doctor Moreau* keep company, for sure, with Enlightenment rationalism and contemporary science, and their imaginative cousins of the dark sublime, Gothic and speculative fiction. But they are also quintessentially of the nineteenth century, reflecting both the "romantic" potency of Erasmus Darwin's imaginable Nature and the equally wonderworking but imperviously unpredictable Nature delivered to high Victorian science and imagination by his grandson Charles.

They reflect too the concerns immortalized in the yearnings of Tennyson's troubled midcentury poem "In Memoriam." The poem's initial lament is of a nature indifferent to the meaning of one's own outrageously dead friend. Nature may be, in all her variety and ingenuity, moving experimentally toward "higher things" but cannot afford to care for any one human she has made, not your mother, not your friend: "So careful of the type she seems, / So careless of the single life." In Mary Shelley's tale, Victor Frankenstein gathers flesh from many dead individuals to create the prototype of a new, larger, hardier species, and Tennyson's speaker dreams his poem will reincarnate his friend as the prototype of a higher race.

Nearly forty years after *The Origin of Species*, three decades after Thomas Huxley debated Bishop Wilberforce on whether his grandfather was an ape, the readers of H. G. Wells's tales hear all around them the even darker terror of Tennyson's speaker: nature actually cares for nothing, acts randomly, makes no distinctions of "higher and lower." And humankind, which insists that its own ethical and creative consciousness does make such meaning, is in this very respect "a monster, a dream, a discord" in nature. Wells's Doctor Moreau duplicates this picture of nature; as his visitor Prendick sees it, only "unspeakable aimlessness" characterizes Moreau's surgical experiments on animal types, and a contempt for the human paradoxically drives his efforts to make humans out of pigs, pumas, rabbits, and, of course, apes.

In 1818, Mary Shelley could subtitle her fable "the Modern Prometheus," self-consciously placing within classic and pedagogical myth the story of a scientist driven to create and certain of his capacity to handle fire. Both Victor Frankenstein and his creature could qualify for the role of Prometheus; they are related not only to the heroes and overreachers of classic and romantic drama, but also to the evolving hero of realistic novels, the sensitive and eager young man from the provinces whose quest to maturity entices him to some fell purpose of modernity in which he is ground up or burned, leaving, however, an elevating spark for the contemplative observer. It is a young story for a young century.

In 1896, Wells pickled his fable in Swiftian satire: the narrator sailed out on the *Lady Vain* and returned in a boat belonging to the schooner *Ipecacuanha*. The "man-making" conducted on Noble's isle by the notorious vivisector Doctor Moreau was varied, here and there, by the "manufacture" of "things," as chance dictated—pure research proceeding not according to goal but according to the random imagination: "was this possible, or that possible? [. . .] You cannot imagine the delight of these strange, colourless intellectual desires." "An exercise in youthful blasphemy" Wells called it in his preface to a 1933 edition of several of his stories (see Parrinder, 243, in the Works Cited section of this text).

Between these two dates, between the flamboyant ambition to create and the colorless desire to manufacture, between Shelley's urgent scientist-God and Wells's indifferent experimenter, lies a century of heated speculation about the nature of the human, the limits and promises of the proliferating natural sciences, and the capacity of the imagination to sustain meanings for the human. Both of these intensely readable and disturbing tales raise scientific and political questions around the related concepts of species and race, and stage debates about education, law, gender, language, and community. Though the reader will encounter in one the elevated diction and romantic feeling of the first years of the nineteenth century and in the other the sometimes savagely naturalistic diction and skepticism of the waning years, these tales are the same story in one further respect. When they are playing God, or nature, creating and manufacturing their children, Victor Frankenstein and Doctor Moreau both see them as human: when those children gaze back at them, as both independent and dependent beings, they abandon them as "unhuman."

* * * *

Mary Shelley was born in 1797 in London to two of the century's most creative and progressive thinkers, William Godwin, author of *An Enquiry Concerning Political Justice* (1793), and Mary Wollstonecraft, author of *A Vindication of the Rights of Woman* (1792). She grew up listening to the animated conversation of writers, scientists, and political activists. When she eloped with and eventually married the poet Percy Bysshe Shelley in 1814–16, she continued that self-education in the Shelley-Byron circle of artists, physicians, and rebels. She wrote *Frankenstein* in 1816–17 within the nourishing but also complex, constraining hospitality of that circle and continued to write and publish novels, biographies, and travel narratives until her death in 1851. Like *Frankenstein*, they explore the distresses of women and the rise and fall of political and social idealism, sometimes with chilling or sympathetic effect. But nothing she wrote afterward quite matches the impact of this compact tale, so imaginatively gruesome, so intellectually ambitious that readers can still scarcely credit a young girl of under twenty with its creation.

For the circles in which Mary Shelley moved, science, art, and politics were the unified toolkit of a revolutionary new birth at which they were assisting, a new world of freedom and equality, making (and made by) the new human being of natural passion and purity emerging from the imagination of eighteenth-century social, moral, and above all, natural philosophy. Linnaeus's *System of Nature* (1735) had mapped the location of the human in terms of its continuities with other species of mammalian primates, and had newly framed an old debate about the nature of the human, its innate or acquired characteristics. In the public sphere, global exploration and imperial ideology fueled sometimes toxic speculations on the links among races on the imagined ladder of progressively better-made humans.

And in the private sphere, education philosophers, from Jean Jacques Rousseau to the Godwins and their daughter, conducted in the safety of writing what Roger Shattuck has called "the forbidden experiment": to isolate, observe, and reconstruct the "natural" human being. Shattuck's fascinating account of the efforts of doctors to understand and educate the "wild boy" found living abandoned (but self-educated to survive) in the forest near the town of Aveyron in 1800 suggests that much of the educated community's interest in such cases was grounded in the desire for a license of some sort, at last, to conduct this forbidden experiment.

Closer to home, the ideas of two scientist-poets would be the key to the emergence of *Frankenstein*. In 1802, the chemist-anatomist Humphry Davy began a famous series of lectures, demonstrations, and publications that consolidated a theory of matter as electrically charged atoms. Pursuing the basis of the electrochemical motions of the body along these lines, he excited the educated world with speculations about the capacity of science to touch, and even manipulate, the springs of the "vital force" itself, an excitement increased that same year by the headline-making experiments of Luigi Galvini. As Iwan Rhys Morus has compellingly shown, the spectacular successes of Davy, and later his assistant Michael Farraday, helped produce a culture around the new science whose theatricalism was both scientifically necessary — to make visible the invisible force and "fluid" under study — and ideologically central to the scientific humanism then emerging around the beneficial control of nature. It was this too-confident humanism that *Frankenstein* would challenge.

Meanwhile, the botanist Erasmus Darwin, in works published between 1789 and 1803, popularized the first strands of a theory of gradualist perfectabilitarian evolution — sea to land, plant toward human, "imitation" toward rational and creative volition—allowing indeed for cycles of improvement and degeneration but emphasizing everywhere the promise of a luminous renewability in an ever-plastic and electrically fluid matter:

> Hence when a Monarch or a mushroom dies,
> Awhile extinct the organic matter lies,
> But, as a few short hours or years revolve;
> Alchemic powers the changing mass dissolve. [. . .]
> The wrecks of Death are but a change of forms;
> Emerging matter from the grave returns,
> Feels new desires, with new sensations burns [. . .]

> The Temple of Nature (1803), Canto IV, 382–5, 398–400

For Erasmus Darwin the new-desiring body emerges from the grave at the benign volition of timely nature, her rich alchemy combining new molecules within hours, and new plants and animals and finally humans over the years. And nature evolves ever-more complex technologies of "making" as well, from dimly spontaneous generation, through single-organism replication and hermaphrodite coupling, to the sexual intercourse that produces, through its counterpointing of infinitely variable male and female, "the most perfect orders of animals," (E. Darwin 37) culminating in the poetry of parenting and the "sympathetic society" (40) whose crowning achievement is the "human."

The intuition here is a grand synthesis of all the forces of universal "making": from the acids and alkalis, to the planets and stars, to the bodies of humans, what attracts and repels also generates. What the scientist Benjamin Franklin calls Positive and Negative, Darwin muses, let us call vitreous and resinous electrical ethers, (66) or "for greater ease of conversing on this subject, let us call these two ethers . . . the masculine and the feminine ethers" (76).

The 1831 introduction to *Frankenstein* mentions Erasmus Darwin's influence only for his reported (but probably apocryphal) electrical stimulation of a piece of vermicelli to voluntary motion. But contemporary scholars, led by Anne Mellor, have pinpointed this collaborative bow to evolutionary time and this centering of the human on the sympathetic intercourse of male and female bodies and forces as the real contribution of the first Darwin to the nineteenth century's first and still most influential analysis of the making of humans. For Erasmus Darwin, the "solitary generation" of the sort Victor Frankenstein pursues is primitive, vastly inferior to the heterosexual reproduction for which his paradoxically more natural creature yearns, a bane to the "sympathetic society" that is both the cause and effect of the human. Feminist critical readings (see Gilbert and Gubar, Chapter 7, and Mellor in the Works Cited section of this book) as well as

Marxist (see Moretti, Chapter 3) and postcolonialist (see Spivak) critics, have found fertile analytic territory in the way the individual or the community can seem alternately to be artificial or monstrous in the novel's kaleidoscope of the human. And those who study the role of the nineteenth-century novel itself in the making of humans, that is, reading humans, have put *Frankenstein* back where it belongs in the tradition of the novel itself (see Levine, Chapter 2, and Stewart, Chapter 5).

While the natural philosophers were experimenting with the interaction of matter and motion, the body and its "spark of life," the moral philosophers were continuing their interrogation of the interaction between matter and mind, the body and its self-consciousness. The theory of this interaction, ancient as Greek philosophy, is suffering and its fulcrum is pain: consciousness as matter's response to the stimulus of pain. The management of the response refines consciousness to ever-higher registers of complexity, so that in the further precincts of Cartesian dualism, the mastering mind may almost contemplate itself free of the body. But a natural wariness of this untethering is evident, for instance, in Edmund Burke's influential 1757 *Enquiry on the Origin of our Ideas of the Sublime and the Beautiful*, which recognizes pain and terror as the sharpest sensations of the body's consciousness, and praises the "sublime" experiences of solitude, obscurity, and magnitude — as the root of consciousness, the origin of representation of the self to the self, and the origin of art, the representation of this representation.

Gothic fiction is a powerful form of this representation. Horace Walpole's *The Castle of Otranto* (1765) featured the armored fragments of a gigantic body that crushed or incarcerated the flesh while it solicited the overreaching mind of its outlaw hero Manfred. The fascination of the early English Gothic with the torturers of the Inquisition was an oblique tribute to the science as well as the aesthetics of the management of pain and terror. Wells's readers will find the tribute directly stated in the chilling chapter called "Doctor Moreau Explains." The portrait of religious professionals who imagine they are licensed by a torturing deity to conduct "the forbidden experiment" on a series of bodies terrorized in a pain-bath into hyperconsciousness prepares the way for the Gothic figure of the licensed professionals of electricity demonstrations and the vivisecting laboratory.

Mary Shelley's novel largely obscures the physical sufferings of the no doubt hideously pained body of the monster, and of his murdered victims, the better to allow the remorseful Victor Frankenstein to claim the consciousness-making privilege of pain. The sufferings of this responsible spectator of torture and death are described with a physician's careful attention to blood pressure, temperature changes, and nerve and lung convulsions — all meant as a cunning guide to the evoked experience of that other willing and responsible perpetrator and spectator of these tortures, the writer and the reader.

The creature's awakening to the invasion of pain "on all sides" (page 84) enters him into competition with the suffering creator. Looking at the wornout and postconscious body of Victor at the end, the creature feels an envy but also a curious access of power. His own body, it seems, is of a magnitude beyond the natural shocks that flesh is heir to, and so therefore is his suffering, and his consciousness. In an unimaginable arctic solitude, he decides he will go to work on this body, unmaking it down to ashes. This pain may reverse the evolution that produced him, but the thrust of the story suggests rather another, more obscure stage in the series of his still human being, attuned by the pain of the fire to a deeper consciousness, a new form of thinking: "my spirit will sleep in peace, or if it thinks, it will not surely think thus" (page 171).

*   *   *   *

In the half-century between the work of Erasmus Darwin and that of his grandson Charles, the geologists, physicists, and paleontologists hollowed out a vast space–time continuum, a cosmic evolution within which an experimenting planet earth could conduct the organic evolution that goes to the making of humans. In 1831, as Mary Shelley revised *Frankenstein* to a more fatalistic perspective on a less knowable universe, Charles Darwin set sail on the *Beagle* to make and ponder the observations that would be published in 1859 as *The Origin of Species*. Charles Lyell's 1830–33 *Principles of Geology* both enlarged the domain of evolution and opened a dangerous window on the mutability, the chance-wrought extinction of species. In 1844, Robert Chambers's *The Vestiges of the Natural History of Creation* burst upon an increasingly science-literate and debate-sharpened Victorian public. In the words of historian G. M. Young, this book "issued in elaborate secrecy and attributed by a wild surmise to Prince Albert, was a national sensation; translated into golden verses by Tennyson, evolution almost became a national creed" (74).

Charles Darwin rather hedged his bets about how the dynamic exposed in *Origins* applied to the natural making and cultural remaking of humans, but the golden verses of "In Memoriam" faced the prospect, trusting, if faintly, the larger hope of ongoing spiritual evolution. And so did the speeches and essays of "Darwin's bulldog," Thomas Henry Huxley. Within months of the publication of *Origins*, Huxley claimed the intelligent ape as his grandfather in a famous Oxford debate, and in a series of brilliant essays and books from the 1864 *Man's Place in Nature* through the 1893 *Evolution and Ethics*, this brilliant teacher and writer became a primary cultural spokesperson and interpreter of the enigmatic interaction between the "cosmic process" and the "ethical process" that went into the making of humans.

Huxley recognized this interaction was no gentle meshing but an often frightful grinding of gears. The golden rule, Erasmus Darwin's poetry of parenting and sympathetic society, has now been put in its place in nature by the iron laws of cosmic process articulated by Thomas Malthus, Charles Darwin, and Lord Kelvin governing population, resources, the struggle for existence, and the squandering of heat energy by matter in action. The protagonist of Thomas Hardy's *Jude the Obscure* discovers in shock that "what was good for God's gardeners was bad for God's birds" (15). Worse still, the Prolegomenon to Huxley's *Evolution and Ethics* argues, the inhabitants of the garden of civil society must disconnect their emotional kinship not only with blackbirds and slugs and toads but with other human "trespassers" as well. Huxley's brightest pupil, H. G. Wells, learned the lesson.

Born in 1866 in the soon-to-be-industrial suburb of Bromley, Wells was an ambitious teenager who rejected both the feckless passivity of his low-earning, cricket-playing father and the punitive Christianity and yearnings after gentility of his managing mother. But his inchoate sense of resistant freethinking crystallized only after he won a scholarship to the Normal School of Science in London and spent a year listening to Thomas Huxley's lectures, educated, shaped, even, as Norman and Joanne MacKenzie suggest, "bewitched" (57) by the figure of the great science educator. What Huxley provided, the MacKenzies propose, was a way both to create with and to critique the scientific and the religious imagination that his culture had stimulated in him. Both the first Darwin and the later Darwin's first popularizers had given a benign spin to the evolutionary process, as if humanist progress had simply replaced divine purpose in a still human-friendly universe. But the Huxleyan universe was edgier, deeply strange, in fact, and attuned as never before to the processes of estrangement, extinction, and exhaustion on the far side of the cycles of nature. It was a scientific vision for an age whose spirit and study in philosophy, social politics, and art focused increasingly on degeneration. Mary Shelley's *Frankenstein* had moralized on the likely degeneration of human morality if improperly parented, but fin de siècle degeneration theory, as William Greenslade's 1994 study charts it, uncovered and anticipated a reversal of cosmic process, starting with the backsliding not of the soul, but the body, the race, the planet, and time itself.

By turns eerily energetic and morosely self-lacerating, hopeful and despairing, the spirit of the age made room for passionate expansion and experiment—and also the terror attendant on what Freud would recognize as the return of the repressed after a strenuously imposed Victorian adulthood. Max Nordau's all too eagerly received 1895 book *Degeneration,* on the other hand, posited a species-body rapidly aging, too fatigued by the century's new pace of discovery to combat the microorganisms of mysticism, hysteria, imitation, sensation-craving, and other parasites that the well body hosts without damage (527).

A host of vivid scenes in popular novels recorded the titillating reversions that grounded the perversions of the time. Ayesha in H. Rider Haggard's *She* (1887) was reincarnated in youthful splendor, only to shrivel into an object both wizened in age and simian in shape. Robert Louis Stevenson's Dr Jekyll (1886) reversed under chemical persuasion into the imp-and-ape-like Mr. Hyde. Wilde's Dorian Gray, the living picture of beautiful manhood, transferred the magnitude and solitude and obscurity of his true evolution to the dark sublime of his hidden portrait (1890). In this company, H. G. Wells made his international name between 1895 and 1897 with three parables of mad scientists helpless against or complicit with the devolving universe and a humankind in the unmaking: the species broken in half and cooling off with the dying sun of *The Time Machine*; not just hiding but disappearing in *The Invisible Man*; and relaxing to its creeping, biting, barking origins in *The Island of Doctor Moreau,* whose bloody shambles of a laboratory exactly matches the "filthy workshop of creation" imagined by Mary Shelley 78 years before.

Wells actually wrote references to *Frankenstein* into the first draft of the fable about "beast people" he had been imagining perhaps even since *Gulliver's Travels* captured his imagination as a teenager. The 1894 draft shows Moreau himself fishing the apparently dead body of the narrator Prendick out of the sea because he is "piqued by death" and pondering some reanimating techniques. Since Prendick recovers on his own, he becomes simply a "bother" to the scientist (see Philmus, 105). In the entirely rewritten version published in 1896, however, Wells has adjusted the focus of the fable to a different transformation. The great anatomist Moreau, in his sublime maturity, is no more interested in the Gothic foolishness of reanimation than the matured Victor Frankenstein is in the Gothic foolishness of alchemy. He is not even interested in the wicked surgical degenerative transformation of humans into animals, as the terrified Prendick first fears after a brief glimpse of the bloody figure on Moreau's lab table. He is dedicated, like all good experimentors, including nature herself, to making humans—excise and graft, cut and paste, transfix and train: "I wanted to find the extreme limit of plasticity in a living shape. . . . I will make a rational creature of my own" (pages 225 and 228).

Moreau asserts that it's only by chance he has chosen the human form as the limit case for plasticity and rationality, a necessary logic for a Darwinian agnostic. Postcolonial critics see Moreau as another imperialist importer of educational disciplines to the primitive races with dark skins. And readers may also recognize a post-Marxian picture of class struggle here, vividly particularized in Coral Lansbury's 1985 study of English working-class revulsion over vivisection as a new form of the educated classes' aggression upon the bodies of the poor—an aggression first associated with body-snatching dissecting doctors like, well, Victor Frankenstein.

A more directly Frankensteinian reading would suggest that Moreau wishes to evade the "natural" reproduction of humanity through commerce with heterosexuality and the body. Moreau's life is an emphatically bachelor one in the revised version, and it seems no accident that the subject of the project underway, the creature that finally ends the experiment and the experimenter, is female. Or that the agonized creatures from Moreau's laboratory recognize an important difference between Moreau and the degraded assistant Montgomery, and the newly arrived and appalled Prendick. All three are men, all three hold the "whip" of reason, but one of them walks weeping into the sea from which he came, one of them "bleeds and weeps" (page 234) and has a body. Moreau and Montgomery wield the surgical and chemical apparatus in the house of pain, and the educational inoculations of rules and punishments of postoperative treatment, having consciously severed themselves from the body and its illuminating pain. As such, they seem to the beast people to be immortal beings, neither made nor unmakable. But Prendick, bleeding and weeping, seems like themselves, "made," an inexact motley being, the one who is many, an always reversible equation.

In the end, however, the novel's picture of "the human" eludes even its maker. As the "ethical process" of Wells's story depicts it, the making of humans in *Moreau*, as in *Frankenstein*, is or ought to be an exercise in community, where the energies of sexual and social commerce, family feeling and companionate work, can check as well as inspire pure creaturely desire. But the final pages of both novels make it clear that humankind is also *unheimlich*, uncanny, not the measure of the human being. The human being's place is in the cosmic process too, at the extremes of Burke's Gothic "magnitude," in *Frankenstein*'s winds and waves, in *Moreau*'s winds and stars.

At the end, the narrator of *The Island of Doctor Moreau* recommends the humane companionship of "wise books" (page 268) but rare is the twenty-first-century reader who comes to these texts without the prior acquaintance of film treatments of one or both. None reproduce the novel faithfully, of course; filmmakers invent according to their medium, their generation, not to mention their budget. James Whale's 1930s *Frankenstein* films subtract the arctic sublime and add the pursuing mobs and the electrified bride. Hammer Films's 1957 *Curse of Frankenstein* offered not just a monomaniac but a murderous Victor. The 1994 version from Kenneth Branagh, whose creature fisted the beating heart from the body of Elizabeth Frankenstein, went the distance of fashionable special effects. *The Island of Lost Souls* (1932) offers the gimlet-eyed Charles Laughton as a voyeuristic Moreau in an elegantly chiaroscuro jungle like *Paradise Lost*. The 1977 version, with Bert Lancaster's earnest scientist next door, is well lit and not Gothic, while John Frankenheimer's 1996 film stars Marlon Brando in an elegant fantasia of freaks. Little remains of the nineteenth century's philosophical and satirical seriousness in these adaptations, which are keyed to the scenic staging of the punishment of the overreacher. Indeed, it might be argued that to recover in the genre of film the true depth of the "making humans" argument in *Frankenstein* and *The Island of Doctor Moreau*, we must go to the more subtle realizations of the "artificial person" in the *Alien* and *Terminator* films, in Ridley Scott's *Blade Runner* and Steven Spielberg's *A.I.*, and the unnerving new world of digitally created film-humans.

A NOTE ON THE TEXTS
Judith Wilt

The canons of good editorial practice used to hold that the best text was the one that incorporated the author's final vision/revision. Increasingly, however, practice favors the "first" text, true to its cultural and biographical context, rather than a later, authorized text, in which the writer is often at work "modernizing" the original child of his or her brain. And of course the best practice would be to provide all texts and variations, with the editor favoring none among them. This volume reprints the first text of each of these novels, the 1818 edition of *Frankenstein*, published in London by Lackington, Hughes, Harding, Mavor and Jones, and the 1896 English edition of *The Island of Doctor Moreau*, published in London by William Heinemann. The frontispiece accompanying *Moreau* is from this edition; the frontispiece accompanying *Frankenstein* is from the 1831 edition published in London by H. Colburn and R. Bentley.

*   *   *   *

Frankenstein first emerged as a brief ghost story in the summer of 1816, product of a cowriting or competitive writing game among friends looking for an evening's entertainment. Urged by her husband, Mary Shelley then developed her story into a novel with ties to the eighteenth-century epistolary tradition, a heavy dose of the Romantic sublime, and a significant editorial/stylistic contribution from Percy Shelley, including a preface describing the origin of the tale in private amusement. This 1818 edition was supplanted in 1831 by a revised edition in the one-volume form, popular at the time, in which Mary Shelley, widowed, disillusioned, and financially troubled, remoralized the complex, aggressive, and in some ways contradictory Victor Frankenstein into the victim of an indifferent and mechanical universe.

Modern scholarship on the text of *Frankenstein* begins with James Rieger's 1974 edition for Bobbs-Merrill Co. (reprinted by the University of Chicago Press in 1982), which urgently introduced the issue of Percy Shelley's collaborative and perhaps even "authoritative" hand in reading and making corrections in the first edition. Anne K. Mellor's still central critical biography of 1988 included an appendix on Percy's revisions and contributions, stressing the improvements in diction and coherence in a way that, as Charles Robinson remarks, inadvertently gave more credit to Percy than Mellor intended. Mellor's extraordinarily clear and accessible treatment of the revisions in her 1990 contribution to the MLA-published *Approaches to Teaching Frankenstein* corrected this impression.

Still more influential was Mellor's chapter about Mary Shelley's own revisions in the 1831 edition, drawing attention to changes that deepen the earlier version's rhetoric of fatalism and destiny, and both soften the incestuous edge of the relationship between Victor and Elizabeth and subtly renege on the implied hope that the loving bourgeois family can resist the forces that threaten it (173–76). The intellectual and literary historian Marilyn Butler has continued the study of this important issue. Her Oxford World Classics edition of 1994 reprints the key passages which demonstrate that the later edition gives Victor Frankenstein a more admirable and ideal and explicitly more religious consciousness. In 1996, Garland Press issued, as volumes IX and X of its reprint series of *The Manuscripts of the Younger Romantics,* a full scale facsimile of *The "Frankenstein" Notebooks,* including the available draft manuscripts, typescript with handwritten alterations, and the text of the 1818 edition edited by Charles E. Robinson. I've made grateful use of all these sources for text and notes.

*   *   *   *

H. G. Wells began writing a tale called "Mourget," then "Doctor Moreau," in late 1894. In this version, of which the Wells Collection at the University of Illinois has 112 consecutive handwritten pages, the vivisecting surgeon had a wife who longs for the intellectual comforts of London, and a child who likes to kill flies. In this draft, Wells first wrote in and then deleted two references to *Frankenstein.* Robert Philmus believes that the tale was originally longer than the 112 pages of this manuscript, which ends at the bottom of a page with the startlingly apt but unfortunately not surviving remark from Moreau's assistant Montgomery that he'd like to go back to London to see the paintings in the newly built National Gallery of Art because, unlike his colleague and the beast people, "the people in pictures *are* human beings" (Philmus 137).

Wells abandoned this draft after a few months and began a new one on the same theme, eventually published in 1896, that sharpens the concept away from the Gothic puzzle motif that framed the first version and toward the Swiftian satire and Huxleyan debate it now represents. He also created for it an "introduction," written by the narrator's nephew, Charles Edward Prendick, who testifies in standard fashion to the evidence favoring the truth of the story, and a final "note" that, in its explicit reference to Wells's *Saturday Review Essay* of the year before, "The Limits of Individual Plasticity," may be presumed to be in Charles Edward Prendick's voice — or in Wells's voice.

Perhaps because of this confusion in the note, and probably because he thought the DeFoe-like introduction too old-fashioned, Wells deleted both in the Heinemann edition for colonial readers, and omitted both for the "modern" edition of his collected works, the Atlantic Edition published in 1924 by T. Fisher Unwin (New York) and Charles Scribner's Sons (New York). Popular editions almost immediately began to restore both the introduction and the note. Of the two key contemporary scholarly editions, Robert Philmus's *The Island of Doctor Moreau: A Variorum Text* (1993) reprints the first edition in its slightly altered American version, but with the variants from all editions, and Leon Stover's *The Island of Doctor Moreau: A Critical Text of the 1896 London First Edition, with an Introduction and Appendices* (1996) reprints the London first edition. I'm indebted to both works, which contain the fruits of a long acquaintance with and argument over Wells and his texts. Philmus also reprints the fascinating "first Moreau" of the 1894 manuscript fragment, and Stover includes several pertinent Wells essays.

Part One

FRANKENSTEIN AND
THE ISLAND OF DOCTOR MOREAU

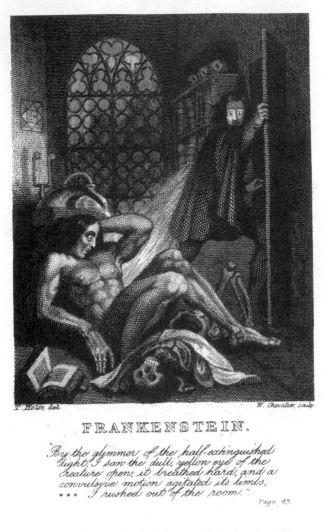

FRANKENSTEIN.

"By the glimmer of the half-extinguished light, I saw the dull, yellow eye of the creature open; it breathed hard, and a convulsive motion agitated its limbs.
* * * I rushed out of the room.".

Page 43.

London, Published by H: Colburn and R. Bentley, 1831.

The original frontispiece for the 1831 H. Colburn and R. Bentley edition of *Frankenstein*, depicting the first movements of Dr. Frankenstein's creature.

Frankenstein

or,

The Modern Prometheus

Mary Shelley

Did I request thee, Maker, from my clay
To mould Me man? Did I solicit thee
From darkness to promote me?—
                    Paradise Lost *(x. 743–5)*

TO WILLIAM GODWIN,
Author of Political Justice, Caleb Williams, &c.
These Volumes are respectfully inscribed by
THE AUTHOR

PREFACE[1]

The event on which this fiction is founded has been supposed, by Dr Darwin, and some of the physiological writers of Germany, as not of impossible occurrence.[2] I shall not be supposed as according the remotest degree of serious faith to such an imagination; yet, in assuming it as the basis of a work of fancy, I have not considered myself as merely weaving a series of supernatural terrors. The event on which the interest of the story depends is exempt from the disadvantages of a mere tale of spectres or enchantment. It was recommended by the novelty of the situations which it developes; and, however impossible as a physical fact, affords a point of view to the imagination for the delineating of human passions more comprehensive and commanding than any which the ordinary relations of existing events can yield.

I have thus endeavoured to preserve the truth of the elementary principles of human nature, while I have not scrupled to innovate upon their combinations. The *Iliad*, the tragic poetry of Greece, —Shakespeare, in the *Tempest* and *Midsummer Night's Dream,* —and most especially Milton, in *Paradise Lost,* conform to this rule; and the most humble novelist, who seeks to confer or receive amusement from his labours, may, without presumption, apply to prose fiction a licence, or rather a rule, from the adoption of which so many exquisite combinations of human feeling have resulted in the highest specimens of poetry.

The circumstance on which my story rests was suggested in casual conversation. It was commenced, partly as a source of amusement, and partly as an expedient for exercising any untried resources of mind. Other motives were mingled with these, as the work proceeded. I am by no means indifferent to the manner in which whatever moral tendencies exist in the sentiments or characters it contains shall affect the reader; yet my chief concern in this respect has been limited to the avoiding the enervating effects of the novels of the present day, and to the exhibition of the amiableness of

---

Frankenstein: or, The Modern Prometheus. London: Lackington, Hughes, Harding, Mavor, & Jones, 1818.

[1] The preface was written by Percy Bysshe Shelley, who in conversation, reading drafts and writing suggested emendations, and shepherding the 1818 text through publication, was an active assistant to his wife. See A Note on the Texts. [Ed.]

[2] See selections from the work of Erasmus Darwin in Part Two, Contexts. Among the influential German physiologists whose work was discussed in the Shelley circle were Blumenback, Rudolphi, and Tiedemann. See also Butler's "Radical Science" in Part Three, Contemporary Views. [Ed.]

domestic affection, and the excellence of universal virtue. The opinions which naturally spring from the character and situation of the hero are by no means to be conceived as existing always in my own conviction, nor is any inference justly to be drawn from the following pages as prejudicing any philosophical doctrine of whatever kind.

It is a subject also of additional interest to the author, that this story was begun in the majestic region where the scene is principally laid, and in society which cannot cease to be regretted. I passed the summer of 1816 in the environs of Geneva. The season was cold and rainy, and in the evenings we crowded around a blazing wood fire, and occasionally amused ourselves with some German stories of ghosts, which happened to fall into our hands. These tales excited in us a playful desire of imitation. Two other friends (a tale from the pen of one of whom would be far more acceptable to the public than any thing I can ever hope to produce) and myself agreed to write each a story, founded on some supernatural occurrence.[3]

The weather, however, suddenly became serene; and my two friends left me on a journey among the Alps, and lost, in the magnificent scenes which they present, all memory of their ghostly visions. The following tale is the only one which has been completed.

---

[3] Mary Shelley describes the genesis of the story more fully in the Author's Introduction to the Standard Edition of *Frankenstein* (1831); see Part Two, Contexts. [Ed.]

VOLUME 1

LETTER I

To Mrs *SAVILLE*, England.
St Petersburgh, Dec. 11th, 17—.

You will rejoice to hear that no disaster has accompanied the commencement of an enterprise which you have regarded with such evil forebodings. I arrived here yesterday; and my first task is to assure my dear sister of my welfare, and increasing confidence in the success of my undertaking.

I am already far north of London; and as I walk in the streets of Petersburgh, I feel a cold northern breeze play upon my cheeks, which braces my nerves, and fills me with delight. Do you understand this feeling? This breeze, which has travelled from the regions towards which I am advancing, gives me a foretaste of those icy climes. Inspirited by this wind of promise, my day dreams become more fervent and vivid. I try in vain to be persuaded that the pole is the seat of frost and desolation; it ever presents itself to my imagination as the region of beauty and delight. There, Margaret, the sun is for ever visible; its broad disk just skirting the horizon, and diffusing a perpetual splendour. There—for with your leave, my sister, I will put some trust in preceding navigators—there snow and frost are banished; and, sailing over a calm sea, we may be wafted to a land surpassing in wonders and in beauty every region hitherto discovered on the habitable globe. Its productions and features may be without example, as the phænomena of the heavenly bodies undoubtedly are in those undiscovered solitudes. What may not be expected in a country of eternal light? I may there discover the wondrous power which attracts the needle; and may regulate a thousand celestial observations, that require only this voyage to render their seeming eccentricities consistent for ever. I shall satiate my ardent curiosity with the sight of a part of the world never before visited, and may tread a land never before imprinted by the foot of man. These are my enticements, and they are sufficient to conquer all fear of danger or death, and to induce me to commence this laborious voyage with the joy a child feels when he embarks in a little boat, with his holiday mates, on an expedition of discovery up his native river. But, supposing all these conjectures to be false, you cannot contest the inestimable benefit which I shall confer on all mankind to the last generation, by discovering a passage near the pole to those countries, to reach which at present so many months are requisite; or by ascertaining the secret of the magnet, which, if at all possible, can only be effected by an undertaking such as mine.[4]

These reflections have dispelled the agitation with which I began my letter, and I feel my heart glow with an enthusiasm which elevates me to heaven; for nothing contributes so much to tranquillize the mind as a steady purpose,—a point on which the soul may fix its intellectual eye. This expedition has been the favourite dream of my early years. I have read with ardour the accounts of the various voyages which have been made in the prospect of arriving at the North Pacific Ocean through the seas which surround the pole. You may remember, that a history of all the voyages made for purposes of discovery composed the whole of our good uncle Thomas's library. My education was neglected, yet I was passionately fond of reading. These volumes were my study day and night, and my familiarity with them increased that regret which I had felt, as a child, on learning that my father's dying injunction had forbidden my uncle to allow me to embark in a sea-faring life.

These visions faded when I perused, for the first time, those poets whose effusions entranced my soul, and lifted it to heaven. I also became a poet, and for one year lived in a Paradise of my own creation; I imagined that I also might obtain a niche in the temple where the names of Homer and Shakespeare are consecrated. You are well acquainted with my failure, and how heavily I bore the disappointment. But just at that time I inherited the fortune of my cousin, and my thoughts were turned into the channel of their earlier bent.

Six years have passed since I resolved on my present undertaking. I can, even now, remember the hour from which I dedicated myself to this great enterprise. I commenced by inuring my body to hardship. I accompanied the whale-fishers on several expeditions to the North Sea; I voluntarily endured cold, famine, thirst, and want of sleep; I often worked harder than the common sailors during the day, and devoted my nights to the study of mathematics, the theory of medicine, and those branches of physical science from which a naval adventurer might derive the greatest practical advantage. Twice I actually hired myself as an under-mate in a Greenland whaler, and acquitted myself to admiration. I must own I felt a little proud, when my captain offered me the second dignity in the vessel, and entreated me to remain with the greatest earnestness; so valuable did he consider my services.

---

[4] Early Romantic science sought a unifying theory of forces such as magnetism and electricity; for Erasmus Darwin, such "polar" forces, or "fluids," also functioned in the making of humans as the polar powers, and fluids, of the "masculine" and "feminine"; see selections from *Zoönomia* and *The Temple of Nature* in Part Two, Contexts. [Ed.]

And now, dear Margaret, do I not deserve to accomplish some great purpose. My life might have been passed in ease and luxury; but I preferred glory to every enticement that wealth placed in my path. Oh, that some encouraging voice would answer in the affirmative! My courage and my resolution is firm; but my hopes fluctuate, and my spirits are often depressed. I am about to proceed on a long and difficult voyage; the emergencies of which will demand all my fortitude: I am required not only to raise the spirits of others, but sometimes to sustain my own, when theirs are failing.

This is the most favourable period for travelling in Russia. They fly quickly over the snow in their sledges; the motion is pleasant, and, in my opinion, far more agreeable than that of an English stage-coach. The cold is not excessive, if you are wrapt in furs, a dress which I have already adopted; for there is a great difference between walking the deck and remaining seated motionless for hours, when no exercise prevents the blood from actually freezing in your veins. I have no ambition to lose my life on the post-road between St Petersburgh and Archangel. *exotic lands*

I shall depart for the latter town in a fortnight or three weeks; and my intention is to hire a ship there, which can easily be done by paying the insurance for the owner, and to engage as many sailors as I think necessary among those who are accustomed to the whale-fishing. I do not intend to sail until the month of June: and when shall I return? Ah, dear sister, how can I answer this question? If I succeed, many, many months, perhaps years, will pass before you and I may meet. If I fail, you will see me again soon, or never. *dramatic*

Farewell, my dear, excellent, Margaret. Heaven shower down blessings on you, and save me, that I may again and again testify my gratitude for all your love and kindness.

Your affectionate brother,
R. WALTON.

LETTER II

To Mrs SAVILLE, England.
Archangel, 28th March, 17—.

How slowly the time passes here, encompassed as I am by frost and snow; yet a second step is taken towards my enterprise. I have hired a vessel, and am occupied in collecting my sailors; those whom I have already engaged appear to be men on whom I can depend, and are certainly possessed of dauntless courage.

But I have one want which I have never yet been able to satisfy; and the absence of the object of which I now feel as a most severe evil. I have no friend, Margaret: when I am glowing with the enthusiasm of success, there will be none to participate my joy; if I am assailed by disappointment, no one will endeavour to sustain me in dejection. I shall commit my thoughts to paper, it is true; but that is a poor medium for the communication of feeling. I desire the company of a man who could sympathize with me; whose eyes would reply to mine. You may deem me romantic, my dear sister, but I bitterly feel the want of a friend. I have no one near me, gentle yet courageous, possessed of a cultivated as well as of a capacious mind, whose tastes are like my own, to approve or amend my plans. How would such a friend repair the faults of your poor brother! I am too ardent in execution, and too impatient of difficulties. But it is a still greater evil to me that I am self-educated: for the first fourteen years of my life I ran wild on a common, and read nothing but our uncle Thomas's books of voyages. At that age I became acquainted with the celebrated poets of our own country; but it was only when it had ceased to be in my power to derive its most important benefits from such a conviction, that I perceived the necessity of becoming acquainted with more languages than that of my native country. Now I am twenty-eight, and am in reality more illiterate than many school-boys of fifteen. It is true that I have thought more, and that my day dreams are more extended and magnificent; but they want (as the painters call it) *keeping;* and I greatly need a friend who would have sense enough not to despise me as romantic, and affection enough for me to endeavour to regulate my mind.[5]

Well, these are useless complaints; I shall certainly find no friend on the wide ocean, nor even here in Archangel, among merchants and seamen. Yet some feelings, unallied to the dross of human nature, beat even in these rugged bosoms. My lieutenant, for instance, is a man of wonderful courage and enterprise; he is madly desirous of glory. He is an Englishman, and in the midst of national and professional prejudices, unsoftened by cultivation, retains some of the noblest endowments of humanity. I first became acquainted with him on board a whale vessel: finding that he was unemployed in this city, I easily engaged him to assist in my enterprise.

The master is a person of an excellent disposition, and is remarkable in the ship for his gentleness, and the mildness of his discipline. He is, indeed, of so amiable a nature, that he will not hunt (a favourite, and almost the

---

[5] That is, Walton desires a friend with an artist's or architect's eye, a training in "perspective," the proper relationship between near and far objects, between dreams and their "regulation." [Ed.]

Ⓓ = overdramatized

only amusement here), because he cannot endure to spill blood. He is, moreover, heroically <u>generous</u>. Some years ago he loved a young Russian lady, of moderate fortune; and having amassed a considerable sum in prize-money, the father of the girl consented to the match. He saw his mistress once before the destined ceremony; but she was bathed in tears, and, throwing herself at his feet, entreated him to spare her, confessing at the same time that she loved another, but that he was poor, and that her father would never consent to the union. My generous friend reassured the suppliant, and on being informed of the name of her lover instantly abandoned his pursuit. <u>He had already bought a farm with his money, on which he had designed to pass the remainder of his life; but he bestowed the whole on his rival, together with the remains of his prize-money to purchase stock, and then himself solicited the young woman's father to consent to her marriage with her lover.</u> But the old man decidedly refused, thinking himself bound in honour to my friend; who, when he found the father inexorable, quitted his country, nor returned until he heard that his former mistress was married according to her inclinations. 'What a (noble) fellow!' you will exclaim. He is so; but then he has passed all his life on board a vessel, and has scarcely an idea beyond the rope and the shroud.

A romantic story

But do not suppose that, because I complain a little, or because I can conceive a consolation for my toils which I may never know, that I am wavering in my resolutions. Those are as fixed as fate; and my voyage is only now delayed until the <u>weather</u> shall permit my embarkation. The winter has been dreadfully severe; but the spring promises well, and it is considered as a remarkably early season; so that, perhaps, I may sail sooner than I expected. I shall do nothing rashly; you know me sufficiently to confide in my prudence and considerateness whenever the safety of others is committed to my care.

I cannot describe to you my sensations on the near prospect of my undertaking. It is impossible to communicate to you a conception of the trembling sensation, half pleasurable and half fearful, with which I am preparing to depart. <u>I am going to unexplored regions, to 'the land of mist and snow;'[6] but I shall kill no (albatross), therefore do not be alarmed for my safety.</u>   joke?

Shall I meet you again, after having traversed immense seas, and returned by the most southern cape of Africa or America? I dare not expect such success, yet I cannot bear to look on the reverse side of the picture. Continue to write to me by every opportunity: <u>I may receive your letters (though the chance is very <u>doubtful</u>) on some occasions when I need them</u>

Ⓓ

---

[6] Line 403 of S. T. Coleridge's "The Rime of the Ancient Mariner" (1798). [Ed.]

most to support my spirits. I love you very tenderly. Remember me with affection, should you never hear from me again.

> *Your affectionate brother,*
> ROBERT WALTON.

LETTER III

To Mrs SAVILLE, England.
July 7th, 17—.
MY DEAR SISTER,

I write a few lines in haste, to say that I am safe, and well advanced on my voyage. This letter will reach England by a merchant-man now on its homeward voyage from Archangel; more fortunate than I, who may not see my native land, perhaps, for many years. I am, however, in good spirits: my men are bold, and apparently firm of purpose; nor do the floating sheets of ice that continually pass us, indicating the dangers of the region towards which we are advancing, appear to dismay them. We have already reached a very high latitude; but it is the height of summer, and although not so warm as in England, the southern gales, which blow us speedily towards those shores which I so ardently desire to attain, breathe a degree of renovating warmth which I had not expected.

No incidents have hitherto befallen us, that would make a figure in a letter. One or two stiff gales, and the breaking of a mast, are accidents which experienced navigators scarcely remember to record; and I shall be well content, if nothing worse happen to us during our voyage.

Adieu, my dear Margaret. Be assured, that for my own sake, as well as yours, I will not rashly encounter danger. I will be cool, persevering, and prudent.

Remember me to all my English friends.

> *Most affectionately yours,*
> R. W.

LETTER IV

To Mrs SAVILLE, England.
August 5th, 17—

So strange an accident has happened to us, that I cannot forbear recording it, although it is very probable that you will see me before these papers can come into your possession.

Last Monday (July 31st), we were nearly surrounded by ice, which closed in the ship on all sides, scarcely leaving her the sea room in which she floated. Our situation was somewhat dangerous, especially as we were compassed round by a very thick fog. We accordingly lay to, hoping that some change would take place in the atmosphere and weather.

About two o'clock the mist cleared away, and we beheld, stretched out in every direction, vast and irregular plains of ice, which seemed to have no end. Some of my comrades groaned, and my own mind began to grow watchful with anxious thoughts, when a strange sight suddenly attracted our attention, and diverted our solicitude from our own situation. We perceived a low carriage, fixed on a sledge and drawn by dogs, pass on towards the north, at the distance of half a mile: a being which had the shape of a man, but apparently of gigantic stature, sat in the sledge, and guided the dogs. We watched the rapid progress of the traveller with our telescopes, until he was lost among the distant inequalities of the ice.

This appearance excited our unqualified wonder. We were, as we believed, many hundred miles from any land; but this apparition seemed to denote that it was not, in reality so distant as we had supposed. Shut in, however, by ice, it was impossible to follow his track, which we had observed with the greatest attention.

About two hours after this occurrence, we heard the ground sea,[7] and before night the ice broke, and freed our ship. We, however, lay to until the morning, fearing to encounter in the dark those large loose masses which float about after the breaking up of the ice. I profited of this time to rest for a few hours.

In the morning, however, as soon as it was light, I went upon deck, and found all the sailors busy on one side of the vessel, apparently talking to some one in the sea. It was, in fact, a sledge, like that we had seen before, which had drifted towards us in the night, on a large fragment of ice. Only one dog remained alive; but there was a human being within it, whom the sailors were persuading to enter the vessel. He was not, as the other traveller seemed to be, a savage inhabitant of some undiscovered island, but an European.[8] When I appeared on deck, the master said, 'Here is our captain, and he will not allow you to perish on the open sea.'

On perceiving me, the stranger addressed me in English, although with a foreign accent. 'Before I come on board your vessel,' said he, 'will you have the kindness to inform me whither you are bound?'

---

[7] Ground swell, a heaving of the sea. [Ed.]

[8] Both *Frankenstein* and *The Island of Doctor Moreau* reflect the standard cultural dichotomy between the savage or fantastic "island" and the mobile shipboard "civilization" of the European. Daniel DeFoe's *Robinson Crusoe* (1719) is the common ancestor. [Ed.]

You may conceive my astonishment on hearing such a question addressed to me from a man on the brink of destruction, and to whom I should have supposed that my vessel would have been a resource which he would not have exchanged for the most precious wealth the earth can afford. I replied, however, that we were on a voyage of discovery towards the northern pole.

Upon hearing this he appeared satisfied, and consented to come on board. Good God! Margaret, if you had seen the man who thus capitulated for his safety, your surprise would have been boundless. His limbs were nearly frozen, and his body dreadfully emaciated by fatigue and suffering. I never saw a man in so wretched a condition. We attempted to carry him into the cabin; but as soon as he had quitted the fresh air, he fainted. We accordingly brought him back to the deck, and restored him to animation by rubbing him with brandy, and forcing him to swallow a small quantity. As soon as he shewed signs of life, we wrapped him up in blankets, and placed him near the chimney of the kitchen-stove. By slow degrees he recovered, and ate a little soup, which restored him wonderfully.

Two days passed in this manner before he was able to speak; and I often feared that his sufferings had deprived him of understanding. When he had in some measure recovered, I removed him to my own cabin, and attended on him as much as my duty would permit. I never saw a more interesting creature: his eyes have generally an expression of wildness, and even madness; but there are moments when, if any one performs an act of kindness towards him, or does him any the most trifling service, his whole countenance is lighted up, as it were, with a beam of benevolence and sweetness that I never saw equalled. But he is generally melancholy and despairing; and sometimes he gnashes his teeth, as if impatient of the weight of woes that oppresses him.

When my guest was a little recovered, I had great trouble to keep off the men, who wished to ask him a thousand questions; but I would not allow him to be tormented by their idle curiosity, in a state of body and mind whose restoration evidently depended upon entire repose. Once, however, the lieutenant asked, Why he had come so far upon the ice in so strange a vehicle?

His countenance instantly assumed an aspect of the deepest gloom; and he replied, 'To seek one who fled from me.'

'And did the man whom you pursued travel in the same fashion?'

'Yes.'

'Then I fancy we have seen him; for, the day before we picked you up, we saw some dogs drawing a sledge, with a man in it, across the ice.'

This aroused the stranger's attention; and he asked a multitude of questions concerning the route which the dæmon, as he called him, had pursued. Soon after, when he was alone with me, he said, 'I have, doubtless, excited your curiosity, as well as that of these good people; but you are too considerate to make inquiries.'

'Certainly; it would indeed be very impertinent and inhuman in me to trouble you with any inquisitiveness of mine.'

'And yet you rescued me from a strange and perilous situation; you have benevolently restored me to life.'

Soon after this he inquired, if I thought that the breaking up of the ice had destroyed the other sledge? I replied, that I could not answer with any degree of certainty; for the ice had not broken until near midnight, and the traveller might have arrived at a place of safety before that time; but of this I could not judge.

From this time the stranger seemed very eager to be upon deck, to watch for the sledge which had before appeared; but I have persuaded him to remain in the cabin, for he is far too weak to sustain the rawness of the atmosphere. But I have promised that some one should watch for him, and give him instant notice if any new object should appear in sight.

Such is my journal of what relates to this strange occurrence up to the present day. The stranger has gradually improved in health, but is very silent, and appears uneasy when any one except myself enters his cabin. Yet his manners are so conciliating and gentle, that the sailors are all interested in him, although they have had very little communication with him. For my own part, I begin to love him as a brother; and his constant and deep grief fills me with sympathy and compassion. He must have been a noble creature in his better days, being even now in wreck so attractive and amiable.

I said in one of my letters, my dear Margaret, that I should find no friend on the wide ocean; yet I have found a man who, before his spirit had been broken by misery, I should have been happy to have possessed as the brother of my heart.

I shall continue my journal concerning the stranger at intervals, should I have any fresh incidents to record.

August 13th, 17—.

My affection for my guest increases every day. He excites at once my admiration and my pity to an astonishing degree. How can I see so noble a creature destroyed by misery without feeling the most poignant grief? He is so gentle, yet so wise; his mind is so cultivated; and when he speaks, although his words are culled with the choicest art, yet they flow with rapidity and unparalleled eloquence.

He is now much recovered from his illness, and is continually on the deck, apparently watching for the sledge that preceded his own. Yet, although unhappy, he is not so utterly occupied by his own misery, but that he interests himself deeply in the employments of others. He has asked me many questions concerning my design; and I have related my little history frankly to him. He appeared pleased with the confidence, and suggested several alterations in my plan, which I shall find exceedingly useful. There is no pedantry in his manner; but all he does appears to spring solely from the interest he instinctively takes in the welfare of those who surround him. He is often overcome by gloom, and then he sits by himself, and tries to overcome all that is sullen or unsocial in his humour. These paroxysms pass from him like a cloud from before the sun, though his dejection never leaves him. I have endeavoured to win his confidence; and I trust that I have succeeded. One day I mentioned to him the desire I had always felt of finding a friend who might sympathize with me, and direct me by his counsel. I said, I did not belong to that class of men who are offended by advice. 'I am self-educated, and perhaps I hardly rely sufficiently upon my own powers. I wish therefore that my companion should be wiser and more experienced than myself, to confirm and support me; nor have I believed it impossible to find a true friend.'

'I agree with you,' replied the stranger, 'in believing that friendship is not only a desirable, but a possible acquisition. I once had a friend, the most noble of human creatures, and am entitled, therefore, to judge respecting friendship. You have hope, and the world before you, and have no cause for despair. But I—I have lost every thing, and cannot begin life anew.'

As he said this, his countenance became expressive of a calm settled grief, that touched me to the heart. But he was silent, and presently retired to his cabin.

Even broken in spirit as he is, no one can feel more deeply than he does the beauties of nature. The starry sky, the sea, and every sight afforded by these wonderful regions, seems still to have the power of elevating his soul from earth. Such a man has a double existence: he may suffer misery, and be overwhelmed by disappointments; yet when he has retired into himself, he will be like a celestial spirit, that has a halo around him, within whose circle no grief or folly ventures. Will you laugh at the enthusiasm I express concerning this divine wanderer? If you do, you must have certainly lost that simplicity which was once your characteristic charm. Yet, if you will, smile at the warmth of my expressions, while I find every day new causes for repeating them.

August 19th, 17—.

Yesterday the stranger said to me, 'You may easily perceive, Captain Walton, that I have suffered great and unparalleled misfortunes. I had determined, once, that the memory of these evils should die with me; but you have won me to alter my determination. You seek for knowledge and wisdom, as I once did; and I ardently hope that the gratification of your wishes may not be a serpent to sting you, as mine has been. I do not know that the relation of my misfortunes will be useful to you, yet, if you are inclined, listen to my tale. I believe that the strange incidents connected with it will afford a view of nature, which may enlarge your faculties and understanding. You will hear of powers and occurrences, such as you have been accustomed to believe impossible: but I do not doubt that my tale conveys in its series internal evidence of the truth of the events of which it is composed.'

You may easily conceive that I was much gratified by the offered communication; yet I could not endure that he should renew his grief by a recital of his misfortunes. I felt the greatest eagerness to hear the promised narrative, partly from curiosity, and partly from a strong desire to ameliorate his fate, if it were in my power. I expressed these feelings in my answer.

'I thank you,' he replied, 'for your sympathy, but it is useless; my fate is nearly fulfilled. I wait but for one event, and then I shall repose in peace. I understand your feeling,' continued he, perceiving that I wished to interrupt him; 'but you are mistaken, my friend, if thus you will allow me to name you; nothing can alter my destiny: listen to my history, and you will perceive how irrevocably it is determined.'

He then told me, that he would commence his narrative the next day when I should be at leisure. This promise drew from me the warmest thanks. I have resolved every night, when I am not engaged, to record, as nearly as possible in his own words, what he has related during the day. If I should be engaged, I will at least make notes. This manuscript will doubtless afford you the greatest pleasure: but to me, who know him, and who hear it from his own lips, with what interest and sympathy shall I read it in some future day!

CHAPTER I

I am by birth a Genevese; and my family is one of the most distinguished of that republic. My ancestors had been for many years counsellors and syndics;[9] and my father had filled several public situations with honour and reputation. He was respected by all who knew him for his integrity and indefatigable attention to public business. He passed his younger days perpetually occupied by the affairs of his country; and it was not until the decline of life that he thought of marrying, and bestowing on the state sons who might carry his virtues and his name down to posterity.

---

[9] Republican Geneva was governed by legislators and magistrates (syndics). [Ed.]

As the circumstances of his marriage illustrate his character, I cannot refrain from relating them. One of his most intimate friends was a merchant, who, from a flourishing state, fell, through numerous mischances, into poverty. This man, whose name was Beaufort, was of a proud and unbending disposition, and could not bear to live in poverty and oblivion in the same country where he had formerly been distinguished for his rank and magnificence. Having paid his debts, therefore, in the most honourable manner, he retreated with his daughter to the town of Lucerne, where he lived unknown and in wretchedness. My father loved Beaufort with the truest friendship, and was deeply grieved by his retreat in these unfortunate circumstances. He grieved also for the loss of his society, and resolved to seek him out and endeavour to persuade him to begin the world again through his credit and assistance.

Beaufort had taken effectual measures to conceal himself; and it was ten months before my father discovered his abode. Overjoyed at this discovery, he hastened to the house, which was situated in a mean street, near the Reuss. But when he entered, misery and despair alone welcomed him. Beaufort had saved but a very small sum of money from the wreck of his fortunes; but it was sufficient to provide him with sustenance for some months, and in the mean time he hoped to procure some respectable employment in a merchant's house. The interval was consequently spent in inaction; his grief only became more deep and rankling, when he had leisure for reflection; and at length it took so fast hold of his mind, that at the end of three months he lay on a bed of sickness, incapable of any exertion.

His daughter attended him with the greatest tenderness; but she saw with despair that their little fund was rapidly decreasing, and that there was no other prospect of support. But Caroline Beaufort possessed a mind of an uncommon mould; and her courage rose to support her in her adversity. She procured plain work; she plaited straw; and by various means contrived to earn a pittance scarcely sufficient to support life.

Several months passed in this manner. Her father grew worse; her time was more entirely occupied in attending him; her means of subsistence decreased; and in the tenth month her father died in her arms, leaving her an orphan and a beggar. This last blow overcame her; and she knelt by Beaufort's coffin, weeping bitterly, when my father entered the chamber. He came like a protecting spirit to the poor girl, who committed herself to his care, and after the interment of his friend he conducted her to Geneva, and placed her under the protection of a relation. Two years after this event Caroline became his wife.

When my father became a husband and a parent, he found his time so occupied by the duties of his new situation, that he relinquished many of his public employments, and devoted himself to the education of his children. Of these I was the eldest, and the destined successor to all his labours and utility. No creature could have more tender parents than mine. My improvement and health were their constant care, especially as I remained for several years their only child. But before I continue my narrative, I must record an incident which took place when I was four years of age.

My father had a sister, whom he tenderly loved, and who had married early in life an Italian gentleman. Soon after her marriage, she had accompanied her husband into his native country, and for some years my father had very little communication with her. About the time I mentioned she died; and a few months afterwards he received a letter from her husband, acquainting him with his intention of marrying an Italian lady, and requesting my father to take charge of the infant Elizabeth, the only child of his deceased sister. 'It is my wish,' he said, 'that you should consider her as your own daughter, and educate her thus. Her mother's fortune is secured to her, the documents of which I will commit to your keeping. Reflect upon this proposition; and decide whether you would prefer educating your niece yourself to her being brought up by a stepmother.'[10]

My father did not hesitate, and immediately went to Italy, that he might accompany the little Elizabeth to her future home. I have often heard my mother say, that she was at that time the most beautiful child she had ever seen, and shewed signs even then of a gentle and affectionate disposition. These indications, and a desire to bind as closely as possible the ties of domestic love, determined my mother to consider Elizabeth as my future wife; a design which she never found reason to repent.

From this time Elizabeth Lavenza became my playfellow, and, as we grew older, my friend. She was docile and good tempered, yet gay and playful as a summer insect. Although she was lively and animated, her feelings were strong and deep, and her disposition uncommonly affectionate. No one could better enjoy liberty, yet no one could submit with more grace than she did to constraint and caprice. Her imagination was luxuriant, yet her capability of application was great. Her person was the image of her mind; her hazel eyes, although as lively as a bird's, possessed an attractive softness. Her figure was light and airy; and, though capable of enduring great fatigue, she appeared the most fragile creature in the world. While I admired

---

[10]An example of an important concept altered by Mary Shelley in the 1831 revision. Here, Elizabeth is Victor's first cousin, a quasi-incestuous kin-spirit like the female alter-egos of Byron's "Manfred" (1817) and Shelley's "Epipsychidion" (1821), while in the later version she is a stranger, the orphaned daughter of a Milanese nobleman. See Mellor (1988) on this effort to normalize the presentation of the family. [Ed.]

her understanding and fancy, I loved to tend on her, as I should on a favourite animal; and I never saw so much grace both of person and mind united to so little pretension.

Every one adored Elizabeth. If the servants had any request to make, it was always through her intercession. We were strangers to any species of disunion and dispute; for although there was a great dissimilitude in our characters, there was an harmony in that very dissimilitude. I was more calm and philosophical than my companion; yet my temper was not so yielding. My application was of longer endurance; but it was not so severe whilst it endured. I delighted in investigating the facts relative to the actual world; she busied herself in following the aërial creations of the poets. The world was to me a secret, which I desired to discover; to her it was a vacancy, which she sought to people with imaginations of her own.

My brothers were considerably younger than myself; but I had a friend in one of my schoolfellows, who compensated for this deficiency. Henry Clerval was the son of a merchant of Geneva, an intimate friend of my father. He was a boy of singular talent and fancy. I remember, when he was nine years old, he wrote a fairy tale, which was the delight and amazement of all his companions. His favourite study consisted in books of chivalry and romance; and when very young, I can remember, that we used to act plays composed by him out of these favourite books, the principal characters of which were Orlando, Robin Hood, Amadis, and St George.[11]

No youth could have passed more happily than mine. My parents were indulgent, and my companions amiable. Our studies were never forced; and by some means we always had an end placed in view, which excited us to ardour in the prosecution of them. It was by this method, and not by emulation, that we were urged to application. Elizabeth was not incited to apply herself to drawing, that her companions might not outstrip her; but through the desire of pleasing her aunt, by the representation of some favourite scene done by her own hand. We learned Latin and English, that we might read the writings in those languages; and so far from study being made odious to us through punishment, we loved application, and our amusements would have been the labours of other children. Perhaps we did not read so many books, or learn languages so quickly, as those who are disciplined according to the ordinary methods; but what we learned was impressed the more deeply on our memories.

---

[11] *Orlando Furioso* (1532) is a romance epic by Lodovico Ariosto; *Amadis de Gaul* (1508) is a romance translated into English by Robert Southey in 1803; St. George and Robin Hood are legendary English heroes. The latter would appear, historicized, a year after *Frankenstein*, in Walter Scott's wildly popular novel *Ivanhoe*. [Ed.]

In this description of our domestic circle I include Henry Clerval; for he was constantly with us. He went to school with me, and generally passed the afternoon at our house; for being an only child, and destitute of companions at home, his father was well pleased that he should find associates at our house; and we were never completely happy when Clerval was absent.

I feel pleasure in dwelling on the recollections of childhood, before misfortune had tainted my mind, and changed its bright visions of extensive usefulness into gloomy and narrow reflections upon self. But, in drawing the picture of my early days, I must not omit to record those events which led, by insensible steps to my after tale of misery: for when I would account to myself for the birth of that passion, which afterwards ruled my destiny, I find it arose, like a mountain river, from ignoble and almost forgotten sources; but, swelling as it proceeded, it became the torrent which, in its course, has swept away all my hopes and joys.

Natural philosophy is the genius that has regulated my fate; I desire therefore, in this narration, to state those facts which led to my predilection for that science. When I was thirteen years of age, we all went on a party of pleasure to the baths near Thonon: the inclemency of the weather obliged us to remain a day confined to the inn. In this house I chanced to find a volume of the works of Cornelius Agrippa. I opened it with apathy; the theory which he attempts to demonstrate, and the wonderful facts which he relates, soon changed this feeling into enthusiasm. A new light seemed to dawn upon my mind; and, bounding with joy, I communicated my discovery to my father. I cannot help remarking here the many opportunities instructors possess of directing the attention of their pupils to useful knowledge, which they utterly neglect. My father looked carelessly at the title-page of my book, and said, 'Ah! Cornelius Agrippa! My dear Victor, do not waste your time upon this; it is sad trash.'

If, instead of this remark, my father had taken the pains to explain to me, that the principles of Agrippa had been entirely exploded, and that a modern system of science had been introduced, which possessed much greater powers than the ancient, because the powers of the latter were chimerical, while those of the former were real and practical; under such circumstances, I should certainly have thrown Agrippa aside, and, with my imagination warmed as it was, should probably have applied myself to the more rational theory of chemistry which has resulted from modern discoveries. It is even possible, that the train of my ideas would never have received the fatal impulse that led to my ruin. But the cursory glance my father had taken of my volume by no means assured me that he was acquainted with its contents; and I continued to read with the greatest avidity.

When I returned home, my first care was to procure the whole works of this author, and afterwards of Paracelsus and Albertus Magnus.[12] I read and studied the wild fancies of these writers with delight; they appeared to me treasures known to few beside myself; and although I often wished to communicate these secret stores of knowledge to my father, yet his indefinite censure of my favourite Agrippa always withheld me. I disclosed my discoveries to Elizabeth, therefore, under a promise of strict secrecy; but she did not interest herself in the subject, and I was left by her to pursue my studies alone.[13]

It may appear very strange, that a disciple of Albertus Magnus should arise in the eighteenth century; but our family was not scientifical, and I had not attended any of the lectures given at the schools of Geneva. My dreams were therefore undisturbed by reality; and I entered with the greatest diligence into the search of the philosopher's stone and the elixir of life. But the latter obtained my most undivided attention: wealth was an inferior object; but what glory would attend the discovery, if I could banish disease from the human frame, and render man invulnerable to any but a violent death!

Nor were these my only visions. The raising of ghosts or devils was a promise liberally accorded by my favourite authors; the fulfillment of which I most eagerly sought; and if my incantations were always unsuccessful, I attributed the failure rather to my own inexperience and mistake, than to a want of skill or fidelity in my instructors.

The natural phænomena that take place every day before our eyes did not escape my examinations. Distillation, and the wonderful effects of steam, processes of which my favourite authors were utterly ignorant, excited my astonishment; but my utmost wonder was engaged by some experiments on an airpump, which I saw employed by a gentleman whom we were in the habit of visiting.

The ignorance of the early philosophers on these and several other points served to decrease their credit with me: but I could not entirely throw them aside, before some other system should occupy their place in my mind.

---

[12] Cornelius Agrippa, Paracelsus, and Albertus Magnus were philosophers whose early scientific studies and experiments were perceived as magic, or worse. Albertus was a thirteenth-century Dominican theologian who studied plant science and the brain, Paracelsus (Theophrastus Bombastus von Hohenheim, 1490–1541), a Swiss physician and chemist; and Agrippa (1486–1535), the German author of *De Occulta Philosophia* (1529). [Ed.]

[13] Theodore Roszak's 1995 novel *The Memoirs of Elizabeth Frankenstein* persuasively imagines an Elizabeth who did join Victor in these studies and went on to perfect them in concert with other students of ancient wisdoms, especially female ones. [Ed.]

When I was about fifteen years old, we had retired to our house near Belrive, when we witnessed a most violent and terrible thunder-storm. It advanced from behind the mountains of Jura; and the thunder burst at once with frightful loudness from various quarters of the heavens. I remained, while the storm lasted, watching its progress with curiosity and delight. As I stood at the door, on a sudden I beheld a stream of fire issue from an old and beautiful oak, which stood about twenty yards from our house; and so soon as the dazzling light vanished, the oak had disappeared, and nothing remained but a blasted stump. When we visited it the next morning, we found the tree shattered in a singular manner. It was not splintered by the shock, but entirely reduced to thin ribbands of wood. I never beheld any thing so utterly destroyed.

The catastrophe of this tree excited my extreme astonishment; and I eagerly inquired of my father the nature and origin of thunder and lightning. He replied, 'Electricity;' describing at the same time the various effects of that power. He constructed a small electrical machine, and exhibited a few experiments; he made also a kite, with a wire and string, which drew down that fluid from the clouds.[14]

This last stroke completed the overthrow of Cornelius Agrippa, Albertus Magnus, and Paracelsus, who had so long reigned the lords of my imagination. But by some fatality I did not feel inclined to commence the study of any modern system; and this disinclination was influenced by the following circumstance.

My father expressed a wish that I should attend a course of lectures upon natural philosophy, to which I cheerfully consented. Some accident prevented my attending these lectures until the course was nearly finished. The lecture, being therefore one of the last, was entirely incomprehensible to me. The professor discoursed with the greatest fluency of potassium and boron, of sulphates and oxyds, terms to which I could affix no idea; and I became disgusted with the science of natural philosophy, although I still read Pliny and Buffon with delight, authors, in my estimation, of nearly equal interest and utility.[15]

My occupations at this age were principally the mathematics, and most of the branches of study appertaining to that science. I was busily employed in learning languages; Latin was already familiar to me, and I began

---

[14] An allusion to Benjamin Franklin's famous discoveries detailed in his *Experiments and Observations in Electricity* (1751). Percy and Mary Shelley followed with interest the development of early electrochemical theories and experiments by Erasmus Darwin, Humphry Davy, and Luigi Galvini; see Introduction. [Ed.]

[15] Pliny the Elder (c. 23–79), Roman author of *Historiae Naturalis;* Georges Louis Leclerc, comte de Buffon (1707–1788), author of the 44-volume *Histoire Naturelle.* [Ed.]

to read some of the easiest Greek authors without the help of a lexicon. I also perfectly understood English and German. This is the list of my accomplishments at the age of seventeen; and you may conceive that my hours were fully employed in acquiring and maintaining a knowledge of this various literature.

Another task also devolved upon me, when I became the instructor of my brothers. Ernest was six years younger than myself, and was my principal pupil. He had been afflicted with ill health from his infancy, through which Elizabeth and I had been his constant nurses: his disposition was gentle, but he was incapable of any severe application. William, the youngest of our family, was yet an infant, and the most beautiful little fellow in the world; his lively blue eyes, dimpled cheeks, and endearing manners, inspired the tenderest affection.

Such was our domestic circle, from which care and pain seemed for ever banished. My father directed our studies, and my mother partook of our enjoyments. Neither of us possessed the slightest pre-eminence over the other; the voice of command was never heard amongst us; but mutual affection engaged us all to comply with and obey the slightest desire of each other. *perfection*

CHAPTER II

When I had attained the age of seventeen, my parents resolved that I should become a student at the university of Ingolstadt.[16] I had hitherto attended the schools of Geneva; but my father thought it necessary, for the completion of my education, that I should be made acquainted with other customs than those of my native country. My departure was therefore fixed at an early date; but, before the day resolved upon could arrive, the first misfortune of my life occurred — an omen, as it were, of my future misery.

Elizabeth had caught the scarlet fever; but her illness was not severe, and she quickly recovered. During her confinement, many arguments had been urged to persuade my mother to refrain from attending upon her. She had, at first, yielded to our entreaties; but when she heard that her favourite was recovering, she could no longer debar herself from her society, and entered her chamber long before the danger of infection was past. The consequences of this imprudence were fatal. On the third day my mother sick-

---

[16] Bavarian University founded in 1472, important to the Catholic Counter-Reformation and later the birthplace of the Illuminati, a secret society of freethinkers holding deistic and republican beliefs. [Ed.]

ened; her fever was very malignant, and the looks of her attendants prognosticated the worst event. On her death-bed the fortitude and benignity of this admirable woman did not desert her. She joined the hands of Elizabeth and myself: 'My children,' she said, 'my firmest hopes of future happiness were placed on the prospect of your union. This expectation will now be the consolation of your father. Elizabeth, my love, you must supply my place to your younger cousins. Alas! I regret that I am taken from you; and, happy and beloved as I have been, is it not hard to quit you all? But these are not thoughts befitting me; I will endeavour to resign myself cheerfully to death, and will indulge a hope of meeting you in another world.' She died calmly; and her countenance expressed affection even in death. I need not describe the feelings of those whose dearest ties are rent by that most irreparable evil, the void that presents itself to the soul, and the despair that is exhibited on the countenance. It is so long before the mind can persuade itself that she, whom we saw every day, and whose very existence appeared a part of our own, can have departed for ever—that the brightness of a beloved eye can have been extinguished, and the sound of a voice so familiar, and dear to the ear, can be hushed, never more to be heard. These are the reflections of the first days; but when the lapse of time proves the reality of the evil, then the actual bitterness of grief commences. Yet from whom has not that rude hand rent away some dear connexion; and why should I describe a sorrow which all have felt, and must feel? The time at length arrives, when grief is rather an indulgence than a necessity; and the smile that plays upon the lips, although it may be deemed a sacrilege, is not banished. My mother was dead, but we had still duties which we ought to perform; we must continue our course with the rest, and learn to think ourselves fortunate, whilst one remains whom the spoiler has not seized.

My journey to Ingolstadt, which had been deferred by these events, was now again determined upon. I obtained from my father a respite of some weeks. This period was spent sadly; my mother's death, and my speedy departure, depressed our spirits; but Elizabeth endeavoured to renew the spirit of cheerfulness in our little society. Since the death of her aunt, her mind had acquired new firmness and vigour. She determined to fulfil her duties with the greatest exactness; and she felt that that most imperious duty, of rendering her uncle and cousins happy, had devolved upon her. She consoled me, amused her uncle, instructed my brothers; and I never beheld her so enchanting as at this time, when she was continually endeavouring to contribute to the happiness of others, entirely forgetful of herself.

The day of my departure at length arrived. I had taken leave of all my friends, excepting Clerval, who spent the last evening with us. He bitterly lamented that he was unable to accompany me: but his father could not be persuaded to part with him, intending that he should become a partner with him in business, in compliance with his favourite theory, that learning was superfluous in the commerce of ordinary life. Henry had a refined mind; he had no desire to be idle, and was well pleased to become his father's partner, but he believed that a man might be a very good trader, and yet possess a cultivated understanding.

We sat late, listening to his complaints, and making many little arrangements for the future. The next morning early I departed. Tears gushed from the eyes of Elizabeth; they proceeded partly from sorrow at my departure, and partly because she reflected that the same journey was to have taken place three months before, when a mother's blessing would have accompanied me.

I threw myself into the chaise that was to convey me away, and indulged in the most melancholy reflections. I, who had ever been surrounded by amiable companions, continually engaged in endeavouring to bestow mutual pleasure, I was now alone. In the university, whither I was going, I must form my own friends, and be my own protector. My life had hitherto been remarkably secluded and domestic; and this had given me invincible repugnance to new countenances. I loved my brothers, Elizabeth, and Clerval; these were 'old familiar faces;'[17] but I believed myself totally unfitted for the company of strangers. Such were my reflections as I commenced my journey; but as I proceeded, my spirits and hopes rose. I ardently desired the acquisition of knowledge. I had often, when at home, thought it hard to remain during my youth cooped up in one place, and had longed to enter the world, and take my station among other human beings. Now my desires were complied with, and it would, indeed, have been folly to repent.

I had sufficient leisure for these and many other reflections during my journey to Ingolstadt, which was long and fatiguing. At length the high white steeple of the town met my eyes. I alighted, and was conducted to my solitary apartment, to spend the evening as I pleased.

The next morning I delivered my letters of introduction, and paid a visit to some of the principal professors, and among others to M. Krempe, professor of natural philosophy. He received me with politeness, and asked me several questions concerning my progress in the different branches of science appertaining to natural philosophy. I mentioned, it is true, with fear and trembling, the only authors I had ever read upon those subjects. The professor stared: 'Have you,' he said, 'really spent your time in studying such nonsense?'

---

[17] Title of a 1798 poem by Charles Lamb (1775–1834). [Ed.]

I replied in the affirmative. 'Every minute,' continued M. Krempe with warmth, 'every instant that you have wasted on those books is utterly and entirely lost. You have burdened your memory with exploded systems, and useless names. Good God! in what desert land have you lived, where no one was kind enough to inform you that these fancies, which you have so greedily imbibed, are a thousand years old, and as musty as they are ancient? I little expected in this enlightened and scientific age to find a disciple of Albertus Magnus and Paracelsus. My dear Sir, you must begin your studies entirely anew.'

So saying, he stept aside, and wrote down a list of several books treating of natural philosophy, which he desired me to procure, and dismissed me, after mentioning that in the beginning of the following week he intended to commence a course of lectures upon natural philosophy in its general relations, and that M. Waldman, a fellow-professor, would lecture upon chemistry the alternate days that he missed.

I returned home, not disappointed, for I had long considered those authors useless whom the professor had so strongly reprobated; but I did not feel much inclined to study the books which I procured at his recommendation. M. Krempe was a little squat man, with a gruff voice and repulsive countenance; the teacher, therefore, did not prepossess me in favour of his doctrine. Besides, I had a contempt for the uses of modern natural philosophy. It was very different, when the masters of the science sought immortality and power; such views, although futile, were grand: but now the scene was changed. The ambition of the inquirer seemed to limit itself to the annihilation of those visions on which my interest in science was chiefly founded. I was required to exchange chimeras of boundless grandeur for realities of little worth.

Such were my reflections during the first two or three days spent almost in solitude. But as the ensuing week commenced, I thought of the information which M. Krempe had given me concerning the lectures. And although I could not consent to go and hear that little conceited fellow deliver sentences out of a pulpit, I recollected what he had said of M. Waldman, whom I had never seen, as he had hitherto been out of town.

Partly from curiosity, and partly from idleness, I went into the lecturing room, which M. Waldman entered shortly after.[18] This professor was very

---

[18] The charismatic Waldman and this lecture are based on Humphry Davy's introductory lecture to a course in chemistry given at the recently founded Royal Institution on June 21, 1802, and immediately published as *A Discourse, Introductory to a Course of Lectures on Chemistry*. For Davy's impact, and Shelley's use of him in her novel, see Mellor (1988), especially "A Feminist Critique of Science." [Ed.]

unlike his colleague. He appeared about fifty years of age, but with an aspect expressive of the greatest benevolence; a few gray hairs covered his temples, but those at the back of his head were nearly black. His person was short, but remarkably erect; and his voice the sweetest I had ever heard. He began his lecture by a recapitulation of the history of chemistry and the various improvements made by different men of learning, pronouncing with fervour the names of the most distinguished discoverers. He then took a cursory view of the present state of the science, and explained many of its elementary terms. After having made a few preparatory experiments, he concluded with a panegyric upon modern chemistry, the terms of which I shall never forget: —

'The ancient teachers of this science,' said he, 'promised impossibilities, and performed nothing. The modern masters promise very little; they know that metals cannot be transmuted, and that the elixir of life is a chimera. But these philosophers, whose hands seem only made to dabble in dirt, and their eyes to pore over the microscope or crucible, have indeed performed miracles. They penetrate into the recesses of nature, and shew how she works in her hiding places. They ascend into the heavens; they have discovered how the blood circulates, and the nature of the air we breathe.[19] They have acquired new and almost unlimited powers; they can command the thunders of heaven, mimic the earthquake, and even mock the invisible world with its own shadows.'

I departed highly pleased with the professor and his lecture, and paid him a visit the same evening. His manners in private were even more mild and attractive than in public; for there was a certain dignity in his mien during his lecture, which in his own house was replaced by the greatest affability and kindness. He heard with attention my little narration concerning my studies, and smiled at the names of Cornelius Agrippa, and Paracelsus, but without the contempt that M. Krempe had exhibited. He said, that 'these were men to whose indefatigable zeal modern philosophers were indebted for most of the foundations of their knowledge. They had left to us, as an easier task, to give new names, and arrange in connected classifications, the facts which they in a great degree had been the instruments of bringing to light. The labours of men of genius, however erroneously directed, scarcely ever fail in ultimately turning to the solid advantage of mankind.' I listened to his statement, which was delivered without any presumption or affectation; and then added, that his lecture had removed my

---

[19] William Harvey (1578–1657) discovered the circulation of the blood in 1628; Robert Boyle (1627–91) elaborated the properties of the air, and published *The Skeptical Chemist* (1661), challenging the science of "the ancient teachers." [Ed.]

prejudices against modern chemists; and I, at the same time, requested his advice concerning the books I ought to procure.

'I am happy,' said M. Waldman, 'to have gained a disciple; and if your application equals your ability, I have no doubt of your success. Chemistry is that branch of natural philosophy in which the greatest improvements have been and may be made; it is on that account that I have made it my peculiar study; but at the same time I have not neglected the other branches of science. A man would make but a very sorry chemist, if he attended to that department of human knowledge alone. If your wish is to become really a man of science, and not merely a petty experimentalist, I should advise you to apply to every branch of natural philosophy, including mathematics.'

He then took me into his laboratory, and explained to me the uses of his various machines; instructing me as to what I ought to procure, and promising me the use of his own, when I should have advanced far enough in the science not to derange their mechanism. He also gave me the list of books which I had requested; and I took my leave.

Thus ended a day memorable to me; it decided my future destiny.

CHAPTER III

From this day natural philosophy, and particularly chemistry, in the most comprehensive sense of the term, became nearly my sole occupation. I read with ardour those works, so full of genius and discrimination, which modern inquirers have written on these subjects. I attended the lectures, and cultivated the acquaintance, of the men of science of the university; and I found even in M. Krempe a great deal of sound sense and real information, combined, it is true, with a repulsive physiognomy and manners, but not on that account the less valuable. In M. Waldman I found a true friend. His gentleness was never tinged by dogmatism; and his instructions were given with an air of frankness and good nature, that banished every idea of pedantry. It was, perhaps, the amiable character of this man that inclined me more to that branch of natural philosophy which he professed, than an intrinsic love for the science itself. But this state of mind had place only in the first steps towards knowledge: the more fully I entered into the science, the more exclusively I pursued it for its own sake. That application, which at first had been a matter of duty and resolution, now became so ardent and eager, that the stars often disappeared in the light of morning whilst I was yet engaged in my laboratory.

As I applied so closely, it may be easily conceived that I improved rapidly. My ardour was indeed the astonishment of the students; and my proficiency, that of the masters. Professor Krempe often asked me, with a sly smile, how Cornelius Agrippa went on? whilst M. Waldman expressed the most heartfelt exultation in my progress. Two years passed in this manner, during which I paid no visit to Geneva, but was engaged, heart and soul, in the pursuit of some discoveries, which I hoped to make. None but those who have experienced them can conceive of the enticements of science. In other studies you go as far as others have gone before you, and there is nothing more to know; but in a scientific pursuit there is continual food for discovery and wonder. A mind of moderate capacity, which closely pursues one study, must infallibly arrive at great proficiency in that study; and I, who continually sought the attainment of one object of pursuit, and was solely wrapt up in this, improved so rapidly, that, at the end of two years, I made some discoveries in the improvement of some chemical instruments, which procured me great esteem and admiration at the university. When I had arrived at this point, and had become as well acquainted with the theory and practice of natural philosophy as depended on the lessons of any of the professors at Ingolstadt, my residence there being no longer conducive to my improvements, I thought of returning to my friends and my native town, when an incident happened that protracted my stay.

One of the phænomena which had peculiarly attracted my attention was the structure of the human frame, and, indeed, any animal endued with life. Whence, I often asked myself, did the principle of life proceed? It was a bold question, and one which has ever been considered as a mystery; yet with how many things are we upon the brink of becoming acquainted, if cowardice or carelessness did not restrain our inquiries. I revolved these circumstances in my mind, and determined thenceforth to apply myself more particularly to those branches of natural philosophy which relate to physiology. Unless I had been animated by an almost supernatural enthusiasm, my application to this study would have been irksome, and almost intolerable. To examine the causes of life, we must first have recourse to death. I became acquainted with the science of anatomy: but this was not sufficient; I must also observe the natural decay and corruption of the human body. In my education my father had taken the greatest precautions that my mind should be impressed with no supernatural horrors. I do not ever remember to have trembled at a tale of superstition, or to have feared the apparition of a spirit. Darkness had no effect upon my fancy; and a church-yard was to me merely the receptacle of bodies deprived of life, which, from being the seat of beauty and strength, had become food for the worm. Now I was led to examine the cause and progress of this decay, and forced to spend days and nights in vaults and charnel houses. My attention was fixed upon every object the most insupportable to the delicacy of the human feelings. I saw how the fine form of man was degraded and wasted; I beheld the corruption of death succeed to the blooming cheek of life; I saw how the worm inherited the wonders of the eye and brain. I paused, examining and analysing all the minutiæ of causation, as exemplified in the change from life to death, and death to life, until from the midst of this darkness a sudden light broke in upon me—a light so brilliant and wondrous, yet so simple, that while I became dizzy with the immensity of the prospect which it illustrated, I was surprised that among so many men of genius, who had directed their inquiries towards the same science, that I alone should be reserved to discover so astonishing a secret.

Remember, I am not recording the vision of a madman. The sun does not more certainly shine in the heavens, than that which I now affirm is true. Some miracle might have produced it, yet the stages of the discovery were distinct and probable. After days and nights of incredible labour and fatigue, I succeeded in discovering the cause of generation and life; nay, more, I became myself capable of bestowing animation upon lifeless matter.

The astonishment which I had at first experienced on this discovery soon gave place to delight and rapture. After so much time spent in painful labour, to arrive at once at the summit of my desires, was the most gratifying consummation of my toils. But this discovery was so great and overwhelming, that all the steps by which I had been progressively led to it were obliterated, and I beheld only the result. What had been the study and desire of the wisest men since the creation of the world, was now within my grasp. Not that, like a magic scene, it all opened upon me at once: the information I had obtained was of a nature rather to direct my endeavours so soon as I should point them towards the object of my search, than to exhibit that object already accomplished. I was like the Arabian who had been buried with the dead, and found a passage to life aided only by one glimmering, and seemingly ineffectual, light.[20]

I see by your eagerness, and the wonder and hope which your eyes express, my friend, that you expect to be informed of the secret with which I am acquainted; that cannot be: listen patiently until the end of my story, and you will easily perceive why I am reserved upon that subject. I will not lead you on, unguarded and ardent as I then was, to your destruction and infallible misery. Learn from me, if not by my precepts, at least by my example, how dangerous is the acquirement of knowledge, and how much

---

[20] Buried alive with the corpse of his wife, Sinbad follows a distant light to the surface, in Sinbad's Fourth Voyage, *A Thousand and One Nights*. [Ed.]

happier that man is who believes his native town to be the world, than he who aspires to become greater than his nature will allow.

When I found so astonishing a power placed within my hands, I hesitated a long time concerning the manner in which I should employ it. Although I possessed the capacity of bestowing animation, yet to prepare a frame for the reception of it, with all its intricacies of fibres, muscles, and veins, still remained a work of inconceivable difficulty and labour. I doubted at first whether I should attempt the creation of a being like myself or one of simpler organization; but my imagination was too much exalted by my first success to permit me to doubt of my ability to give life to an animal as complex and wonderful as man. The materials at present within my command hardly appeared adequate to so arduous an undertaking; but I doubted not that I should ultimately succeed. I prepared myself for a multitude of reverses; my operations might be incessantly baffled, and at last my work be imperfect: yet, when I considered the improvement which every day takes place in science and mechanics, I was encouraged to hope my present attempts would at least lay the foundations of future success. Nor could I consider the magnitude and complexity of my plan as any argument of its impracticability. It was with these feelings that I began the creation of a human being. As the minuteness of the parts formed a great hindrance to my speed, I resolved, contrary to my first intention, to make the being of a gigantic stature; that is to say, about eight feet in height, and proportionably large. After having formed this determination, and having spent some months in successfully collecting and arranging my materials, I began.

No one can conceive the variety of feelings which bore me onwards, like a hurricane, in the first enthusiasm of success. Life and death appeared to me ideal bounds, which I should first break through, and pour a torrent of light into our dark world. A new species would bless me as its creator and source; many happy and excellent natures would owe their being to me. No father could claim the gratitude of his child so completely as I should deserve theirs. Pursuing these reflections, I thought, that if I could bestow animation upon lifeless matter, I might in process of time (although I now found it impossible) renew life where death had apparently devoted the body to corruption.[21]

These thoughts supported my spirits, while I pursued my undertaking with unremitting ardour. My cheek had grown pale with study, and my person had become emaciated with confinement. Sometimes, on the very brink of certainty, I failed; yet still I clung to the hope which the next day

---

[21] Luigi Galvini had demonstrated electrically induced motion in the dead body of a cow in 1802; his nephew John Aldini had similar, if eerie, success with the corpse of a criminal in experiments conducted in 1803 and 1804. [Ed.]

or the next hour might realize. One secret which I alone possessed was the hope to which I had dedicated myself; and the moon gazed on my midnight labours, while, with unrelaxed and breathless eagerness, I pursued nature to her hiding places. Who shall conceive the horrors of my secret toil, as I dabbled among the unhallowed damps of the grave, or tortured the living animal to animate the lifeless clay?[22] My limbs now tremble, and my eyes swim with the remembrance; but then a resistless, and almost frantic impulse, urged me forward; I seemed to have lost all soul or sensation but for this one pursuit. It was indeed but a passing trance, that only made me feel with renewed acuteness so soon as, the unnatural stimulus ceasing to operate, I had returned to my old habits. I collected bones from charnel houses; and disturbed, with profane fingers, the tremendous secrets of the human frame. In a solitary chamber, or rather cell, at the top of the house, and separated from all the other apartments by a gallery and staircase, I kept my workshop of filthy creation; my eyeballs were starting from their sockets in attending to the details of my employment. The dissecting room and the slaughter-house furnished many of my materials; and often did my human nature turn with loathing from my occupation, whilst, still urged on by an eagerness which perpetually increased, I brought my work near to a conclusion.

The summer months passed while I was thus engaged, heart and soul, in one pursuit. It was a most beautiful season; never did the fields bestow a more plentiful harvest, or the vines yield a more luxuriant vintage: but my eyes were insensible to the charms of nature. And the same feelings which made me neglect the scenes around me caused me also to forget those friends who were so many miles absent, and whom I had not seen for so long a time. I knew my silence disquieted them; and I well remembered the words of my father: 'I know that while you are pleased with yourself, you will think of us with affection, and we shall hear regularly from you. You must pardon me, if I regard any interruption in your correspondence as a proof that your other duties are equally neglected.'

I knew well therefore what would be my father's feelings; but I could not tear my thoughts from my employment, loathsome in itself, but which had taken an irresistible hold of my imagination. I wished, as it were, to procrastinate all that related to my feelings of affection until the great object, which swallowed up every habit of my nature, should be completed.

I then thought that my father would be unjust if he ascribed my neglect to vice, or faultiness on my part; but I am now convinced that he was

---

[22] This suggests that animal vivisection as well as the dissection of dead humans provided Victor Frankenstein with some of his knowledge, and even some of his materials, another moment that connects *Frankenstein* with *The Island of Doctor Moreau*. [Ed.]

justified in conceiving that I should not be altogether free from blame. A human being in perfection ought always to preserve a calm and peaceful mind, and never to allow passion or a transitory desire to disturb his tranquillity. I do not think that the pursuit of knowledge is an exception to this rule. If the study to which you apply yourself has a tendency to weaken your affections, and to destroy your taste for those simple pleasures in which no alloy can possibly mix, then that study is certainly unlawful, that is to say, not befitting the human mind. If this rule were always observed; if no man allowed any pursuit whatsoever to interfere with the tranquillity of his domestic affections, Greece had not been enslaved; Cæsar would have spared his country; America would have been discovered more gradually; and the empires of Mexico and Peru had not been destroyed.

But I forget that I am moralizing in the most interesting part of my tale: and your looks remind me to proceed.

My father made no reproach in his letters; and only took notice of my silence by inquiring into my occupations more particularly than before. Winter, spring, and summer, passed away during my labours; but I did not watch the blossom or the expanding leaves—sights which before always yielded me supreme delight, so deeply was I engrossed in my occupation. The leaves of that year had withered before my work drew near to a close; and now every day shewed me more plainly how well I had succeeded. But my enthusiasm was checked by my anxiety, and I appeared rather like one doomed by slavery to toil in the mines, or any other unwholesome trade, than an artist occupied by his favourite employment. Every night I was oppressed by a slow fever, and I became nervous to a most painful degree; a disease that I regretted the more because I had hitherto enjoyed most excellent health, and had always boasted of the firmness of my nerves. But I believed that exercise and amusement would soon drive away such symptoms; and I promised myself both of these, when my creation should be complete.

CHAPTER IV

It was on a dreary night of November, that I beheld the accomplishment of my toils. With an anxiety that almost amounted to agony, I collected the instruments of life around me, that I might infuse a spark of being into the lifeless thing that lay at my feet. It was already one in the morning; the rain pattered dismally against the panes, and my candle was nearly burnt out, when, by the glimmer of the half-extinguished light, I saw the dull yellow eye of the creature open; it breathed hard, and a convulsive motion agitated its limbs.

How can I describe my emotions at this catastrophe, or how delineate the wretch whom with such infinite pains and care I had endeavoured to form? His limbs were in proportion, and I had selected his features as beautiful. Beautiful!—Great God! His yellow skin scarcely covered the work of muscles and arteries beneath; his hair was of a lustrous black, and flowing; his teeth of a pearly whiteness; but these luxuriances only formed a more horrid contrast with his watery eyes, that seemed almost of the same colour as the dun white sockets in which they were set, his shrivelled complexion, and straight black lips.

The different accidents of life are not so changeable as the feelings of human nature. I had worked hard for nearly two years, for the sole purpose of infusing life into an inanimate body. For this I had deprived myself of rest and health. I had desired it with an ardour that far exceeded moderation; but now that I had finished, the beauty of the dream vanished, and breathless horror and disgust filled my heart. Unable to endure the aspect of the being I had created, I rushed out of the room, and continued a long time traversing my bed-chamber, unable to compose my mind to sleep. At length lassitude succeeded to the tumult I had before endured; and I threw myself on the bed in my clothes, endeavouring to seek a few moments of forgetfulness. But it was in vain: I slept indeed, but I was disturbed by the wildest dreams. I thought I saw Elizabeth, in the bloom of health, walking in the streets of Ingolstadt. Delighted and surprised, I embraced her; but as I imprinted the first kiss on her lips, they became livid with the hue of death; her features appeared to change, and I thought that I held the corpse of my dead mother in my arms; a shroud enveloped her form, and I saw the grave-worms crawling in the folds of the flannel. I started from my sleep with horror; a cold dew covered my forehead, my teeth chattered, and every limb became convulsed; when, by the dim and yellow light of the moon, as it forced its way through the window-shutters, I beheld the wretch—the miserable monster whom I had created. He held up the curtain of the bed; and his eyes, if eyes they may be called, were fixed on me. His jaws opened, and he muttered some inarticulate sounds, while a grin wrinkled his cheeks. He might have spoken, but I did not hear; one hand was stretched out, seemingly to detain me, but I escaped, and rushed down stairs. I took refuge in the court-yard belonging to the house which I inhabited; where I remained during the rest of the night, walking up and down in the greatest agitation, listening attentively, catching and fearing each sound as if it were to announce the approach of the demoniacal corpse to which I had so miserably given life.

Oh! no mortal could support the horror of that countenance. A mummy again endued with animation could not be so hideous as that wretch. I had gazed on him while unfinished; he was ugly then; but when those muscles and joints were rendered capable of motion, it became a thing such as even Dante could not have conceived.[23]

I passed the night wretchedly. Sometimes my pulse beat so quickly and hardly, that I felt the palpitation of every artery; at others, I nearly sank to the ground through languor and extreme weakness. Mingled with this horror, I felt the bitterness of disappointment: dreams that had been my food and pleasant rest for so long a space, were now become a hell to me; and the change was so rapid, the overthrow so complete!

Morning, dismal and wet, at length dawned, and discovered to my sleepless and aching eyes the church of Ingolstadt, its white steeple and clock, which indicated the sixth hour. The porter opened the gates of the court, which had that night been my asylum, and I issued into the streets, pacing them with quick steps, as if I sought to avoid the wretch whom I feared every turning of the street would present to my view. I did not dare return to the apartment which I inhabited, but felt impelled to hurry on, although wetted by the rain, which poured from a black and comfortless sky.

I continued walking in this manner for some time, endeavouring, by bodily exercise, to ease the load that weighed upon my mind. I traversed the streets, without any clear conception of where I was, or what I was doing. My heart palpitated in the sickness of fear; and I hurried on with irregular steps, not daring to look about me:

Like one who, on a lonely road,
    Doth walk in fear and dread,
And, having once turn'd round, walks on,
    And turns no more his head;
Because he knows a frightful fiend
    Doth close behind him tread.[24]

Continuing thus, I came at length opposite to the inn at which the various diligences and carriages usually stopped. Here I paused, I knew not why; but I remained some minutes with my eyes fixed on a coach that was coming towards me from the other end of the street. As it drew nearer, I observed that it was the Swiss diligence: it stopped just where I was standing; and, on the door being opened, I perceived Henry Clerval, who, on

---

[23] The first book of Dante Alighieri's *Divine Comedy*, "The Inferno" (1321) contains many scenes where humans are confronted or tormented by devils in the shape of their own monstrous deeds or natures. [Ed.]

[24] Coleridge's "Ancient Mariner." [Mary Shelley's note. These are lines 446–51. Ed.]

seeing me, instantly sprung out. 'My dear Frankenstein,' exclaimed he, 'how glad I am to see you! how fortunate that you should be here at the very moment of my alighting!'

Nothing could equal my delight on seeing Clerval; his presence brought back to my thoughts my father, Elizabeth, and all those scenes of home so dear to my recollection. I grasped his hand, and in a moment forgot my horror and misfortune; I felt suddenly, and for the first time during many months, calm and serene joy. I welcomed my friend, therefore, in the most cordial manner, and we walked towards my college. Clerval continued talking for some time about our mutual friends, and his own good fortune in being permitted to come to Ingolstadt. 'You may easily believe,' said he, 'how great was the difficulty to persuade my father that it was not absolutely necessary for a merchant not to understand any thing except book-keeping; and indeed, I believe I left him incredulous to the last, for his constant answer to my unwearied entreaties was the same as that of the Dutch school-master in *The Vicar of Wakefield:* "I have ten thousand florins a year without Greek, I eat heartily without Greek." [25] But his affection for me at length overcame his dislike of learning, and he has permitted me to undertake a voyage of discovery to the land of knowledge.'

'It gives me the greatest delight to see you; but tell me how you left my father, brothers, and Elizabeth.'

'Very well, and very happy, only a little uneasy that they hear from you so seldom. By the bye, I mean to lecture you a little upon their account myself.—But, my dear Frankenstein,' continued he, stopping short, and gazing full in my face, 'I did not before remark how very ill you appear; so thin and pale; you look as if you had been watching for several nights.'

'You have guessed right; I have lately been so deeply engaged in one occupation, that I have not allowed myself sufficient rest, as you see: but I hope, I sincerely hope, that all these employments are now at an end, and that I am at length free.'

I trembled excessively; I could not endure to think of, and far less to allude to the occurrences of the preceding night. I walked with a quick pace, and we soon arrived at my college. I then reflected, and the thought made me shiver, that the creature whom I had left in my apartment might still be there, alive, and walking about. I dreaded to behold this monster; but I feared still more that Henry should see him. Entreating him therefore to remain a few minutes at the bottom of the stairs, I darted up towards my own room. My hand was already on the lock of the door before I recollected myself. I then paused; and a cold shivering came over me. I threw the door

---

[25] Oliver Goldsmith's novel (1776), Chapter 20. [Ed.]

forcibly open, as children are accustomed to do when they expect a spectre to stand in waiting for them on the other side; but nothing appeared. I stepped fearfully in: the apartment was empty; and my bedroom was also freed from its hideous guest. I could hardly believe that so great a good-fortune could have befallen me; but when I became assured that my enemy had indeed fled, I clapped my hands for joy, and ran down to Clerval.

We ascended into my room, and the servant presently brought break-fast; but I was unable to contain myself. It was not joy only that possessed me; I felt my flesh tingle with excess of sensitiveness, and my pulse beat rapidly. I was unable to remain for a single instant in the same place; I jumped over the chairs, clapped my hands, and laughed aloud. Clerval at first attributed my unusual spirits to joy on his arrival; but when he ob-served me more attentively, he saw a wildness in my eyes for which he could not account; and my loud, unrestrained, heartless laughter, fright-ened and astonished him.

'My dear Victor,' cried he, 'what, for God's sake, is the matter? Do not laugh in that manner. How ill you are! What is the cause of all this?'

'Do not ask me,' cried I, putting my hands before my eyes, for I thought I saw the dreaded spectre glide into the room; '*he* can tell. —Oh, save me! save me!' I imagined that the monster seized me; I struggled furiously, and fell down in a fit.

Poor Clerval! what must have been his feelings? A meeting, which he an-ticipated with such joy, so strangely turned to bitterness. But I was not the witness of his grief; for I was lifeless, and did not recover my senses for a long, long time.

This was the commencement of a nervous fever, which confined me for several months. During all that time Henry was my only nurse. I afterwards learned that, knowing my father's advanced age, and unfitness for so long a journey, and how wretched my sickness would make Elizabeth, he spared them this grief by concealing the extent of my disorder. He knew that I could not have a more kind and attentive nurse than himself; and, firm in the hope he felt of my recovery, he did not doubt that, instead of doing harm, he performed the kindest action that he could towards them.

But I was in reality very ill; and surely nothing but the unbounded and unremitting attentions of my friend could have restored me to life. The form of the monster on whom I had bestowed existence was for ever be-fore my eyes, and I raved incessantly concerning him. Doubtless my words surprised Henry: he at first believed them to be the wanderings of my dis-turbed imagination; but the pertinacity with which I continually recurred to the same subject persuaded him that my disorder indeed owed its origin to some uncommon and terrible event.

By very slow degrees, and with frequent relapses, that alarmed and grieved my friend, I recovered. I remember the first time I became capable of observing outward objects with any kind of pleasure, I perceived that the fallen leaves had disappeared, and that the young buds were shooting forth from the trees that shaded my window. It was a divine spring; and the season contributed greatly to my convalescence. I felt also sentiments of joy and affection revive in my bosom; my gloom disappeared, and in a short time I became as cheerful as before I was attacked by the fatal passion.

'Dearest Clerval,' exclaimed I, 'how kind, how very good you are to me. This whole winter, instead of being spent in study, as you promised yourself, has been consumed in my sick room. How shall I ever repay you? I feel the greatest remorse for the disappointment of which I have been the occasion; but you will forgive me.'

'You will repay me entirely, if you do not discompose yourself, but get well as fast as you can; and since you appear in such good spirits, I may speak to you on one subject, may I not?'

I trembled. One subject! What could it be? Could he allude to an object on whom I dared not even think?

'Compose yourself,' said Clerval, who observed my change of colour, 'I will not mention it, if it agitates you; but your father and cousin would be very happy if they received a letter from you in your own hand-writing. They hardly know how ill you have been, and are uneasy at your long silence.'

'Is that all? my dear Henry. How could you suppose that my first thought would not fly towards those dear, dear friends whom I love, and who are so deserving of my love.'

'If this is your present temper, my friend, you will perhaps be glad to see a letter that has been lying here some days for you: it is from your cousin, I believe.'

CHAPTER V

Clerval then put the following letter into my hands.

To V. FRANKENSTEIN.
'MY DEAR COUSIN,

'I cannot describe to you the uneasiness we have all felt concerning your health. We cannot help imagining that your friend Clerval conceals the extent of your disorder: for it is now several months since we have seen your hand-writing; and all this time you have been obliged to dictate your letters to Henry. Surely, Victor, you must have been exceedingly ill; and this makes us all very wretched, as much so nearly as after the death of your dear mother. My uncle was almost persuaded that you were indeed dangerously ill, and could hardly be restrained from undertaking a journey to Ingolstadt. Clerval always writes that you are getting better; I eagerly hope that you will confirm this intelligence soon in your own hand-writing; for indeed, indeed, Victor, we are all very miserable on this account. Relieve us from this fear, and we shall be the happiest creatures in the world. Your father's health is now so vigorous, that he appears ten years younger since last winter. Ernest also is so much improved, that you would hardly know him: he is now nearly sixteen, and has lost that sickly appearance which he had some years ago; he is grown quite robust and active.

'My uncle and I conversed a long time last night about what profession Ernest should follow. His constant illness when young has deprived him of the habits of application; and now that he enjoys good health, he is continually in the open air, climbing the hills, or rowing on the lake. I therefore proposed that he should be a farmer; which you know, Cousin, is a favourite scheme of mine. A farmer's is a very healthy happy life; and the least hurtful, or rather the most beneficial profession of any. My uncle had an idea of his being educated as an advocate, that through his interest he might become a judge. But, besides that he is not at all fitted for such an occupation, it is certainly more creditable to cultivate the earth for the sustenance of man, than to be the confidant, and sometimes the accomplice, of his vices; which is the profession of a lawyer. I said, that the employments of a prosperous farmer, if they were not a more honourable, they were at least a happier species of occupation than that of a judge, whose misfortune it was always to meddle with the dark side of human nature. My uncle smiled, and said, that I ought to be an advocate myself, which put an end to the conversation on that subject.

'And now I must tell you a little story that will please, and perhaps amuse you. Do you not remember Justine Moritz? Probably you do not; I will relate her history, therefore, in a few words. Madame Moritz, her mother, was a widow with four children, of whom Justine was the third. This girl had always been the favourite of her father; but, through a strange perversity, her mother could not endure her, and, after the death of M. Moritz, treated her very ill. My aunt observed this; and, when Justine was twelve years of age, prevailed on her mother to allow her to live at her house. The republican institutions of our country have produced simpler and happier manners than those which prevail in the great monarchies that surround it. Hence there is less distinction between the several classes of its inhabitants; and the lower orders being neither so poor nor so despised, their manners are more refined and moral. A servant in Geneva does not mean the same thing as a servant in France and England. Justine, thus received in our family, learned the duties of a servant; a condition which, in our fortunate country, does not include the idea of ignorance, and a sacrifice of the dignity of a human being. *antislavery discourse*

'After what I have said, I dare say you well remember the heroine of my little tale: for Justine was a great favourite of yours; and I recollect you once remarked, that if you were in an ill humour, one glance from Justine could dissipate it, for the same reason that Ariosto gives concerning the beauty of Angelica—she looked so frank-hearted and happy.[26] My aunt conceived a great attachment for her, by which she was induced to give her an education superior to that which she had at first intended. This benefit was fully repaid; Justine was the most grateful little creature in the world: I do not mean that she made any professions, I never heard one pass her lips; but you could see by her eyes that she almost adored her protectress. Although her disposition was gay, and in many respects inconsiderate, yet she paid the greatest attention to every gesture of my aunt. She thought her the model of all excellence, and endeavoured to imitate her phraseology and manners, so that even now she often reminds me of her.

'When my dearest aunt died, every one was too much occupied in their own grief to notice poor Justine, who had attended her during her illness with the most anxious affection. Poor Justine was very ill; but other trials were reserved for her.

'One by one, her brothers and sister died; and her mother, with the exception of her neglected daughter, was left childless. The conscience of the woman was troubled; she began to think that the deaths of her favourites was a judgment from heaven to chastise her partiality. She was a Roman Catholic; and I believe her confessor confirmed the idea which she had conceived. Accordingly, a few months after your departure for Ingolstadt, Justine was called home by her repentant mother. Poor girl! she wept when she quitted our house: she was much altered since the death of my aunt; grief had given softness and a winning mildness to her manners, which had before been remarkable for vivacity. Nor was her residence at her mother's house of a nature to restore her gaiety. The poor woman was very vacillating in her repentance. She sometimes begged Justine to forgive her unkindness, but much oftener accused her of having caused the deaths of her brothers and sister. Perpetual fretting at length threw Madame Moritz into a decline, which at first increased her irritability, but she is now at peace for ever. She died on the first approach of cold weather, at the beginning of this last winter. Justine has returned to us; and I assure you I love her tenderly.

---

[26] Angelica is the heroine of Ariosto's *Orlando Furioso*. [Ed.]

She is very clever and gentle, and extremely pretty; as I mentioned before, her mien and her expressions continually remind me of my dear aunt.

'I must say also a few words to you, my dear cousin, of little darling William. I wish you could see him; he is very tall of his age, with sweet laughing blue eyes, dark eye-lashes, and curling hair. When he smiles, two little dimples appear on each cheek, which are rosy with health. He has already had one or two little *wives*, but Louisa Biron is his favourite, a pretty little girl of five years of age.

'Now, dear Victor, I dare say you wish to be indulged in a little gossip concerning the good people of Geneva. The pretty Miss Mansfield has already received the congratulatory visits on her approaching marriage with a young Englishman, John Melbourne, Esq. Her ugly sister, Manon, married M. Duvillard, the rich banker, last autumn. Your favourite schoolfellow, Louis Manoir, has suffered several misfortunes since the departure of Clerval from Geneva. But he has already recovered his spirits, and is reported to be on the point of marrying a very lively pretty Frenchwoman, Madame Tavernier. She is a widow, and much older than Manoir; but she is very much admired, and a favourite with every body.

'I have written myself into good spirits, dear cousin; yet I cannot conclude without again anxiously inquiring concerning your health. Dear Victor, if you are not very ill, write yourself, and make your father and all of us happy; or—I cannot bear to think of the other side of the question; my tears already flow. Adieu, my dearest cousin.

'ELIZABETH LAVENZA.
'Geneva, March 18th, 17—.'

'Dear, dear Elizabeth!' I exclaimed when I had read her letter, 'I will write instantly, and relieve them from the anxiety they must feel.' I wrote, and this exertion greatly fatigued me; but my convalescence had commenced, and proceeded regularly. In another fortnight I was able to leave my chamber.

One of my first duties on my recovery was to introduce Clerval to the several professors of the university. In doing this, I underwent a kind of rough usage, ill befitting the wounds that my mind had sustained. Ever since the fatal night, the end of my labours, and the beginning of my misfortunes, I had conceived a violent antipathy even to the name of natural philosophy. When I was otherwise quite restored to health, the sight of a chemical instrument would renew all the agony of my nervous symptoms. Henry saw this, and had removed all my apparatus from my view. He had also changed my apartment; for he perceived that I had acquired a dislike for the room which had previously been my laboratory. But these cares of Clerval were made of no avail when I visited the professors. M. Waldman inflicted torture when he praised, with kindness and warmth, the astonishing progress I had made in the sciences. He soon perceived that I disliked the subject; but, not guessing the real cause, he attributed my feelings to modesty, and changed the subject from my improvement to the science itself, with a desire, as I evidently saw, of drawing me out. What could I do? He meant to please, and he tormented me. I felt as if he had placed carefully, one by one, in my view those instruments which were to be afterwards used in putting me to a slow and cruel death. I writhed under his words, yet dared not exhibit the pain I felt. Clerval, whose eyes and feelings were always quick in discerning the sensations of others, declined the subject, alleging, in excuse, his total ignorance; and the conversation took a more general turn. I thanked my friend from my heart, but I did not speak. I saw plainly that he was surprised, but he never attempted to draw my secret from me; and although I loved him with a mixture of affection and reverence that knew no bounds, yet I could never persuade myself to confide to him that event which was so often present to my recollection, but which I feared the detail to another would only impress more deeply.

M. Krempe was not equally docile; and in my condition at that time, of almost insupportable sensitiveness, his harsh blunt encomiums gave me even more pain than the benevolent approbation of M. Waldman. 'D——n the fellow!' cried he; 'why, M. Clerval, I assure you he has outstript us all. Aye, stare if you please; but it is nevertheless true. A youngster who, but a few years ago, believed Cornelius Agrippa as firmly as the gospel, has now set himself at the head of the university; and if he is not soon pulled down, we shall all be out of countenance. —Aye, aye,' continued he, observing my face expressive of suffering, 'M. Frankenstein is modest; an excellent quality in a young man. Young men should be diffident of themselves, you know, M. Clerval; I was myself when young: but that wears out in a very short time.'

M. Krempe had now commenced an eulogy on himself, which happily turned the conversation from a subject that was so annoying to me.

Clerval was no natural philosopher. His imagination was too vivid for the minutiæ of science. Languages were his principal study; and he sought, by acquiring their elements, to open a field for self-instruction on his return to Geneva. Persian, Arabic, and Hebrew, gained his attention, after he had made himself perfectly master of Greek and Latin. For my own part, idleness had ever been irksome to me; and now that I wished to fly from reflection, and hated my former studies, I felt great relief in being the fellow-pupil with my friend, and found not only instruction but consolation in the works of the orientalists. Their melancholy is soothing, and their joy elevating to a degree I never experienced in studying the authors of any other country. When you read their writings, life appears to consist

contrast

in a warm sun and garden of roses,—in the smiles and frowns of a fair enemy, and the fire that consumes your own heart. How different from the
manly and heroical poetry of Greece and Rome.

Summer passed away in these occupations, and my return to Geneva was
fixed for the latter end of autumn; but being delayed by several accidents,
winter and snow arrived, the roads were deemed impassable, and my journey was retarded until the ensuing spring. I felt this delay very bitterly; for
I longed to see my native town, and my beloved friends. My return had only
been delayed so long from an unwillingness to leave Clerval in a strange
place, before he had become acquainted with any of its inhabitants. The
winter, however, was spent cheerfully; and although the spring was uncommonly late, when it came, its beauty compensated for its dilatoriness.

The month of May had already commenced, and I expected the letter
daily which was to fix the date of my departure, when Henry proposed a
pedestrian tour in the environs of Ingolstadt that I might bid a personal
farewell to the country I had so long inhabited. I acceded with pleasure to
this proposition: I was fond of exercise, and Clerval had always been my
favourite companion in the rambles of this nature that I had taken among
the scenes of my native country.

We passed a fortnight in these perambulations: my health and spirits
had long been restored, and they gained additional strength from the salu-
brious air I breathed, the natural incidents of our progress, and the conversation of my friend. Study had before secluded me from the intercourse
of my fellow-creatures, and rendered me unsocial; but Clerval called forth
the better feelings of my heart; he again taught me to love the aspect of nature, and the cheerful faces of children. Excellent friend! how sincerely did
you love me, and endeavour to elevate my mind, until it was on a level with
your own. A selfish pursuit had cramped and narrowed me, until your gentleness and affection warmed and opened my senses; I became the same

eulogy

happy creature who, a few years ago, loving and beloved by all, had no sorrow or care. When happy, inanimate nature had the power of bestowing on
me the most delightful sensations. A serene sky and verdant fields filled me
with ecstacy. The present season was indeed divine; the flowers of spring
bloomed in the hedges, while those of summer were already in bud: I was
undisturbed by thoughts which during the preceeding year had pressed
upon me, notwithstanding my endeavours to throw them off, with an invincible burden.

love

Henry rejoiced in my gaiety, and sincerely sympathized in my feelings:
he exerted himself to amuse me, while he expressed the sensations that
filled his soul. The resources of his mind on this occasion were truly astonishing: his conversation was full of imagination; and very often, in imitation of the Persian and Arabic writers, he invented tales of wonderful

fancy and passion. At other times he repeated my favourite poems, or drew me out into arguments, which he supported with great ingenuity.

We returned to our college on a Sunday afternoon: the peasants were dancing, and every one we met appeared gay and happy. My own spirits were high, and I bounded along with feelings of unbridled joy and hilarity.

whon . . .

CHAPTER VI

On my return, I found the following letter from my father: —

'To *V. FRANKENSTEIN.*
'*MY DEAR VICTOR,*

'You have probably waited impatiently for a letter to fix the date of your return to us; and I was at first tempted to write only a few lines, merely mentioning the day on which I should expect you. But that would be a cruel kindness, and I dare not do it. What would be your surprise, my son, when you expected a happy and gay welcome, to behold, on the contrary, tears and wretchedness? And how, Victor, can I relate our misfortune? Absence cannot have rendered you callous to our joys and griefs; and how shall I inflict pain on an absent child? I wish to prepare you for the woeful news, but I know it is impossible; even now your eye skims over the page, to seek the words which are to convey to you the horrible tidings.

'William is dead! — that sweet child, whose smiles delighted and warmed my heart, who was so gentle, yet so gay! Victor, he is murdered!

'I will not attempt to console you; but will simply relate the circumstances of the transaction.

'Last Thursday (May 7th) I, my niece, and your two brothers, went to walk in Plainpalais. The evening was warm and serene, and we prolonged our walk farther than usual. It was already dusk before we thought of returning; and then we discovered that William and Ernest, who had gone on before, were not to be found. We accordingly rested on a seat until they should return. Presently Ernest came, and inquired if we had seen his brother: he said, that they had been playing together, that William had run away to hide himself, and that he vainly sought for him, and afterwards waited for him a long time, but that he did not return.

'This account rather alarmed us, and we continued to search for him until night fell, when Elizabeth conjectured that he might have returned to the house. He was not there. We returned again, with torches; for I could not rest, when I thought that my sweet boy had lost himself, and was exposed to all the damps and dews of night: Elizabeth also suffered extreme

innocence

anguish. About five in the morning I discovered my lovely boy, whom the night before I had seen blooming and active in health, stretched on the grass livid and motionless: the print of the murderer's finger was on his neck.

'He was conveyed home, and the anguish that was visible in my countenance betrayed the secret to Elizabeth. She was very earnest to see the corpse. At first I attempted to prevent her; but she persisted, and entering the room where it lay, hastily examined the neck of the victim, and clasping her hands exclaimed, "O God! I have murdered my darling infant!'

'She fainted, and was restored with extreme difficulty. When she again lived, it was only to weep and sigh. She told me, that that same evening William had teazed her to let him wear a very valuable miniature that she possessed of your mother. This picture is gone, and was doubtless the temptation which urged the murderer to the deed. We have no trace of him at present, although our exertions to discover him are unremitted; but they will not restore my beloved William.

'Come, dearest Victor; you alone can console Elizabeth. She weeps continually, and accuses herself unjustly as the cause of his death; her words pierce my heart. We are all unhappy; but will not that be an additional motive for you, my son, to return and be our comforter? Your dear mother! Alas, Victor! I now say, Thank God she did not live to witness the cruel, miserable death of her youngest darling!

'Come, Victor; not brooding thoughts of vengeance against the assassin, but with feelings of peace and gentleness, that will heal, instead of festering the wounds of our minds. Enter the house of mourning, my friend, but with kindness and affection for those who love you, and not with hatred for your enemies.

warning

> '*Your affectionate and afflicted father,*
> ALPHONSE FRANKENSTEIN.
> '*Geneva, May 12th, 17—.*'

Clerval, who had watched my countenance as I read this letter, was surprised to observe the despair that succeeded to the joy I at first expressed on receiving news from my friends. I threw the letter on the table, and covered my face with my hands.

'My dear Frankenstein,' exclaimed Henry, when he perceived me weep with bitterness, 'are you always to be unhappy? My dear friend, what has happened?'

I motioned to him to take up the letter, while I walked up and down the room in the extremest agitation. Tears also gushed from the eyes of Clerval, as he read the account of my misfortune.

'I can offer you no consolation, my friend,' said he; 'your disaster is irreparable. What do you intend to do?'

'To go instantly to Geneva: come with me, Henry, to order the horses.'

During our walk, Clerval endeavoured to raise my spirits. He did not do this by common topics of consolation, but by exhibiting the truest sympathy. 'Poor William!' said he, 'that dear child; he now sleeps with his angel mother. His friends mourn and weep, but he is at rest: he does not now feel the murderer's grasp; a sod covers his gentle form, and he knows no pain. He can no longer be a fit subject for pity; the survivors are the greatest sufferers, and for them time is the only consolation. Those maxims of the Stoics, that death was no evil, and that the mind of man ought to be superior to despair on the eternal absence of a beloved object, ought not to be urged. Even Cato wept over the dead body of his brother.'

Clerval spoke thus as we hurried through the streets; the words impressed themselves on my mind, and I remembered them afterwards in solitude. But now, as soon as the horses arrived, I hurried into a cabriole,[27] and bade farewell to my friend.

My journey was very melancholy. At first I wished to hurry on, for I longed to console and sympathize with my loved and sorrowing friends; but when I drew near my native town, I slackened my progress. I could hardly sustain the multitude of feelings that crowded into my mind. I passed through scenes familiar to my youth, but which I had not seen for nearly six years. How altered every thing might be during that time? One sudden and desolating change had taken place; but a thousand little circumstances might have by degrees worked other alterations, which, although they were done more tranquilly, might not be the less decisive. Fear overcame me; I dared not advance, dreading a thousand nameless evils that made me tremble, although I was unable to define them.

I remained two days at Lausanne, in this painful state of mind. I contemplated the lake: the waters were placid; all around was calm, and the snowy mountains, 'the palaces of nature,'[28] were not changed. By degrees the calm and heavenly scene restored me, and I continued my journey towards Geneva.

The road ran by the side of the lake, which became narrower as I approached my native town. I discovered more distinctly the black sides of Jura, and the bright summit of Mont Blanc; I wept like a child: 'Dear mountains! my own beautiful lake! how do you welcome your wanderer? Your summits are clear; the sky and lake are blue and placid. Is this to prognosticate peace, or to mock at my unhappiness?'

I fear, my friend, that I shall render myself tedious by dwelling on these preliminary circumstances; but they were days of comparative happiness,

---

[27] A two-wheeled, horsedrawn carriage. [Ed.]

[28] From Canto III of Byron's *Child Harold's Pilgrimage* (1816), lxii, 591. [Ed.]

and I think of them with pleasure. My country, my beloved country! who but a native can tell the delight I took in again beholding thy streams, thy mountains, and, more than all, thy lovely lake.

Yet, as I drew nearer home, grief and fear again overcame me. Night also closed around; and when I could hardly see the dark mountains, I felt still more gloomily. The picture appeared a vast and dim scene of evil, and I foresaw obscurely that I was destined to become the most wretched of human beings. Alas! I prophesied truly, and failed only in one single circumstance, that in all the misery I imagined and dreaded, I did not conceive the hundredth part of the anguish I was destined to endure.

It was completely dark when I arrived in the environs of Geneva; the gates of the town were already shut; and I was obliged to pass the night at Secheron, a village half a league to the east of the city. The sky was serene; and, as I was unable to rest, I resolved to visit the spot where my poor William had been murdered. As I could not pass through the town, I was obliged to cross the lake in a boat to arrive at Plainpalais. During this short voyage I saw the lightnings playing on the summit of Mont Blanc in the most beautiful figures. The storm appeared to approach rapidly; and, on landing, I ascended a low hill, that I might observe its progress. It advanced; the heavens were clouded, and I soon felt the rain coming slowly in large drops, but its violence quickly increased.

I quitted my seat, and walked on, although the darkness and storm increased every minute, and the thunder burst with a terrific crash over my head. It was echoed from Salève, the Juras, and the Alps of Savoy; vivid flashes of lightning dazzled my eyes, illuminating the lake, making it appear like a vast sheet of fire; then for an instant every thing seemed of a pitchy darkness, until the eye recovered itself from the preceding flash. The storm, as is often the case in Switzerland, appeared at once in various parts of the heavens. The most violent storm hung exactly north of the town, over that part of the lake which lies between the promontory of Belrive and the village of Copêt. Another storm enlightened Jura with faint flashes; and another darkened and sometimes disclosed the Môle, a peaked mountain to the east of the lake.

While I watched the storm, so beautiful yet terrific, I wandered on with a hasty step. This noble war in the sky elevated my spirits; I clasped my hands, and exclaimed aloud, 'William, dear angel! this is thy funeral, this thy dirge!' As I said these words, I perceived in the gloom a figure which stole from behind a clump of trees near me; I stood fixed, gazing intently: I could not be mistaken. A flash of lightning illuminated the object, and discovered its shape plainly to me; its gigantic stature, and the deformity of its aspect, more hideous than belongs to humanity, instantly informed me that it was the wretch, the filthy dæmon to whom I had given life. What did he there? Could he be (I shuddered at the conception) the murderer of my brother? No sooner did that idea cross my imagination, than I became convinced of its truth; my teeth chattered, and I was forced to lean against a tree for support. The figure passed me quickly, and I lost it in the gloom. Nothing in human shape could have destroyed that fair child. *He* was the murderer! I could not doubt it. The mere presence of the idea was an irresistible proof of the fact. I thought of pursuing the devil; but it would have been in vain, for another flash discovered him to me hanging among the rocks of the nearly perpendicular ascent of Mont Salêve, a hill that bounds Plainpalais on the south. He soon reached the summit, and disappeared.

I remained motionless. The thunder ceased; but the rain still continued, and the scene was enveloped in an impenetrable darkness. I revolved in my mind the events which I had until now sought to forget: the whole train of my progress towards the creation; the appearance of the work of my own hands alive at my bed side; its departure. Two years had now nearly elapsed since the night on which he first received life; and was this his first crime? Alas! I had turned loose into the world a depraved wretch, whose delight was in carnage and misery; had he not murdered my brother?

No one can conceive the anguish I suffered during the remainder of the night, which I spent, cold and wet, in the open air. But I did not feel the inconvenience of the weather; my imagination was busy in scenes of evil and despair. I considered the being whom I had cast among mankind, and endowed with the will and power to effect purposes of horror, such as the deed which he had now done, nearly in the light of my own vampire, my own spirit let loose from the grave, and forced to destroy all that was dear to me.

Day dawned; and I directed my steps towards the town. The gates were open; and I hastened to my father's house. My first thought was to discover what I knew of the murderer, and cause instant pursuit to be made. But I paused when I reflected on the story that I had to tell. A being whom I myself had formed, and endued with life, had met me at midnight among the precipices of an inaccessible mountain. I remembered also the nervous fever with which I had been seized just at the time that I dated my creation, and which would give an air of delirium to a tale otherwise so utterly improbable. I well knew that if any other had communicated such a relation to me, I should have looked upon it as the ravings of insanity. Besides, the strange nature of the animal would elude all pursuit, even if I were so far credited as to persuade my relatives to commence it. Besides, of what use would be pursuit? Who could arrest a creature capable of scaling the overhanging sides of Mont Salêve? These reflections determined me, and I resolved to remain silent.

It was about five in the morning when I entered my father's house. I told the servants not to disturb the family, and went into the library to attend their usual hour of rising.

Six years had elapsed, passed as a dream but for one indelible trace, and I stood in the same place where I had last embraced my father before my departure for Ingolstadt. Beloved and respectable parent! He still remained to me. I gazed on the picture of my mother, which stood over the mantel-piece. It was an historical subject, painted at my father's desire, and represented Caroline Beaufort in an agony of despair, kneeling by the coffin of her dead father. Her garb was rustic, and her cheek pale; but there was an air of dignity and beauty, that hardly permitted the sentiment of pity. Below this picture was a miniature of William; and my tears flowed when I looked upon it. While I was thus engaged, Ernest entered: he had heard me arrive, and hastened to welcome me. He expressed a sorrowful delight to see me: 'Welcome, my dearest Victor,' said he. 'Ah! I wish you had come three months ago, and then you would have found us all joyous and delighted. But we are now unhappy; and, I am afraid, tears instead of smiles will be your welcome. Our father looks so sorrowful: this dreadful event seems to have revived in his mind his grief on the death of Mamma. Poor Elizabeth also is quite inconsolable.' Ernest began to weep as he said these words.

'Do not,' said I, 'welcome me thus; try to be more calm, that I may not be absolutely miserable the moment I enter my father's house after so long an absence. But, tell me, how does my father support his misfortunes? and how is my poor Elizabeth?'

'She indeed requires consolation; she accused herself of having caused the death of my brother, and that made her very wretched. But since the murderer has been discovered —'

'The murderer discovered! Good God! how can that be? who could attempt to pursue him? It is impossible; one might as well try to overtake the winds, or confine a mountain-stream with a straw.'

'I do not know what you mean; but we were all very unhappy when she was discovered. No one would believe it at first; and even now Elizabeth will not be convinced, notwithstanding all the evidence. Indeed, who would credit that Justine Moritz, who was so amiable, and fond of all the family, could all at once become so extremely wicked?'

'Justine Moritz! Poor, poor girl, is she the accused? But it is wrongfully; every one knows that; no one believes it, surely, Ernest?'

'No one did at first; but several circumstances came out, that have almost forced conviction upon us: and her own behaviour has been so confused, as to add to the evidence of facts a weight that, I fear, leaves no hope for doubt. But she will be tried to-day, and you will then hear all.'

He related that, the morning on which the murder of poor William had been discovered, Justine had been taken ill, and confined to her bed; and, after several days, one of the servants, happening to examine the apparel she had worn on the night of the murder, had discovered in her pocket the picture of my mother, which had been judged to be the temptation of the murderer. The servant instantly shewed it to one of the others, who, without saying a word to any of the family, went to a magistrate; and, upon their deposition, Justine was apprehended. On being charged with the fact, the poor girl confirmed the suspicion in a great measure by her extreme confusion of manner.

This was a strange tale, but it did not shake my faith; and I replied earnestly, 'You are all mistaken; I know the murderer. Justine, poor, good Justine is innocent.'

At that instant my father entered. I saw unhappiness deeply impressed on his countenance, but he endeavoured to welcome me cheerfully; and, after we had exchanged our mournful greeting, would have introduced some other topic than that of our disaster, had not Ernest exclaimed, 'Good God, Papa! Victor says that he knows who was the murderer of poor William.'

'We do also, unfortunately,' replied my father; 'for indeed I had rather have been for ever ignorant than have discovered so much depravity and ingratitude in one I valued so highly.'

'My dear father, you are mistaken; Justine is innocent.'

'If she is, God forbid that she should suffer as guilty. She is to be tried to-day, and I hope, I sincerely hope, that she will be acquitted.'

This speech calmed me. I was firmly convinced in my own mind that Justine, and indeed every human being, was guiltless of this murder. I had no fear, therefore, that any circumstantial evidence could be brought forward strong enough to convict her; and, in this assurance, I calmed myself, expecting the trial with eagerness, but without prognosticating an evil result.

We were soon joined by Elizabeth. Time had made great alterations in her form since I had last beheld her. Six years before she had been a pretty, good-humoured girl, whom every one loved and caressed. She was now a woman in stature and expression of countenance, which was uncommonly lovely. An open and capacious forehead gave indications of a good understanding, joined to great frankness of disposition. Her eyes were hazel, and expressive of mildness, now through recent affliction allied to sadness. Her hair was of a rich dark auburn, her complexion fair, and her figure slight and graceful. She welcomed me with the greatest affection. 'Your arrival, my dear cousin,' said she, 'fills me with hope. You perhaps will find some means to justify my poor guiltless Justine. Alas! who is safe, if she be convicted of crime? I rely on her innocence as certainly as I do upon my own. Our misfortune is doubly hard to us; we have not only lost that lovely darling boy, but this poor girl, whom I sincerely love, is to be torn away by even a worse fate. If she is condemned, I never shall know joy more. But she will not, I am sure she will not; and then I shall be happy again, even after the sad death of my little William.'

'She is innocent, my Elizabeth,' said I, 'and that shall be proved; fear nothing, but let your spirits be cheered by the assurance of her acquittal.'

'How kind you are! every one else believes in her guilt, and that made me wretched; for I knew that it was impossible: and to see every one else prejudiced in so deadly a manner, rendered me hopeless and despairing.' She wept.

'Sweet niece,' said my father, 'dry your tears. If she is, as you believe, innocent, rely on the justice of our judges, and the activity with which I shall prevent the slightest shadow of partiality.'

CHAPTER VII

We passed a few sad hours, until eleven o'clock, when the trial was to commence. My father and the rest of the family being obliged to attend as witnesses, I accompanied them to the court. During the whole of this wretched mockery of justice, I suffered living torture. It was to be decided, whether the result of my curiosity and lawless devices would cause the death of two of my fellow-beings: one a smiling babe, full of innocence and joy; the other far more dreadfully murdered, with every aggravation of infamy that could make the murder memorable in horror. Justine also was a girl of merit, and possessed qualities which promised to render her life happy: now all was to be obliterated in an ignominious grave; and I the cause! A thousand times rather would I have confessed myself guilty of the crime ascribed to Justine; but I was absent when it was committed, and such a declaration would have been considered as the ravings of a madman, and would not have exculpated her who suffered through me.

The appearance of Justine was calm. She was dressed in mourning; and her countenance, always engaging, was rendered, by the solemnity of her feelings, exquisitely beautiful. Yet she appeared confident in innocence, and did not tremble, although gazed on and execrated by thousands; for all the kindness which her beauty might otherwise have excited, was obliterated in the minds of the spectators by the imagination of the enormity she was supposed to have committed. She was tranquil, yet her tranquillity was evidently constrained; and as her confusion had before been adduced as a proof of her guilt, she worked up her mind to an appearance of courage. When she entered the court, she threw her eyes round it, and quickly discovered where we were seated. A tear seemed to dim her eye when she saw us; but she quickly recovered herself, and a look of sorrowful affection seemed to attest her utter guiltlessness.

The trial began; and after the advocate against her had stated the charge, several witnesses were called. Several strange facts combined against her, which might have staggered any one who had not such proof of her innocence as I had. She had been out the whole of the night on which the murder had been committed, and towards morning had been perceived by a market-woman not far from the spot where the body of the murdered child had been afterwards found. The woman asked her what she did there; but she looked very strangely, and only returned a confused and unintelligible answer. She returned to the house about eight o'clock; and when one inquired where she had passed the night, she replied, that she had been looking for the child, and demanded earnestly, if any thing had been heard concerning him. When shewn the body, she fell into violent hysterics, and kept her bed for several days. The picture was then produced, which the servant had found in her pocket; and when Elizabeth, in a faltering voice, proved that it was the same which, an hour before the child had been missed, she had placed round his neck, a murmur of horror and indignation filled the court.

Justine was called on for her defence. As the trial had proceeded, her countenance had altered. Surprise, horror, and misery, were strongly expressed. Sometimes she struggled with her tears; but when she was desired to plead, she collected her powers, and spoke in an audible although variable voice: —

'God knows,' she said, 'how entirely I am innocent. But I do not pretend that my protestations should acquit me: I rest my innocence on a plain and simple explanation of the facts which have been adduced against me; and I hope the character I have always borne will incline my judges to a favourable interpretation, where any circumstance appears doubtful or suspicious.'

She then related that, by the permission of Elizabeth, she had passed the evening of the night on which the murder had been committed, at the house of an aunt at Chêne, a village situated at about a league from Geneva. On her return, at about nine o'clock, she met a man, who asked her if she had seen any thing of the child who was lost. She was alarmed by this account, and passed several hours in looking for him, when the gates of Geneva were shut, and she was forced to remain several hours of the night in a barn belonging to a cottage, being unwilling to call up the inhabitants, to whom she was well known. Unable to rest or sleep, she quitted her asylum early, that she might again endeavour to find my brother. If she had gone near the spot where his body lay, it was without her knowledge. That she had been bewildered when questioned by the market-woman, was not surprising, since she had passed a sleepless night, and the fate of poor William was yet uncertain. Concerning the picture she could give no account.

'I know,' continued the unhappy victim, 'how heavily and fatally this one circumstance weighs against me, but I have no power of explaining it; and when I have expressed my utter ignorance, I am only left to conjecture concerning the probabilities by which it might have been placed in my pocket. But here also I am checked. I believe that I have no enemy on earth, and none surely would have been so wicked as to destroy me wantonly. Did the murderer place it there? I know of no opportunity afforded him for so doing; or if I had, why should he have stolen the jewel, to part with it again so soon?

'I commit my cause to the justice of my judges, yet I see no room for hope. I beg permission to have a few witnesses examined concerning my character; and if their testimony shall not overweigh my supposed guilt, I must be condemned, although I would pledge my salvation on my innocence.'

Several witnesses were called, who had known her for many years, and they spoke well of her; but fear, and hatred of the crime of which they supposed her guilty, rendered them timorous, and unwilling to come forward. Elizabeth saw even this last resource, her excellent dispositions and irreproachable conduct, about to fail the accused, when, although violently agitated, she desired permission to address the court.

'I am,' said she, 'the cousin of the unhappy child who was murdered, or rather his sister, for I was educated by and have lived with his parents ever since and even long before his birth. It may therefore be judged indecent in me to come forward on this occasion; but when I see a fellow-creature about to perish through the cowardice of her pretended friends, I wish to be allowed to speak, that I may say what I know of her character. I am well acquainted with the accused. I have lived in the same house with her, at one time for five, and at another for nearly two years. During all that period she appeared to me the most amiable and benevolent of human creatures. She nursed Madame Frankenstein, my aunt, in her last illness with the greatest affection and care; and afterwards attended her own mother during a tedious illness, in a manner that excited the admiration of all who knew her. After which she again lived in my uncle's house, where she was beloved by all the family. She was warmly attached to the child who is now dead, and acted towards him like a most affectionate mother. For my own part, I do not hesitate to say, that, notwithstanding all the evidence produced against her, I believe and rely on her perfect innocence. She had no temptation for such an action: as to the bauble on which the chief proof rests, if she had earnestly desired it, I should have willingly given it to her; so much do I esteem and value her.'

Excellent Elizabeth! A murmur of approbation was heard; but it was excited by her generous interference, and not in favour of poor Justine, on whom the public indignation was turned with renewed violence, charging her with the blackest ingratitude. She herself wept as Elizabeth spoke, but she did not answer. My own agitation and anguish was extreme during the whole trial. I believed in her innocence; I knew it. Could the dæmon, who had (I did not for a minute doubt) murdered my brother, also in his hellish sport have betrayed the innocent to death and ignominy. I could not sustain the horror of my situation; and when I perceived that the popular voice, and the countenances of the judges, had already condemned my unhappy victim, I rushed out of the court in agony. The tortures of the accused did not equal mine; she was sustained by innocence, but the fangs of remorse tore my bosom, and would not forego their hold.

I passed a night of unmingled wretchedness. In the morning I went to the court; my lips and throat were parched. I dared not ask the fatal question; but I was known, and the officer guessed the cause of my visit. The ballots had been thrown; they were all black, and Justine was condemned.

I cannot pretend to describe what I then felt. I had before experienced sensations of horror; and I have endeavoured to bestow upon them adequate expressions, but words cannot convey an idea of the heart-sickening despair that I then endured. The person to whom I addressed myself added, that Justine had already confessed her guilt. 'That evidence,' he observed, 'was hardly required in so glaring a case, but I am glad of it; and, indeed, none of our judges like to condemn a criminal upon circumstantial evidence, be it ever so decisive.'

When I returned home, Elizabeth eagerly demanded the result.

'My cousin,' replied I, 'it is decided as you may have expected; all judges had rather that ten innocent should suffer, than that one guilty should escape. But she had confessed.'

This was a dire blow to poor Elizabeth, who had relied with firmness upon Justine's innocence. 'Alas!' said she, 'how shall I ever again believe in human benevolence? Justine, whom I loved and esteemed as my sister, how could she put on those smiles of innocence only to betray; her mild eyes seemed incapable of any severity or ill-humour, and yet she has committed a murder.'

Soon after we heard that the poor victim had expressed a wish to see my cousin. My father wished her not to go; but said, that he left it to her own judgment and feelings to decide. 'Yes,' said Elizabeth, 'I will go, although she is guilty; and you, Victor, shall accompany me: I cannot go alone.' The idea of this visit was torture to me, yet I could not refuse.

We entered the gloomy prison-chamber, and beheld Justine sitting on some straw at the further end; her hands were manacled, and her head rested on her knees. She rose on seeing us enter; and when we were left alone with her, she threw herself at the feet of Elizabeth, weeping bitterly. My cousin wept also.

'Oh, Justine!' said she, 'why did you rob me of my last consolation. I relied on your innocence; and although I was then very wretched, I was not so miserable as I am now.'

'And do you also believe that I am so very, very wicked? Do you also join with my enemies to crush me?' Her voice was suffocated with sobs.

'Rise, my poor girl,' said Elizabeth, 'why do you kneel, if you are innocent? I am not one of your enemies; I believed you guiltless, notwithstanding every evidence, until I heard that you had yourself declared your guilt. That report, you say, is false; and be assured, dear Justine, that nothing can shake my confidence in you for a moment, but your own confession.'

'I did confess; but I confessed a lie. I confessed, that I might obtain absolution; but now that falsehood lies heavier at my heart than all my other sins. The God of heaven forgive me! Ever since I was condemned, my confessor has besieged me; he threatened and menaced, until I almost began to think that I was the monster that he said I was. He threatened excommunication and hell fire in my last moments, if I continued obdurate. Dear lady, I had none to support me; all looked on me as a wretch doomed to ignominy and perdition. What could I do? In an evil hour I subscribed to a lie; and now only am I truly miserable.'

She paused, weeping, and then continued—'I thought with horror, my sweet lady, that you should believe your Justine, whom your blessed aunt had so highly honoured, and whom you loved, was a creature capable of a crime which none but the devil himself could have perpetrated. Dear William! dearest blessed child! I soon shall see you again in heaven, where we shall all be happy; and that consoles me, going as I am to suffer ignominy and death.'

'Oh, Justine! forgive me for having for one moment distrusted you. Why did you confess? But do not mourn, my dear girl; I will every where proclaim your innocence, and force belief. Yet you must die; you, my playfellow, my companion, my more than sister. I never can survive so horrible a misfortune.'

'Dear, sweet Elizabeth, do not weep. You ought to raise me with thoughts of a better life, and elevate me from the petty cares of this world of injustice and strife. Do not you, excellent friend, drive me to despair.'

'I will try to comfort you; but this, I fear, is an evil too deep and poignant to admit of consolation, for there is no hope. Yet heaven bless thee, my dearest Justine, with resignation, and a confidence elevated beyond this world.

Oh! how I hate its shews and mockeries! when one creature is murdered, another is immediately deprived of life in a slow torturing manner; then the executioners, their hands yet reeking with the blood of innocence, believe that they have done a great deed. They call this *retribution*. Hateful name! When that word is pronounced, I know greater and more horrid punishments are going to be inflicted than the gloomiest tyrant has ever invented to satiate his utmost revenge. Yet this is not consolation for you, my Justine, unless indeed that you may glory in escaping from so miserable a den. Alas! I would I were in peace with my aunt and my lovely William, escaped from a world which is hateful to me, and the visages of men which I abhor.'

Justine smiled languidly. 'This, dear lady, is despair, and not resignation. I must not learn the lesson that you would teach me. Talk of something else, something that will bring peace, and not increase of misery.'

During this conversation I had retired to a corner of the prison-room, where I could conceal the horrid anguish that possessed me. Despair! Who dared talk of that? The poor victim, who on the morrow was to pass the dreary boundary between life and death, felt not as I did, such deep and bitter agony. I gnashed my teeth, and ground them together, uttering a groan that came from my inmost soul. Justine started. When she saw who it was, she approached me, and said, 'Dear Sir, you are very kind to visit me; you, I hope, do not believe that I am guilty.'

I could not answer. 'No, Justine,' said Elizabeth; 'he is more convinced of your innocence than I was; for even when he heard that you had confessed, he did not credit it.'

'I truly thank him. In these last moments I feel the sincerest gratitude towards those who think of me with kindness. How sweet is the affection of others to such a wretch as I am! It removes more than half my misfortune; and I feel as if I could die in peace, now that my innocence is acknowledged by you, dear lady, and your cousin.'

Thus the poor sufferer tried to comfort others and herself. She indeed gained the resignation she desired. But I, the true murderer, felt the never-dying worm alive in my bosom, which allowed of no hope or consolation. Elizabeth also wept, and was unhappy; but hers also was the misery of innocence, which, like a cloud that passes over the fair moon, for a while hides, but cannot tarnish its brightness. Anguish and despair had penetrated into the core of my heart; I bore a hell within me, which nothing could extinguish. We staid several hours with Justine; and it was with great difficulty that Elizabeth could tear herself away. 'I wish,' cried she, 'that I were to die with you; I cannot live in this world of misery.'

Justine assumed an air of cheerfulness, while she with difficulty repressed her bitter tears. She embraced Elizabeth, and said, in a voice of half-suppressed emotion, 'Farewell, sweet lady, dearest Elizabeth, my beloved and only friend; may heaven in its bounty bless and preserve you; may this be the last misfortune that you will ever suffer. Live, and be happy, and make others so.'

As we returned, Elizabeth said, 'You know not, my dear Victor, how much I am relieved, now that I trust in the innocence of this unfortunate girl. I never could again have known peace, if I had been deceived in my reliance on her. For the moment that I did believe her guilty, I felt an anguish that I could not have long sustained. Now my heart is lightened. The innocent suffers; but she whom I thought amiable and good has not betrayed the trust I reposed in her, and I am consoled.'

Amiable cousin! such were your thoughts, mild and gentle as your own dear eyes and voice. But I—I was a wretch, and none ever conceived of the misery that I then endured.

END OF VOLUME 1.

VOLUME 2

CHAPTER I

Nothing is more painful to the human mind, than, after the feelings have been worked up by a quick succession of events, the dead calmness of inaction and certainty which follows, and deprives the soul both of hope and fear. Justine died; she rested; and I was alive. The blood flowed freely in my veins, but a weight of despair and remorse pressed on my heart, which nothing could remove. Sleep fled from my eyes; I wandered like an evil spirit, for I had committed deeds of mischief beyond description horrible, and more, much more, (I persuaded myself) was yet behind. Yet my heart overflowed with kindness, and the love of virtue. I had begun life with benevolent intentions, and thirsted for the moment when I should put them in practice, and make myself useful to my fellow-beings. Now all was blasted: instead of that serenity of conscience, which allowed me to look back upon the past with self-satisfaction, and from thence to gather promise of new hopes, I was seized by remorse and the sense of guilt, which hurried me away to a hell of intense tortures, such as no language can describe.

This state of mind preyed upon my health, which had entirely recovered from the first shock it had sustained. I shunned the face of man; all sound of joy or complacency was torture to me; solitude was my only consolation — deep, dark, death-like solitude.

My father observed with pain the alteration perceptible in my disposition and habits, and endeavoured to reason with me on the folly of giving way to immoderate grief. 'Do you think, Victor,' said he, 'that I do not suffer also? No one could love a child more than I loved your brother;' (tears came into his eyes as he spoke); 'but is it not a duty to the survivors, that we should refrain from augmenting their unhappiness by an appearance of immoderate grief? It is also a duty owed to yourself; for excessive sorrow prevents improvement or enjoyment, or even the discharge of daily usefulness, without which no man is fit for society.'

This advice, although good, was totally inapplicable to my case; I should have been the first to hide my grief, and console my friends, if remorse had not mingled its bitterness with my other sensations. Now I could only answer my father with a look of despair, and endeavour to hide myself from his view.

About this time we retired to our house at Belrive. This change was particularly agreeable to me. The shutting of the gates regularly at ten o'clock, and the impossibility of remaining on the lake after that hour, had rendered our residence within the walls of Geneva very irksome to me. I was now free. Often, after the rest of the family had retired for the night, I took the boat, and passed many hours upon the water. Sometimes, with my sails set, I was carried by the wind; and sometimes, after rowing into the middle of the lake, I left the boat to pursue its own course, and gave way to my own miserable reflections. I was often tempted, when all was at peace around me, and I the only unquiet thing that wandered restless in a scene so beautiful and heavenly, if I except some bat, or the frogs, whose harsh and interrupted croaking was heard only when I approached the shore — often, I say, I was tempted to plunge into the silent lake, that the waters might close over me and my calamities for ever. But I was restrained, when I thought of the heroic and suffering Elizabeth, whom I tenderly loved, and whose existence was bound up in mine. I thought also of my father, and surviving brother: should I by my base desertion leave them exposed and unprotected to the malice of the fiend whom I had let loose among them?

At these moments I wept bitterly, and wished that peace would revisit my mind only that I might afford them consolation and happiness. But that could not be. Remorse extinguished every hope. I had been the author of unalterable evils; and I lived in daily fear, lest the monster whom I had created should perpetrate some new wickedness. I had an obscure feeling that all was not over, and that he would still commit some signal crime, which by its enormity should almost efface the recollection of the past. There was always scope for fear, so long as any thing I loved remained behind. My abhorrence of this fiend cannot be conceived. When I thought of him, I gnashed my teeth, my eyes became inflamed, and I ardently wished to extinguish that life which I had so thoughtlessly bestowed. When I reflected on his crimes and malice, my hatred and revenge burst all bounds of moderation. I would have made a pilgrimage to the highest peak of the Andes, could I, when there, have precipitated him to their base. I wished to see him again, that I might wreak the utmost extent of anger on his head, and avenge the deaths of William and Justine.

Our house was the house of mourning. My father's health was deeply shaken by the horror of the recent events. Elizabeth was sad and desponding; she no longer took delight in her ordinary occupations; all pleasure seemed to her sacrilege toward the dead; eternal woe and tears she then thought was the just tribute she should pay to innocence so blasted and destroyed. She was no longer that happy creature, who in earlier youth wandered with me on the banks of the lake, and talked with ecstacy of our future prospects. She had become grave, and often conversed of the inconstancy of fortune, and the instability of human life.

'When I reflect, my dear cousin,' said she, 'on the miserable death of Justine Moritz, I no longer see the world and its works as they before appeared to me. Before, I looked upon the accounts of vice and injustice, that I read in books or heard from others, as tales of ancient days, or imaginary evils; at least they were remote, and more familiar to reason than to the imagination; but now misery has come home, and men appear to me as monsters thirsting for each other's blood. Yet I am certainly unjust. Every body believed that poor girl to be guilty; and if she could have committed the crime for which she suffered, assuredly she would have been the most depraved of human creatures. For the sake of a few jewels, to have murdered the son of her benefactor and friend, a child whom she had nursed from its birth, and appeared to love as if it had been her own! I could not consent to the death of any human being; but certainly I should have thought such a creature unfit to remain in the society of men. Yet she was innocent. I know, I feel she was innocent; you are of the same opinion, and that confirms me. Alas! Victor, when falsehood can look so like the truth, who can assure themselves of certain happiness? I feel as if I were walking on the edge of a precipice, towards which thousands are crowding, and endeavouring to plunge me into the abyss. William and Justine were assassinated, and the murderer escapes; he walks about the world free, and perhaps respected. But even if I were condemned to suffer on the scaffold for the same crimes, I would not change places with such a wretch.'

I listened to this discourse with the extremest agony. I, not in deed, but in effect, was the true murderer. Elizabeth read my anguish in my countenance, and kindly taking my hand said, 'My dearest cousin, you must calm yourself. These events have affected me, God knows how deeply; but I am not so wretched as you are. There is an expression of despair, and sometimes of revenge, in your countenance, that makes me tremble. Be calm, my dear Victor; I would sacrifice my life to your peace. We surely shall be happy: quiet in our native country, and not mingling in the world, what can disturb our tranquillity?'

She shed tears as she said this, distrusting the very solace that she gave; but at the same time she smiled, that she might chase away the fiend that lurked in my heart. My father, who saw in the unhappiness that was painted in my face only an exaggeration of that sorrow which I might naturally feel, thought that an amusement suited to my taste would be the best means of restoring to me my wonted serenity. It was from this cause that he had removed to the country; and, induced by the same motive, he now proposed that we should all make an excursion to the valley of Chamounix. I had been there before, but Elizabeth and Ernest never had; and both had often expressed an earnest desire to see the scenery of this place, which had been described to them as so wonderful and sublime. Accordingly we departed from Geneva on this tour about the middle of the month of August, nearly two months after the death of Justine.

The weather was uncommonly fine; and if mine had been a sorrow to be chased away by any fleeting circumstance, this excursion would certainly have had the effect intended by my father. As it was, I was somewhat interested in the scene; it sometimes lulled, although it could not extinguish my grief. During the first day we travelled in a carriage. In the morning we had seen the mountains at a distance, towards which we gradually advanced. We perceived that the valley through which we wound, and which was formed by the river Arve, whose course we followed, closed in upon us by degrees; and when the sun had set, we beheld immense mountains and precipices overhanging us on every side, and heard the sound of the river raging among rocks, and the dashing of waterfalls around.

The next day we pursued our journey upon mules; and as we ascended still higher, the valley assumed a more magnificent and astonishing character. Ruined castles hanging on the precipices of piny mountains; the impetuous Arve, and cottages every here and there peeping forth from among the trees, formed a scene of singular beauty. But it was augmented and rendered sublime by the mighty Alps, whose white and shining pyramids and domes towered above all, as belonging to another earth, the habitations of another race of beings.[29]

We passed the bridge of Pelissier, where the ravine, which the river forms, opened before us, and we began to ascend the mountain that overhangs it. Soon after we entered the valley of Chamounix. This valley is more wonderful and sublime, but not so beautiful and picturesque as that of Servox, through which we had just passed. The high and snowy mountains were its immediate boundaries; but we saw no more ruined castles and fertile fields. Immense glaciers approached the road; we heard the rumbling thunder of the falling avalanche, and marked the smoke of its passage. Mont Blanc, the supreme and magnificent Mont Blanc, raised itself from the surrounding *aiguilles*,[30] and its tremendous *dome* overlooked the valley.

During this journey, I sometimes joined Elizabeth, and exerted myself to point out to her the various beauties of the scene. I often suffered my mule to lag behind, and indulged in the misery of reflection. At other times

---

[29] Mary and Percy Shelley took this journey to Chamounix while she was writing *Frankenstein* in the summer of 1816. Victor's earlier glimpse of the lightning-shot landscape and its nonhuman inhabitant (p. 64) prepares us for another meeting here. Percy captured a similar theme in the poem he wrote about this experience: "awful scene/ Where Power in likeness of the Arve comes down/ From the ice gulphs that gird his secret throne, / Bursting through these dark mountains like the flame/ Of lightning through the tempest" ("Mont Blanc," ll. 14–18). [Ed.]

[30] Sharply pointed peaks; "aiguilles" is French for "needles." [Ed.]

I spurred on the animal before my companions, that I might forget them, the world, and, more than all, myself. When at a distance, I alighted, and threw myself on the grass, weighed down by horror and despair. At eight in the evening I arrived at Chamounix. My father and Elizabeth were very much fatigued; Ernest, who accompanied us, was delighted, and in high spirits: the only circumstance that detracted from his pleasure was the south wind, and the rain it seemed to promise for the next day.

We retired early to our apartments, but not to sleep; at least I did not. I remained many hours at the window, watching the pallid lightning that played above Mont Blanc, and listening to the rushing of the Arve, which ran below my window.

CHAPTER II

The next day, contrary to the prognostications of our guides, was fine, although clouded. We visited the source of the Arveiron, and rode about the valley until evening. These sublime and magnificent scenes afforded me the greatest consolation that I was capable of receiving. They elevated me from all littleness of feeling; and although they did not remove my grief, they subdued and tranquillized it. In some degree, also, they diverted my mind from the thoughts over which it had brooded for the last month. I returned in the evening, fatigued, but less unhappy, and conversed with my family with more cheerfulness than had been my custom for some time. My father was pleased, and Elizabeth overjoyed. 'My dear cousin,' said she, 'you see what happiness you diffuse when you are happy; do not relapse again!'

The following morning the rain poured down in torrents, and thick mists hid the summits of the mountains. I rose early, but felt unusually melancholy. The rain depressed me; my old feelings recurred, and I was miserable. I knew how disappointed my father would be at this sudden change, and I wished to avoid him until I had recovered myself so far as to be enabled to conceal those feelings that overpowered me. I knew that they would remain that day at the inn; and as I had never inured myself to rain, moisture, and cold, I resolved to go alone to the summit to Montanvert. I remembered the effect that the view of the tremendous and ever-moving glacier had produced upon my mind when I first saw it. It had then filled me with a sublime ecstacy that gave wings to the soul, and allowed it to soar from the obscure world to light and joy. The sight of the awful and majestic in nature had indeed always the effect of solemnizing my mind, and causing me to forget the passing cares of life. I determined to go alone, for *unon*

I was well acquainted with the path, and the presence of another would destroy the solitary grandeur of the scene.

The ascent is precipitous, but the path is cut into continual and short windings, which enable you to surmount the perpendicularity of the mountain. It is a scene terrifically desolate. In a thousand spots the traces of the winter avalanche may be perceived, where trees lie broken and strewed on the ground; some entirely destroyed, others bent, leaning upon the jutting rocks of the mountain, or transversely upon other trees. The path, as you ascend higher, is intersected by ravines of snow, down which stones continually roll from above; one of them is particularly dangerous, as the slightest sound, such as even speaking in a loud voice, produces a concussion of air sufficient to draw destruction upon the head of the speaker. The pines are not tall or luxuriant, but they are sombre, and add an air of severity to the scene. I looked on the valley beneath; vast mists were rising from the rivers which ran through it, and curling in thick wreaths around the opposite mountains, whose summits were hid in the uniform clouds, while rain poured from the dark sky, and added to the melancholy impression I received from the objects around me. Alas! why does man boast of sensibilities superior to those apparent in the brute; it only renders them more necessary beings.[31] If our impulses were confined to hunger, thirst, and desire, we might be nearly free; but now we are moved by every wind that blows, and a chance word or scene that that word may convey to us.

> We rest; a dream has power to poison sleep.
> We rise; one wand'ring thought pollutes the day.
> We feel, conceive, or reason; laugh, or weep,
> Embrace fond woe, or cast our cares away;
> It is the same: for, be it joy or sorrow,
> The path of its departure still is free.
> Man's yesterday may ne'er be like his morrow;
> Nought may endure but mutability![32]

nature

It was nearly noon when I arrived at the top of the ascent. For some time I sat upon the rock that overlooks the sea of ice. A mist covered both that and the surrounding mountains. Presently a breeze dissipated the cloud, and I descended upon the glacier. The surface is very uneven, rising like the waves of a troubled sea, descending low, and interspersed by rifts that sink deep. The field of ice is almost a league in width, but I spent nearly two hours in crossing it. The opposite mountain is a bare perpendicular rock.

---

[31] More contingent and vulnerable beings. [Ed.]

[32] The last two stanzas of Percy Shelley's "Mutability" (1816). [Ed.]

From the side where I now stood Montanvert was exactly opposite, at the distance of a league; and above it rose Mont Blanc, in awful majesty. I remained in a recess of rock, gazing on this wonderful and stupendous scene. The sea, or rather the vast river of ice, wound among its dependent mountains, whose aerial summits hung over its recesses. Their icy and glittering peaks shone in the sunlight over the clouds. My heart, which was before sorrowful, now swelled with something like joy; I exclaimed — 'Wandering spirits, if indeed ye wander, and do not rest in your narrow beds, allow me this faint happiness, or take me, as your companion, away from the joys of life.'

As I said this, I suddenly beheld the figure of a man, at some distance, advancing towards me with superhuman speed. He bounded over the crevices in the ice, among which I had walked with caution; his stature also, as he approached, seemed to exceed that of man. I was troubled: a mist came over my eyes, and I felt a faintness seize me; but I was quickly restored by the cold gale of the mountains. I perceived, as the shape came nearer, (sight tremendous and abhorred!) that it was the wretch whom I had created. I trembled with rage and horror, resolving to wait his approach, and then close with him in mortal combat. He approached; his countenance bespoke bitter anguish, combined with disdain and malignity, while its unearthly ugliness rendered it almost too horrible for human eyes. But I scarcely observed this; anger and hatred had at first deprived me of utterance, and I recovered only to overwhelm him with words expressive of furious detestation and contempt.

'Devil!' I exclaimed, 'do you dare approach me? and do not you fear the fierce vengeance of my arm wreaked on your miserable head? Begone, vile insect! or rather stay, that I may trample you to dust! and, oh, that I could, with the extinction of your miserable existence, restore those victims whom you have so diabolically murdered!'

'I expected this reception,' said the dæmon. 'All men hate the wretched; how then must I be hated, who am miserable beyond all living things! Yet you, my creator, detest and spurn me, thy creature, to whom thou art bound by ties only dissoluble by the annihilation of one of us. You purpose to kill me. How dare you sport thus with life? Do your duty towards me, and I will do mine towards you and the rest of mankind. If you will comply with my conditions, I will leave them and you at peace; but if you refuse, I will glut the maw of death, until it be satiated with the blood of your remaining friends.'

'Abhorred monster! fiend that thou art! the tortures of hell are too mild a vengeance for thy crimes. Wretched devil! you reproach me with your creation; come on then, that I may extinguish the spark which I so negligently bestowed.'

My rage was without bounds; I sprang on him, impelled by all the feelings which can arm one being against the existence of another.

He easily eluded me, and said,

'Be calm! I entreat you to hear me, before you give vent to your hatred on my devoted head. Have I not suffered enough, that you seek to increase my misery? Life, although it may only be an accumulation of anguish, is dear to me, and I will defend it. Remember thou hast made me more powerful than thyself; my height is superior to thine; my joints more supple. But I will not be tempted to set myself in opposition to thee. I am thy creature, and I will be even mild and docile to my natural lord and king, if thou wilt also perform thy part, the which thou owest me. Oh, Frankenstein, be not equitable to every other, and trample upon me alone, to whom thy justice, and even thy clemency and affection, is most due. Remember, that I am thy creature: I ought to be thy Adam; but I am rather the fallen angel, whom thou drivest from joy for no misdeed. Every where I see bliss, from which I alone am irrevocably excluded. I was benevolent and good; misery made me a fiend. Make me happy, and I shall again be virtuous.'

'Begone! I will not hear you. There can be no community between you and me; we are enemies. Begone, or let us try our strength in a fight, in which one must fall.'

'How can I move thee? Will no entreaties cause thee to turn a favourable eye upon thy creature, who implores thy goodness and compassion. Believe me, Frankenstein: I was benevolent; my soul glowed with love and humanity: but am I not alone, miserably alone? You, my creator, abhor me; what hope can I gather from your fellow-creatures, who owe me nothing? they spurn and hate me. The desert mountains and dreary glaciers are my refuge. I have wandered here many days; the caves of ice, which I only do not fear, are a dwelling to me, and the only one which man does not grudge. These bleak skies I hail, for they are kinder to me than your fellow-beings. If the multitude of mankind knew of my existence, they would do as you do, and arm themselves for my destruction. Shall I not then hate them who abhor me? I will keep no terms with my enemies. I am miserable, and they shall share my wretchedness. Yet it is in your power to recompense me, and deliver them from an evil which it only remains for you to make so great, that not only you and your family, but thousands of others, shall be swallowed up in the whirlwinds of its rage. Let your compassion be moved, and do not disdain me. Listen to my tale: when you have heard that, abandon or commiserate me, as you shall judge that I deserve. But hear me. The guilty are allowed, by human laws, bloody as they may be, to speak in their own defence before they are condemned. Listen to me, Frankenstein. You accuse me of murder; and yet you would, with a satisfied conscience, destroy your own creature. Oh, praise the eternal justice of man! Yet I ask you not to spare me: listen to me; and then, if you can, and if you will, destroy the work of your hands.'

'Why do you call to my remembrance circumstances of which I shudder to reflect, that I have been the miserable origin and author? Cursed be the day, abhorred devil, in which you first saw light! Cursed (although I curse myself) be the hands that formed you! You have made me wretched beyond expression. You have left me no power to consider whether I am just to you, or not. Begone! relieve me from the sight of your detested form.'

'Thus I relieve thee, my creator,' he said, and placed his hated hands before my eyes, which I flung from me with violence; 'thus I take from thee a sight which you abhor. Still thou canst listen to me, and grant me thy compassion. By the virtues that I once possessed, I demand this from you. Hear my tale; it is long and strange, and the temperature of this place is not fitting to your fine sensations; come to the hut upon the mountain. The sun is yet high in the heavens; before it descends to hide itself behind yon snowy precipices, and illuminate another world, you will have heard my story, and can decide. On you it rests, whether I quit for ever the neighbourhood of man, and lead a harmless life, or become the scourge of your fellow-creatures, and the author of your own speedy ruin.'

As he said this, he led the way across the ice: I followed. My heart was full, and I did not answer him; but, as I proceeded, I weighed the various arguments that he had used, and determined at least to listen to his tale. I was partly urged by curiosity, and compassion confirmed my resolution. I had hitherto supposed him to be the murderer of my brother, and I eagerly sought a confirmation or denial of this opinion. For the first time, also, I felt what the duties of a creator towards his creature were, and that I ought to render him happy before I complained of his wickedness. These motives urged me to comply with his demand. We crossed the ice, therefore, and ascended the opposite rock. The air was cold, and the rain again began to descend: we entered the hut, the fiend with an air of exultation, I with a heavy heart, and depressed spirits. But I consented to listen; and, seating myself by the fire which my odious companion had lighted, he thus began his tale.

CHAPTER III

'It is with considerable difficulty that I remember the original æra of my being: all the events of that period appear confused and indistinct. A strange multiplicity of sensations seized me, and I saw, felt, heard, and smelt, at the same time; and it was, indeed, a long time before I learned to distinguish between the operations of my various senses. By degrees, I remember, a stronger light pressed upon my nerves, so that I was obliged to shut my eyes. Darkness then came over me, and troubled me; but hardly had I felt this, when, by opening my eyes, as I now suppose, the light poured in upon me again. I walked, and, I believe, descended; but I presently found a great alteration in my sensations. Before, dark and opaque bodies had surrounded me, impervious to my touch or sight; but I now found that I could wander on at liberty, with no obstacles which I could not either surmount or avoid. The light became more and more oppressive to me; and, the heat wearying me as I walked, I sought a place where I could receive shade. This was the forest near Ingolstadt; and here I lay by the side of a brook resting from my fatigue, until I felt tormented by hunger and thirst. This roused me from my nearly dormant state, and I ate some berries which I found hanging on the trees, or lying on the ground. I slaked my thirst at the brook; and then lying down, was overcome by sleep.

'It was dark when I awoke; I felt cold also, and half-frightened as it were instinctively, finding myself so desolate. Before I had quitted your apartment, on a sensation of cold, I had covered myself with some clothes; but these were insufficient to secure me from the dews of night. I was a poor, helpless, miserable wretch; I knew, and could distinguish, nothing; but, feeling pain invade me on all sides, I sat down and wept.

'Soon a gentle light stole over the heavens, and gave me a sensation of pleasure. I started up, and beheld a radiant form rise from among the trees. I gazed with a kind of wonder. It moved slowly, but it enlightened my path; and I again went out in search of berries. I was still cold, when under one of the trees I found a huge cloak, with which I covered myself, and sat down upon the ground. No distinct ideas occupied my mind; all was confused. I felt light, and hunger, and thirst, and darkness; innumerable sounds rung in my ears, and on all sides various scents saluted me: the only object that I could distinguish was the bright moon, and I fixed my eyes on that with pleasure.

'Several changes of day and night passed, and the orb of night had greatly lessened when I began to distinguish my sensations from each other. I gradually saw plainly the clear stream that supplied me with drink, and the trees that shaded me with their foliage. I was delighted when I first discovered that a pleasant sound, which often saluted my ears, proceeded from the throats of the little winged animals who had often intercepted the light from my eyes. I began also to observe, with greater accuracy, the forms that surrounded me, and to perceive the boundaries of the radiant roof of light which canopied me. Sometimes I tried to imitate the pleasant songs of the birds, but was unable. Sometimes I wished to express my sensations in my own mode, but the uncouth and inarticulate sounds which broke from me frightened me into silence again.

'The moon had disappeared from the night, and again, with a lessened form, shewed itself, while I still remained in the forest. My sensations had, by this time, become distinct, and my mind received every day additional ideas. My eyes became accustomed to the light, and to perceive objects in their right forms; I distinguished the insect from the herb, and, by degrees, one herb from another. I found that the sparrow uttered none but harsh notes, whilst those of the blackbird and thrush were sweet and enticing.

'One day, when I was oppressed by cold, I found a fire which had been left by some wandering beggars, and was overcome with delight at the warmth I experienced from it. In my joy I thrust my hand into the live embers, but quickly drew it out again with a cry of pain. How strange, I thought, that the same cause should produce such opposite effects! I examined the materials of the fire, and to my joy found it to be composed of wood. I quickly collected some branches; but they were wet, and would not burn. I was pained at this, and sat still watching the operation of the fire. The wet wood which I had placed near the heat dried, and itself became inflamed. I reflected on this; and, by touching the various branches, I discovered the cause, and busied myself in collecting a great quantity of wood, that I might dry it, and have a plentiful supply of fire. When night came on, and brought sleep with it, I was in the greatest fear lest my fire should be extinguished. I covered it carefully with dry wood and leaves, and placed wet branches upon it; and then, spreading my cloak, I lay on the ground, and sunk into sleep.

'It was morning when I awoke, and my first care was to visit the fire. I uncovered it, and a gentle breeze quickly fanned it into a flame. I observed this also, and contrived a fan of branches, which roused the embers when they were nearly extinguished. When night came again, I found, with pleasure, that the fire gave light as well as heat, and that the discovery of this element was useful to me in my food; for I found some of the offals that the travellers had left had been roasted, and tasted much more savoury than the berries I gathered from the trees. I tried, therefore, to dress my food in the same manner, placing it on the live embers. I found that the berries were spoiled by this operation, and the nuts and roots much improved.

'Food, however, became scarce; and I often spent the whole day searching in vain for a few acorns to assuage the pangs of hunger. When I found this, I resolved to quit the place that I had hitherto inhabited, to seek for one where the few wants I experienced would be more easily satisfied. In this emigration, I exceedingly lamented the loss of the fire which I had obtained through accident, and knew not how to re-produce it. I gave several hours to the serious consideration of this difficulty; but I was obliged to relinquish all attempt to supply it; and, wrapping myself up in my cloak, I struck across the wood towards the setting sun. I passed three days in these rambles, and at length discovered the open country. A great fall of snow had taken place the night before, and the fields were of one uniform white; the appearance was disconsolate, and I found my feet chilled by the cold damp substance that covered the ground.

'It was about seven in the morning, and I longed to obtain food and shelter; at length I perceived a small hut, on a rising ground, which had doubtless been built for the convenience of some shepherd. This was a new sight to me; and I examined the structure with great curiosity. Finding the door open, I entered. An old man sat in it, near a fire, over which he was preparing his breakfast. He turned on hearing a noise; and, perceiving me, shrieked loudly, and, quitting the hut, ran across the fields with a speed of which his debilitated form hardly appeared capable. His appearance, different from any I had ever before seen, and his flight, somewhat surprised me. But I was enchanted by the appearance of the hut: here the snow and rain could not penetrate; the ground was dry; and it presented to me then as exquisite and divine a retreat as Pandæmonium appeared to the dæmons of hell after their sufferings in the lake of fire.[33] I greedily devoured the remnants of the shepherd's breakfast, which consisted of bread, cheese, milk, and wine; the latter, however, I did not like. [Then] overcome by fatigue, I lay down among some straw, and fell asleep.

'It was noon when I awoke; and, allured by the warmth of the sun, which shone brightly on the white ground, I determined to recommence my travels; and, depositing the remains of the peasant's breakfast in a wallet I found, I proceeded across the fields for several hours, until at sunset I arrived at a village. How miraculous did this appear! the huts, the neater cottages, and stately houses, engaged my admiration by turns. The vegetables in the gardens, the milk and cheese that I saw placed at the windows of some of the cottages, allured my appetite. One of the best of these I entered; but I had hardly placed my foot within the door, before the children shrieked, and one of the women fainted. The whole village was roused; some fled, some attacked me, until, grievously bruised by stones and many other kinds of missile weapons, I escaped to the open country, and fearfully took refuge in a low hovel, quite bare, and making a wretched appearance after the palaces I had beheld in the village. This hovel, however, joined a cottage of a neat and pleasant appearance; but, after my late dearly-bought experience, I dared not enter it. My place of refuge was constructed of wood, but so low, that I could with difficulty sit upright in it. No wood, however, was placed on the earth, which formed the floor, but it was dry;

---

[33] Milton's *Paradise Lost* (1667) I, 670 and following. [Ed.]

and although the wind entered it by innumerable chinks, I found it an agreeable asylum from the snow and rain.

'Here then I retreated, and lay down, happy to have found a shelter, however miserable, from the inclemency of the season, and still more from the barbarity of man.

'As soon as morning dawned, I crept from my kennel, that I might view the adjacent cottage, and discover if I could remain in the habitation I had found. It was situated against the back of the cottage, and surrounded on the sides which were exposed by a pig-stye and a clear pool of water. One part was open, and by that I had crept in; but now I covered every crevice by which I might be perceived with stones and wood, yet in such a manner that I might move them on occasion to pass out: all the light I enjoyed came through the stye, and that was sufficient for me.

'Having thus arranged my dwelling, and carpeted it with clean straw, I retired; for I saw the figure of a man at a distance, and I remembered too well my treatment the night before, to trust myself in his power. I had first, however, provided for my sustenance for that day, by a loaf of coarse bread, which I purloined, and a cup with which I could drink, more conveniently than from my hand, of the pure water which flowed by my retreat. The floor was a little raised, so that it was kept perfectly dry, and by its vicinity to the chimney of the cottage it was tolerably warm.

'Being thus provided, I resolved to reside in this hovel, until something should occur which might alter my determination. It was indeed a paradise, compared to the bleak forest, my former residence, the rain-dropping branches, and dank earth. I ate my breakfast with pleasure, and was about to remove a plank to procure myself a little water, when I heard a step, and, looking through a small chink, I beheld a young creature, with a pail on her head, passing before my hovel. The girl was young and of gentle demeanour, unlike what I have since found cottagers and farm-house servants to be. Yet she was meanly dressed, a coarse blue petticoat and a linen jacket being her only garb; her fair hair was plaited, but not adorned; she looked patient, yet sad. I lost sight of her; and in about a quarter of an hour she returned, bearing the pail, which was now partly filled with milk. As she walked along, seemingly incommoded by the burden, a young man met her, whose countenance expressed a deeper despondence. Uttering a few sounds with an air of melancholy, he took the pail from her head, and bore it to the cottage himself. She followed, and they disappeared. Presently I saw the young man again, with some tools in his hand, cross the field behind the cottage; and the girl was also busied, sometimes in the house, and sometimes in the yard.

'On examining my dwelling, I found that one of the windows of the cottage had formerly occupied a part of it, but the panes had been filled up with wood. In one of these was a small and almost imperceptible chink, through which the eye could just penetrate. Through this crevice, a small room was visible, white-washed and clean, but very bare of furniture. In one corner, near a small fire, sat an old man, leaning his head on his hands in a disconsolate attitude. The young girl was occupied in arranging the cottage; but presently she took something out of a drawer, which employed her hands, and she sat down beside the old man, who, taking up an instrument, began to play, and to produce sounds, sweeter than the voice of the thrush or the nightingale. It was a lovely sight, even to me, poor wretch! who had never beheld aught beautiful before. The silver hair and benevolent countenance of the aged cottager, won my reverence; while the gentle manners of the girl enticed my love. He played a sweet mournful air, which I perceived drew tears from the eyes of his amiable companion, of which the old man took no notice, until she sobbed audibly; he then pronounced a few sounds, and the fair creature, leaving her work, knelt at his feet. He raised her, and smiled with such kindness and affection, that I felt sensations of a peculiar and overpowering nature: they were a mixture of pain and pleasure, such as I had never before experienced, either from hunger or cold, warmth or food; and I withdrew from the window, unable to bear these emotions.

'Soon after this the young man returned, bearing on his shoulders a load of wood. The girl met him at the door, helped to relieve him of his burden, and, taking some of the fuel into the cottage, placed it on the fire; then she and the youth went apart into a nook of the cottage, and he shewed her a large loaf and a piece of cheese. She seemed pleased; and went into the garden for some roots and plants, which she placed in water, and then upon the fire. She afterwards continued her work, whilst the young man went into the garden, and appeared busily employed in digging and pulling up roots. After he had been employed thus about an hour, the young woman joined him, and they entered the cottage together.

'The old man had, in the mean time, been pensive; but, on the appearance of his companions, he assumed a more cheerful air, and they sat down to eat. The meal was quickly dispatched. The young woman was again occupied in arranging the cottage; the old man walked before the cottage in the sun for a few minutes, leaning on the arm of the youth. Nothing could exceed in beauty the contrast between these two excellent creatures. One was old, with silver hairs and a countenance beaming with benevolence and love: the younger was slight and graceful in his figure, and his features were moulded with the finest symmetry; yet his eyes and attitude expressed the utmost sadness and despondency. The old man returned to the cottage; and the youth, with tools different from those he had used in the morning, directed his steps across the fields.

'Night quickly shut in; but, to my extreme wonder, I found that the cottagers had a means of prolonging light, by the use of tapers, and was delighted to find, that the setting of the sun did not put an end to the pleasure I experienced in watching my human neighbours. In the evening, the young girl and her companion were employed in various occupations which I did not understand; and the old man again took up the instrument, which produced the divine sounds that had enchanted me in the morning. So soon as he had finished, the youth began, not to play, but to utter sounds that were monotonous, and neither resembling the harmony of the old man's instrument or the songs of the birds; I since found that he read aloud, but at that time I knew nothing of the science of words or letters.

'The family, after having been thus occupied for a short time, extinguished their lights, and retired, as I conjectured, to rest.

CHAPTER IV

'I lay on my straw, but I could not sleep. I thought of the occurrences of the day. What chiefly struck me was the gentle manners of these people; and I longed to join them, but dared not. I remembered too well the treatment I had suffered the night before from the barbarous villagers, and resolved, whatever course of conduct I might hereafter think it right to pursue, that for the present I would remain quietly in my hovel, watching, and endeavouring to discover the motives which influenced their actions.

'The cottagers arose the next morning before the sun. The young woman arranged the cottage, and prepared the food; and the youth departed after the first meal.

'This day was passed in the same routine as that which preceded it. The young man was constantly employed out of doors, and the girl in various laborious occupations within. The old man, whom I soon perceived to be blind, employed his leisure hours on his instrument, or in contemplation. Nothing could exceed the love and respect which the younger cottagers exhibited towards their venerable companion. They performed towards him every little office of affection and duty with gentleness; and he rewarded them by his benevolent smiles.

'They were not entirely happy. The young man and his companion often went apart, and appeared to weep. I saw no cause for their unhappiness; but I was deeply affected by it. If such lovely creatures were miserable, it was less strange that I, an imperfect and solitary being, should be wretched. Yet why were these gentle beings unhappy? They possessed a delightful house (for such it was in my eyes), and every luxury; they had a fire to warm them when chill, and delicious viands when hungry; they were dressed in excellent clothes; and, still more, they enjoyed one another's company and speech, interchanging each day looks of affection and kindness. What did their tears imply? Did they really express pain? I was at first unable to solve these questions; but perpetual attention, and time, explained to me many appearances which were at first enigmatic.

'A considerable period elapsed before I discovered one of the causes of the uneasiness of this amiable family; it was poverty: and they suffered that evil in a very distressing degree. Their nourishment consisted entirely of the vegetables of their garden, and the milk of one cow, who gave very little during the winter, when its masters could scarcely procure food to support it. They often, I believe, suffered the pangs of hunger very poignantly, especially the two younger cottagers; for several times they placed food before the old man, when they reserved none for themselves.

'This trait of kindness moved me sensibly. I had been accustomed, during the night, to steal a part of their store for my own consumption; but when I found that in doing this I inflicted pain on the cottagers, I abstained, and satisfied myself with berries, nuts, and roots, which I gathered from a neighbouring wood.

'I discovered also another means through which I was enabled to assist their labours. I found that the youth spent a great part of each day in collecting wood for the family fire; and, during the night, I often took his tools, the use of which I quickly discovered, and brought home firing sufficient for the consumption of several days.

'I remember, the first time that I did this, the young woman, when she opened the door in the morning, appeared greatly astonished on seeing a great pile of wood on the outside. She uttered some words in a loud voice, and the youth joined her, who also expressed surprise. I observed, with pleasure, that he did not go to the forest that day, but spent it in repairing the cottage and cultivating the garden.

'By degrees I made a discovery of still greater moment. I found that these people possessed a method of communicating their experience and feelings to one another by articulate sounds. I perceived that the words they spoke sometimes produced pleasure or pain, smiles or sadness, in the minds and countenances of the hearers. This was indeed a godlike science, and I ardently desired to become acquainted with it. But I was baffled in every attempt I made for this purpose. Their pronunciation was quick; and the words they uttered, not having any apparent connexion with visible objects, I was unable to discover any clue by which I could unravel the mystery of their reference. By great application, however, and after having remained during the space of several revolutions of the moon in my hovel, I discovered the names that were given to some of the most familiar objects of discourse: I learned and applied the words *fire, milk, bread,* and *wood.* I learned also the names of the cottagers themselves. The youth and his companion had each of them several names, but the old man had only one, which was *father.* The girl was called *sister,* or *Agatha;* and the youth *Felix, brother,* or *son.* I cannot describe the delight I felt when I learned the ideas appropriated to each of these sounds, and was able to pronounce them. I distinguished several other words, without being able as yet to understand or apply them; such as *good, dearest, unhappy.*

'I spent the winter in this manner. The gentle manners and beauty of the cottagers greatly endeared them to me: when they were unhappy, I felt depressed; when they rejoiced, I sympathized in their joys. I saw few human beings beside them; and if any other happened to enter the cottage, their harsh manners and rude gait only enhanced to me the superior accomplishments of my friends. The old man, I could perceive, often endeavoured to encourage his children, as sometimes I found that he called them, to cast off their melancholy. He would talk in a cheerful accent, with an expression of goodness that bestowed pleasure even upon me. Agatha listened with respect, her eyes sometimes filled with tears, which she endeavoured to wipe away unperceived; but I generally found that her countenance and tone were more cheerful after having listened to the exhortations of her father. It was not thus with Felix. He was always the saddest of the groupe; and, even to my unpractised senses, he appeared to have suffered more deeply than his friends. But if his countenance was more sorrowful, his voice was more cheerful than that of his sister, especially when he addressed the old man.

'I could mention innumerable instances, which, although slight, marked the dispositions of these amiable cottagers. In the midst of poverty and want, Felix carried with pleasure to his sister the first little white flower that peeped out from beneath the snowy ground. Early in the morning before she had risen, he cleared away the snow that obstructed her path to the milk-house, drew water from the well, and brought the wood from the outhouse, where, to his perpetual astonishment, he found his store always replenished by an invisible hand. In the day, I believe, he worked sometimes for a neighbouring farmer, because he often went forth, and did not return until dinner, yet brought no wood with him. At other times he worked in the garden; but, as there was little to do in the frosty season, he read to the old man and Agatha.

'This reading had puzzled me extremely at first; but, by degrees, I discovered that he uttered many of the same sounds when he read as when he talked. I conjectured, therefore, that he found on the paper signs for speech which he understood, and I ardently longed to comprehend these also; but how was that possible, when I did not even understand the sounds for which they stood as signs? I improved, however, sensibly in this science, but not sufficiently to follow up any kind of conversation, although I applied my whole mind to the endeavour: for I easily perceived that, although I eagerly longed to discover myself to the cottagers, I ought not to make the attempt until I had first become master of their language; which knowledge might enable me to make them overlook the deformity of my figure; for with this also the contrast perpetually presented to my eyes had made me acquainted.

'I had admired the perfect forms of my cottagers—their grace, beauty, and delicate complexions: but how was I terrified, when I viewed myself in a transparent pool! At first I started back, unable to believe that it was indeed I who was reflected in the mirror; and when I became fully convinced that I was in reality the monster that I am, I was filled with the bitterest sensations of despondence and mortification. Alas! I did not yet entirely know the fatal effects of this miserable deformity.

'As the sun became warmer, and the light of day longer, the snow vanished, and I beheld the bare trees and the black earth. From this time Felix was more employed; and the heart-moving indications of impending famine disappeared. Their food, as I afterwards found, was coarse, but it was wholesome; and they procured a sufficiency of it. Several new kinds of plants sprung up in the garden, which they dressed; and these signs of comfort increased daily as the season advanced.

'The old man, leaning on his son, walked each day at noon, when it did not rain, as I found it was called when the heavens poured forth its waters. This frequently took place; but a high wind quickly dried the earth, and the season became far more pleasant than it had been.

'My mode of life in my hovel was uniform. During the morning I attended the motions of the cottagers; and when they were dispersed in various occupations, I slept: the remainder of the day was spent in observing my friends. When they had retired to rest, if there was any moon, or the night was star-light, I went into the woods, and collected my own food and fuel for the cottage. When I returned, as often as it was necessary, I cleared their path from the snow, and performed those offices that I had seen done by Felix. I afterwards found that these labours, performed by an invisible hand, greatly astonished them; and once or twice I heard them, on these occasions, utter the words *good spirit, wonderful;* but I did not then understand the signification of these terms.

'My thoughts now became more active, and I longed to discover the motives and feelings of these lovely creatures; I was inquisitive to know why Felix appeared so miserable, and Agatha so sad. I thought (foolish wretch!) that it might be in my power to restore happiness to these deserving people. When I slept, or was absent, the forms of the venerable blind father, the gentle Agatha, and the excellent Felix, flitted before me. I looked upon them as superior beings, who would be the arbiters of my future destiny. I formed in my imagination a thousand pictures of presenting myself to them, and their reception of me. I imagined that they would be disgusted, until, by my gentle demeanour and conciliating words, I should first win their favour, and afterwards their love.

'These thoughts exhilarated me, and led me to apply with fresh ardour to the acquiring the art of language. My organs were indeed harsh, but supple; and although my voice was very unlike the soft music of their tones, yet I pronounced such words as I understood with tolerable ease. It was as the ass and the lap-dog; yet surely the gentle ass, whose intentions were affectionate, although his manners were rude, deserved better treatment than blows and execration.[34]

'The pleasant showers and genial warmth of spring greatly altered the aspect of the earth. Men, who before this change seemed to have been hid in caves, dispersed themselves, and were employed in various arts of cultivation. The birds sang in more cheerful notes, and the leaves began to bud forth on the trees. Happy, happy earth! fit habitation for gods, which, so short a time before, was bleak, damp, and unwholesome. My spirits were elevated by the enchanting appearance of nature; the past was blotted from my memory, the present was tranquil, and the future gilded by bright rays of hope, and anticipations of joy.

CHAPTER V

'I now hasten to the more moving part of my story. I shall relate events that impressed me with feelings which, from what I was, have made me what I am.

'Spring advanced rapidly; the weather became fine, and the skies cloudless. It surprised me, that what before was desert and gloomy should now bloom with the most beautiful flowers and verdure. My senses were gratified and refreshed by a thousand scents of delight, and a thousand sights of beauty.

'It was on one of these days, when my cottagers periodically rested from labour—the old man played on his guitar, and the children listened to

---

[34]LaFontaine, *Fables* (1678, 1694), the fable of the Ass and the Lapdog. [Ed.]

him—I observed that the countenance of Felix was melancholy beyond expression: he sighed frequently; and once his father paused in his music, and I conjectured by his manner that he inquired the cause of his son's sorrow. Felix replied in a cheerful accent, and the old man was recommencing his music, when some one tapped at the door.

'It was a lady on horseback, accompanied by a countryman as a guide. The lady was dressed in a dark suit, and covered with a thick black veil. Agatha asked a question; to which the stranger only replied by pronouncing, in a sweet accent, the name of Felix. Her voice was musical, but unlike that of either of my friends. On hearing this word, Felix came up hastily to the lady; who, when she saw him, threw up her veil, and I beheld a countenance of angelic beauty and expression. Her hair of a shining raven black, and curiously braided; her eyes were dark, but gentle, although animated; her features of a regular proportion, and her complexion wondrously fair, each cheek tinged with a lovely pink.

'Felix seemed ravished with delight when he saw her, every trait of sorrow vanished from his face, and it instantly expressed a degree of ecstatic joy, of which I could hardly have believed it capable; his eyes sparkled, as his cheek flushed with pleasure; and at that moment I thought him as beautiful as the stranger. She appeared affected by different feelings; wiping a few tears from her lovely eyes, she held out her hand to Felix, who kissed it rapturously, and called her, as well as I could distinguish, his sweet Arabian. She did not appear to understand him, but smiled. He assisted her to dismount, and, dismissing her guide, conducted her into the cottage. Some conversation took place between him and his father; and the young stranger knelt at the old man's feet, and would have kissed his hand, but he raised her, and embraced her affectionately.

'I soon perceived, that although the stranger uttered articulate sounds, and appeared to have a language of her own, she was neither understood by, or herself understood, the cottagers. They made many signs which I did not comprehend; but I saw that her presence diffused gladness through the cottage, dispelling their sorrow as the sun dissipates the morning mists. Felix seemed peculiarly happy, and with smiles of delight welcomed his Arabian. Agatha, the ever-gentle Agatha, kissed the hands of the lovely stranger; and, pointing to her brother, made signs which appeared to me to mean that he had been sorrowful until she came. Some hours passed thus, while they, by their countenances, expressed joy, the cause of which I did not comprehend. Presently I found, by the frequent recurrence of one sound which the stranger repeated after them, that she was endeavouring to learn their language; and the idea instantly occurred to me, that I should make use of the same instructions to the same end. The stranger learned about twenty words at the first lesson, most of them indeed were those which I had before understood, but I profited by the others.

'As night came on, Agatha and the Arabian retired early. When they separated, Felix kissed the hand of the stranger, and said, "Good night, sweet Safie." He sat up much longer, conversing with his father; and, by the frequent repetition of her name, I conjectured that their lovely guest was the subject of their conversation. I ardently desired to understand them, and bent every faculty towards that purpose, but found it utterly impossible.

The next morning Felix went out to his work; and, after the usual occupations of Agatha were finished, the Arabian sat at the feet of the old man, and, taking his guitar, played some airs so entrancingly beautiful, that they at once drew tears of sorrow and delight from my eyes. She sang, and her voice flowed in a rich cadence, swelling or dying away, like a nightingale of the woods.   *Orientalism*

'When she had finished, she gave the guitar to Agatha, who at first declined it. She played a simple air, and her voice accompanied it in sweet accents, but unlike the wondrous strain of the stranger. The old man appeared enraptured, and said some words, which Agatha endeavoured to explain to Safie, and by which he appeared to wish to express that she bestowed on him the greatest delight by her music.

'The days now passed as peaceably as before, with the sole alteration, that joy had taken place of sadness in the countenances of my friends. Safie was always gay and happy; she and I improved rapidly in the knowledge of language, so that in two months I began to comprehend most of the words uttered by my protectors.

'In the meanwhile also the black ground was covered with herbage, and the green banks interspersed with innumerable flowers, sweet to the scent and the eyes, stars of pale radiance among the moonlight woods; the sun became warmer, the nights clear and balmy; and my nocturnal rambles were an extreme pleasure to me, although they were considerably shortened by the late setting and early rising of the sun; for I never ventured abroad during daylight, fearful of meeting with the same treatment as I had formerly endured in the first village which I entered.

'My days were spent in close attention, that I might more speedily master the language; and I may boast that I improved more rapidly than the Arabian, who understood very little, and conversed in broken accents, whilst I comprehended and could imitate almost every word that was spoken.

'While I improved in speech, I also learned the science of letters, as it was taught to the stranger; and this opened before me a wide field for wonder and delight.

'The book from which Felix instructed Safie was Volney's *Ruins of Empires*.[35] I should not have understood the purport of this book, had not Felix, in reading it, given very minute explanations. He had chosen this work, he said, because the declamatory style was framed in imitation of the eastern authors. Through this work I obtained a cursory knowledge of history, and a view of the several empires at present existing in the world; it gave me an insight into the manners, governments, and religions of the different nations of the earth. I heard of the slothful Asiatics; of the stupendous genius and mental activity of the Grecians; of the wars and wonderful virtue of the early Romans—of their subsequent degeneration—of the decline of that mighty empire; of chivalry, christianity, and kings. I heard of the discovery of the American hemisphere, and wept with Safie over the hapless fate of its original inhabitants.

'These wonderful narrations inspired me with strange feelings. Was man, indeed, at once so powerful, so virtuous, and magnificent, yet so vicious and base? He appeared at one time a mere scion of the evil principle, and at another as all that can be conceived of noble and godlike. To be a great and virtuous man appeared the highest honour that can befall a sensitive being; to be base and vicious, as many on record have been, appeared the lowest degradation, a condition more abject than that of the blind mole or harmless worm. For a long time I could not conceive how one man could go forth to murder his fellow, or even why there were laws and governments; but when I heard details of vice and bloodshed, my wonder ceased, and I turned away with disgust and loathing.

'Every conversation of the cottagers now opened new wonders to me. While I listened to the instructions which Felix bestowed upon the Arabian, the strange system of human society was explained to me. I heard of the division of property, of immense wealth and squalid poverty; of rank, descent, and noble blood.

'The words induced me to turn towards myself. I learned that the possessions most esteemed by your fellow creatures were, high and unsullied descent united with riches. A man might be respected with only one of these acquisitions; but without either he was considered, except in very rare instances, as a vagabond and a slave, doomed to waste his powers for the profit of the chosen few. And what was I? Of my creation and creator I was absolutely ignorant; but I knew that I possessed no money, no friends, no kind of property. I was, besides, endowed with a figure hideously de-

---

[35] *The Ruins, or a Survey of the Revolutions of Empires* (1791), by Constantin François Chasseboeuf, comte de Volney, a powerful polemic on the rise and fall of ancient and modern empires. [Ed.]

formed and loathsome; I was not even of the same nature as man. I was more agile than they, and could subsist upon coarser diet; I bore the extremes of heat and cold with less injury to my frame; my stature far exceeded theirs. When I looked around, I saw and heard of none like me. Was I then a monster, a blot upon the earth, from which all men fled, and whom all men disowned?

'I cannot describe to you the agony that these reflections inflicted upon me; I tried to dispel them, but sorrow only increased with knowledge. Oh, that I had for ever remained in my native wood, nor known or felt beyond the sensations of hunger, thirst, and heat!

'Of what a strange nature is knowledge! It clings to the mind, when it has once seized on it, like a lichen on the rock. I wished sometimes to shake off all thought and feeling; but I learned that there was but one means to overcome the sensation of pain, and that was death—a state which I feared yet did not understand. I admired virtue and good feelings, and loved the gentle manners and amiable qualities of my cottagers; but I was shut out from intercourse with them, except through means which I obtained by stealth, when I was unseen and unknown, and which rather increased than satisfied the desire I had of becoming one among my fellows. The gentle words of Agatha, and the animated smiles of the charming Arabian, were not for me. The mild exhortations of the old man, and the lively conversation of the loved Felix, were not for me. Miserable, unhappy wretch!

'Other lessons were impressed upon me even more deeply. I heard of the difference of sexes; of the birth and growth of children; how the father doated on the smiles of the infant, and the lively sallies of the older child; how all the life and cares of the mother were wrapt up in the precious charge; how the mind of youth expanded and gained knowledge; of brother, sister, and all the various relationships which bind one human being to another in mutual bonds.

'But where were my friends and relations? No father had watched my infant days, no mother had blessed me with smiles and caresses; or if they had, all my past life was now a blot, a blind vacancy in which I distinguished nothing. From my earliest remembrance I had been as I then was in height and proportion. I had never yet seen a being resembling me, or who claimed any intercourse with me. What was I? The question again recurred, to be answered only with groans.

'I will soon explain to what these feelings tended; but allow me now to return to the cottagers, whose story excited in me such various feelings of indignation, delight, and wonder, but which all terminated in additional love and reverence for my protectors (for so I loved, in an innocent, half painful self-deceit, to call them).

CHAPTER VI

'Some time elapsed before I learned the history of my friends. It was one which could not fail to impress itself deeply on my mind, unfolding as it did a number of circumstances each interesting and wonderful to one so utterly inexperienced as I was.

'The name of the old man was De Lacey. He was descended from a good family in France, where he had lived for many years in affluence, respected by his superiors, and beloved by his equals. His son was bred in the service of his country; and Agatha had ranked with ladies of the highest distinction. A few months before my arrival, they had lived in a large and luxurious city, called Paris, surrounded by friends, and possessed of every enjoyment which virtue, refinement of intellect, or taste, accompanied by a moderate fortune, could afford.

'The father of Safie had been the cause of their ruin. He was a Turkish merchant, and had inhabited Paris for many years, when, for some reason which I could not learn, he became obnoxious to the government. He was seized and cast into prison the very day that Safie arrived from Constantinople to join him. He was tried, and condemned to death. The injustice of his sentence was very flagrant; all Paris was indignant; and it was judged that his religion and wealth, rather than the crime alleged against him, had been the cause of his condemnation.

'Felix had been present at the trial; his horror and indignation were uncontrollable, when he heard the decision of the court. He made, at that moment, a solemn vow to deliver him, and then looked around for the means. After many fruitless attempts to gain admittance to the prison, he found a strongly grated window in an unguarded part of the building, which lighted the dungeon of the unfortunate Mahometan; who, loaded with chains, waited in despair the execution of the barbarous sentence. Felix visited the grate at night, and made known to the prisoner his intentions in his favour. The Turk, amazed and delighted, endeavoured to kindle the zeal of his deliverer by promises of reward and wealth. Felix rejected his offers with contempt; yet when he saw the lovely Safie, who was allowed to visit her father, and who, by her gestures, expressed her lively gratitude, the youth could not help owning to his own mind, that the captive possessed a treasure which would fully reward his toil and hazard.

'The Turk quickly perceived the impression that his daughter had made on the heart of Felix, and endeavoured to secure him more entirely in his interests by the promise of her hand in marriage, so soon as he should be conveyed to a place of safety. Felix was too delicate to accept this offer; yet he looked forward to the probability of that event as to the consummation of his happiness.

'During the ensuing days, while the preparations were going forward for the escape of the merchant, the zeal of Felix was warmed by several letters that he received from this lovely girl, who found means to express her thoughts in the language of her lover by the aid of an old man, a servant of her father's, who understood French. She thanked him in the most ardent terms for his intended services towards her father; and at the same time she gently deplored her own fate.

'I have copies of these letters; for I found means, during my residence in the hovel, to procure the implements of writing; and the letters were often in the hands of Felix or Agatha. Before I depart, I will give them to you, they will prove the truth of my tale; but at present, as the sun is already far declined, I shall only have time to repeat the substance of them to you.

'Safie related, that her mother was a Christian Arab, seized and made a slave by the Turks; recommended by her beauty, she had won the heart of the father of Safie, who married her. The young girl spoke in high and enthusiastic terms of her mother, who, born in freedom spurned the bondage to which she was now reduced. She instructed her daughter in the tenets of her religion, and taught her to aspire to higher powers of intellect, and an independence of spirit, forbidden to the female followers of Mahomet. This lady died; but her lessons were indelibly impressed on the mind of Safie, who sickened at the prospect of again returning to Asia, and the being immured within the walls of a haram, allowed only to occupy herself with puerile amusements, ill suited to the temper of her soul, now accustomed to grand ideas and a noble emulation for virtue. The prospect of marrying a Christian, and remaining in a country where women were allowed to take a rank in society, was enchanting to her. *orientalist*

'The day for the execution of the Turk was fixed; but, on the night previous to it, he had quitted prison, and before morning was distant many leagues from Paris. Felix had procured passports in the name of his father, sister, and himself. He had previously communicated his plan to the former, who aided the deceit by quitting his house, under the pretence of a journey, and concealed himself, with his daughter, in an obscure part of Paris.

'Felix conducted the fugitives through France to Lyons, and across Mont Cenis to Leghorn, where the merchant had decided to wait a favourable opportunity of passing into some part of the Turkish dominions.

'Safie resolved to remain with her father until the moment of his departure, before which time the Turk renewed his promise that she should be united to his deliverer; and Felix remained with them in expectation of that event; and in the mean time he enjoyed the society of the Arabian, who exhibited towards him the simplest and tenderest affection. They conversed with one another through the means of an interpreter, and sometimes with the interpretation of looks; and Safie sang to him the divine airs of her native country.

'The Turk allowed this intimacy to take place, and encouraged the hopes of the youthful lovers, while in his heart he had formed far other plans. He loathed the idea that his daughter should be united to a Christian; but he feared the resentment of Felix if he should appear lukewarm; for he knew that he was still in the power of his deliverer, if he should choose to betray him to the Italian state which they inhabited. He revolved a thousand plans by which he should be enabled to prolong the deceit until it might be no longer necessary, and secretly to take his daughter with him when he departed. His plans were greatly facilitated by the news which arrived from Paris.

'The government of France were greatly enraged at the escape of their victim, and spared no pains to detect and punish his deliverer. The plot of Felix was quickly discovered, and De Lacey and Agatha were thrown into prison. The news reached Felix, and roused him from his dream of pleasure. His blind and aged father, and his gentle sister, lay in a noisome dungeon, while he enjoyed the free air, and the society of her whom he loved. This idea was torture to him. He quickly arranged with the Turk, that if the latter should find a favourable opportunity for escape before Felix could return to Italy, Safie should remain as a boarder at a convent at Leghorn; and then, quitting the lovely Arabian, he hastened to Paris, and delivered himself up to the vengeance of the law, hoping to free De Lacey and Agatha by this proceeding.

'He did not succeed. They remained confined for five months before the trial took place; the result of which deprived them of their fortune, and condemned them to a perpetual exile from their native country.

'They found a miserable asylum in the cottage in Germany, where I discovered them. Felix soon learned that the treacherous Turk, for whom he and his family endured such unheard-of oppression, on discovering that his deliverer was thus reduced to poverty and impotence, became a traitor to good feeling and honour, and had quitted Italy with his daughter, insultingly sending Felix a pittance of money to aid him, as he said, in some plan of future maintenance.

'Such were the events that preyed on the heart of Felix, and rendered him, when I first saw him, the most miserable of his family. He could have endured poverty, and when this distress had been the meed of his virtue, he would have gloried in it: but the ingratitude of the Turk, and the loss of his beloved Safie, were misfortunes more bitter and irreparable. The arrival of the Arabian now infused new life into his soul.

'When the news reached Leghorn, that Felix was deprived of his wealth and rank, the merchant commanded his daughter to think no more of her lover, but to prepare to return with him to her native country. The generous nature of Safie was outraged by this command; she attempted to expostulate with her father, but he left her angrily, reiterating his tyrannical mandate.

'A few days after, the Turk entered his daughter's apartment, and told her hastily, that he had reason to believe that his residence at Leghorn had been divulged, and that he should speedily be delivered up to the French government; he had, consequently, hired a vessel to convey him to Constantinople, for which city he should sail in a few hours. He intended to leave his daughter under the care of a confidential servant, to follow at her leisure with the greater part of his property, which had not yet arrived at Leghorn.

'When alone, Safie resolved in her own mind the plan of conduct that it would become her to pursue in this emergency. A residence in Turkey was abhorrent to her; her religion and feelings were alike adverse to it. By some papers of her father's, which fell into her hands, she heard of the exile of her lover, and learned the name of the spot where he then resided. She hesitated some time, but at length she formed her determination. Taking with her some jewels that belonged to her, and a small sum of money, she quitted Italy, with an attendant, a native of Leghorn, but who understood the common language of Turkey, and departed for Germany.

'She arrived in safety at a town about twenty leagues from the cottage of De Lacey, when her attendant fell dangerously ill. Safie nursed her with the most devoted affection; but the poor girl died, and the Arabian was left alone, unacquainted with the language of the country, and utterly ignorant of the customs of the world. She fell, however, into good hands. The Italian had mentioned the name of the spot for which they were bound; and, after her death, the woman of the house in which they had lived took care that Safie should arrive in safety at the cottage of her lover.

CHAPTER VII

'Such was the history of my beloved cottagers. It impressed me deeply. I learned, from the views of social life which it developed, to admire their virtues, and to deprecate the vices of mankind.

'As yet I looked upon crime as a distant evil; benevolence and generosity were ever present before me, inciting within me a desire to become an actor in the busy scene where so many admirable qualities were called forth and displayed. But, in giving an account of the progress of my intellect, I must not omit a circumstance which occurred in the beginning of the month of August of the same year.

'One night, during my accustomed visit to the neighbouring wood, where I collected my own food, and brought home firing for my protectors, I found on the ground a leathern portmanteau, containing several articles of dress and some books. I eagerly seized the prize, and returned with it to my hovel. Fortunately the books were written in the language the elements of which I had acquired at the cottage; they consisted of *Paradise Lost*, a volume of *Plutarch's Lives*, and the *Sorrows of Werter*.[36] The possession of these treasures gave me extreme delight; I now continually studied and exercised my mind upon these histories, whilst my friends were employed in their ordinary occupations.

'I can hardly describe to you the effect of these books. They produced in me an infinity of new images and feelings, that sometimes raised me to ecstacy, but more frequently sunk me into the lowest dejection. In the *Sorrows of Werter*, besides the interest of its simple and affecting story, so many opinions are canvassed, and so many lights thrown upon what had hitherto been to me obscure subjects, that I found in it a never-ending source of speculation and astonishment. The gentle and domestic manners it described, combined with lofty sentiments and feelings, which had for their object something out of self, accorded well with my experience among my protectors, and with the wants which were for ever alive in my own bosom. But I thought Werter himself a more divine being than I had ever beheld or imagined; his character contained no pretension, but it sunk deep. The disquisitions upon death and suicide were calculated to fill me with wonder. I did not pretend to enter into the merits of the case, yet I inclined towards the opinions of the hero, whose extinction I wept, without precisely understanding it.

'As I read, however, I applied much personally to my own feelings and condition. I found myself similar, yet at the same time strangely unlike the beings concerning whom I read, and to whose conversation I was a listener. I sympathized with, and partly understood them, but I was unformed in mind; I was dependent on none, and related to none. "The path of my departure was free;"[37] and there was none to lament my annihilation. My

---

[36] Milton's *Paradise Lost*. Plutarch's *Parallel Lives* (c. AD 100) details the lives of Greek and Roman statesmen and heroes; Johan von Goethe's *The Sorrows of Young Werther* (1774), the story of a young poet and an unconsummated love affair, is a landmark text for romantic sensibility. [Ed.]

[37] From Percy Shelley's "Mutability." [Ed.]

person was hideous, and my stature gigantic: what did this mean? Who was I? What was I? Whence did I come? What was my destination? These questions continually recurred, but I was unable to solve them.

'The volume of *Plutarch's Lives* which I possessed, contained the histories of the first founders of the ancient republics. This book had a far different effect upon me from the *Sorrows of Werter*. I learned from Werter's imaginations despondency and gloom: but Plutarch taught me high thoughts; he elevated me above the wretched sphere of my own reflections, to admire and love the heroes of past ages. Many things I read surpassed my understanding and experience. I had a very confused knowledge of kingdoms, wide extents of country, mighty rivers, and boundless seas. But I was perfectly unacquainted with towns, and large assemblages of men. The cottage of my protectors had been the only school in which I had studied human nature; but this book developed new and mightier scenes of action. I read of men concerned in public affairs governing or massacring their species. I felt the greatest ardour for virtue rise within me, and abhorrence for vice, as far as I understood the signification of those terms, relative as they were, as I applied them, to pleasure and pain alone. Induced by these feelings, I was of course led to admire peaceable law-givers, Numa, Solon, and Lycurgus, in preference to Romulus and Theseus.[38] The patriarchal lives of my protectors caused these impressions to take a firm hold on my mind; perhaps, if my first introduction to humanity had been made by a young soldier, burning for glory and slaughter, I should have been imbued with different sensations.

'But *Paradise Lost* excited different and far deeper emotions. I read it, as I had read the other volumes which had fallen into my hands, as a true history. It moved every feeling of wonder and awe, that the picture of an omnipotent God warring with his creatures was capable of exciting. I often referred the several situations, as their similarity struck me, to my own. Like Adam, I was created apparently united by no link to any other being in existence; but his state was far different from mine in every other respect. He had come forth from the hands of God a perfect creature, happy and prosperous, guarded by the especial care of his Creator; he was allowed to converse with, and acquire knowledge from beings of a superior nature: but I was wretched, helpless, and alone. Many times I considered Satan as the fitter emblem of my condition; for often, like him, when I viewed the bliss of my protectors, the bitter gall of envy rose within me.

---

[38] Lycurgus, Athenian statesman and reformer (c. 390–324 BC); Numa Pompilius (715–673 BC), second king of Rome; Solon (sixth century BC), Athenian statesman and poet. Romulus and Theseus are legendary heroes of Rome and Greece. [Ed.]

'Another circumstance strengthened and confirmed these feelings. Soon after my arrival in the hovel, I discovered some papers in the pocket of the dress which I had taken from your laboratory. At first I had neglected them; but now that I was able to decypher the characters in which they were written, I began to study them with diligence. It was your journal of the four months that preceded my creation. You minutely described in these papers every step you took in the progress of your work; this history was mingled with accounts of domestic occurrences. You, doubtless, recollect these papers. Here they are. Every thing is related in them which bears reference to my accursed origin; the whole detail of that series of disgusting circumstances which produced it is set in view; the minutest description of my odious and loathsome person is given, in language which painted your own horrors, and rendered mine ineffaceable. I sickened as I read. "Hateful day when I received life!" I exclaimed in agony. "Cursed creator! Why did you form a monster so hideous that even you turned from me in disgust? God in pity made man beautiful and alluring, after his own image; but my form is a filthy type of yours, more horrid from its very resemblance. Satan had his companions, fellow-devils, to admire and encourage him; but I am solitary and detested."

'These were the reflections of my hours of despondency and solitude; but when I contemplated the virtues of the cottagers, their amiable and benevolent dispositions, I persuaded myself that when they should become acquainted with my admiration of their virtues, they would compassionate me, and overlook my personal deformity. Could they turn from their door one, however monstrous, who solicited their compassion and friendship? I resolved, at least, not to despair, but in every way to fit myself for an interview with them which would decide my fate. I postponed this attempt for some months longer; for the importance attached to its success inspired me with a dread lest I should fail. Besides, I found that my understanding improved so much with every day's experience, that I was unwilling to commence this undertaking until a few more months should have added to my wisdom.

'Several changes, in the mean time, took place in the cottage. The presence of Safie diffused happiness among its inhabitants; and I also found that a greater degree of plenty reigned there. Felix and Agatha spent more time in amusement and conversation, and were assisted in their labours by servants. They did not appear rich, but they were contented and happy; their feelings were serene and peaceful, while mine became every day more tumultuous. Increase of knowledge only discovered to me more clearly what a wretched outcast I was. I cherished hope, it is true; but it vanished, when I beheld my person reflected in water, or my shadow in the moon-shine, even as that frail image and that inconstant shade.

'I endeavoured to crush these fears, and to fortify myself for the trial which in a few months I resolved to undergo; and sometimes I allowed my thoughts, unchecked by reason, to ramble in the fields of Paradise, and dared to fancy amiable and lovely creatures sympathizing with my feelings and cheering my gloom; their angelic countenances breathed smiles of consolation. But it was all a dream: no Eve soothed my sorrows, or shared my thoughts; I was alone. I remembered Adam's supplication to his Creator; but where was mine? he had abandoned me, and, in the bitterness of my heart, I cursed him.

'Autumn passed thus. I saw, with surprise and grief, the leaves decay and fall, and nature again assume the barren and bleak appearance it had worn when I first beheld the woods and the lovely moon. Yet I did not heed the bleakness of the weather; I was better fitted by my conformation for the endurance of cold than heat. But my chief delights were the sight of the flowers, the birds, and all the gay apparel of summer; when those deserted me, I turned with more attention towards the cottagers. Their happiness was not decreased by the absence of summer. They loved, and sympathized with one another; and their joys, depending on each other, were not interrupted by the casualties that took place around them. The more I saw of them, the greater became my desire to claim their protection and kindness; my heart yearned to be known and loved by these amiable creatures: to see their sweet looks turned towards me with affection, was the utmost limit of my ambition. I dared not think that they would turn them from me with disdain and horror. The poor that stopped at their door were never driven away. I asked, it is true, for greater treasures than a little food or rest; I required kindness and sympathy; but I did not believe myself utterly unworthy of it.

'The winter advanced, and an entire revolution of the seasons had taken place since I awoke into life. My attention, at this time, was solely directed towards my plan of introducing myself into the cottage of my protectors. I revolved many projects; but that on which I finally fixed was, to enter the dwelling when the blind old man should be alone. I had sagacity enough to discover, that the unnatural hideousness of my person was the chief object of horror with those who had formerly beheld me. My voice, although harsh, had nothing terrible in it; I thought, therefore, that if, in the absence of his children, I could gain the good-will and mediation of the old De Lacy,[39] I might, by his means, be tolerated by my younger protectors.

'One day, when the sun shone on the red leaves that strewed the ground, and diffused cheerfulness, although it denied warmth, Safie, Agatha, and

---

[39] This is the first of five places where the 1818 edition has changed De Lacey to De Lacy. Later editions restore the first spelling; see Robinson. [Ed.]

Felix, departed on a long country walk, and the old man, at his own desire, was left alone in the cottage. When his children had departed, he took up his guitar, and played several mournful, but sweet airs, more sweet and mournful than I had ever heard him play before. At first his countenance was illuminated with pleasure, but, as he continued, thoughtfulness and sadness succeeded; at length, laying aside the instrument, he sat absorbed in reflection.

'My heart beat quick; this was the hour and moment of trial, which would decide my hopes, or realize my fears. The servants were gone to a neighbouring fair. All was silent in and around the cottage: it was an excellent opportunity; yet, when I proceeded to execute my plan, my limbs failed me, and I sunk to the ground. Again I rose; and, exerting all the firmness of which I was master, removed the planks which I had placed before my hovel to conceal my retreat. The fresh air revived me, and, with renewed determination, I approached the door of their cottage.

'I knocked. "Who is there?" said the old man—"Come in."

'I entered; "Pardon this intrusion," said I, "I am a traveller in want of a little rest; you would greatly oblige me, if you would allow me to remain a few minutes before the fire."

'"Enter," said De Lacy; "and I will try in what manner I can relieve your wants; but, unfortunately, my children are from home, and, as I am blind, I am afraid I shall find it difficult to procure food for you."

'"Do not trouble yourself, my kind host, I have food; it is warmth and rest only that I need."

'I sat down, and a silence ensued. I knew that every minute was precious to me, yet I remained irresolute in what manner to commence the interview; when the old man addressed me—

'"By your language, stranger, I suppose you are my countryman;—are you French?"

'"No; but I was educated by a French family, and understand that language only. I am now going to claim the protection of some friends, whom I sincerely love, and of whose favour I have some hopes."

'"Are these Germans?"

'"No, they are French. But let us change the subject. I am an unfortunate and deserted creature; I look around, and I have no relation or friend upon earth. These amiable people to whom I go have never seen me, and know little of me. I am full of fears; for if I fail there, I am an outcast in the world for ever."

'"Do not despair. To be friendless is indeed to be unfortunate; but the hearts of men, when unprejudiced by any obvious self-interest, are full of brotherly love and charity. Rely, therefore, on your hopes; and if these friends are good and amiable, do not despair."

'"They are kind—they are the most excellent creatures in the world; but, unfortunately, they are prejudiced against me. I have good dispositions; my life has been hitherto harmless, and, in some degree, beneficial; but a fatal prejudice clouds their eyes, and where they ought to see a feeling and kind friend, they behold only a detestable monster."

'"That is indeed unfortunate; but if you are really blameless, cannot you undeceive them?"

'"I am about to undertake that task; and it is on that account that I feel so many overwhelming terrors. I tenderly love these friends; I have, unknown to them, been for many months in the habits of daily kindness towards them; but they believe that I wish to injure them, and it is that prejudice which I wish to overcome."

'"Where do these friends reside?"

'"Near this spot."

'The old man paused, and then continued, "If you will unreservedly confide to me the particulars of your tale, I perhaps may be of use in undeceiving them. I am blind, and cannot judge of your countenance, but there is something in your words which persuades me that you are sincere. I am poor, and an exile; but it will afford me true pleasure to be in any way serviceable to a human creature."

'"Excellent man! I thank you, and accept your generous offer. You raise me from the dust by this kindness; and I trust that, by your aid, I shall not be driven from the society and sympathy of your fellow-creatures."

'"Heaven forbid! even if you were really criminal; for that can only drive you to desperation, and not instigate you to virtue. I also am unfortunate; I and my family have been condemned, although innocent: judge, therefore, if I do not feel for your misfortunes."

'"How can I thank you, my best and only benefactor? from your lips first have I heard the voice of kindness directed towards me; I shall be for ever grateful; and your present humanity assures me of success with those friends whom I am on the point of meeting."

'"May I know the names and residence of those friends?"

'I paused. This, I thought, was the moment of decision, which was to rob me of, or bestow happiness on me for ever. I struggled vainly for firmness sufficient to answer him, but the effort destroyed all my remaining strength, I sank on the chair, and sobbed aloud. At that moment I heard the steps of my younger protectors. I had not a moment to lose; but, seizing the hand of the old man, I cried, "Now is the time!—save and protect me! You and your family are the friends whom I seek. Do not you desert me in the hour of trial!"

'"Great God!" exclaimed the old man, "who are you?"

'At that instant the cottage door was opened, and Felix, Safie and Agatha entered. Who can describe their horror and consternation on beholding me? Agatha fainted; and Safie, unable to attend to her friend, rushed out of the cottage. Felix darted forward, and with supernatural force tore me from his father, to whose knees I clung: in a transport of fury, he dashed me to the ground, and struck me violently with a stick. I could have torn him limb from limb, as the lion rends the antelope. But my heart sunk within me as with bitter sickness, and I refrained. I saw him on the point of repeating his blow, when, overcome by pain and anguish, I quitted the cottage, and in the general tumult escaped unperceived to my hovel.

CHAPTER VIII

'Cursed, cursed creator! Why did I live? Why, in that instant, did I not extinguish the spark of existence which you had so wantonly bestowed? I know not; despair had not yet taken possession of me; my feelings were those of rage and revenge. I could with pleasure have destroyed the cottage and its inhabitants, and have glutted myself with their shrieks and misery.

'When night came, I quitted my retreat, and wandered in the wood; and now, no longer restrained by the fear of discovery, I gave vent to my anguish in fearful howlings. I was like a wild beast that had broken the toils; destroying the objects that obstructed me, and ranging through the wood with a stag-like swiftness. Oh! what a miserable night I passed! the cold stars shone in mockery, and the bare trees waved their branches above me: now and then the sweet voice of a bird burst forth amidst the universal stillness. All, save I, were at rest or in enjoyment: I, like the arch fiend, bore a hell within me;[40] and, finding myself unsympathized with, wished to tear up the trees, spread havoc and destruction around me, and then to have sat down and enjoyed the ruin.

'But this was a luxury of sensation that could not endure; I became fatigued with excess of bodily exertion, and sank on the damp grass in the sick impotence of despair. There was none among the myriads of men that existed who would pity or assist me; and should I feel kindness towards my enemies? No: from that moment I declared everlasting war against the species, and, more than all, against him who had formed me, and sent me forth to this insupportable misery.

'The sun rose; I heard the voices of men, and knew that it was impossible to return to my retreat during that day. Accordingly I hid myself in

---

[40] Paraphrasing Satan in *Paradise Lost:* "which way shall I fly/Infinite wrath, and infinite despair?/Which way I fly is Hell; myself am Hell" (IV, 73–75). [Ed.]

some thick underwood, determining to devote the ensuing hours to reflection on my situation.

'The pleasant sunshine, and the pure air of day, restored me to some degree of tranquillity; and when I considered what had passed at the cottage, I could not help believing that I had been too hasty in my conclusions. I had certainly acted imprudently. It was apparent that my conversation had interested the father in my behalf, and I was a fool in having exposed my person to the horror of his children. I ought to have familiarized the old De Lacy to me, and by degrees have discovered myself to the rest of his family, when they should have been prepared for my approach. But I did not believe my errors to be irretrievable; and, after much consideration, I resolved to return to the cottage, seek the old man, and by my representations win him to my party.

'These thoughts calmed me, and in the afternoon I sank into a profound sleep; but the fever of my blood did not allow me to be visited by peaceful dreams. The horrible scene of the preceding day was for ever acting before my eyes; the females were flying, and the enraged Felix tearing me from his father's feet. I awoke exhausted; and, finding that it was already night, I crept forth from my hiding-place, and went in search of food.

'When my hunger was appeased, I directed my steps towards the well-known path that conducted to the cottage. All there was at peace. I crept into my hovel, and remained in silent expectation of the accustomed hour when the family arose. That hour past, the sun mounted high in the heavens, but the cottagers did not appear. I trembled violently, apprehending some dreadful misfortune. The inside of the cottage was dark, and I heard no motion; I cannot describe the agony of this suspence.

'Presently two countrymen passed by; but, pausing near the cottage, they entered into conversation, using violent gesticulations; but I did not understand what they said, as they spoke the language of the country, which differed from that of my protectors. Soon after, however, Felix approached with another man: I was surprised, as I knew that he had not quitted the cottage that morning, and waited anxiously to discover, from his discourse, the meaning of these unusual appearances.

'"Do you consider," said his companion to him, "that you will be obliged to pay three months' rent, and to lose the produce of your garden? I do not wish to take any unfair advantage, and I beg therefore that you will take some days to consider of your determination."

'"It is utterly useless," replied Felix, "we can never again inhabit your cottage. The life of my father is in the greatest danger, owing to the dreadful circumstance that I have related. My wife and my sister will never recover their horror. I entreat you not to reason with me any more. Take possession of your tenement, and let me fly from this place."

'Felix trembled violently as he said this. He and his companion entered the cottage, in which they remained for a few minutes, and then departed. I never saw any of the family of De Lacy more.

'I continued for the remainder of the day in my hovel in a state of utter and stupid despair. My protectors had departed, and had broken the only link that held me to the world. For the first time the feelings of revenge and hatred filled my bosom, and I did not strive to control them; but, allowing myself to be borne away by the stream, I bent my mind towards injury and death. When I thought of my friends, of the mild voice of De Lacy, the gentle eyes of Agatha, and the exquisite beauty of the Arabian, these thoughts vanished, and a gush of tears somewhat soothed me. But again, when I reflected that they had spurned and deserted me, anger returned, a rage of anger; and, unable to injure any thing human, I turned my fury towards inanimate objects. As night advanced, I placed a variety of combustibles around the cottage; and, after having destroyed every vestige of cultivation in the garden, I waited with forced impatience until the moon had sunk to commence my operations.

'As the night advanced, a fierce wind arose from the woods, and quickly dispersed the clouds that had loitered in the heavens: the blast tore along like a mighty avalanche, and produced a kind of insanity in my spirits, that burst all bounds of reason and reflection. I lighted the dry branch of a tree, and danced with fury around the devoted cottage, my eyes still fixed on the western horizon, the edge of which the moon nearly touched. A part of its orb was at length hid, and I waved my brand; it sunk, and, with a loud scream, I fired the straw, and heath, and bushes, which I had collected. The wind fanned the fire, and the cottage was quickly enveloped by the flames, which clung to it, and licked it with their forked and destroying tongues.

'As soon as I was convinced that no assistance could save any part of the habitation, I quitted the scene, and sought for refuge in the woods.

'And now, with the world before me, whither should I bend my steps?[41] I resolved to fly far from the scene of my misfortunes; but to me, hated and despised, every country must be equally horrible. At length the thought of you crossed my mind. I learned from your papers that you were my father, my creator; and to whom could I apply with more fitness than to him who had given me life? Among the lessons that Felix had bestowed upon Safie geography had not been omitted: I had learned from these the relative situations of the different countries of the earth. You had mentioned Geneva as the name of your native town; and towards this place I resolved to proceed.

---

[41] Paraphrasing the final lines of *Paradise Lost;* as Adam and Eve depart the Garden, "The World was all before them, where to choose/Their place of rest" (XII, 646–47). [Ed.]

'But how was I to direct myself? I knew that I must travel in a south-westerly direction to reach my destination; but the sun was my only guide. I did not know the names of the towns that I was to pass through, nor could I ask information from a single human being; but I did not despair. From you only could I hope for succour, although towards you I felt no sentiment but that of hatred. Unfeeling, heartless creator! you had endowed me with perceptions and passions, and then cast me abroad an object for the scorn and horror of mankind. But on you only had I any claim for pity and redress, and from you I determined to seek that justice which I vainly attempted to gain from any other being that wore the human form.

'My travels were long, and the sufferings I endured intense. It was late in autumn when I quitted the district where I had so long resided. I travelled only at night, fearful of encountering the visage of a human being. Nature decayed around me, and the sun became heatless; rain and snow poured around me; mighty rivers were frozen; the surface of the earth was hard, and chill, and bare, and I found no shelter. Oh, earth! how often did I imprecate curses on the cause of my being! The mildness of my nature had fled, and all within me was turned to gall and bitterness. The nearer I approached to your habitation, the more deeply did I feel the spirit of revenge enkindled in my heart. Snow fell, and the waters were hardened, but I rested not. A few incidents now and then directed me, and I possessed a map of the country; but I often wandered wide from my path. The agony of my feelings allowed me no respite: no incident occurred from which my rage and misery could not extract its food; but a circumstance that happened when I arrived on the confines of Switzerland, when the sun had recovered its warmth, and the earth again began to look green, confirmed in an especial manner the bitterness and horror of my feelings.

'I generally rested during the day, and travelled only when I was secured by night from the view of man. One morning, however, finding that my path lay through a deep wood, I ventured to continue my journey after the sun had risen; the day, which was one of the first of spring, cheered even me by the loveliness of its sunshine and the balminess of the air. I felt emotions of gentleness and pleasure, that had long appeared dead, revive within me. Half surprised by the novelty of these sensations, I allowed myself to be borne away by them; and, forgetting my solitude and deformity, dared to be happy. Soft tears again bedewed my cheeks, and I even raised my humid eyes with thankfulness towards the blessed sun which bestowed such joy upon me.

'I continued to wind among the paths of the wood, until I came to its boundary, which was skirted by a deep and rapid river, into which many of the trees bent their branches, now budding with the fresh spring. Here I paused, not exactly knowing what path to pursue, when I heard the sound of voices, that induced me to conceal myself under the shade of a cypress. I was scarcely hid, when a young girl came running towards the spot where I was concealed, laughing as if she ran from some one in sport. She continued her course along the precipitous sides of the river, when suddenly her foot slipt, and she fell into the rapid stream. I rushed from my hiding-place, and, with extreme labour from the force of the current, saved her, and dragged her to shore. She was senseless; and I endeavoured, by every means in my power, to restore animation, when I was suddenly interrupted by the approach of a rustic, who was probably the person from whom she had playfully fled. On seeing me, he darted towards me, and, tearing the girl from my arms, hastened towards the deeper parts of the wood. I followed speedily, I hardly knew why; but when the man saw me draw near, he aimed a gun, which he carried, at my body, and fired. I sunk to the ground, and my injurer, with increased swiftness, escaped into the wood.

'This was then the reward of my benevolence! I had saved a human being from destruction, and, as a recompence, I now writhed under the miserable pain of a wound, which shattered the flesh and bone. The feelings of kindness and gentleness, which I had entertained but a few moments before, gave place to hellish rage and gnashing of teeth. Inflamed by pain, I vowed eternal hatred and vengeance to all mankind. But the agony of my wound overcame me; my pulses paused, and I fainted.

'For some weeks I led a miserable life in the woods, endeavouring to cure the wound which I had received. The ball had entered my shoulder, and I knew not whether it had remained there or passed through; at any rate I had no means of extracting it. My sufferings were augmented also by the oppressive sense of the injustice and ingratitude of their infliction. My daily vows rose for revenge—a deep and deadly revenge, such as would alone compensate for the outrages and anguish I had endured.

'After some weeks my wound healed, and I continued my journey. The labours I endured were no longer to be alleviated by the bright sun or gentle breezes of spring; all joy was but a mockery, which insulted my desolate state, and made me feel more painfully that I was not made for the enjoyment of pleasure.

'But my toils now drew near a close; and, two months from this time, I reached the environs of Geneva.

'It was evening when I arrived, and I retired to a hiding-place among the fields that surround it, to meditate in what manner I should apply to you. I was oppressed by fatigue and hunger, and far too unhappy to enjoy the gentle breezes of evening, or the prospect of the sun setting behind the stupendous mountains of Jura.

'At this time a slight sleep relieved me from the pain of reflection, which was disturbed by the approach of a beautiful child, who came running into

William

the recess I had chosen with all the sportiveness of infancy. Suddenly, as I gazed on him, an idea seized me, that this little creature was unprejudiced, and had lived too short a time to have imbibed a horror of deformity. If, therefore, I could seize him, and educate him as my companion and friend, I should not be so desolate in this peopled earth.

'Urged by this impulse, I seized on the boy as he passed, and drew him towards me. As soon as he beheld my form, he placed his hands before his eyes, and uttered a shrill scream: I drew his hand forcibly from his face, and said, "Child, what is the meaning of this? I do not intend to hurt you; listen to me."

'He struggled violently; "Let me go," he cried; "monster! ugly wretch! you wish to eat me, and tear me to pieces—You are an ogre—Let me go, or I will tell my papa."

'"Boy, you will never see your father again; you must come with me."

'"Hideous monster! let me go; My papa is a Syndic—he is M. Frankenstein—he would punish you. You dare not keep me."

'"Frankenstein! you belong then to my enemy—to him towards whom I have sworn eternal revenge; you shall be my first victim."

'The child still struggled, and loaded me with epithets which carried despair to my heart: I grasped his throat to silence him, and in a moment he lay dead at my feet.

'I gazed on my victim, and my heart swelled with exultation and hellish triumph: clapping my hands, I exclaimed, "I, too, can create desolation; my enemy is not impregnable; this death will carry despair to him, and a thousand other miseries shall torment and destroy him."

'As I fixed my eyes on the child, I saw something glittering on his breast. I took it; it was a portrait of a most lovely woman. In spite of my malignity, it softened and attracted me. For a few moments I gazed with delight on her dark eyes fringed by deep lashes, and her lovely lips; but presently my rage returned: I remembered that I was for ever deprived of the delights that such beautiful creatures could bestow; and that she whose resemblance I contemplated would, in regarding me, have changed that air of divine benignity to one expressive of disgust and affright.

'Can you wonder that such thoughts transported me with rage? I only wonder that at that moment, instead of venting my sensations in exclamations and agony, I did not rush among mankind, and perish in the attempt to destroy them.

'While I was overcome by these feelings, I left the spot where I had committed the murder, and was seeking a more secluded hiding-place, when I perceived a woman passing near me. She was young, not indeed so beautiful as her whose portrait I held, but of an agreeable aspect, and blooming in the loveliness of youth and health. Here, I thought, is one of those whose smiles are bestowed on all but me; she shall not escape: thanks to the lessons of Felix, and the sanguinary laws of man, I have learned how to work mischief. I approached her unperceived, and placed the portrait securely in one of the folds of her dress.

'For some days I haunted the spot where these scenes had taken place; sometimes wishing to see you, sometimes resolved to quit the world and its miseries for ever. At length I wandered towards these mountains, and have ranged through their immense recesses, consumed by a burning passion which you alone can gratify. We may not part until you have promised to comply with my requisition. I am alone, and miserable; man will not associate with me; but one as deformed and horrible as myself would not deny herself to me. My companion must be of the same species, and have the same defects. This being you must create.'

request

CHAPTER IX

The being finished speaking, and fixed his looks upon me in expectation of a reply. But I was bewildered, perplexed, and unable to arrange my ideas sufficiently to understand the full extent of his proposition. He continued—

'You must create a female for me, with whom I can live in the interchange of those sympathies necessary for my being. This you alone can do; and I demand it of you as a right which you must not refuse.'

The latter part of his tale had kindled anew in me the anger that had died away while he narrated his peaceful life among the cottagers, and, as he said this, I could no longer suppress the rage that burned within me.

'I do refuse it,' I replied; 'and no torture shall ever extort a consent from me. You may render me the most miserable of men, but you shall never make me base in my own eyes. Shall I create another like yourself, whose joint wickedness might desolate the world. Begone! I have answered you; you may torture me, but I will never consent.'

'You are in the wrong,' replied the fiend; 'and, instead of threatening, I am content to reason with you. I am malicious because I am miserable; am I not shunned and hated by all mankind? You, my creator, would tear me to pieces, and triumph; remember that, and tell me why I should pity man more than he pities me? You would not call it murder, if you could precipitate me into one of those ice-rifts, and destroy my frame, the work of your own hands. Shall I respect man, when he contemns me? Let him live with me in the interchange of kindness, and, instead of injury, I would bestow every benefit upon him with tears of gratitude at his acceptance. But that cannot be; the human senses are insurmountable barriers to our union. Yet mine shall not be the submission of abject slavery. I will revenge my injuries: if I cannot inspire love, I will cause fear; and chiefly towards you my arch-enemy, because my creator, do I swear inextinguishable hatred. Have a care: I will work at your destruction, nor finish until I desolate your heart, so that you curse the hour of your birth.'

A fiendish rage animated him as he said this; his face was wrinkled into contortions too horrible for human eyes to behold; but presently he calmed himself, and proceeded —

'I intended to reason. This passion is detrimental to me; for you do not reflect that you are the cause of its excess. If any being felt emotions of benevolence towards me, I should return them an hundred and an hundred fold; for that one creature's sake, I would make peace with the whole kind! But I now indulge in dreams of bliss that cannot be realized. What I ask of you is reasonable and moderate; I demand a creature of another sex, but as hideous as myself: the gratification is small, but it is all that I can receive, and it shall content me. It is true, we shall be monsters, cut off from all the world; but on that account we shall be more attached to one another. Our lives will not be happy, but they will be harmless, and free from the misery I now feel. Oh! my creator, make me happy; let me feel gratitude towards you for one benefit! Let me see that I excite the sympathy of some existing thing; do not deny me my request!'

I was moved. I shuddered when I thought of the possible consequences of my consent; but I felt that there was some justice in his argument. His tale, and the feelings he now expressed, proved him to be a creature of fine sensations; and did I not, as his maker, owe him all the portion of happiness that it was in my power to bestow? He saw my change of feeling, and continued —

'If you consent, neither you nor any other human being shall ever see us again: I will go to the vast wilds of South America. My food is not that of man; I do not destroy the lamb and the kid, to glut my appetite; acorns and berries afford me sufficient nourishment. My companion will be of the same nature as myself, and will be content with the same fare. We shall make our bed of dried leaves; the sun will shine on us as on man, and will ripen our food. The picture I present to you is peaceful and human, and you must feel that you could deny it only in the wantonness of power and cruelty. Pitiless as you have been towards me, I now see compassion in your eyes; let me seize the favourable moment, and persuade you to promise what I so ardently desire.'

'You propose,' replied I, 'to fly from the habitations of man, to dwell in those wilds where the beasts of the field will be your only companions. How can you, who long for the love and sympathy of man, persevere in this exile? You will return, and again seek their kindness, and you will meet with their detestation; your evil passions will be renewed, and you will then have a companion to aid you in the task of destruction. This may not be; cease to argue the point, for I cannot consent.'

'How inconstant are your feelings! but a moment ago you were moved by my representations, and why do you again harden yourself to my complaints? I swear to you, by the earth which I inhabit, and by you that made me, that, with the companion you bestow, I will quit the neighbourhood of man, and dwell, as it may chance, in the most savage of places. My evil passions will have fled, for I shall meet with sympathy; my life will flow quietly away, and, in my dying moments, I shall not curse my maker.'

His words had a strange effect upon me. I compassionated him, and sometimes felt a wish to console him; but when I looked upon him, when I saw the filthy mass that moved and talked, my heart sickened, and my feelings were altered to those of horror and hatred. I tried to stifle these sensations; I thought, that as I could not sympathize with him, I had no right to withhold from him the small portion of happiness which was yet in my power to bestow.

'You swear,' I said, 'to be harmless; but have you not already shewn a degree of malice that should reasonably make me distrust you? May not even this be a feint that will increase your triumph by affording a wider scope for your revenge?'

'How is this? I thought I had moved your compassion, and yet you still refuse to bestow on me the only benefit that can soften my heart, and render me harmless. If I have no ties and no affections, hatred and vice must be my portion; the love of another will destroy the cause of my crimes, and I shall become a thing, of whose existence every one will be ignorant. My vices are the children of a forced solitude that I abhor; and my virtues will necessarily arise when I live in communion with an equal. I shall feel the affections of a sensitive being, and become linked to the chain of existence and events, from which I am now excluded.'

I paused some time to reflect on all he had related, and the various arguments which he had employed. I thought of the promise of virtues which he had displayed on the opening of his existence, and the subsequent blight of all kindly feeling by the loathing and scorn which his protectors had manifested towards him. His power and threats were not omitted in my calculations: a creature who could exist in the ice caves of the glaciers, and hide himself from pursuit among the ridges of inaccessible precipices, was a being possessing faculties it would be vain to cope with. After a long pause of reflection, I concluded, that the justice due both to him and my fellow-creatures demanded of me that I should comply with his request. Turning to him, therefore, I said —

'I consent to your demand, on your solemn oath to quit Europe for ever, and every other place in the neighbourhood of man, as soon as I shall deliver into your hands a female who will accompany you in your exile.'

'I swear,' he cried, 'by the sun, and by the blue sky of heaven, that if you grant my prayer, while they exist you shall never behold me again. Depart to your home, and commence your labours: I shall watch their progress with unutterable anxiety; and fear not but that when you are ready I shall appear.'

Saying this, he suddenly quitted me, fearful, perhaps, of any change in my sentiments. I saw him descend the mountain with greater speed than the flight of an eagle, and quickly lost him among the undulations of the sea of ice.

His tale had occupied the whole day; and the sun was upon the verge of the horizon when he departed. I knew that I ought to hasten my descent towards the valley, as I should soon be encompassed in darkness; but my heart was heavy, and my steps slow. The labour of winding among the little paths of the mountains, and fixing my feet firmly as I advanced, perplexed me, occupied as I was by the emotions which the occurrences of the day had produced. Night was far advanced, when I came to the half-way resting-place, and seated myself beside the fountain. The stars shone at intervals, as the clouds passed from over them; the dark pines rose before me, and every here and there a broken tree lay on the ground: it was a scene of wonderful solemnity, and stirred strange thoughts within me. I wept bitterly; and, clasping my hands in agony, I exclaimed, 'Oh! stars, and clouds, and winds, ye are all about to mock me: if ye really pity me, crush sensation and memory; let me become as nought; but if not, depart, depart and leave me in darkness.'

These were wild and miserable thoughts; but I cannot describe to you how the eternal twinkling of the stars weighed upon me, and how I listened to every blast of wind, as if it were a dull ugly siroc on its way to consume me.[42]

Morning dawned before I arrived at the village of Chamounix; but my presence, so haggard and strange, hardly calmed the fears of my family, who had waited the whole night in anxious expectation of my return.

The following day we returned to Geneva. The intention of my father in coming had been to divert my mind, and to restore me to my lost tranquillity; but the medicine had been fatal. And, unable to account for the excess of misery I appeared to suffer, he hastened to return home, hoping the

---

[42] The sirocco is a hot and blighting wind that blows from Africa into southern Europe. [Ed.]

quiet and monotony of a domestic life would by degrees alleviate my sufferings from whatsoever cause they might spring.

For myself, I was passive in all their arrangements; and the gentle affection of my beloved Elizabeth was inadequate to draw me from the depth of my despair. The promise I had made to the dæmon weighed upon my mind, like Dante's iron cowl on the heads of the hellish hypocrites.[43] All pleasures of earth and sky passed before me like a dream, and that thought only had to me the reality of life. Can you wonder, that sometimes a kind of insanity possessed me, or that I saw continually about me a multitude of filthy animals inflicting on me incessant torture, that often extorted screams and bitter groans?

By degrees, however, these feelings became calmed. I entered again into the every-day scene of life, if not with interest, at least with some degree of tranquillity.

END OF VOLUME 2.

---

[43] Dante's *Inferno*, XXIII, 58 and following. [Ed.]

VOLUME 3

CHAPTER I

Day after day, week after week, passed away on my return to Geneva; and I could not collect the courage to recommence my work. I feared the vengeance of the disappointed fiend, yet I was unable to overcome my repugnance to the task which was enjoined me. I found that I could not compose a female without again devoting several months to profound study and laborious disquisition. I had heard of some discoveries having been made by an English philosopher, the knowledge of which was material to my success, and I sometimes thought of obtaining my father's consent to visit England for this purpose; but I clung to every pretence of delay, and could not resolve to interrupt my returning tranquillity. My health, which had hitherto declined, was now much restored; and my spirits, when unchecked by the memory of my unhappy promise, rose proportionably. My father saw this change with pleasure, and he turned his thoughts towards the best method of eradicating the remains of my melancholy, which every now and then would return by fits, and with a devouring blackness overcast the approaching sunshine. At these moments I took refuge in the most perfect solitude. I passed whole days on the lake alone in a little boat, watching the clouds, and listening to the rippling of the waves, silent and listless. But the fresh air and bright sun seldom failed to restore me to some degree of composure; and, on my return, I met the salutations of my friends with a readier smile and a more cheerful heart.

It was after my return from one of these rambles that my father, calling me aside, thus addressed me: —

'I am happy to remark, my dear son, that you have resumed your former pleasures, and seem to be returning to yourself. And yet you are still unhappy, and still avoid our society. For some time I was lost in conjecture as to the cause of this; but yesterday an idea struck me, and if it is well founded, I conjure you to avow it. Reserve on such a point would be not only useless, but draw down treble misery on us all.'

I trembled violently at this exordium, and my father continued —

'I confess, my son, that I have always looked forward to your marriage with your cousin as the tie of our domestic comfort, and the stay of my declining years. You were attached to each other from your earliest infancy; you studied together, and appeared, in dispositions and tastes, entirely suited to one another. But so blind is the experience of man, that what I conceived to be the best assistants to my plan may have entirely destroyed it. You, perhaps, regard her as your sister, without any wish that she might become your wife. Nay, you may have met with another whom you may love; and, considering yourself as bound in honour to your cousin, this struggle may occasion the poignant misery which you appear to feel.'

'My dear father, re-assure yourself. I love my cousin tenderly and sincerely. I never saw any woman who excited, as Elizabeth does, my warmest admiration and affection. My future hopes and prospects are entirely bound up in the expectation of our union.'

'The expression of your sentiments on this subject, my dear Victor, gives me more pleasure than I have for some time experienced. If you feel thus, we shall assuredly be happy, however present events may cast a gloom over us. But it is this gloom, which appears to have taken so strong a hold of your mind, that I wish to dissipate. Tell me, therefore, whether you object to an immediate solemnization of the marriage. We have been unfortunate, and recent events have drawn us from that every-day tranquillity befitting my years and infirmities. You are younger; yet I do not suppose, possessed as you are of a competent fortune, that an early marriage would at all interfere with any future plans of honour and utility that you may have formed. Do not suppose, however, that I wish to dictate happiness to you, or that a delay on your part would cause me any serious uneasiness. Interpret my words with candour, and answer me, I conjure you, with confidence and sincerity.'

I listened to my father in silence, and remained for some time incapable of offering any reply. I revolved rapidly in my mind a multitude of thoughts, and endeavoured to arrive at some conclusion. Alas! to me the idea of an immediate union with my cousin was one of horror and dismay. I was bound by a solemn promise, which I had not yet fulfilled, and dared not break; or, if I did, what manifold miseries might not impend over me and my devoted family! Could I enter into a festival with this deadly weight yet hanging round my neck, and bowing me to the ground. I must perform my engagement, and let the monster depart with his mate, before I allowed myself to enjoy the delight of an union from which I expected peace.

I remembered also the necessity imposed upon me of either journeying to England, or entering into a long correspondence with those philosophers of that country, whose knowledge and discoveries were of indispensable use to me in my present undertaking. The latter method of obtaining the desired intelligence was dilatory and unsatisfactory: besides, any variation was agreeable to me, and I was delighted with the idea of spending a year or two in change of scene and variety of occupation, in absence from my family; during which period some event might happen which would restore me to them in peace and happiness: my promise might be fulfilled, and the monster have departed; or some accident might occur to destroy him, and put an end to my slavery for ever.

These feelings dictated my answer to my father. I expressed a wish to visit England; but, concealing the true reasons of this request, I clothed my desires under the guise of wishing to travel and see the world before I sat down for life within the walls of my native town.

I urged my entreaty with earnestness, and my father was easily induced to comply; for a more indulgent and less dictatorial parent did not exist upon earth. Our plan was soon arranged. I should travel to Strasburgh, where Clerval would join me. Some short time would be spent in the towns of Holland, and our principal stay would be in England. We should return by France; and it was agreed that the tour should occupy the space of two years.

My father pleased himself with the reflection, that my union with Elizabeth should take place immediately on my return to Geneva. 'These two years,' said he, 'will pass swiftly, and it will be the last delay that will oppose itself to your happiness. And, indeed, I earnestly desire that period to arrive, when we shall all be united, and neither hopes or fears arise to disturb our domestic calm.'

'I am content,' I replied, 'with your arrangement. By that time we shall both have become wiser, and I hope happier, than we at present are.' I sighed; but my father kindly forbore to question me further concerning the cause of my dejection. He hoped that new scenes, and the amusement of travelling, would restore my tranquillity.

I now made arrangements for my journey; but one feeling haunted me, which filled me with fear and agitation. During my absence I should leave my friends unconscious of the existence of their enemy, and unprotected from his attacks, exasperated as he might be by my departure. But he had promised to follow me wherever I might go; and would he not accompany me to England? This imagination was dreadful in itself, but soothing, inasmuch as it supposed the safety of my friends. I was agonized with the idea of the possibility that the reverse of this might happen. But through the whole period during which I was the slave of my creature, I allowed myself to be governed by the impulses of the moment; and my present sensations strongly intimated that the fiend would follow me, and exempt my family from the danger of his machinations.

It was in the latter end of August that I departed, to pass two years of exile. Elizabeth approved of the reasons of my departure, and only regretted that she had not the same opportunities of enlarging her experience, and cultivating her understanding. She wept, however, as she bade me farewell, and entreated me to return happy and tranquil. 'We all,' said she, 'depend upon you; and if you are miserable, what must be our feelings?'

I threw myself into the carriage that was to convey me away, hardly knowing whither I was going, and careless of what was passing around. I remembered only, and it was with a bitter anguish that I reflected on it, to order that my chemical instruments should be packed to go with me: for I resolved to fulfil my promise while abroad, and return, if possible, a free man. Filled with dreary imaginations, I passed through many beautiful and majestic scenes; but my eyes were fixed and unobserving. I could only think of the bourne of my travels, and the work which was to occupy me whilst they endured.

After some days spent in listless indolence, during which I traversed many leagues, I arrived at Strasburgh, where I waited two days for Clerval. He came. Alas, how great was the contrast between us! He was alive to every new scene; joyful when he saw the beauties of the setting sun, and more happy when he beheld it rise, and recommence a new day. He pointed out to me the shifting colours of the landscape, and the appearances of the sky. 'This is what it is to live;' he cried, 'now I enjoy existence! But you, my dear Frankenstein, wherefore are you desponding and sorrowful?' In truth, I was occupied by gloomy thoughts, and neither saw the descent of the evening star, nor the golden sun-rise reflected in the Rhine. —And you, my friend, would be far more amused with the journal of Clerval, who observed the scenery with an eye of feeling and delight, than to listen to my reflections. I, a miserable wretch, haunted by a curse that shut up every avenue to enjoyment.

We had agreed to descend the Rhine in a boat from Strasburgh to Rotterdam, whence we might take shipping for London. During this voyage, we passed by many willowy islands, and saw several beautiful towns. We staid a day at Manheim, and, on the fifth from our departure from Strasburgh, arrived at Mayence. The course of the Rhine below Mayence becomes much more picturesque. The river descends rapidly, and winds between hills, not high, but steep, and of beautiful forms. We saw many ruined castles standing on the edges of precipices, surrounded by black woods, high and inaccessible. This part of the Rhine, indeed, presents a singularly variegated landscape. In one spot you view rugged hills, ruined castles overlooking tremendous precipices, with the dark Rhine rushing beneath; and, on the sudden turn of a promontory, flourishing vineyards, with green sloping banks, and a meandering river, and populous towns, occupy the scene.

We travelled at the time of the vintage, and heard the song of the labourers, as we glided down the stream. Even I, depressed in mind, and my spirits continually agitated by gloomy feelings, even I was pleased. I lay at the bottom of the boat, and, as I gazed on the cloudless blue sky, I seemed to drink in a tranquillity to which I had long been a stranger. And if these were

nature

my sensations, who can describe those of Henry? He felt as if he had been transported to Fairy-land, and enjoyed a happiness seldom tasted by man. 'I have seen,' he said, 'the most beautiful scenes of my own country; I have visited the lakes of Lucerne and Uri, where the snowy mountains descend almost perpendicularly to the water, casting black and impenetrable shades, which would cause a gloomy and mournful appearance, were it not for the most verdant islands that relieve the eye by their gay appearance; I have seen this lake agitated by a tempest, when the wind tore up whirlwinds of water, and gave you an idea of what the water-spout must be on the great ocean, and the waves dash with fury the base of the mountain, where the priest and his mistress were overwhelmed by an avalanche, and where their dying voices are still said to be heard amid the pauses of the nightly wind; I have seen the mountains of La Valais, and the Pays de Vaud: but this country, Victor, pleases me more than all those wonders. The mountains of Switzerland are more majestic and strange; but there is a charm in the banks of this divine river, that I never before saw equalled. Look at that castle which overhangs yon precipice; and that also on the island, almost concealed amongst the foliage of those lovely trees; and now that group of labourers coming from among their vines; and that village half-hid in the recess of the mountain. Oh, surely, the spirit that inhabits and guards this place has a source more in harmony with man, than those who pile the glacier, or retire to the inaccessible peaks of the mountains of our own country.'

Clerval! beloved friend! even now it delights me to record your words, and to dwell on the praise of which you are so eminently deserving. He was a being formed in the 'very poetry of nature.' [44] His wild and enthusiastic imagination was chastened by the sensibility of his heart. His soul overflowed with ardent affections, and his friendship was of that devoted and wondrous nature that the worldly-minded teach us to look for only in the imagination. But even human sympathies were not sufficient to satisfy his eager mind. The scenery of external nature, which others regard only with admiration, he loved with ardour:

> ———— 'The sounding cataract
> Haunted *him* like a passion: the tall rock,
> The mountain, and the deep and gloomy wood,
> Their colours and their forms, were then to him
> An appetite: a feeling, and a love,

---

[44] Leigh Hunt's "Rimini" [Mary Shelley's note. *The Story of Rimini* (1818), about Paolo and Francesca, famous lovers in Dante's *Inferno*. Ed.]

That had no need of a remoter charm,
By thought supplied, or any interest
Unborrowed from the eye.'[45]

gives away
end

And where does he now exist? Is this gentle and lovely being lost for ever? Has this mind so replete with ideas, imaginations fanciful and magnificent, which formed a world, whose existence depended on the life of its creator; has this mind perished? Does it now only exist in my memory? No, it is not thus; your form so divinely wrought, and beaming with beauty, has decayed, but your spirit still visits and consoles your unhappy friend.

Pardon this gush of sorrow; these ineffectual words are but a slight tribute to the unexampled worth of Henry, but they soothe my heart, overflowing with the anguish which his remembrance creates. I will proceed with my tale.

Beyond Cologne we descended to the plains of Holland; and we resolved to post the remainder of our way; for the wind was contrary, and the stream of the river was too gentle to aid us.

Our journey here lost the interest arising from beautiful scenery; but we arrived in a few days at Rotterdam, whence we proceeded by sea to England. It was on a clear morning, in the latter days of December, that I first saw the white cliffs of Britain. The banks of the Thames presented a new scene; they were flat, but fertile, and almost every town was marked by the remembrance of some story. We saw Tilbury Fort, and remembered the Spanish armada; Gravesend, Woolwich, and Greenwich, places which I had heard of even in my country.

At length we saw the numerous steeples of London, St Paul's towering above all, and the Tower famed in English history.

CHAPTER II

London was our present point of rest; we determined to remain several months in this wonderful and celebrated city. Clerval desired the intercourse of the men of genius and talent who flourished at this time; but this was with me a secondary object; I was principally occupied with the means of obtaining the information necessary for the completion of my promise, and quickly availed myself of the letters of introduction that I had brought with me, addressed to the most distinguished natural philosophers.

---

[45] Wordsworth's "Tintern Abbey" [Mary Shelley's note. From "Lines Composed a Few Miles above Tintern Abbey" (1798), 76–83. Ed.]

If this journey had taken place during my days of study and happiness, it would have afforded me inexpressible pleasure. But a blight had come over my existence, and I only visited these people for the sake of the information they might give me on the subject in which my interest was so terribly profound. Company was irksome to me; when alone, I could fill my mind with the sights of heaven and earth; the voice of Henry soothed me, and I could thus cheat myself into a transitory peace. But busy uninteresting joyous faces brought back despair to my heart. I saw an insurmountable barrier placed between me and my fellow-men; this barrier was sealed with the blood of William and Justine; and to reflect on the events connected with those names filled my soul with anguish.

But in Clerval I saw the image of my former self; he was inquisitive, and anxious to gain experience and instruction. The difference of manners which he observed was to him an inexhaustible source of instruction and amusement. He was for ever busy; and the only check to his enjoyments was my sorrowful and dejected mien. I tried to conceal this as much as possible, that I might not debar him from the pleasures natural to one who was entering on a new scene of life, undisturbed by any care or bitter recollection. I often refused to accompany him, alleging another engagement, that I might remain alone. I now also began to collect the materials necessary for my new creation, and this was to me like the torture of single drops of water continually falling on the head. Every thought that was devoted to it was an extreme anguish, and every word that I spoke in allusion to it caused my lips to quiver, and my heart to palpitate.

After passing some months in London, we received a letter from a person in Scotland, who had formerly been our visitor at Geneva. He mentioned the beauties of his native country, and asked us if those were not sufficient allurements to induce us to prolong our journey as far north as Perth, where he resided. Clerval eagerly desired to accept this invitation; and I, although I abhorred society, wished to view again mountains and streams, and all the wondrous works with which Nature adorns her chosen dwelling-places.

We had arrived in England at the beginning of October, and it was now February. We accordingly determined to commence our journey towards the north at the expiration of another month. In this expedition we did not intend to follow the great road to Edinburgh, but to visit Windsor, Oxford, Matlock, and the Cumberland lakes, resolving to arrive at the completion of this tour about the end of July. I packed my chemical instruments, and the materials I had collected, resolving to finish my labours in some obscure nook in the northern highlands of Scotland.

We quitted London on the 27th of March, and remained a few days at Windsor, rambling in its beautiful forest. This was a new scene to us mountaineers; the majestic oaks, the quantity of game, and the herds of stately deer, were all novelties to us.

From thence we proceeded to Oxford. As we entered this city, our minds were filled with the remembrance of the events that had been transacted there more than a century and a half before. It was here that Charles I had collected his forces. This city had remained faithful to him, after the whole nation had forsaken his cause to join the standard of parliament and liberty. The memory of that unfortunate king, and his companions, the amiable Falkland, the insolent Gower, his queen, and son, gave a peculiar interest to every part of the city, which they might be supposed to have inhabited:[46] The spirit of elder days found a dwelling here, and we delighted to trace its footsteps. If these feelings had not found an imaginary gratification, the appearance of the city had yet in itself sufficient beauty to obtain our admiration. The colleges are ancient and picturesque; the streets are almost magnificent; and the lovely Isis, which flows beside it through meadows of exquisite verdure, is spread forth into a placid expanse of waters, which reflects its majestic assemblage of towers, and spires, and domes, embosomed among aged trees.

I enjoyed this scene; and yet my enjoyment was embittered both by the memory of the past, and the anticipation of the future. I was formed for peaceful happiness. During my youthful days discontent never visited my mind; and if I was ever overcome by *ennui*, the sight of what is beautiful in nature, or the study of what is excellent and sublime in the productions of man, could always interest my heart, and communicate elasticity to my spirits. But I am a blasted tree; the bolt has entered my soul; and I felt then that I should survive to exhibit, what I shall soon cease to be—a miserable spectacle of wrecked humanity, pitiable to others, and abhorrent to myself.

We passed a considerable period at Oxford, rambling among its environs, and endeavouring to identify every spot which might relate to the most animating epoch of English history. Our little voyages of discovery were often prolonged by the successive objects that presented themselves. We visited the tomb of the illustrious Hampden, and the field on which that patriot fell.[47] For a moment my soul was elevated from its debasing and miserable fears to contemplate the divine ideas of liberty and self-sacrifice, of which these sights were the monuments and the remembrancers. For an

---

[46] Lucius Carey, second Viscount Falkland (1610–43), heroic Royalist killed at the Battle of Newbury, a prototype for Godwin's character Falkland in *Caleb Williams* (1794). "Gower," is George Goring, Baron Goring (1608–57), who fought as a Royalist after twice switching sides. [Ed.]

[47] John Hampden (1594–1643), leader of the parliamentary opposition to Charles I, killed at Chalgrove Field near Oxford. [Ed.]

antislavery

instant I dared to shake off my chains, and look around me with a free and lofty spirit; but the iron had eaten into my flesh, and I sank again, trembling and hopeless, into my miserable self.

We left Oxford with regret, and proceeded to Matlock, which was our next place of rest. The country in the neighbourhood of this village resembled, to a greater degree, the scenery of Switzerland; but every thing is on a lower scale, and the green hills want the crown of distant white Alps, which always attend on the piny mountains of my native country. We visited the wondrous cave, and the little cabinets of natural history, where the curiosities are disposed in the same manner as in the collections at Servox and Chamounix. The latter name made me tremble, when pronounced by Henry; and I hastened to quit Matlock, with which that terrible scene was thus associated.

From Derby still journeying northward, we passed two months in Cumberland and Westmoreland. I could now almost fancy myself among the Swiss mountains. The little patches of snow which yet lingered on the northern sides of the mountains, the lakes, and the dashing of the rocky streams, were all familiar and dear sights to me. Here also we made some acquaintances, who almost contrived to cheat me into happiness. The delight of Clerval was proportionably greater than mine; his mind expanded in the company of men of talent, and he found in his own nature greater capacities and resources than he could have imagined himself to have possessed while he associated with his inferiors. 'I could pass my life here,' said he to me; 'and among these mountains I should scarcely regret Switzerland and the Rhine.'

But he found that a traveller's life is one that includes much pain amidst its enjoyments. His feelings are for ever on the stretch; and when he begins to sink into repose, he finds himself obliged to quit that on which he rests in pleasure for something new, which again engages his attention, and which also he forsakes for other novelties.

We had scarcely visited the various lakes of Cumberland and Westmoreland, and conceived an affection for some of the inhabitants, when the period of our appointment with our Scotch friend approached, and we left them to travel on. For my own part I was not sorry. I had now neglected my promise for some time, and I feared the effects of the dæmon's disappointment. He might remain in Switzerland, and wreak his vengeance on my relatives. This idea pursued me, and tormented me at every moment from which I might otherwise have snatched repose and peace. I waited for my letters with feverish impatience; if they were delayed, I was miserable, and overcome by a thousand fears; and when they arrived, and I saw the superscription of Elizabeth or my father, I hardly dared to read and ascertain my fate. Sometimes I thought that the fiend followed me, and might expedite my remissness by murdering my companion. When these thoughts possessed me, I would not quit Henry for a moment, but followed him as his shadow, to protect him from the fancied rage of his destroyer. I felt as if I had committed some great crime, the consciousness of which haunted me. I was guiltless, but I had indeed drawn down a horrible curse upon my head, as mortal as that of crime.

I visited Edinburgh with languid eyes and mind; and yet that city might have interested the most unfortunate being. Clerval did not like it so well as Oxford; for the antiquity of the latter city was more pleasing to him. But the beauty and regularity of the new town of Edinburgh, its romantic castle, and its environs, the most delightful in the world, Arthur's Seat, St. Bernard's Well, and the Pentland Hills, compensated him for the change, and filled him with cheerfulness and admiration. But I was impatient to arrive at the termination of my journey.

We left Edinburgh in a week, passing through Coupar, St Andrews, and along the banks of the Tay, to Perth, where our friend expected us. But I was in no mood to laugh and talk with strangers, or enter into their feelings or plans with the good humour expected from a guest; and accordingly I told Clerval that I wished to make the tour of Scotland alone. 'Do you,' said I, 'enjoy yourself, and let this be our rendezvous. I may be absent a month or two; but do not interfere with my motions, I entreat you: leave me to peace and solitude for a short time; and when I return, I hope it will be with a lighter heart, more congenial to your own temper.'

Henry wished to dissuade me; but, seeing me bent on this plan; ceased to remonstrate. He entreated me to write often. 'I had rather be with you,' he said, 'in your solitary rambles, than with these Scotch people, whom I do not know: hasten then, my dear friend, to return, that I may again feel myself somewhat at home, which I cannot do in your absence.'

Having parted from my friend, I determined to visit some remote spot of Scotland, and finish my work in solitude. I did not doubt but that the monster followed me, and would discover himself to me when I should have finished, that he might receive his companion.

With this resolution I traversed the northern highlands, and fixed on one of the remotest of the Orkneys as the scene [of my] labours. It was a place fitted for such a work, being hardly more than a rock, whose high sides were continually beaten upon by the waves. The soil was barren, scarcely affording pasture for a few miserable cows, and oatmeal for its inhabitants, which consisted of five persons, whose gaunt and scraggy limbs gave tokens of their miserable fare. Vegetables and bread, when they indulged in such luxuries, and even fresh water, was to be procured from the main land, which was about five miles distant.

On the whole island there were but three miserable huts, and one of these was vacant when I arrived. This I hired. It contained but two rooms, and these exhibited all the squalidness of the most miserable penury. The thatch had fallen in, the walls were unplastered, and the door was off its hinges. I ordered it to be repaired, bought some furniture, and took possession; an incident which would, doubtless, have occasioned some surprise, had not all the senses of the cottagers been benumbed by want and squalid poverty. As it was, I lived ungazed at and unmolested, hardly thanked for the pittance of food and clothes which I gave; so much does suffering blunt even the coarsest sensations of men.

In this retreat I devoted the morning to labour; but in the evening, when the weather permitted, I walked on the stony beach of the sea, to listen to the waves as they roared, and dashed at my feet. It was a monotonous, yet ever-changing scene. I thought of Switzerland; it was far different from this desolate and appalling landscape. Its hills are covered with vines, and its cottages are scattered thickly in the plains. Its fair lakes reflect a blue and gentle sky; and, when troubled by the winds, their tumult is but as the play of a lively infant, when compared to the roarings of the giant ocean.

In this manner I distributed my occupations when I first arrived; but, as I proceeded in my labour, it became every day more horrible and irksome to me. Sometimes I could not prevail on myself to enter my laboratory for several days; and at other times I toiled day and night in order to complete my work. It was indeed a filthy process in which I was engaged. During my first experiment, a kind of enthusiastic frenzy had blinded me to the horror of my employment; my mind was intently fixed on the sequel of my labour, and my eyes were shut to the horror of my proceedings. But now I went to it in cold blood, and my heart often sickened at the work of my hands.

Thus situated, employed in the most detestable occupation, immersed in a solitude where nothing could for an instant call my attention from the actual scene in which I was engaged, my spirits became unequal; I grew restless and nervous. Every moment I feared to meet my persecutor. Sometimes I sat with my eyes fixed on the ground, fearing to raise them lest they should encounter the object which I so much dreaded to behold. I feared to wander from the sight of my fellow-creatures, lest when alone he should come to claim his companion.

In the mean time I worked on, and my labour was already considerably advanced. I looked towards its completion with a tremulous and eager hope, which I dared not trust myself to question, but which was intermixed with obscure forebodings of evil, that made my heart sicken in my bosom.

CHAPTER III

I sat one evening in my laboratory; the sun had set, and the moon was just rising from the sea; I had not sufficient light for my employment, and I remained idle, in a pause of consideration of whether I should leave my labour for the night, or hasten its conclusion by an unremitting attention to it. As I sat, a train of reflection occurred to me, which led me to consider the effects of what I was now doing. Three years before I was engaged in the same manner, and had created a fiend whose unparalleled barbarity had desolated my heart, and filled it for ever with the bitterest remorse. I was now about to form another being, of whose dispositions I was alike ignorant; she might become ten thousand times more malignant than her mate, and delight, for its own sake, in murder and wretchedness. He had sworn to quit the neighbourhood of man, and hide himself in deserts; but she had not; and she, who in all probability was to become a thinking and reasoning animal, might refuse to comply with a compact made before her creation. They might even hate each other; the creature who already lived loathed his own deformity, and might he not conceive a greater abhorrence for it when it came before his eyes in the female form? She also might turn with disgust from him to the superior beauty of man; she might quit him, and he be again alone, exasperated by the fresh provocation of being deserted by one of his own species.

Even if they were to leave Europe, and inhabit the deserts of the new world, yet one of the first results of those sympathies for which the dæmon thirsted would be children, and a race of devils would be propagated upon the earth, who might make the very existence of the species of man a condition precarious and full of terror. Had I a right, for my own benefit, to inflict this curse upon everlasting generations? I had before been moved by the sophisms of the being I had created; I had been struck senseless by his fiendish threats: but now, for the first time, the wickedness of my promise burst upon me; I shuddered to think that future ages might curse me as their pest, whose selfishness had not hesitated to buy its own peace at the price perhaps of the existence of the whole human race.

I trembled, and my heart failed within me; when, on looking up, I saw, by the light of the moon, the dæmon at the casement. A ghastly grin wrinkled his lips as he gazed on me, where I sat fulfilling the task which he had allotted to me. Yes, he had followed me in my travels; he had loitered in forests, hid himself in caves, or taken refuge in wide and desert heaths; and he now came to mark my progress, and claim the fulfilment of my promise.

As I looked on him, his countenance expressed the utmost extent of malice and treachery. I thought with a sensation of madness on my promise of

creating another like to him, and, trembling with passion, tore to pieces the
thing on which I was engaged. The wretch saw me destroy the creature on
whose future existence he depended for happiness, and, with a howl of
devilish despair and revenge, withdrew.

I left the room, and, locking the door, made a solemn vow in my own
heart never to resume my labours; and then, with trembling steps, I sought
my own apartment. I was alone; none were near me to dissipate the gloom,
and relieve me from the sickening oppression of the most terrible reveries.

Several hours passed, and I remained near my window gazing on the
sea; it was almost motionless, for the winds were hushed, and all nature
reposed under the eye of the quiet moon. A few fishing vessels alone
specked the water, and now and then the gentle breeze wafted the sound of
voices, as the fishermen called to one another. I felt the silence, although I
was hardly conscious of its extreme profundity, until my ear was suddenly
arrested by the paddling of oars near the shore, and a person landed close
to my house.

In a few minutes after, I heard the creaking of my door, as if some one
endeavoured to open it softly. I trembled from head to foot; I felt a presentiment of who it was, and wished to rouse one of the peasants who dwelt in
a cottage not far from mine; but I was overcome by the sensation of helplessness, so often felt in frightful dreams, when you in vain endeavour to fly
from an impending danger, and was rooted to the spot.

Presently I heard the sound of footsteps along the passage; the door
opened, and the wretch whom I dreaded appeared. Shutting the door, he
approached me, and said, in a smothered voice—

'You have destroyed the work which you began; what is it that you intend? Do you dare to break your promise? I have endured toil and misery:
I left Switzerland with you; I crept along the shores of the Rhine, among its
willow islands, and over the summits of its hills. I have dwelt many months
in the heaths of England, and among the deserts of Scotland. I have endured
incalculable fatigue, and cold, and hunger; do you dare destroy my hopes?'

'Begone! I do break my promise; never will I create another like yourself, equal in deformity and wickedness.'

'Slave, I before reasoned with you, but you have proved yourself unworthy of my condescension. Remember that I have power; you believe yourself miserable, but I can make you so wretched that the light of day will be
hateful to you. You are my creator, but I am your master;—obey!'

'The hour of my weakness is past, and the period[48] of your power is
arrived. Your threats cannot move me to do an act of wickedness; but they

---

[48] Concluding moment. [Ed.]

confirm me in a resolution of not creating you a companion in vice. Shall I, in cool blood, set loose upon the earth a dæmon, whose delight is in death and wretchedness. Begone! I am firm, and your words will only exasperate my rage.'

The monster saw my determination in my face, and gnashed his teeth in the impotence of anger. 'Shall each man,' cried he, 'find a wife for his bosom, and each beast have his mate, and I be alone? I had feelings of affection, and they were requited by detestation and scorn. Man, you may hate; but beware! Your hours will pass in dread and misery, and soon the bolt will fall which must ravish from you your happiness for ever. Are you to be happy, while I grovel in the intensity of my wretchedness? You can blast my other passions; but revenge remains—revenge, henceforth dearer than light or food! I may die; but first you, my tyrant and tormentor, shall curse the sun that gazes on your misery. Beware; for I am fearless, and therefore powerful. I will watch with the wiliness of a snake, that I may sting with its venom. Man, you shall repent of the injuries you inflict.'

'Devil, cease; and do not poison the air with these sounds of malice. I have declared my resolution to you, and I am no coward to bend beneath words. Leave me; I am inexorable.'

'It is well. I go; but remember, I shall be with you on your wedding-night.'

I started forward, and exclaimed, 'Villain! before you sign my death-warrant, be sure that you are yourself safe.'

I would have seized him; but he eluded me, and quitted the house with precipitation: in a few moments I saw him in his boat, which shot across the waters with an arrowy swiftness, and was soon lost amidst the waves.

All was again silent; but his words rung in my ears. I burned with rage to pursue the murderer of my peace, and precipitate him into the ocean. I walked up and down my room hastily and perturbed, while my imagination conjured up a thousand images to torment and sting me. Why had I not followed him, and closed with him in mortal strife? But I had suffered him to depart, and he had directed his course towards the main land. I shuddered to think who might be the next victim sacrificed to his insatiate revenge. And then I thought again of his words—'I will be with you on your wedding-night.' That then was the period fixed for the fulfilment of my destiny. In that hour I should die, and at once satisfy and extinguish his malice. The prospect did not move me to fear; yet when I thought of my beloved Elizabeth,—of her tears and endless sorrow, when she should find her lover so barbarously snatched from her,—tears, the first I had shed for many months, streamed from my eyes, and I resolved not to fall before my enemy without a bitter struggle.

The night passed away, and the sun rose from the ocean; my feelings became calmer, if it may be called calmness, when the violence of rage sinks into the depths of despair. I left the house, the horrid scene of the last night's contention, and walked on the beach of the sea, which I almost regarded as an insuperable barrier between me and my fellow-creatures; nay, a wish that such should prove the fact stole across me. I desired that I might pass my life on that barren rock, wearily it is true, but uninterrupted by any sudden shock of misery. If I returned, it was to be sacrificed, or to see those whom I most loved die under the grasp of a dæmon whom I had myself created.

I walked about the isle like a restless spectre, separated from all it loved, and miserable in the separation. When it became noon, and the sun rose higher, I lay down on the grass, and was overpowered by a deep sleep. I had been awake the whole of the preceding night, my nerves were agitated, and my eyes inflamed by watching and misery. The sleep into which I now sunk refreshed me; and when I awoke, I again felt as if I belonged to a race of human beings like myself, and I began to reflect upon what had passed with greater composure; yet still the words of the fiend rung in my ears like a death-knell, they appeared like a dream, yet distinct and oppressive as a reality.

The sun had far descended, and I still sat on the shore, satisfying my appetite, which had become ravenous, with an oaten cake, when I saw a fishing-boat land close to me, and one of the men brought me a packet; it contained letters from Geneva, and one from Clerval, entreating me to join him. He said that nearly a year had elapsed since we had quitted Switzerland, and France was yet unvisited. He entreated me, therefore, to leave my solitary isle, and meet him at Perth, in a week from that time, when we might arrange the plan of our future proceedings. This letter in a degree recalled me to life, and I determined to quit my island at the expiration of two days.

Yet, before I departed, there was a task to perform, on which I shuddered to reflect: I must pack my chemical instruments; and for that purpose I must enter the room which had been the scene of my odious work, and I must handle those utensils, the sight of which was sickening to me. The next morning, at day-break, I summoned sufficient courage, and unlocked the door of my laboratory. The remains of the half-finished creature, whom I had destroyed, lay scattered on the floor, and I almost felt as if I had mangled the living flesh of a human being. I paused to collect myself, and then entered the chamber. With trembling hand I conveyed the instruments out of the room; but I reflected that I ought not to leave the relics of my work to excite the horror and suspicion of the peasants, and I accordingly put them into a basket, with a great quantity of stones, and laying them up, determined to throw them into the sea that very night; and in the mean time I sat upon the beach, employed in cleaning and arranging my chemical apparatus.

Nothing could be more complete than the alteration that had taken place in my feelings since the night of the appearance of the dæmon. I had before regarded my promise with a gloomy despair, as a thing that, with whatever consequences, must be fulfilled; but I now felt as if a film had been taken from before my eyes, and that I, for the first time, saw clearly. The idea of renewing my labours did not for one instant occur to me; the threat I had heard weighed on my thoughts, but I did not reflect that a voluntary act of mine could avert it. I had resolved in my own mind, that to create another like the fiend I had first made would be an act of the basest and most atrocious selfishness; and I banished from my mind every thought that could lead to a different conclusion.

Between two and three in the morning the moon rose; and I then, putting my basket aboard a little skiff, sailed out about four miles from the shore. The scene was perfectly solitary: a few boats were returning towards land, but I sailed away from them. I felt as if I was about the commission of a dreadful crime, and avoided with shuddering anxiety any encounter with my fellow-creatures. At one time the moon, which had before been clear, was suddenly overspread by a thick cloud, and I took advantage of the moment of darkness, and cast my basket into the sea; I listened to the gurgling sound as it sunk, and then sailed away from the spot. The sky became clouded; but the air was pure, although chilled by the north-east breeze that was then rising. But it refreshed me, and filled me with such agreeable sensations, that I resolved to prolong my stay on the water, and fixing the rudder in a direct position, stretched myself at the bottom of the boat. Clouds hid the moon, every thing was obscure, and I heard only the sound of the boat, as its keel cut through the waves; the murmur lulled me, and in a short time I slept soundly.

I do not know how long I remained in this situation, but when I awoke I found that the sun had already mounted considerably. The wind was high, and the waves continually threatened the safety of my little skiff. I found that the wind was north-east, and must have driven me far from the coast from which I had embarked. I endeavoured to change my course, but quickly found that if I again made the attempt the boat would be instantly filled with water. Thus situated, my only resource was to drive before the wind. I confess that I felt a few sensations of terror. I had no compass with me, and was so little acquainted with the geography of this part of the world that the sun was of little benefit to me. I might be driven into the wide Atlantic, and feel all the tortures of starvation, or be swallowed up in the immeasurable waters that roared and buffeted around me. I had already been out many hours, and felt the torment of a burning thirst, a prelude to

solitary nature

my other sufferings. I looked on the heavens, which were covered by clouds that flew before the wind only to be replaced by others: I looked upon the sea, it was to be my grave. 'Fiend,' I exclaimed, 'your task is already fulfilled!' I thought of Elizabeth, of my father, and of Clerval; and sunk into a reverie, so despairing and frightful, that even now, when the scene is on the point of closing before me for ever, I shudder to reflect on it.

Some hours passed thus; but by degrees, as the sun declined towards the horizon, the wind died away into a gentle breeze, and the sea became free from breakers. But these gave place to a heavy swell; I felt sick, and hardly able to hold the rudder, when suddenly I saw a line of high land towards the south.

Almost spent, as I was, by fatigue, and the dreadful suspense I endured for several hours, this sudden certainty of life rushed like a flood of warm joy to my heart, and tears gushed from my eyes.

How mutable are our feelings, and how strange is that clinging love we have of life even in the excess of misery! I constructed another sail with a part of my dress, and eagerly steered my course towards the land. It had a wild and rocky appearance; but as I approached nearer, I easily perceived the traces of cultivation. I saw vessels near the shore, and found myself suddenly transported back to the neighbourhood of civilized man. I eagerly traced the windings of the land, and hailed a steeple which I at length saw issuing from behind a small promontory. As I was in a state of extreme debility, I resolved to sail directly towards the town as a place where I could most easily procure nourishment. Fortunately I had money with me. As I turned the promontory, I perceived a small neat town and a good harbour, which I entered, my heart bounding with joy at my unexpected escape.

As I was occupied in fixing the boat and arranging the sails, several people crowded towards the spot. They seemed very much surprised at my appearance; but, instead of offering me any assistance, whispered together with gestures that at any other time might have produced in me a slight sensation of alarm. As it was, I merely remarked that they spoke English; and I therefore addressed them in that language: 'My good friends,' said I, 'will you be so kind as to tell me the name of this town, and inform me where I am?'

'You will know that soon enough,' replied a man with a gruff voice. 'May be you are come to a place that will not prove much to your taste; but you will not be consulted as to your quarters, I promise you.'

I was exceedingly surprised on receiving so rude an answer from a stranger; and I was also disconcerted on perceiving the frowning and angry countenances of his companions. 'Why do you answer me so roughly?' I replied: 'surely it is not the custom of Englishmen to receive strangers so inhospitably.'

'I do not know,' said the man, 'what the custom of the English may be; but it is the custom of the Irish to hate villains.'[49]

While this strange dialogue continued, I perceived the crowd rapidly increase. Their faces expressed a mixture of curiosity and anger, which annoyed, and in some degree alarmed me. I inquired the way to the inn; but no one replied. I then moved foward, and a murmuring sound arose from the crowd as they followed and surrounded me; when an ill-looking man approaching, tapped me on the shoulder, and said, 'Come, Sir, you must follow me to Mr Kirwin's, to give an account of yourself.'

'Who is Mr Kirwin? Why am I to give an account of myself? Is not this a free country?'

'Aye, Sir, free enough for honest folks. Mr Kirwin is a magistrate; and you are to give an account of the death of a gentleman who was found murdered here last night.'

This answer startled me; but I presently recovered myself. I was innocent; that could easily be proved: accordingly I followed my conductor in silence, and was led to one of the best houses in the town. I was ready to sink from fatigue and hunger; but, being surrounded by a crowd, I thought it politic to rouse all my strength, that no physical debility might be construed into apprehension or conscious guilt. Little did I then expect the calamity that was in a few moments to overwhelm me, and extinguish in horror and despair all fear of ignominy or death.

I must pause here; for it requires all my fortitude to recall the memory of the frightful events which I am about to relate, in proper detail, to my recollection.

CHAPTER IV

I was soon introduced into the presence of the magistrate, an old benevolent man, with calm and mild manners. He looked upon me, however, with some degree of severity; and then, turning towards my conductors, he asked who appeared as witnesses on this occasion.

About half a dozen men came forward; and one being selected by the magistrate, he deposed, that he had been out fishing the night before with

---

[49] The lands of England's first Empire, Scotland to the north and Ireland and Wales to the west, are the traditional locations for the extreme deeds and mental states of English Gothic fiction. The heroine of Jane Austen's satiric *Northanger Abbey*, written in the late 1790s and posthumously published in 1817, recognizes the possibility of Gothic plots in the northern and western "extremities" of the country, though she asserts that England itself is civilized and secure. [Ed.]

his son and brother-in-law, Daniel Nugent, when, about ten o'clock, they observed a strong northerly blast rising, and they accordingly put in for port. It was a very dark night, as the moon had not yet risen; they did not land at the harbour, but, as they had been accustomed, at a creek about two miles below. He walked on first, carrying a part of the fishing tackle, and his companions followed him at some distance. As he was proceeding along the sands, he struck his foot against something, and fell all his length on the ground. His companions came up to assist him; and, by the light of their lantern, they found that he had fallen on the body of a man, who was to all appearance dead. Their first supposition was, that it was the corpse of some person who had been drowned, and was thrown on shore by the waves; but, upon examination, they found that the clothes were not wet, and even that the body was not then cold. They instantly carried it to the cottage of an old woman near the spot, and endeavoured, but in vain, to restore it to life. He appeared to be a handsome young man, about five and twenty years of age. He had apparently been strangled; for there was no sign of any violence, except the black mark of fingers on his neck.

The first part of this deposition did not in the least interest me; but when the mark of the fingers was mentioned, I remembered the murder of my brother, and felt myself extremely agitated; my limbs trembled, and a mist came over my eyes, which obliged me to lean on a chair for support. The magistrate observed me with a keen eye, and of course drew an unfavourable augury from my manner.

The son confirmed his father's account: but when Daniel Nugent was called, he swore positively that, just before the fall of his companion, he saw a boat, with a single man in it, at a short distance from the shore; and, as far as he could judge by the light of a few stars, it was the same boat in which I had just landed.

A woman deposed, that she lived near the beach, and was standing at the door of her cottage, waiting for the return of the fishermen, about an hour before she heard of the discovery of the body, when she saw a boat, with only one man in it, push off from that part of the shore where the corpse was afterwards found.

Another woman confirmed the account of the fishermen having brought the body into her house; it was not cold. They put it into a bed, and rubbed it; and Daniel went to the town for an apothecary, but life was quite gone.

Several other men were examined concerning my landing; and they agreed, that, with the strong north wind that had arisen during the night, it was very probable that I had beaten about for many hours, and had been obliged to return nearly to the same spot from which I had departed. Besides, they observed that it appeared that I had brought the body from another place, and it was likely, that as I did not appear to know the shore,

I might have put into the harbour ignorant of the distance of the town of——from the place where I had deposited the corpse.

Mr Kirwin, on hearing this evidence, desired that I should be taken into the room where the body lay for interment, that it might be observed what effect the sight of it would produce upon me. This idea was probably suggested by the extreme agitation I had exhibited when the mode of the murder had been described. I was accordingly conducted, by the magistrate and several other persons, to the inn. I could not help being struck by the strange coincidences that had taken place during this eventful night; but, knowing that I had been conversing with several persons in the island I had inhabited about the time that the body had been found, I was perfectly tranquil as to the consequences of the affair.

I entered the room where the corpse lay, and was led up to the coffin. How can I describe my sensations on beholding it? I feel yet parched with horror, nor can I reflect on that terrible moment without shuddering and agony, that faintly reminds me of the anguish of the recognition. The trial, the presence of the magistrate and witnesses, passed like a dream from my memory, when I saw the lifeless form of Henry Clerval stretched before me. I gasped for breath; and, throwing myself on the body, I exclaimed, 'Have my murderous machinations deprived you also, my dearest Henry, of life? Two I have already destroyed; other victims await their destiny: but you, Clerval, my friend, my benefactor' —

The human frame could no longer support the agonizing suffering that I endured, and I was carried out of the room in strong convulsions.

A fever succeeded to this. I lay for two months on the point of death: my ravings, as I afterwards heard, were frightful; I called myself the murderer of William, of Justine, and of Clerval. Sometimes I entreated my attendants to assist me in the destruction of the fiend by whom I was tormented; and, at others, I felt the fingers of the monster already grasping my neck, and screamed aloud with agony and terror. Fortunately, as I spoke my native language, Mr Kirwin alone understood me; but my gestures and bitter cries were sufficient to affright the other witnesses.

Why did I not die? More miserable than man ever was before, why did I not sink into forgetfulness and rest? Death snatches away many blooming children, the only hopes of their doating parents: how many brides and youthful lovers have been one day in the bloom of health and hope, and the next a prey for worms and the decay of the tomb! Of what materials was I made, that I could thus resist so many shocks, which, like the turning of the wheel, continually renewed the torture.

But I was doomed to live; and, in two months, found myself as awaking from a dream, in a prison, stretched on a wretched bed, surrounded by gaolers, turnkeys, bolts, and all the miserable apparatus of a dungeon. It was morning, I remember, when I thus awoke to understanding: I had forgotten the particulars of what had happened, and only felt as if some great misfortune had suddenly overwhelmed me; but when I looked around, and saw the barred windows, and the squalidness of the room in which I was, all flashed across my memory, and I groaned bitterly.

This sound disturbed an old woman who was sleeping in a chair beside me. She was a hired nurse, the wife of one of the turnkeys, and her countenance expressed all those bad qualities which often characterize that class. The lines of her face were hard and rude, like that of persons accustomed to see without sympathizing in sights of misery. Her tone expressed her entire indifference; she addressed me in English, and the voice struck me as one that I had heard during my sufferings:

'Are you better now, Sir?' said she.

I replied in the same language, with a feeble voice, 'I believe I am; but if it be all true, if indeed I did not dream, I am sorry that I am still alive to feel this misery and horror.'

'For that matter,' replied the old woman, 'if you mean about the gentleman you murdered, I believe that it were better for you if you were dead, for I fancy it will go hard with you; but you will be hung when the next sessions come on. However, that's none of my business, I am sent to nurse you, and get you well; I do my duty with a safe conscience, it were well if every body did the same.'

I turned with loathing from the woman who could utter so unfeeling a speech to a person just saved, on the very edge of death; but I felt languid, and unable to reflect on all that had passed. The whole series of my life appeared to me as a dream; I sometimes doubted if indeed it were all true, for it never presented itself to my mind with the force of reality.

As the images that floated before me became more distinct, I grew feverish; a darkness pressed around me; no one was near me who soothed me with the gentle voice of love; no dear hand supported me. The physician came and prescribed medicines, and the old woman prepared them for me; but utter carelessness was visible in the first, and the expression of brutality was strongly marked in the visage of the second. Who could be interested in the fate of a murderer, but the hangman who would gain his fee?

These were my first reflections; but I soon learned that Mr Kirwin had shewn me extreme kindness. He had caused the best room in the prison to be prepared for me (wretched indeed was the best); and it was he who had provided a physician and a nurse. It is true, he seldom came to see me; for, although he ardently desired to relieve the sufferings of every human creature, he did not wish to be present at the agonies and miserable ravings of a murderer. He came, therefore, sometimes to see that I was not neglected; but his visits were short, and at long intervals.

One day, when I was gradually recovering, I was seated in a chair, my eyes half open, and my cheeks livid like those in death, I was overcome by gloom and misery, and often reflected I had better seek death than remain miserably pent up only to be let loose in a world replete with wretchedness. At one time I considered whether I should not declare myself guilty, and suffer the penalty of the law, less innocent than poor Justine had been. Such were my thoughts, when the door of my apartment was opened, and Mr Kirwin entered. His countenance expressed sympathy and compassion; he draw a chair close to mine, and addressed me in French —

'I fear that this place is very shocking to you; can I do any thing to make you more comfortable?'

'I thank you; but all that you mention is nothing to me: on the whole earth there is no comfort which I am capable of receiving.'

'I know that the sympathy of a stranger can be but of little relief to one borne down as you are by so strange a misfortune. But you will, I hope, soon quit this melancholy abode; for, doubtless, evidence can easily be brought to free you from the criminal charge.'

'That is my least concern: I am, by a course of strange events, become the most miserable of mortals. Persecuted and tortured as I am and have been, can death be any evil to me?'

'Nothing indeed could be more unfortunate and agonizing than the strange chances that have lately occurred. You were thrown, by some surprising accident, on this shore, renowned for its hospitality; seized immediately, and charged with murder. The first sight that was presented to your eyes was the body of your friend, murdered in so unaccountable a manner, and placed, as it were, by some fiend across your path.'

As Mr Kirwin said this, notwithstanding the agitation I endured on this retrospect of my sufferings, I also felt considerable surprise at the knowledge he seemed to possess concerning me. I suppose some astonishment was exhibited in my countenance; for Mr Kirwin hastened to say —

'It was not until a day or two after your illness that I thought of examining your dress, that I might discover some trace by which I could send to your relations an account of your misfortune and illness. I found several letters, and, among others, one which I discovered from its commencement to be from your father. I instantly wrote to Geneva: nearly two months have elapsed since the departure of my letter. — But you are ill; even now you tremble: you are unfit for agitation of any kind.'

'This suspense is a thousand times worse than the most horrible event: tell me what new scene of death has been acted, and whose murder I am now to lament.'

'Your family is perfectly well,' said Mr Kirwin, with gentleness; 'and some one, a friend, is come to visit you.'

I know not by what chain of thought the idea presented itself, but it instantly darted into my mind that the murderer had come to mock at my misery, and taunt me with the death of Clerval, as a new incitement for me to comply with his hellish desires. I put my hand before my eyes, and cried out in agony—

'Oh! take him away! I cannot see him; for God's sake, do not let him enter!'

Mr Kirwin regarded me with a troubled countenance. He could not help regarding my exclamation as a presumption of my guilt, and said, in rather a severe tone—

'I should have thought, young man, that the presence of your father would have been welcome, instead of inspiring such violent repugnance.'

'My father!' cried I, while every feature and every muscle was relaxed from anguish to pleasure. 'Is my father, indeed, come? How kind, how very kind. But where is he, why does he not hasten to me?'

My change of manner surprised and pleased the magistrate; perhaps he thought that my former exclamation was a momentary return of delirium, and now he instantly resumed his former benevolence. He rose, and quitted the room with my nurse, and in a moment my father entered it.

Nothing, at this moment, could have given me greater pleasure than the arrival of my father. I stretched out my hand to him, and cried—

'Are you then safe—and Elizabeth—and Ernest?'

My father calmed me with assurances of their welfare, and endeavoured, by dwelling on these subjects so interesting to my heart, to raise my desponding spirits; but he soon felt that a prison cannot be the abode of cheerfulness. 'What a place is this that you inhabit, my son!' said he, looking mournfully at the barred windows, and wretched appearance of the room. 'You travelled to seek happiness, but a fatality seems to pursue you. And poor Clerval—'

The name of my unfortunate and murdered friend was an agitation too great to be endured in my weak state; I shed tears.

'Alas! yes, my father,' replied I; 'some destiny of the most horrible kind hangs over me, and I must live to fulfil it, or surely I should have died on the coffin of Henry.'

We were not allowed to converse for any length of time, for the precarious state of my health rendered every precaution necessary that could insure tranquillity. Mr Kirwin came in, and insisted that my strength should not be exhausted by too much exertion. But the appearance of my father was to me like that of my good angel, and I gradually recovered my health.

As my sickness quitted me, I was absorbed by a gloomy and black melancholy, that nothing could dissipate. The image of Clerval was for ever before me, ghastly and murdered. More than once the agitation into which these reflections threw me made my friends dread a dangerous relapse. Alas! why did they preserve so miserable and detested a life? It was surely that I might fulfil my destiny, which is now drawing to a close. Soon, oh, very soon, will death extinguish these throbbings, and relieve me from the mighty weight of anguish that bears me to the dust; and, in executing the award of justice, I shall also sink to rest. Then the appearance of death was distant, although the wish was ever present to my thoughts; and I often sat for hours motionless and speechless, wishing for some mighty revolution that might bury me and my destroyer in its ruins.

The season of the assizes approached. I had already been three months in prison; and although I was still weak, and in continual danger of a relapse, I was obliged to travel nearly a hundred miles to the county-town, where the court was held. Mr Kirwin charged himself with every care of collecting witnesses, and arranging my defence. I was spared the disgrace of appearing publicly as a criminal, as the case was not brought before the court that decides on life and death. The grand jury rejected the bill, on its being proved that I was on the Orkney Islands at the hour the body of my friend was found, and a fortnight after my removal I was liberated from prison.

My father was enraptured on finding me freed from the vexations of a criminal charge, that I was again allowed to breathe the fresh atmosphere, and allowed to return to my native country. I did not participate in these feelings; for to me the walls of a dungeon or a palace were alike hateful. The cup of life was poisoned for ever; and although the sun shone upon me, as upon the happy and gay of heart, I saw around me nothing but a dense and frightful darkness, penetrated by no light but the glimmer of two eyes that glared upon me. Sometimes they were the expressive eyes of Henry, languishing in death, the dark orbs nearly covered by the lids, and the long black lashes that fringed them; sometimes it was the watery clouded eyes of the monster, as I first saw them in my chamber at Ingolstadt.

My father tried to awaken in me the feelings of affection. He talked of Geneva, which I should soon visit—of Elizabeth, and Ernest; but these words only drew deep groans from me. Sometimes, indeed, I felt a wish for happiness; and thought, with melancholy delight, of my beloved cousin; or longed, with a devouring *maladie du pays*,[50] to see once more the blue lake and rapid Rhone, that had been so dear to me in early childhood: but my general state of feeling was a torpor, in which a prison was as welcome a residence as the divinest scene in nature; and these fits were seldom interrupted, but by paroxysms of anguish and despair. At these moments I often endeavoured to put an end to the existence I loathed; and it required

---

[50] Homesickness. [Ed.]

unceasing attendance and vigilance to restrain me from committing some dreadful act of violence.

I remember, as I quitted the prison, I heard one of the men say, 'He may be innocent of the murder, but he has certainly a bad conscience.' These words struck me. A bad conscience! yes, surely I had one. William, Justine, and Clerval, had died through my infernal machinations; 'And whose death,' cried I, 'is to finish the tragedy? Ah! my father, do not remain in this wretched country; take me where I may forget myself, my existence, and all the world.'

My father easily acceded to my desire; and, after having taken leave of Mr Kirwin, we hastened to Dublin. I felt as if I was relieved from a heavy weight, when the packet sailed with a fair wind from Ireland, and I had quitted for ever the country which had been to me the scene of so much misery.

It was midnight. My father slept in the cabin; and I lay on the deck, looking at the stars, and listening to the dashing of the waves. I hailed the darkness that shut Ireland from my sight, and my pulse beat with a feverish joy, when I reflected that I should soon see Geneva. The past appeared to me in the light of a frightful dream; yet the vessel in which I was, the wind that blew me from the detested shore of Ireland, and the sea which surrounded me, told me too forcibly that I was deceived by no vision, and that Clerval, my friend and dearest companion, had fallen a victim to me and the monster of my creation. I repassed, in my memory, my whole life; my quiet happiness while residing with my family in Geneva, the death of my mother, and my departure for Ingolstadt. I remembered shuddering at the mad enthusiasm that hurried me on to the creation of my hideous enemy, and I called to mind the night during which he first lived. I was unable to pursue the train of thought; a thousand feelings pressed upon me, and I wept bitterly.

Ever since my recovery from the fever I had been in the custom of taking every night a small quantity of laudanum; for it was by means of this drug only that I was enabled to gain the rest necessary for the preservation of life. Oppressed by the recollection of my various misfortunes, I now took a double dose, and soon slept profoundly. But sleep did not afford me respite from thought and misery; my dreams presented a thousand objects that scared me. Towards morning I was possessed by a kind of night-mare; I felt the fiend's grasp in my neck, and could not free myself from it; groans and cries rung in my ears. My father, who was watching over me, perceiving my restlessness, awoke me, and pointed to the port of Holyhead, which we were now entering.[51]

---

[51] On the Isle of Anglesey, Wales. [Ed.]

CHAPTER V

We had resolved not to go to London, but to cross the country to Portsmouth, and thence to embark for Havre. I preferred this plan principally because I dreaded to see again those places in which I had enjoyed a few moments of tranquillity with my beloved Clerval. I thought with horror of seeing again those persons whom we had been accustomed to visit together, and who might make inquiries concerning an event, the very remembrance of which made me again feel the pang I endured when I gazed on his lifeless form in the inn at———.

As for my father, his desires and exertions were bounded to the again seeing me restored to health and peace of mind. His tenderness and attentions were unremitting; my grief and gloom was obstinate, but he would not despair. Sometimes he thought that I felt deeply the degradation of being obliged to answer a charge of murder, and he endeavoured to prove to me the futility of pride.

'Alas! my father,' said I, 'how little do you know me. Human beings, their feelings and passions, would indeed be degraded, if such a wretch as I felt pride. Justine, poor unhappy Justine, was as innocent as I, and she suffered the same charge; she died for it; and I am the cause of this—I murdered her. William, Justine, and Henry—they all died by my hands.'

My father had often, during my imprisonment, heard me make the same assertion; when I thus accused myself, he sometimes seemed to desire an explanation, and at others he appeared to consider it as caused by delirium, and that, during my illness, some idea of this kind had presented itself to my imagination, the remembrance of which I preserved in my convalescence. I avoided explanation, and maintained a continual silence concerning the wretch I had created. I had a feeling that I should be supposed mad, and this for ever chained my tongue, when I would have given the whole world to have confided the fatal secret.

Upon this occasion my father said, with an expression of unbounded wonder, 'What do you mean, Victor? are you mad? My dear son, I entreat you never to make such an assertion again.'

'I am not mad,' I cried energetically; 'the sun and the heavens, who have viewed my operations, can bear witness of my truth. I am the assassin of those most innocent victims; they died by my machinations. A thousand times would I have shed my own blood, drop by drop, to have saved their lives; but I could not, my father, indeed I could not sacrifice the whole human race.'

The conclusion of this speech convinced my father that my ideas were deranged, and he instantly changed the subject of our conversation, and endeavoured to alter the course of my thoughts. He wished as much as possible to obliterate the memory of the scenes that had taken place in Ireland, and never alluded to them, or suffered me to speak of my misfortunes.

As time passed away I became more calm: misery had her dwelling in my heart, but I no longer talked in the same incoherent manner of my own crimes; sufficient for me was the consciousness of them. By the utmost self-violence, I curbed the imperious voice of wretchedness, which sometimes desired to declare itself to the whole world; and my manners were calmer and more composed than they had ever been since my journey to the sea of ice.

We arrived at Havre on the 8th of May, and instantly proceeded to Paris, where my father had some business which detained us a few weeks. In this city, I received the following letter from Elizabeth: —

'To *VICTOR FRANKENSTEIN*.

'*MY DEAREST FRIEND*,

'It gave me the greatest pleasure to receive a letter from my uncle dated at Paris; you are no longer at a formidable distance, and I may hope to see you in less than a fortnight. My poor cousin, how much you must have suffered! I expect to see you looking even more ill than when you quitted Geneva. This winter has been passed most miserably, tortured as I have been by anxious suspense; yet I hope to see peace in your countenance, and to find that your heart is not totally devoid of comfort and tranquillity.

'Yet I fear that the same feelings now exist that made you so miserable a year ago, even perhaps augmented by time. I would not disturb you at this period, when so many misfortunes weigh upon you; but a conversation that I had with my uncle previous to his departure renders some explanation necessary before we meet.

'Explanation! you may possibly say; what can Elizabeth have to explain? If you really say this, my questions are answered, and I have no more to do than to sign myself your affectionate cousin. But you are distant from me, and it is possible that you may dread, and yet be pleased with this explanation; and, in a probability of this being the case, I dare not any longer postpone writing what, during your absence, I have often wished to express to you, but have never had the courage to begin.

'You well know, Victor, that our union had been the favourite plan of your parents ever since our infancy. We were told this when young, and taught to look forward to it as an event that would certainly take place. We were affectionate playfellows during childhood, and, I believe, dear and valued friends to one another as we grew older. But as brother and sister often entertain a lively affection towards each other, without desiring a more intimate union, may not such also be our case? Tell me, dearest Victor.

Answer me, I conjure you, by our mutual happiness, with simple truth—
Do you not love another?

'You have travelled; you have spent several years of your life at Ingolstadt;
and I confess to you, my friend, that when I saw you last autumn so unhappy,
flying to solitude, from the society of every creature, I could not help supposing that you might regret our connexion, and believe yourself bound in
honour to fulfil the wishes of your parents, although they opposed themselves to your inclinations. But this is false reasoning. I confess to you, my
cousin, that I love you, and that in my airy dreams of futurity you have been
my constant friend and companion. But it is your happiness I desire as well
as my own, when I declare to you, that our marriage would render me eter-
nally miserable, unless it were the dictate of your own free choice. Even
now I weep to think, that, borne down as you are by the cruelest misfortunes,
you may stifle, by the word *honour*, all hope of that love and happiness
which would alone restore you to yourself. I, who have so interested an affection for you, may increase your miseries ten-fold, by being an obstacle
to your wishes. Ah, Victor, be assured that your cousin and playmate has
too sincere a love for you not to be made miserable by this supposition. Be
happy, my friend; and if you obey me in this one request, remain satisfied
that nothing on earth will have the power to interrupt my tranquillity.

'Do not let this letter disturb you; do not answer it tomorrow, or the
next day, or even until you come, if it will give you pain. My uncle will send
me news of your health; and if I see but one smile on your lips when we
meet, occasioned by this or any other exertion of mine, I shall need no
other happiness.

'*ELIZABETH LAVENZA.*
'*Geneva, May 18th, 17—.*'

This letter revived in my memory what I had before forgotten, the threat
of the fiend—'*I will be with you on your wedding-night!*' Such was my sentence, and on that night would the dæmon employ every art to destroy me,
and tear me from the glimpse of happiness which promised partly to console my sufferings. On that night he had determined to consummate his
crimes by my death. Well, be it so; a deadly struggle would then assuredly
take place, in which if he was victorious, I should be at peace, and his power
over me be at an end. If he were vanquished, I should be a free man. Alas!
what freedom? such as the peasant enjoys when his family have been mas-
sacred before his eyes, his cottage burnt, his lands laid waste, and he is turned
adrift, homeless, pennyless, and alone, but free. Such would be my liberty,
except that in my Elizabeth I possessed a treasure; alas! balanced by those
horrors of remorse and guilt, which would pursue me until death.

Sweet and beloved Elizabeth! I read and re-read her letter, and some soft-ened feelings stole into my heart, and dared to whisper paradisaical dreams of love and joy; but the apple was already eaten, and the angel's arm bared to drive me from all hope. Yet I would die to make her happy. If the monster executed his threat, death was inevitable; yet, again, I considered whether my marriage would hasten my fate. My destruction might indeed arrive a few months sooner; but if my torturer should suspect that I postponed it, influenced by his menaces, he would surely find other, and perhaps more dreadful means of revenge. He had vowed *to be with me on my wedding-night,* yet he did not consider that threat as binding him to peace in the mean time; for, as if to shew me that he was not yet satiated with blood, he had murdered Clerval immediately after the enunciation of his threats. I resolved, therefore, that if my immediate union with my cousin would conduce either to hers or my father's happiness, my adversary's designs against my life should not retard it a single hour.

In this state of mind I wrote to Elizabeth. My letter was calm and affec-tionate. 'I fear, my beloved girl,' I said, 'little happiness remains for us on earth; yet all that I may one day enjoy is concentered in you. Chase away your idle fears; to you alone do I consecrate my life, and my endeavours for contentment. I have one secret, Elizabeth, a dreadful one; when revealed to you, it will chill your frame with horror, and then, far from being surprised at my misery, you will only wonder that I survive what I have endured. I will confide this tale of misery and terror to you the day after our marriage shall take place; for, my sweet cousin, there must be perfect confidence between us. But until then, I conjure you, do not mention or allude to it. This I most earnestly entreat, and I know you will comply.'

In about a week after the arrival of Elizabeth's letter, we returned to Geneva. My cousin welcomed me with warm affection; yet tears were in her eyes, as she beheld my emaciated frame and feverish cheeks. I saw a change in her also. She was thinner, and had lost much of that heavenly vivacity that had before charmed me; but her gentleness, and soft looks of compassion, made her a more fit companion for one blasted and miserable as I was.

The tranquillity which I now enjoyed did not endure. Memory brought madness with it; and when I thought on what had passed, a real insanity possessed me; sometimes I was furious, and burnt with rage, sometimes low and despondent. I neither spoke or looked, but sat motionless, bewil-dered by the multitude of miseries that overcame me.

Elizabeth alone had the power to draw me from these fits; her gentle voice would soothe me when transported by passion, and inspire me with human feelings when sunk in torpor. She wept with me, and for me. When reason returned, she would remonstrate, and endeavour to inspire me with resignation. Ah! it is well for the unfortunate to be resigned, but for the guilty there is no peace. The agonies of remorse poison the luxury there is otherwise sometimes found in indulging the excess of grief.

Soon after my arrival my father spoke of my immediate marriage with my cousin. I remained silent.

'Have you, then, some other attachment?'

'None on earth. I love Elizabeth, and look forward to our union with delight. Let the day therefore be fixed; and on it I will consecrate myself, in life or death, to the happiness of my cousin.'

'My dear Victor, do not speak thus. Heavy misfortunes have befallen us; but let us only cling closer to what remains, and transfer our love for those whom we have lost to those who yet live. Our circle will be small, but bound close by the ties of affection and mutual misfortune. And when time shall have softened your despair, new and dear objects of care will be born to replace those of whom we have been so cruelly deprived.'

Such were the lessons of my father. But to me the remembrance of the threat returned: nor can you wonder, that, omnipotent as the fiend had yet been in his deeds of blood, I should almost regard him as invincible; and that when he had pronounced the words, *I shall be with you on your wedding-night,* I should regard the threatened fate as unavoidable. But death was no evil to me, if the loss of Elizabeth were balanced with it; and I therefore, with a contented and even cheerful countenance, agreed with my father, that if my cousin would consent, the ceremony should take place in ten days, and thus put, as I imagined, the seal to my fate.

Great God! if for one instant I had thought what might be the hellish intention of my fiendish adversary, I would rather have banished myself for ever from my native country, and wandered a friendless outcast over the earth, than have consented to this miserable marriage. But, as if possessed of magic powers, the monster had blinded me to his real intentions; and when I thought that I prepared only my own death, I hastened that of a far dearer victim.

As the period fixed for our marriage drew nearer, whether from cowardice or a prophetic feeling, I felt my heart sink within me. But I concealed my feelings by an appearance of hilarity, that brought smiles and joy to the countenance of my father, but hardly deceived the ever-watchful and nicer eye of Elizabeth. She looked forward to our union with placid contentment, not unmingled with a little fear, which past misfortunes had impressed, that what now appeared certain and tangible happiness, might soon dissipate into an airy dream, and leave no trace but deep and everlasting regret.

Preparations were made for the event; congratulatory visits were received; and all wore a smiling appearance. I shut up, as well as I could, in my own heart the anxiety that preyed there, and entered with seeming earnestness into the plans of my father, although they might only serve as the decorations of my tragedy. A house was purchased for us near Cologny, by which we should enjoy the pleasures of the country; and yet be so near Geneva as to see my father every day; who would still reside within the walls, for the benefit of Ernest, that he might follow his studies at the schools.

In the mean time I took every precaution to defend my person, in case the fiend should openly attack me. I carried pistols and a dagger constantly about me, and was ever on the watch to prevent artifice; and by these means gained a greater degree of tranquillity. Indeed, as the period approached, the threat appeared more as a delusion, not to be regarded as worthy to disturb my peace, while the happiness I hoped for in my marriage wore a greater appearance of certainty, as the day fixed for its solemnization drew nearer, and I heard it continually spoken of as an occurrence which no accident could possibly prevent.

Elizabeth seemed happy; my tranquil demeanour contributed greatly to calm her mind. But on the day that was to fulfil my wishes and my destiny, she was melancholy, and a presentiment of evil pervaded her; and perhaps also she thought of the dreadful secret, which I had promised to reveal to her the following day. My father was in the mean time overjoyed, and, in the bustle of preparation, only observed in the melancholy of his niece the diffidence of a bride.

After the ceremony was performed, a large party assembled at my father's; but it was agreed that Elizabeth and I should pass the afternoon and night at Evian, and return to Cologny the next morning. As the day was fair, and the wind favourable, we resolved to go by water.

Those were the last moments of my life during which I enjoyed the feeling of happiness. We passed rapidly along: the sun was hot, but we were sheltered from its rays by a kind of canopy, while we enjoyed the beauty of the scene, sometimes on one side of the lake, where we saw Mont Salêve, the pleasant banks of Montalègre, and at a distance, surmounting all, the beautiful Mont Blanc, and the assemblage of snowy mountains that in vain endeavour to emulate her; sometimes coasting the opposite banks, we saw the mighty Jura opposing its dark side to the ambition that would quit its native country, and an almost insurmountable barrier to the invader who should wish to enslave it.[52]

I took the hand of Elizabeth: 'You are sorrowful, my love. Ah! if you knew what I have suffered, and what I may yet endure, you would endeavour to

---

[52] A possible political reference in this geography: Napoleon's army did in fact invade and conquer the Swiss republics in 1797–98, shortly after the probable time of the story. Readers of the 1818 edition would still be celebrating the defeat of the French imperial ruler at Waterloo (1815) and the restoration of Swiss autonomy and neutrality. [Ed.]

let me taste the quiet, and freedom from despair, that this one day at least permits me to enjoy.'

'Be happy, my dear Victor,' replied Elizabeth; 'there is, I hope, nothing to distress you; and be assured that if a lively joy is not painted on my face, my heart is contented. Something whispers to me not to depend too much on the prospect that is opened before us; but I will not listen to such a sinister voice. Observe how fast we move along, and how the clouds which sometimes obscure, and sometimes rise above the dome of Mont Blanc, render this scene of beauty still more interesting. Look also at the innumerable fish that are swimming in the clear waters, where we can distinguish every pebble that lies at the bottom. What a divine day! how happy and serene all nature appears!'

Thus Elizabeth endeavoured to divert her thoughts and mine from all reflection upon melancholy subjects. But her temper was fluctuating; joy for a few instants shone in her eyes, but it continually gave place to distraction and reverie.

The sun sunk lower in the heavens; we passed the river Drance, and observed its path through the chasms of the higher, and the glens of the lower hills. The Alps here come closer to the lake, and we approached the amphitheatre of mountains which forms its eastern boundary. The spire of Evian shone under the woods that surrounded it, and the range of mountain above mountain by which it was overhung.

The wind, which had hitherto carried us along with amazing rapidity, sunk at sunset to a light breeze; the soft air just ruffled the water, and caused a pleasant motion among the trees as we approached the shore, from which it wafted the most delightful scent of flowers and hay. The sun sunk beneath the horizon as we landed; and as I touched the shore, I felt those cares and fears revive, which soon were to clasp me, and cling to me for ever.

CHAPTER VI

It was eight o'clock when we landed; we walked for a short time on the shore, enjoying the transitory light, and then retired to the inn, and contemplated the lovely scene of waters, woods, and mountains, obscured in darkness, yet still displaying their black outlines.

The wind, which had fallen in the south, now rose with great violence in the west. The moon had reached her summit in the heavens, and was beginning to descend; the clouds swept across it swifter than the flight of the vulture, and dimmed her rays, while the lake reflected the scene of the busy heavens, rendered still busier by the restless waves that were beginning to rise. Suddenly a heavy storm of rain descended.

I had been calm during the day; but so soon as night obscured the shapes of objects, a thousand fears arose in my mind. I was anxious and watchful, while my right hand grasped a pistol which was hidden in my bosom; every sound terrified me; but I resolved that I would sell my life dearly, and not relax the impending conflict until my own life, or that of my adversary, were extinguished.

Elizabeth observed my agitation for some time in timid and fearful silence; at length she said, 'What is it that agitates you, my dear Victor? What is it you fear?'

'Oh! peace, peace, my love,' replied I, 'this night, and all will be safe: but this night is dreadful, very dreadful.'

I passed an hour in this state of mind, when suddenly I reflected how dreadful the combat which I momentarily expected would be to my wife, and I earnestly entreated her to retire, resolving not to join her until I had obtained some knowledge as to the situation of my enemy.

She left me, and I continued some time walking up and down the passages of the house, and inspecting every corner that might afford a retreat to my adversary. But I discovered no trace of him, and was beginning to conjecture that some fortunate chance had intervened to prevent the execution of his menaces; when suddenly I heard a shrill and dreadful scream. It came from the room into which Elizabeth had retired. As I heard it, the whole truth rushed into my mind, my arms dropped, the motion of every muscle and fibre was suspended; I could feel the blood trickling in my veins, and tingling in the extremities of my limbs. This state lasted but for an instant; the scream was repeated, and I rushed into the room.

Great God! why did I not then expire! Why am I here to relate the destruction of the best hope, and the purest creature of earth. She was there, lifeless and inanimate, thrown across the bed, her head hanging down, and her pale and distorted features half covered by her hair. Everywhere I turn I see the same figure—her bloodless arms and relaxed form flung by the murderer on its bridal bier. Could I behold this, and live? Alas! life is obstinate, and clings closest where it is most hated. For a moment only did I lose recollection; I fainted.

When I recovered, I found myself surrounded by the people of the inn; their countenances expressed a breathless terror: but the horror of others appeared only as a mockery, a shadow of the feelings that oppressed me. I escaped from them to the room where lay the body of Elizabeth, my love, my wife, so lately living, so dear, so worthy. She had been moved from the posture in which I had first beheld her; and now, as she lay, her head upon her arm, and a handkerchief thrown across her face and neck, I might have supposed her asleep. I rushed towards her, and embraced her with ardour; but the deathly languor and coldness of the limbs told me, that what I now held in my arms had ceased to be the Elizabeth whom I had loved and cherished. The murderous mark of the fiend's grasp was on her neck, and the breath had ceased to issue from her lips.

While I still hung over her in the agony of despair, I happened to look up. The windows of the room had before been darkened; and I felt a kind of panic on seeing the pale yellow light of the moon illuminate the chamber. The shutters had been thrown back; and, with a sensation of horror not to be described, I saw at the open window a figure the most hideous and abhorred. A grin was on the face of the monster; he seemed to jeer, as with his fiendish finger he pointed towards the corpse of my wife. I rushed towards the window, and drawing a pistol from my bosom, shot; but he eluded me, leaped from his station, and, running with the swiftness of lightning, plunged into the lake.

The report of the pistol brought a crowd into the room. I pointed to the spot where he had disappeared, and we followed the track with boats; nets were cast, but in vain. After passing several hours, we returned hopeless, most of my companions believing it to have been a form conjured by my fancy. After having landed, they proceeded to search the country, parties going in different directions among the woods and vines.

I did not accompany them; I was exhausted: a film covered my eyes, and my skin was parched with the heat of fever. In this state I lay on a bed, hardly conscious of what had happened; my eyes wandered round the room, as if to seek something that I had lost.

At length I remembered that my father would anxiously expect the return of Elizabeth and myself, and that I must return alone. This reflection brought tears into my eyes, and I wept for a long time; but my thoughts rambled to various subjects, reflecting on my misfortunes, and their cause. I was bewildered in a cloud of wonder and horror. The death of William, the execution of Justine, the murder of Clerval, and lastly of my wife; even at that moment I knew not that my only remaining friends were safe from the malignity of the fiend; my father even now might be writhing under his grasp, and Ernest might be dead at his feet. This idea made me shudder, and recalled me to action. I started up, and resolved to return to Geneva with all possible speed.

There were no horses to be procured, and I must return by the lake; but the wind was unfavourable, and the rain fell in torrents. However, it was hardly morning, and I might reasonably hope to arrive by night. I hired men to row, and took an oar myself, for I had always experienced relief from mental torment in bodily exercise. But the overflowing misery I now felt, and the excess of agitation that I endured, rendered me incapable of any exertion. I threw down the oar; and, leaning my head upon my hands, gave way to every gloomy idea that arose. If I looked up, I saw the scenes which were familiar to me in my happier time, and which I had contemplated but the day before in the company of her who was now but a shadow and a recollection. Tears streamed from my eyes. The rain had ceased for a moment, and I saw the fish play in the waters as they had done a few hours before; they had then been observed by Elizabeth. Nothing is so painful to the human mind as a great and sudden change. The sun might shine, or the clouds might lour; but nothing could appear to me as it had done the day before. A fiend had snatched from me every hope of future happiness: no creature had ever been so miserable as I was; so frightful an event is single in the history of man.

But why should I dwell upon the incidents that followed this last overwhelming event. Mine has been a tale of horrors; I have reached their acme, and what I must now relate can but be tedious to you. Know that, one by one, my friends were snatched away; I was left desolate. My own strength is exhausted; and I must tell, in a few words, what remains of my hideous narration.

I arrived at Geneva. My father and Ernest yet lived; but the former sunk under the tidings that I bore. I see him now, excellent and venerable old man! his eyes wandered in vacancy, for they had lost their charm and their delight—his niece, his more than daughter, whom he doated on with all that affection which a man feels, who, in the decline of life, having few affections, clings more earnestly to those that remain. Cursed, cursed be the fiend that brought misery on his grey hairs, and doomed him to waste in wretchedness! He could not live under the horrors that were accumulated around him; an apoplectic fit was brought on, and in a few days he died in my arms.

What then became of me? I know not; I lost sensation, and chains and darkness were the only objects that pressed upon me. Sometimes, indeed, I dreamt that I wandered in flowery meadows and pleasant vales with the friends of my youth; but awoke, and found myself in a dungeon. Melancholy followed, but by degrees I gained a clear conception of my miseries and situation, and was then released from my prison. For they had called me mad; and during many months, as I understood, a solitary cell had been my habitation.

But liberty had been a useless gift to me had I not, as I awakened to reason, at the same time awakened to revenge. As the memory of past misfortunes pressed upon me, I began to reflect on their cause—the monster whom I had created, the miserable dæmon whom I had sent abroad into the world for my destruction. I was possessed by a maddening rage when I thought of him, and desired and ardently prayed that I might have him within my grasp to wreak a great and signal revenge on his cursed head.

Nor did my hate long confine itself to useless wishes; I began to reflect on the best means of securing him; and for this purpose, about a month after my release, I repaired to a criminal judge in the town, and told him that I had an accusation to make; that I knew the destroyer of my family; and that I required him to exert his whole authority for the apprehension of the murderer.

The magistrate listened to me with attention and kindness: 'Be assured, sir,' said he, 'no pains or exertions on my part shall be spared to discover the villain.'

'I thank you,' replied I; 'listen, therefore, to the deposition that I have to make. It is indeed a tale so strange, that I should fear you would not credit it, were there not something in truth which, however wonderful, forces conviction. The story is too connected to be mistaken for a dream, and I have no motive for falsehood.' My manner, as I thus addressed him, was impressive, but calm; I had formed in my own heart a resolution to pursue my destroyer to death; and this purpose quieted my agony, and provisionally reconciled me to life. I now related my history briefly, but with firmness and precision, marking the dates with accuracy, and never deviating into invective or exclamation.

The magistrate appeared at first perfectly incredulous, but as I continued he became more attentive and interested; I saw him sometimes shudder with horror, at others a lively surprise, unmingled with disbelief, was painted on his countenance.

When I had concluded my narration, I said, 'This is the being whom I accuse, and for whose detection and punishment I call upon you to exert your whole power. It is your duty as a magistrate, and I believe and hope that your feelings as a man will not revolt from the execution of those functions on this occasion.'

This address caused a considerable change in the physiognomy of my auditor. He had heard my story with that half kind of belief that is given to a tale of spirits and supernatural events; but when he was called upon to act officially in consequence, the whole tide of his incredulity returned. He, however, answered mildly, 'I would willingly afford you every aid in your pursuit; but the creature of whom you speak appears to have powers which would put all my exertions to defiance. Who can follow an animal which can traverse the sea of ice, and inhabit caves and dens, where no man would venture to intrude? Besides, some months have elapsed since the commission of his crimes, and no one can conjecture to what place he has wandered, or what region he may now inhabit.'

'I do not doubt that he hovers near the spot which I inhabit; and if he has indeed taken refuge in the Alps, he may be hunted like the chamois, and destroyed as a beast of prey. But I perceive your thoughts: you do not credit my narrative, and do not intend to pursue my enemy with the punishment which is his desert.'

As I spoke, rage sparkled in my eyes; the magistrate was intimidated; 'You are mistaken,' said he, 'I will exert myself; and if it is in my power to seize the monster, be assured that he shall suffer punishment proportionate to his crimes. But I fear, from what you have yourself described to be his properties, that this will prove impracticable, and that, while every proper measure is pursued, you should endeavour to make up your mind to disappointment.'

'That cannot be; but all that I can say will be of little avail. My revenge is of no moment to you; yet, while I allow it to be a vice, I confess that it is the devouring and only passion of my soul. My rage is unspeakable, when I reflect that the murderer, whom I have turned loose upon society, still exists. You refuse my just demand: I have but one resource; and I devote myself, either in my life or death, to his destruction.'

I trembled with excess of agitation as I said this; there was a phrenzy in my manner, and something, I doubt not, of that haughty fierceness, which the martyrs of old are said to have possessed. But to a Genevan magistrate, whose mind was occupied by far other ideas than those of devotion and heroism, this elevation of mind had much the appearance of madness. He endeavoured to soothe me as a nurse does a child, and reverted to my tale as the effects of delirium.

'Man,' I cried, 'how ignorant art thou in thy pride of wisdom! Cease; you know not what it is you say.'

I broke from the house angry and disturbed, and retired to meditate on some other mode of action.

CHAPTER VII

My present situation was one in which all voluntary thought was swallowed up and lost. I was hurried away by fury; revenge alone endowed me with strength and composure; it modelled my feelings, and allowed me to be calculating and calm, at periods when otherwise delirium or death would have been my portion.

My first resolution was to quit Geneva for ever; my country, which, when I was happy and beloved, was dear to me, now, in my adversity, became hateful. I provided myself with a sum of money, together with a few jewels which had belonged to my mother, and departed.

And now my wanderings began, which are to cease but with life. I have traversed a vast portion of the earth, and have endured all the hardships which travellers, in deserts and barbarous countries, are wont to meet. How I have lived I hardly know; many times have I stretched my failing limbs upon the sandy plain, and prayed for death. But revenge kept me alive; I dared not die, and leave my adversary in being.

When I quitted Geneva, my first labour was to gain some clue by which I might trace the steps of my fiendish enemy. But my plan was unsettled; and I wandered many hours around the confines of the town, uncertain what path I should pursue. As night approached, I found myself at the entrance of the cemetery where William, Elizabeth, and my father, reposed. I entered it, and approached the tomb which marked their graves. Every thing was silent, except the leaves of the trees, which were gently agitated by the wind; the night was nearly dark; and the scene would have been solemn and affecting even to an uninterested observer. The spirits of the departed seemed to flit around, and to cast a shadow, which was felt but seen not, around the head of the mourner.

The deep grief which this scene had at first excited quickly gave way to rage and despair. They were dead, and I lived; their murderer also lived, and to destroy him I must drag out my weary existence. I knelt on the grass, and kissed the earth, and with quivering lips exclaimed, 'By the sacred earth on which I kneel, by the shades that wander near me, by the deep and eternal grief that I feel, I swear; and by thee, O Night, and by the spirits that preside over thee, I swear to pursue that dæmon, who caused this misery, until he or I shall perish in mortal conflict. For this purpose I will preserve my life: to execute this dear revenge, will I again behold the sun, and tread the green herbage of earth, which otherwise should vanish from my eyes for ever. And I call on you, spirits of the dead; and on you, wandering ministers of vengeance, to aid and conduct me in my work. Let the cursed and hellish monster drink deep of agony; let him feel the despair that now torments me.'

I had begun my adjuration with solemnity, and an awe which almost assured me that the shades of my murdered friends heard and approved my devotion; but the furies possessed me as I concluded, and rage choked my utterance.

I was answered through the stillness of night by a loud and fiendish laugh. It rung on my ears long and heavily; the mountains re-echoed it, and I felt as if all hell surrounded me with mockery and laughter. Surely in that moment I should have been possessed by phrenzy, and have destroyed my miserable existence, but that my vow was heard, and that I was reserved for vengeance. The laughter died away; when a well-known and abhorred voice, apparently close to my ear, addressed me in an audible whisper—'I am satisfied: miserable wretch! you have determined to live, and I am satisfied.'

I darted towards the spot from which the sound proceeded; but the devil eluded my grasp. Suddenly the broad disk of the moon arose, and shone full upon his ghastly and distorted shape, as he fled with more than mortal speed.

I pursued him; and for many months this has been my task. Guided by a slight clue, I followed the windings of the Rhone, but vainly. The blue Mediterranean appeared; and, by a strange chance, I saw the fiend enter by night, and hide himself in a vessel bound for the Black Sea. I took my passage in the same ship; but he escaped, I know not how.

Amidst the wilds of Tartary and Russia, although he still evaded me, I have ever followed in his track. Sometimes the peasants, scared by this horrid apparition, informed me of his path; sometimes he himself, who feared that if I lost all trace I should despair and die, often left some mark to guide me. The snows descended on my head, and I saw the print of his huge step on the white plain. To you first entering on life, to whom care is new, and agony unknown, how can you understand what I have felt, and still feel? Cold, want, and fatigue, were the least pains which I was destined to endure; I was cursed by some devil, and carried about with me my eternal hell; yet still a spirit of good followed and directed my steps, and, when I most murmured, would suddenly extricate me from seemingly insurmountable difficulties. Sometimes, when nature, overcome by hunger, sunk under the exhaustion, a repast was prepared for me in the desert, that restored and inspirited me. The fare was indeed coarse, such as the peasants of the country ate; but I may not doubt that it was set there by the spirits that I had invoked to aid me. Often, when all was dry, the heavens cloudless, and I was parched by thirst, a slight cloud would bedim the sky, shed the few drops that revived me, and vanish.

I followed, when I could, the courses of the rivers; but the dæmon generally avoided these, as it was here that the population of the country chiefly collected. In other places human beings were seldom seen; and I generally subsisted on the wild animals that crossed my path. I had money with me, and gained the friendship of the villagers by distributing it, or bringing with me some food that I had killed, which, after taking a small part, I always presented to those who had provided me with fire and utensils for cooking.

My life, as it passed thus, was indeed hateful to me, and it was during sleep alone that I could taste joy. O blessed sleep! often, when most miserable, I sank to repose, and my dreams lulled me even to rapture. The spirits that guarded me had provided these moments, or rather hours, of happiness, that I might retain strength to fulfil my pilgrimage. Deprived of this respite, I should have sunk under my hardships. During the day I was sustained and inspirited by the hope of night: for in sleep I saw my friends, my wife, and my beloved country; again I saw the benevolent countenance of my father, heard the silver tones of my Elizabeth's voice, and beheld Clerval enjoying health and youth. Often, when wearied by a toilsome march, I persuaded myself that I was dreaming until night should come, and

that I should then enjoy reality in the arms of my dearest friends. What agonizing fondness did I feel for them! how did I cling to their dear forms, as
sometimes they haunted even my waking hours, and persuade myself that
they still lived! At such moments vengeance, that burned within me, died
in my heart, and I pursued my path towards the destruction of the dæmon,
more as a task enjoined by heaven, as the mechanical impulse of some
power of which I was unconscious, than as the ardent desire of my soul.

What his feelings were whom I pursued, I cannot know. Sometimes, indeed, he left marks in writing on the barks of the trees, or cut in stone, that
guided me, and instigated my fury. 'My reign is not yet over,' (these words
were legible in one of these inscriptions); 'you live, and my power is complete. Follow me; I seek the everlasting ices of the north, where you will feel
the misery of cold and frost, to which I am impassive. You will find near
this place, if you follow not too tardily, a dead hare; eat, and be refreshed.
Come on, my enemy; we have yet to wrestle for our lives; but many hard
and miserable hours must you endure, until that period shall arrive.'

Scoffing devil! Again do I vow vengeance; again do I devote thee, miserable fiend, to torture and death. Never will I omit my search, until he or
I perish; and then with what ecstacy shall I join my Elizabeth, and those
who even now prepare for me the reward of my tedious toil and horrible
pilgrimage.

As I still pursued my journey to the northward, the snows thickened,
and the cold increased in a degree almost too severe to support. The peasants were shut up in their hovels, and only a few of the most hardy ventured
forth to seize the animals whom starvation had forced from their hiding-
places to seek for prey. The rivers were covered with ice, and no fish could
be procured; and thus I was cut off from my chief article of maintenance.

The triumph of my enemy increased with the difficulty of my labours.
One inscription that he left was in these words: 'Prepare! your toils only begin: wrap yourself in furs, and provide food, for we shall soon enter upon
a journey where your sufferings will satisfy my everlasting hatred.'

My courage and perseverance were invigorated by these scoffing words;
I resolved not to fail in my purpose; and, calling on heaven to support me,
I continued with unabated fervour to traverse immense deserts, until the
ocean appeared at a distance, and formed the utmost boundary of the horizon. Oh! how unlike it was to the blue seas of the south! Covered with ice,
it was only to be distinguished from land by its superior wildness and
ruggedness. The Greeks wept for joy when they beheld the Mediterranean
from the hills of Asia, and hailed with rapture the boundary of their toils.
I did not weep; but I knelt down, and, with a full heart, thanked my guiding spirit for conducting me in safety to the place where I hoped, notwithstanding my adversary's gibe, to meet and grapple with him.

Some weeks before this period I had procured a sledge and dogs, and thus traversed the snows with inconceivable speed. I know not whether the fiend possessed the same advantages; but I found that, as before I had daily lost ground in the pursuit, I now gained on him; so much so, that when I first saw the ocean, he was but one day's journey in advance, and I hoped to intercept him before he should reach the beach. With new courage, therefore, I pressed on, and in two days arrived at a wretched hamlet on the seashore. I inquired of the inhabitants concerning the fiend, and gained accurate information. A gigantic monster, they said, had arrived the night before, armed with a gun and many pistols; putting to flight the inhabitants of a solitary cottage, through fear of his terrific appearance. He had carried off their store of winter food, and, placing it in a sledge, to draw which he had seized on a numerous drove of trained dogs, he had harnessed them, and the same night, to the joy of the horror-struck villagers, had pursued his journey across the sea in a direction that led to no land; and they conjectured that he must speedily be destroyed by the breaking of the ice, or frozen by the eternal frosts.

On hearing this information, I suffered a temporary access of despair. He had escaped me; and I must commence a destructive and almost endless journey across the mountainous ices of the ocean, —amidst cold that few of the inhabitants could long endure, and which I, the native of a genial and sunny climate, could not hope to survive. Yet at the idea that the fiend should live and be triumphant, my rage and vengeance returned, and, like a mighty tide, overwhelmed every other feeling. After a slight repose, during which the spirits of the dead hovered round, and instigated me to toil and revenge, I prepared for my journey.

I exchanged my land sledge for one fashioned for the inequalities of the frozen ocean; and, purchasing a plentiful stock of provisions, I departed from land.

I cannot guess how many days have passed since then; but I have endured misery, which nothing but the eternal sentiment of a just retribution burning within my heart could have enabled me to support. Immense and rugged mountains of ice often barred up my passage, and I often heard the thunder of the ground sea, which threatened my destruction. But again the frost came, and made the paths of the sea secure.

By the quantity of provision which I had consumed I should guess that I had passed three weeks in this journey; and the continual protraction of hope, returning back upon the heart, often wrung bitter drops of despondency and grief from my eyes. Despair had indeed almost secured her prey, and I should soon have sunk beneath this misery; when once, after the poor animals that carried me had with incredible toil gained the summit of a sloping ice mountain, and one sinking under his fatigue died, I viewed the expanse before me with anguish, when suddenly my eye caught a dark speck upon the dusky plain. I strained my sight to discover what it could be, and uttered a wild cry of ecstacy when I distinguished a sledge, and the distorted proportions of a well-known form within. Oh! with what a burning gush did hope revisit my heart! warm tears filled my eyes, which I hastily wiped away, that they might not intercept the view I had of the dæmon; but still my sight was dimmed by the burning drops, until, giving way to the emotions that oppressed me, I wept aloud.

But this was not the time for delay; I disencumbered the dogs of their dead companion, gave them a plentiful portion of food; and, after an hour's rest, which was absolutely necessary, and yet which was bitterly irksome to me, I continued my route. The sledge was still visible; nor did I again lose sight of it, except at the moments when for a short time some ice rock concealed it with its intervening crags. I indeed perceptibly gained on it; and when, after nearly two days' journey, I beheld my enemy at no more than a mile distant, my heart bounded within me.

But now, when I appeared almost within grasp of my enemy, my hopes were suddenly extinguished, and I lost all trace of him more utterly than I had ever done before. A ground sea was heard; the thunder of its progress, as the waters rolled and swelled beneath me, became every moment more ominous and terrific. I pressed on, but in vain. The wind arose; the sea roared; and, as with the mighty shock of an earthquake, it split, and cracked with a tremendous and overwhelming sound. The work was soon finished: in a few minutes a tumultuous sea rolled between me and my enemy, and I was left drifting on a scattered piece of ice, that was continually lessening, and thus preparing for me a hideous death.

In this manner many appalling hours passed; several of my dogs died; and I myself was about to sink under the accumulation of distress, when I saw your vessel riding at anchor, and holding forth to me hopes of succour and life. I had no conception that vessels ever came so far north, and was astounded at the sight. I quickly destroyed part of my sledge to construct oars; and by these means was enabled, with infinite fatigue, to move my ice-raft in the direction of your ship. I had determined, if you were going southward, still to trust myself to the mercy of the seas, rather than abandon my purpose. I hoped to induce you to grant me a boat with which I could still pursue my enemy. But your direction was northward. You took me on board when my vigour was exhausted, and I should soon have sunk under my multiplied hardship into a death, which I still dread,—for my task is unfulfilled.

Oh! when will my guiding spirit, in conducting me to the dæmon, allow me the rest I so much desire; or must I die, and he yet live? If I do, swear to me, Walton, that he shall not escape; that you will seek him, and satisfy my vengeance in his death. Yet, do I dare ask you to undertake my pilgrimage, to endure the hardships that I have undergone? No; I am not so selfish. Yet, when I am dead, if he should appear; if the ministers of vengeance should conduct him to you, swear that he shall not live—swear that he shall not triumph over my accumulated woes, and live to make another such a wretch as I am. He is eloquent and persuasive; and once his words had even power over my heart: but trust him not. His soul is as hellish as his form, full of treachery and fiend-like malice. Hear him not; call on the manes[53] of William, Justine, Clerval, Elizabeth, my father, and of the wretched Victor, and thrust your sword into his heart. I will hover near, and direct the steel aright.

WALTON, in continuation.
August 26th, 17—.

You have read this strange and terrific story, Margaret; and do you not feel your blood congealed with horror, like that which even now curdles mine? Sometimes, seized with sudden agony, he could not continue his tale; at others, his voice broken, yet piercing, uttered with difficulty the words so replete with agony. His fine and lovely eyes were now lighted up with indignation, now subdued to downcast sorrow, and quenched in infinite wretchedness. Sometimes he commanded his countenance and tones, and related the most horrible incidents with a tranquil voice, suppressing every mark of agitation; then, like a volcano bursting forth, his face would suddenly change to an expression of the wildest rage, as he shrieked out imprecations on his persecutor.

His tale is connected, and told with an appearance of the simplest truth; yet I own to you that the letters of Felix and Safie, which he shewed me, and the apparition of the monster, seen from our ship, brought to me a greater conviction of the truth of his narrative than his asseverations, however earnest and connected. Such a monster has then really existence; I cannot doubt it; yet I am lost in surprise and admiration. Sometimes I endeavoured to gain from Frankenstein the particulars of his creature's formation; but on this point he was impenetrable.

'Are you mad, my friend?' said he, 'or whither does your senseless curiosity lead you? Would you also create for yourself and the world a demoniacal enemy? Or to what do your questions tend? Peace, peace! learn my miseries, and do not seek to increase your own.'

---

[53] Manes are spirits of the family dead in early Roman religion. Victor's reversion to this revenge fantasy powered by the desires of the dead represents a form of cultural degeneration. His final words to Walton in the letter of September 12 show him restored to eighteenth-century values. [Ed.]

Frankenstein discovered that I made notes concerning his history: he asked to see them, and then himself corrected and augmented them in many places; but principally in giving the life and spirit to the conversations he held with his enemy. 'Since you have preserved my narration,' said he, 'I would not that a mutilated one should go down to posterity.'

Thus has a week passed away, while I have listened to the strangest tale that ever imagination formed. My thoughts, and every feeling of my soul, have been drunk up by the interest for my guest, which this tale, and his own elevated and gentle manners have created. I wish to soothe him; yet can I counsel one so infinitely miserable, so destitute of every hope of consolation, to live? Oh, no! the only joy that he can now know will be when he composes his shattered feelings to peace and death. Yet he enjoys one comfort, the offspring of solitude and delirium: he believes, that, when in dreams he holds converse with his friends, and derives from that communion consolation for his miseries, or excitements to his vengeance, that they are not the creations of his fancy, but the real beings who visit him from the regions of a remote world. This faith gives a solemnity to his reveries that render them to me almost as imposing and interesting as truth.

Our conversations are not always confined to his own history and misfortunes. On every point of general literature he displays unbounded knowledge, and a quick and piercing apprehension. His eloquence is forcible and touching; nor can I hear him, when he relates a pathetic incident, or endeavours to move the passions of pity or love, without tears. What a glorious creature must he have been in the days of his prosperity, when he is thus noble and godlike in ruin. He seems to feel his own worth, and the greatness of his fall.

'When younger,' said he, 'I felt as if I were destined for some great enterprise. My feelings are profound; but I possessed a coolness of judgment that fitted me for illustrious achievements. This sentiment of the worth of my nature supported me, when others would have been oppressed; for I deemed it criminal to throw away in useless grief those talents that might be useful to my fellow-creatures. When I reflected on the work I had completed, no less a one than the creation of a sensitive and rational animal, I could not rank myself with the herd of common projectors. But this feeling, which supported me in the commencement of my career, now serves only to plunge me lower in the dust. All my speculations and hopes are as nothing; and, like the archangel who aspired to omnipotence, I am chained in an eternal hell. My imagination was vivid, yet my powers of analysis and application were intense; by the union of these qualities I conceived the idea, and executed the creation of a man. Even now I cannot recollect, without passion, my reveries while the work was incomplete. I trod heaven in my thoughts, now exulting in my powers, now burning with the idea of their effects. From my infancy I was imbued with high hopes and a lofty ambition; but how am I sunk! Oh! my friend, if you had known me as I once was, you would not recognize me in this state of degradation. Despondency rarely visited my heart; a high destiny seemed to bear me on, until I fell, never, never again to rise.'

Must I then lose this admirable being? I have longed for a friend; I have sought one who would sympathize with and love me. Behold, on these desert seas I have found such a one; but, I fear, I have gained him only to know his value, and lose him. I would reconcile him to life, but he repulses the idea.

'I thank you, Walton,' he said, 'for your kind intentions towards so miserable a wretch; but when you speak of new ties, and fresh affections, think you that any can replace those who are gone? Can any man be to me as Clerval was; or any woman another Elizabeth? Even where the affections are not strongly moved by any superior excellence, the companions of our childhood always possess a certain power over our minds, which hardly any later friend can obtain. They know our infantine dispositions, which, however they may be afterwards modified, are never eradicated; and they can judge of our actions with more certain conclusions as to the integrity of our motives. A sister or a brother can never, unless indeed such symptoms have been shewn early, suspect the other of fraud or false dealing, when another friend, however strongly he may be attached, may, in spite of himself, be invaded with suspicion. But I enjoyed friends, dear not only through habit and association, but from their own merits; and, wherever I am, the soothing voice of my Elizabeth, and the conversation of Clerval, will be ever whispered in my ear. They are dead; and but one feeling in such a solitude can persuade me to preserve my life. If I were engaged in any high undertaking or design, fraught with extensive utility to my fellow-creatures, then could I live to fulfil it. But such is not my destiny; I must pursue and destroy the being to whom I gave existence; then my lot on earth will be fulfilled, and I may die.'

September 2nd.

MY BELOVED SISTER,

I write to you, encompassed by peril, and ignorant whether I am ever doomed to see again dear England, and the dearer friends that inhabit it. I am surrounded by mountains of ice, which admit of no escape, and threaten every moment to crush my vessel. The brave fellows, whom I have persuaded to be my companions, look towards me for aid; but I have none to bestow. There is something terribly appalling in our situation, yet my courage and hopes do not desert me. We may survive; and if we do not, I will repeat the lessons of my Seneca, and die with a good heart.

Yet what, Margaret, will be the state of your mind? You will not hear of my destruction, and you will anxiously await my return. Years will pass, and you will have visitings of despair, and yet be tortured by hope. Oh! my beloved sister, the sickening failings of your heart-felt expectations are, in prospect, more terrible to me than my own death. But you have a husband, and lovely children; you may be happy: heaven bless you, and make you so!

My unfortunate guest regards me with the tenderest compassion. He endeavours to fill me with hope; and talks as if life were a possession which he valued. He reminds me how often the same accidents have happened to other navigators, who have attempted this sea, and, in spite of myself, he fills me with cheerful auguries. Even the sailors feel the power of his eloquence; when he speaks, they no longer despair; he rouses their energies, and, while they hear his voice, they believe these vast mountains of ice are mole-hills, which will vanish before the resolutions of man. These feelings are transitory; each day's expectation delayed fills them with fear, and I almost dread a mutiny caused by this despair.

September 5th.

A scene has just passed of such uncommon interest, that although it is highly probable that these papers may never reach you, yet I cannot forbear recording it.

We are still surrounded by mountains of ice, still in imminent danger of being crushed in their conflict. The cold is excessive, and many of my unfortunate comrades have already found a grave amidst this scene of desolation. Frankenstein has daily declined in health: a feverish fire still glimmers in his eyes; but he is exhausted, and, when suddenly roused to any exertion, he speedily sinks again into apparent lifelessness.

I mentioned in my last letter the fears I entertained of a mutiny. This morning, as I sat watching the wan countenance of my friend—his eyes half closed, and his limbs hanging listlessly,—I was roused by half a dozen of the sailors, who desired admission into the cabin. They entered; and their leader addressed me. He told me that he and his companions had been chosen by the other sailors to come in deputation to me, to make me a demand, which, in justice, I could not refuse. We were immured in ice, and should probably never escape; but they feared that if, as was possible, the ice should dissipate, and a free passage be opened, I should be rash enough to continue my voyage, and lead them into fresh dangers, after they might happily have surmounted this. They desired, therefore, that I should engage with a solemn promise, that if the vessel should be freed, I would instantly direct my course southward.

This speech troubled me. I had not despaired; nor had I yet conceived the idea of returning, if set free. Yet could I, in justice, or even in possibility, refuse this demand? I hesitated before I answered; when Frankenstein, who had at first been silent, and, indeed, appeared hardly to have force enough to attend, now roused himself; his eyes sparkled, and his cheeks flushed with momentary vigour. Turning towards the men, he said—

'What do you mean? What do you demand of your captain? Are you then so easily turned from your design? Did you not call this a glorious expedition? and wherefore was it glorious? Not because the way was smooth and placid as a southern sea, but because it was full of dangers and terror; because, at every new incident, your fortitude was to be called forth, and your courage exhibited; because danger and death surrounded, and these dangers you were to brave and overcome. For this was it a glorious, for this was it an honourable undertaking. You were hereafter to be hailed as the benefactors of your species; your name adored, as belonging to brave men who encountered death for honour and the benefit of mankind. And now, behold, with the first imagination of danger, or, if you will, the first mighty and terrific trial of your courage, you shrink away, and are content to be handed down as men who had not strength enough to endure cold and peril; and so, poor souls, they were chilly, and returned to their warm firesides. Why, that requires not this preparation; ye need not have come thus far, and dragged your captain to the shame of a defeat, merely to prove yourselves cowards. Oh! be men, or be more than men. Be steady to your purposes, and firm as a rock. This ice is not made of such stuff as your hearts might be; it is mutable, cannot withstand you, if you say that it shall not. Do not return to your families with the stigma of disgrace marked on your brows. Return as heroes who have fought and conquered, and who know not what it is to turn their backs on the foe.'

He spoke this with a voice so modulated to the different feelings expressed in his speech, with an eye so full of lofty design and heroism, that can you wonder that these men were moved. They looked at one another, and were unable to reply. I spoke; I told them to retire, and consider of what had been said: that I would not lead them further north, if they strenuously desired the contrary; but that I hoped that, with reflection, their courage would return.

They retired, and I turned towards my friend; but he was sunk in languor, and almost deprived of life.

How all this will terminate, I know not; but I had rather die, than return shamefully,—my purpose unfulfilled. Yet I fear such will be my fate; the men, unsupported by ideas of glory and honour, can never willingly continue to endure their present hardships.

September 7th.

The die is cast; I have consented to return, if we are not destroyed. Thus are my hopes blasted by cowardice and indecision; I come back ignorant and disappointed. It requires more philosophy than I possess, to bear this injustice with patience.

September 12th.

It is past; I am returning to England. I have lost my hopes of utility and glory;—I have lost my friend. But I will endeavour to detail these bitter circumstances to you, my dear sister; and, while I am wafted towards England, and towards you, I will not despond.

September 9th,[54] the ice began to move, and roarings like thunder were heard at a distance, as the islands split and cracked in every direction. We were in the most imminent peril; but, as we could only remain passive, my chief attention was occupied by my unfortunate guest, whose illness increased in such a degree, that he was entirely confined to his bed. The ice cracked behind us, and was driven with force towards the north; a breeze sprung from the west, and on the 11th the passage towards the south became perfectly free. When the sailors saw this, and that their return to their native country was apparently assured, a shout of tumultuous joy broke from them, loud and long-continued. Frankenstein, who was dozing, awoke, and asked the cause of the tumult. 'They shout,' I said, 'because they will soon return to England.'

'Do you then really return?'

'Alas! yes; I cannot withstand their demands. I cannot lead them unwillingly to danger, and I must return.'

'Do so, if you will; but I will not. You may give up your purpose; but mine is assigned to me by heaven, and I dare not. I am weak; but surely the spirits who assist my vengeance will endow me with sufficient strength.' Saying this, he endeavoured to spring from the bed, but the exertion was too great for him; he fell back, and fainted.

It was long before he was restored; and I often thought that life was entirely extinct. At length he opened his eyes, but he breathed with difficulty, and was unable to speak. The surgeon gave him a composing draught, and ordered us to leave him undisturbed. In the mean time he told me, that my friend had certainly not many hours to live.

His sentence was pronounced; and I could only grieve, and be patient. I sat by his bed watching him; his eyes were closed, and I thought he slept;

---

[54]The 1818 text reads "September 19th," an error corrected to September 9 in all subsequent editions. [Ed.]

but presently he called to me in a feeble voice, and, bidding me come near, said — 'Alas! the strength I relied on is gone; I feel that I shall soon die, and he, my enemy and persecutor, may still be in being. Think not, Walton, that in the last moments of my existence I feel that burning hatred, and ardent desire of revenge, I once expressed, but I feel myself justified in desiring the death of my adversary. During these last days I have been occupied in examining my past conduct; nor do I find it blameable. In a fit of enthusiastic madness I created a rational creature, and was bound towards him, to assure, as far as was in my power, his happiness and well-being. This was my duty; but there was another still paramount to that. My duties towards my fellow-creatures had greater claims to my attention, because they included a greater proportion of happiness or misery. Urged by this view, I refused, and I did right in refusing, to create a companion for the first creature. He shewed unparalleled malignity and selfishness, in evil: he destroyed my friends; he devoted to destruction beings who possessed exquisite sensations, happiness, and wisdom; nor do I know where this thirst for vengeance may end. Miserable himself, that he may render no other wretched, he ought to die. The task of his destruction was mine, but I have failed. When actuated by selfish and vicious motives, I asked you to undertake my unfinished work; and I renew this request now, when I am only induced by reason and virtue.

'Yet I cannot ask you to renounce your country and friends, to fulfil this task; and now, that you are returning to England, you will have little chance of meeting with him. But the consideration of these points, and the well-balancing of what you may esteem your duties, I leave to you; my judgment and ideas are already disturbed by the near approach of death. I dare not ask you to do what I think right, for I may still be misled by passion.

'That he should live to be an instrument of mischief disturbs me, in other respects this hour, when I momentarily expect my release, is the only happy one which I have enjoyed for several years. The forms of the beloved dead flit before me, and I hasten to their arms. Farewell, Walton! Seek happiness in tranquillity, and avoid ambition, even if it be only the apparently innocent one of distinguishing yourself in science and discoveries. Yet why do I say this? I have myself been blasted in these hopes, yet another may succeed.'

His voice became fainter as he spoke; and at length, exhausted by his effort, he sunk into silence. About half an hour afterwards he attempted again to speak, but was unable; he pressed my hand feebly, and his eyes closed for ever, while the irradiation of a gentle smile passed away from his lips.

Margaret, what comment can I make on the untimely extinction of this glorious spirit? What can I say, that will enable you to understand the depth of my sorrow? All that I should express would be inadequate and feeble. My tears flow; my mind is overshadowed by a cloud of disappointment. But I journey towards England, and I may there find consolation.

I am interrupted. What do these sounds portend? It is midnight; the breeze blows fairly, and the watch on deck scarcely stir. Again, there is a sound as of a human voice, but hoarser; it comes from the cabin where the remains of Frankenstein still lie. I must arise, and examine. Good night, my sister.

Great God! what a scene has just taken place! I am yet dizzy with the re-membrance of it. I hardly know whether I shall have the power to detail it; yet the tale which I have recorded would be incomplete without this final and wonderful catastrophe.

I entered the cabin, where lay the remains of my ill-fated and admirable friend. Over him hung a form which I cannot find words to describe, gigan-tic in stature, yet uncouth and distorted in its proportions. As he hung over the coffin, his face was concealed by long locks of ragged hair; but one vast hand was extended, in colour and apparent texture like that of a mummy. When he heard the sound of my approach, he ceased to utter exclamations of grief and horror, and sprung towards the window. Never did I behold a vision so horrible as his face, of such loathsome, yet appalling hideousness. I shut my eyes involuntarily, and endeavoured to recollect what were my duties with regard to this destroyer. I called on him to stay.

He paused, looking on me with wonder; and, again turning towards the lifeless form of his creator, he seemed to forget my presence, and every fea-ture and gesture seemed instigated by the wildest rage of some uncontrol-lable passion.

'That is also my victim!' he exclaimed; 'in his murder my crimes are consummated; the miserable series of my being is wound to its close! Oh, Frankenstein! generous and self-devoted being! what does it avail that I now ask thee to pardon me? I, who irretrievably destroyed thee by destroy-ing all thou lovedst. Alas! he is cold; he may not answer me.'

His voice seemed suffocated; and my first impulses, which had suggested to me the duty of obeying the dying request of my friend, in destroying his enemy, were now suspended by a mixture of curiosity and compassion. I approached this tremendous being; I dared not again raise my looks upon his face, there was something so scaring and unearthly in his ugli-ness. I attempted to speak, but the words died away on my lips. The mon-ster continued to utter wild and incoherent self-reproaches. At length I gathered resolution to address him, in a pause of the tempest of his pas-sion: 'Your repentance,' I said, 'is now superfluous. If you had listened to the voice of conscience, and heeded the stings of remorse, before you had urged your diabolical vengeance to this extremity, Frankenstein would yet have lived.'

'And do you dream?' said the dæmon; 'do you think that I was then dead to agony and remorse?—He,' he continued, pointing to the corpse, 'he suffered not more in the consummation of the deed;—oh! not the ten-thousandth portion of the anguish that was mine during the lingering detail of its execution. A frightful selfishness hurried me on, while my heart was poisoned with remorse. Think ye that the groans of Clerval were music to my ears? My heart was fashioned to be susceptible of love and sympathy; and, when wrenched by misery to vice and hatred, it did not endure the violence of the change without torture, such as you cannot even imagine.

'After the murder of Clerval, I returned to Switzerland, heart-broken and overcome. I pitied Frankenstein; my pity amounted to horror: I abhorred myself. But when I discovered that he, the author at once of my existence and of its unspeakable torments, dared to hope for happiness; that while he accumulated wretchedness and despair upon me, he sought his own enjoyment in feelings and passions from the indulgence of which I was for ever barred, then impotent envy and bitter indignation filled me with an insatiable thirst for vengeance. I recollected my threat, and resolved that it should be accomplished. I knew that I was preparing for myself a deadly torture; but I was the slave, not the master of an impulse, which I detested, yet could not disobey. Yet when she died!—nay, then I was not miserable. I had cast off all feeling, subdued all anguish to riot in the excess of my despair. Evil thenceforth became my good.[55] Urged thus far, I had no choice but to adapt my nature to an element which I had willingly chosen. The completion of my demoniacal design became an insatiable passion. And now it is ended; there is my last victim!'

I was at first touched by the expressions of his misery; yet when I called to mind what Frankenstein had said of his powers of eloquence and persuasion, and when I again cast my eyes on the lifeless form of my friend, indignation was re-kindled within me! 'Wretch!' I said, 'it is well that you come here to whine over the desolation that you have made. You throw a torch into a pile of buildings, and when they are consumed you sit among the ruins, and lament the fall. Hypocritical fiend! if he whom you mourn still lived, still would he be the object, again would he become the prey of your accursed vengeance. It is not pity that you feel; you lament only because the victim of your malignity is withdrawn from your power.'

'Oh, it is not thus—not thus,' interrupted the being; 'yet such must be the impression conveyed to you by what appears to be the purport of my actions. Yet I seek not a fellow-feeling in my misery. No sympathy may I ever find. When I first sought it, it was the love of virtue, the feelings

---

[55] Again quoting Satan in *Paradise Lost*, IV, 110. [Ed.]

of happiness and affection with which my whole being overflowed, that I wished to be participated. But now, that virtue has become to me a shadow, and that happiness and affection are turned into bitter and loathing despair, in what should I seek for sympathy? I am content to suffer alone, while my sufferings shall endure: when I die, I am well satisfied that abhorrence and opprobrium should load my memory. Once my fancy was soothed with dreams of virtue, of fame, and of enjoyment. Once I falsely hoped to meet with beings, who, pardoning my outward form, would love me for the excellent qualities which I was capable of bringing forth. I was nourished with high thoughts of honour and devotion. But now vice has degraded me beneath the meanest animal. No crime, no mischief, no malignity, no misery, can be found comparable to mine. When I call over the frightful catalogue of my deeds, I cannot believe that I am he whose thoughts were once filled with sublime and transcendant visions of the beauty and the majesty of goodness. But it is even so; the fallen angel becomes a malignant devil. Yet even that enemy of God and man had friends and associates in his desolation; I am quite alone.

'You, who call Frankenstein your friend, seem to have a knowledge of my crimes and his misfortunes. But, in the detail which he gave you of them, he could not sum up the hours and months of misery which I endured, wasting in impotent passions. For whilst I destroyed his hopes, I did not satisfy my own desires. They were for ever ardent and craving; still I desired love and fellowship, and I was still spurned. Was there no injustice in this? Am I to be thought the only criminal, when all human kind sinned against me? Why do you not hate Felix, who drove his friend from his door with contumely? Why do you not execrate the rustic who sought to destroy the saviour of his child? Nay, these are virtuous and immaculate beings! I, the miserable and the abandoned, am an abortion, to be spurned at, and kicked, and trampled on. Even now my blood boils at the recollection of this injustice.

But it is true that I am a wretch. I have murdered the lovely and the helpless; I have strangled the innocent as they slept, and grasped to death his throat who never injured me or any other living thing. I have devoted my creator, the select specimen of all that is worthy of love and admiration among men, to misery; I have pursued him even to that irremediable ruin. There he lies, white and cold in death. You hate me; but your abhorrence cannot equal that with which I regard myself. I look on the hands which executed the deed; I think on the heart in which the imagination of it was conceived, and long for the moment when they will meet my eyes, when it will haunt my thoughts, no more.

'Fear not that I shall be the instrument of future mischief. My work is nearly complete. Neither yours nor any man's death is needed to consummate the series of my being, and accomplish that which must be done; but it requires my own. Do not think that I shall be slow to perform this sacrifice. I shall quit your vessel on the ice-raft which brought me hither, and shall seek the most northern extremity of the globe; I shall collect my funeral pile, and consume to ashes this miserable frame, that its remains may afford no light to any curious and unhallowed wretch, who would create such another as I have been. I shall die. I shall no longer feel the agonies which now consume me, or be the prey of feelings unsatisfied, yet unquenched. He is dead who called me into being; and when I shall be no more, the very remembrance of us both will speedily vanish. I shall no longer see the sun or stars, or feel the winds play on my cheeks. Light, feeling, and sense, will pass away; and in this condition must I find my happiness. Some years ago, when the images which this world affords first opened upon me, when I felt the cheering warmth of summer, and heard the rustling of the leaves and the chirping of the birds, and these were all to me, I should have wept to die; now it is my only consolation. Polluted by crimes, and torn by the bitterest remorse, where can I find rest but in death?

'Farewell! I leave you, and in you the last of human kind whom these eyes will ever behold. Farewell, Frankenstein! If thou wert yet alive, and yet cherished a desire of revenge against me, it would be better satiated in my life than in my destruction. But it was not so; thou didst seek my extinction, that I might not cause greater wretchedness; and if yet, in some mode unknown to me, thou hast not yet ceased to think and feel, thou desirest not my life for my own misery. Blasted as thou wert, my agony was still superior to thine; for the bitter sting of remorse may not cease to rankle in my wounds until death shall close them for ever.

'But soon,' he cried, with sad and solemn enthusiasm, 'I shall die, and what I now feel be no longer felt. Soon these burning miseries will be extinct. I shall ascend my funeral pile triumphantly, and exult in the agony of the torturing flames. The light of that conflagration will fade away; my ashes will be swept into the sea by the winds. My spirit will sleep in peace; or if it thinks, it will not surely think thus. Farewell.'

He sprung from the cabin-window, as he said this, upon the ice-raft which lay close to the vessel. He was soon borne away by the waves, and lost in darkness and distance.

THE END

" I could not distinguish what he said."

The original frontispiece for the 1896 first English and American editions of
The Island of Doctor Moreau, depicting Edward Prendick's first discovery
of Dr. Moreau's creations. The first English edition was published by William
Heinemann; the first American edition by Stone and Kimball.

The Island
of Doctor Moreau

H. G. Wells

Introduction

On February the 1st, 1887, the *Lady Vain* was lost by collision with a derelict when about the latitude 1°s. and longitude 107°w.

On January the 5th, 1888 — that is, eleven months and four days after — my uncle, Edward Prendick, a private gentleman, who certainly went aboard the *Lady Vain* at Callao,[1] and who had been considered drowned, was picked up in latitude 5° 3s. and longitude 101°w. in a small open boat, of which the name was illegible, but which is supposed to have belonged to the missing schooner *Ipecacuanha*.[2] He gave such a strange account of himself that he was supposed demented. Subsequently, he alleged that his mind was a blank from the moment of his escape from the *Lady Vain*. His case was discussed among psychologists at the time as a curious instance of the lapse of memory consequent upon physical and mental stress. The following narrative was found among his papers by the undersigned, his nephew and heir, but unaccompanied by any definite request for publication.

The only island known to exist in the region in which my uncle was picked up is Noble's Isle, a small volcanic islet, and uninhabited. It was visited in 1891 by H.M.S. *Scorpion*. A party of sailors then landed, but found nothing living thereon except certain curious white moths, some hogs and rabbits, and some rather peculiar rats. No specimen was secured of these. So that this narrative is without confirmation in its most essential particular. With that understood, there seems no harm in putting this strange story before the public, in accordance, as I believe, with my uncle's intentions. There is at least this much in its behalf: my uncle passed out of human knowledge about latitude 5°s. and longitude 105°e.,[3] and reappeared in the same part of the ocean after a space of eleven months. In some way he must have lived during the interval. And it seems that a schooner called the *Ipecacuanha*, with a drunken captain, John Davis, did start from Arica[4] with a puma and certain other animals aboard in January 1887, that the vessel was well known at several ports in the South Pacific, and that it finally

---

The Island of Doctor Moreau. London: William Heinemann Ltd., 1896.

[1] A guano port in Peru, near Lima. [Ed.]

[2] *Cephaelis ipecacuanha*, a South American plant used as a purgative or emetic. The Swiftian satire combining guano and ipecacuanha is assumed to be deliberate. [Ed.]

[3] These coordinates put Moreau's island near the Galapagos Islands, where Charles Darwin's observations during the voyage of the Beagle in 1831 confirmed for him the theory of natural selection for evolution. [Ed.]

[4] A port in Chile captured in 1880 from Peru and destroyed. In 1891 it was the scene of a bloody civil war. [Ed.]

disappeared from those seas (with a considerable amount of copra aboard), sailing to its unknown fate from Banya[5] in December 1887, a date that tallies entirely with my uncle's story.

CHARLES EDWARD PRENDICK.

I

In the Dingey of the *Lady Vain*

I do not propose to add anything to what has already been written concerning the loss of the *Lady Vain*. As every one knows, she collided with a derelict when ten days out from Callao. The long-boat with seven of the crew was picked up eighteen days after by H.M. gun-boat *Myrtle,* and the story of their privations has become almost as well known as the far more terrible *Medusa* case.[6] I have now, however, to add to the published story of the *Lady Vain* another as horrible, and certainly far stranger. It has hitherto been supposed that the four men who were in the dingey perished, but this is incorrect. I have the best of evidence for this assertion—I am one of the four men.

But, in the first place, I must state that there never were four men in the dingey; the number was three. Constans, who was 'seen by the captain to jump into the gig' (*Daily News,* March 17, 1887),[7] luckily for us, and unluckily for himself, did not reach us. He came down out of the tangle of ropes under the stays of the smashed bowsprit; some small rope caught his heel as he let go, and he hung for a moment head downward, and then fell and struck a block or spar floating in the water. We pulled towards him, but he never came up.

I say, luckily for us he did not reach us, and I might almost add luckily for himself, for there were only a small breaker[8] of water and some soddened

---

[5]Probably Banka, an island in the Dutch East Indies exporting tin. Substituting east for west longitude, Banka's coordinates are those of Moreau's Noble's Isle. Leon Stover (59) posits a possible contrast between this aggressive commercial scene and the supposedly "noble" experiment to eliminate beastly behavior undertaken by Moreau. [Ed.]

[6]The French frigate *Medusa* was wrecked off Africa in 1816, with the loss of hundreds of sailors; the plight of the survivors was depicted in Gericault's famous painting "The Raft of the Medusa" (1819). [Ed.]

[7]Robert Philmus reports an account in the February 22, not March 17, edition of the *Daily News* of "court proceedings in the case of three shipwrecked North Sea sailors who cannibalized a fourth after drawing lots for who would be the victim (one of the sailors had the middle name Hjalmar)" (Philmus 90). [Ed.]

[8]A small keg or cask. [Ed.]

ship's biscuits with us—so sudden had been the alarm, so unprepared the ship for any disaster. We thought the people on the launch would be better provisioned (though it seems they were not), and we tried to hail them. They could not have heard us, and the next morning when the drizzle cleared—which was not until past midday—we could see nothing of them. We could not stand up to look about us because of the pitching of the boat. The sea ran in great rollers, and we had much ado to keep the boat's head to them. The two other men who had escaped so far with me were a man named Helmar, a passenger like myself, and a seaman whose name I don't know, a short sturdy man with a stammer.

We drifted—famishing, and, after our water had come to an end, tormented by an intolerable thirst, for eight days altogether. After the second day the sea subsided slowly to a glassy calm. It is quite impossible for the ordinary reader to imagine those eight days. He has not—luckily for himself—anything in his memory to imagine with. After the first day we said little to one another and lay in our places in the boat and stared at the horizon, or watched, with eyes that grew larger and more haggard every day, the misery and weakness gaining upon our companions. The sun became pitiless. The water ended on the fourth day, and we were already thinking strange things and saying them with our eyes; but it was, I think, the sixth before Helmar gave voice to the thing we all had in mind. I remember our voices—dry and thin, so that we bent towards one another and spared our words. I stood out against it with all my might, was rather for scuttling the boat and perishing together among the sharks that followed us; but when Helmar said that if his proposal was accepted we should have drink, the sailor came round to him.

I would not draw lots, however, and in the night the sailor whispered to Helmar again and again, and I sat in the bows with my clasp-knife in my hand—though I doubt if I had the stuff in me to fight. And in the morning I agreed to Helmar's proposal, and we handed halfpence to find the odd man.

The lot fell upon the sailor, but he was the strongest of us and would not abide by it, and attacked Helmar with his hands. They grappled together and almost stood up. I crawled along the boat to them, intending to help Helmar by grasping the sailor's leg, but the sailor stumbled with the swaying of the boat, and the two fell upon the gunwale and rolled overboard together. They sank like stones. I remember laughing at that and wondering why I laughed. The laugh caught me suddenly like a thing from without.

I lay across one of the thwarts for I know not how long, thinking that if I had the strength I would drink sea-water and madden myself to die quickly. And even as I lay there, I saw, with no more interest than if it had been a picture, a sail come up towards me over the sky-line. My mind must have been wandering, and yet I remember all that happened quite distinctly. I remember how my head swayed with the seas, and the horizon with the sail above it danced up and down. But I also remember as distinctly that I had a persuasion that I was dead, and that I thought what a jest it was they should come too late by such a little to catch me in my body. *delirious*

For an endless period, as it seemed to me, I lay with my head on the thwart watching the dancing schooner—she was a little ship, schooner-rigged fore and aft—come up out of the sea. She kept tacking to and fro in a widening compass, for she was sailing dead into the wind. It never entered my head to attempt to attract attention, and I do not remember anything distinctly after the sight of her side, until I found myself in a little cabin aft. There's a dim half-memory of being lifted up to the gangway and of a big red countenance, covered with freckles and surrounded with red hair, staring at me over the bulwarks. I also had a disconnected impression of a dark face with extraordinary eyes close to mine, but that I thought was a nightmare, until I met it again. I fancy I recollect some stuff being poured in between my teeth. And that is all.

II
The Man Who Was Going Nowhere

The cabin in which I found myself was small, and rather untidy. A young-ish man with flaxen hair, a bristly straw-coloured moustache and a drooping nether lip was sitting and holding my wrist. For a minute we stared at one another without speaking. He had watery grey eyes, oddly void of expression.

Then just overhead came a sound like an iron bedstead being knocked about and the low angry growling of some large animal. At the same time the man spoke again.

He repeated his question:

'How do you feel now?'

I think I said I felt all right. I could not recollect how I had got there. He must have seen the question in my face, for my voice was inaccessible to me.

'You were picked up in a boat—starving. The name on the boat was the *Lady Vain*, and there were spots of blood on the gunwale.' At the same time my eye caught my hand, so thin that it looked like a dirty skin purse full of loose bones, and all the business of the boat came back to me.

'Have some of this,' said he, and gave me a dose of some scarlet stuff, iced. It tasted like blood, and made me feel stronger. *cannibalism*

'You were in luck,' said he, 'to get picked [up] by a ship with a medical man aboard.' He spoke with a slobbering articulation, with the ghost of a lisp.

'What ship is this?' I said slowly, hoarse from my long silence.

'It's a little trader from Arica and Callao. I never asked where she came from in the beginning. Out of the land of born fools, I guess. I'm a passenger myself from Arica. The silly ass who owns her—he's captain too, named Davis—he's lost his certificate or something. You know the kind of man—calls the thing the *Ipecacuanha*—of all silly infernal names, though when there's much of a sea without any wind she certainly acts according.'

Then the noise overhead began again, a snarling growl and the voice of a human being together. Then another voice telling some 'Heaven-forsaken idiot' to desist.

'You were nearly dead,' said my interlocutor. 'It was a very near thing indeed. But I've put some stuff into you now. Notice your arms sore? Injections. You've been insensible for nearly thirty hours.'

I thought slowly. I was distracted now by the yelping of a number of dogs.

'Am I eligible for solid food?' I asked.

'Thanks to me,' he said. 'Even now the mutton is boiling.'

'Yes,' I said, with assurance; 'I could eat some mutton.'

'But,' said he, with a momentary hesitation, 'you know I'm dying to hear of how you came to be alone in the boat.'

I thought I detected a certain suspicion in his eyes.

'Damn that howling!'

He suddenly left the cabin, and I heard him in violent controversy with some one, who seemed to me to talk gibberish in response to him. The matter sounded as though it ended in blows, but in that I thought my ears were mistaken. Then he shouted at the dogs and returned to the cabin.

'Well?' said he, in the doorway. 'You were just beginning to tell me.'

I told him my name, Edward Prendick, and how I had taken to natural history as a relief from the dulness of my comfortable independence. He seemed interested in this.

'I've done some science myself—I did my Biology at University College—getting out the ovary of the earth-worm and the radula of the snail and all that. Lord! it's ten years ago. But go on, go on—tell me about the boat.'

He was evidently satisfied with the frankness of my story, which I told in concise sentences enough—for I felt horribly weak—and when it was finished he reverted at once to the topic of natural history and his own biological studies. He began to question me closely about Tottenham Court Road and Gower Street.

'Is Caplatzi still flourishing? What a shop that was!'[9]

He had evidently been a very ordinary medical student, and drifted incontinently to the topic of the music-halls. He told me some anecdotes.

'Left it all,' he said, 'ten years ago. How jolly it all used to be! But I made a young ass of myself. . . . Played myself out before I was twenty-one. I daresay it's all different now. . . . But I must look up that ass of a cook and see what he's doing to your mutton.'

The growling overhead was renewed, so suddenly and with so much savage anger that it startled me.

'What's that?' I called after him, but the door had closed.

He came back again with the boiled mutton, and I was so excited by the appetising smell of it, that I forgot the noise of the beast forthwith.

After a day of alternate sleep and feeding I was so far recovered as to be able to get from my bunk to the scuttle and see the green seas trying to keep pace with us. I judged the schooner was running before the wind. Montgomery—that was the name of the flaxen-haired man—came in again as I stood there, and I asked him for some clothes. He lent me some duck[10] things of his own, for those I had worn in the boat, he said, had been thrown overboard. They were rather loose for me, for he was large, and long in his limbs.

He told me casually that the captain was three-parts drunk in his own cabin. As I assumed the clothes I began asking him some questions about the destination of the ship. He said the ship was bound for Hawaii, but that it has to land him first.

'Where?' said I.

'It's an island. . . . Where I live. So far as I know, it hasn't got a name.'

He stared at me with his nether lip dropping, and looked so wilfully stupid of a sudden that it came into my head that he desired to avoid my questions. I had the discretion to ask no more.

III

The Strange Face

We left the cabin and found a man at the companion obstructing our way. He was standing on the ladder with his back to us, peering over the combing of the hatch-way. He was, I could see, a misshapen man, short, broad

midget ?

---

[9] According to Philmus (91), Anthony Caplatzi ran a shop selling scientific instruments on the Tottenham Court Road near the University of London's University College in the 1890s. Wells received a science degree from the university in 1890. [Ed.]

[10] Twilled linen. [Ed.]

and clumsy, with a crooked back, a hairy neck and a head sunk between his shoulders. He was dressed in dark blue serge, and had peculiarly thick coarse black hair. I heard the unseen dogs growl furiously, and forthwith he ducked back, coming into contact with the hand I put out to fend him off from myself. He turned with animal swiftness.

In some indefinable way the black face thus flashed upon me shocked me profoundly. It was a singularly deformed one. The facial part projected, forming something dimly suggestive of a muzzle, and the huge half-open mouth showed as big white teeth as I had ever seen in a human mouth. His eyes were bloodshot at the edges, with scarcely a rim of white round the hazel pupils. There was a curious glow of excitement in his face.

'Confound you!' said Montgomery. 'Why the devil don't you get out of the way?'

The black-faced man started aside without a word.

I went on up the companion, instinctively staring at him as I did so. Montgomery stayed at the foot for a moment.

'You have no business here, you know,' he said, in a deliberate tone. 'Your place is forward.'

The black-faced man cowered. 'They . . . won't have me forward.' He spoke slowly, with a queer hoarse quality in his voice.

'Won't have you forward!' said Montgomery in a menacing voice. 'But I tell you to go.'

He was on the brink of saying something further, then looked up at me suddenly and followed me up the ladder. I had paused half-way through the hatchway, looking back, still astonished beyond measure at the grotesque ugliness of this black-faced creature. I had never beheld such a repulsive and extraordinary face before, and yet — if the contradiction is credible — I experienced at the same time an odd feeling that in some way I *had* already encountered exactly the features and gestures that now amazed me. Afterwards it occurred to me that probably I had seen him as I was lifted aboard, and yet that scarcely satisfied my suspicion of a previous acquaintance. Yet how one could have set eyes on so singular a face and have forgotten the precise occasion passed my imagination.

Montgomery's movement to follow me released my attention, and I turned and looked about me at the flush deck of the little schooner. I was already half prepared by the sounds I had heard for what I saw. Certainly I never beheld a deck so dirty. It was littered with scraps of carrot, shreds of green stuff, and indescribable filth. Fastened by chains to the main mast were a number of grisly staghounds, who now began leaping and barking at me, and by the mizzen a huge puma was cramped in a little iron cage, far too small even to give it turning-room. Further under the starboard bulwark were some big hutches containing a number of rabbits, and a solitary llama was squeezed in a mere box of a cage forward. The dogs were muzzled by leather straps. The only human being on deck was a gaunt and silent sailor at the wheel.

The patched and dirty spankers were tense before the wind, and up aloft the little ship seemed carrying every sail she had. The sky was clear, the sun midway down the western sky; long waves, capped by the breeze with froth, were running with us. We went past the steersman to the taffrail and saw the water come foaming under the stern, and the bubbles go dancing and vanishing in her wake. I turned and surveyed the unsavoury length of the ship.

'Is this an ocean menagerie?' said I.

'Looks like it,' said Montgomery.

'What are these beasts for? Merchandise, curios? Does the captain think he is going to sell them somewhere in the South Seas?'

'It looks like it, doesn't it?' said Montgomery, and turned towards the wake again. *mysterious*

Suddenly we heard a yelp and a volley of furious blasphemy coming from the companion hatchway, and the deformed man with the black face clambered up hurriedly. He was immediately followed by a heavy red-haired man in a white cap. At the sight of the former the staghounds, who had all tired of barking at me by this time, became furiously excited, howling and leaping against their chains. The black hesitated before them, and this gave the red-haired man time to come up with him and deliver a tremendous blow between the shoulder-blades. The poor devil went down like a felled ox, and rolled in the dirt among the furiously excited dogs. It was lucky for him they were muzzled. The red-haired man gave a yawp of exultation and stood staggering and, as it seemed to me, in serious danger of either going backwards down the companion hatchway, or forwards upon his victim.

So soon as the second man had appeared, Montgomery had started violently. 'Steady on there!' he cried, in a tone of remonstrance. A couple of sailors appeared on the forecastle.

The black-faced man, howling in a singular voice, rolled about under the feet of the dogs. No one attempted to help him. The brutes did their best to worry him, butting their muzzles at him. There was a quick dance of their lithe grey bodies over the clumsy prostrate figure. The sailors forward shouted to them as though it was admirable sport. Montgomery gave an angry exclamation, and went striding down the deck. I followed him.

In another second the black-faced man had scrambled up and was staggering forward. He stumbled up against the bulwark by the main shrouds, where he remained panting and glaring over his shoulder at the dogs. The red-haired man laughed a satisfied laugh. *creepy*

'Look here, captain,' said Montgomery, with his lisp a little accentuated, gripping the elbows of the red-haired man; 'this won't do.'

I stood behind Montgomery. The captain came half round and regarded him with the dull and solemn eyes of a drunken man.

'Wha' won't do?' he said; and added, after looking sleepily into Montgomery's face for a minute, 'Blasted Sawbones!'

With a sudden movement he shook his arms free, and after two ineffectual attempts stuck his freckled fists into his side-pockets.

'That man's a passenger,' said Montgomery. 'I'd advise you to keep your hands off him.'

'Go to hell!' said the captain loudly. He suddenly turned and staggered towards the side. 'Do what I like on my own ship,' he said.

I think Montgomery might have left him then—seeing the brute was drunk. But he only turned a shade paler, and followed the captain to the bulwarks.

'Look here, captain,' he said. 'That man of mine is not to be ill-treated. He has been hazed ever since he came aboard.'

For a minute alcoholic fumes kept the captain speechless.

'Blasted Sawbones!' was all he considered necessary.

I could see that Montgomery had one of those slow pertinacious tempers that will warm day after day to a white heat and never again cool to forgiveness, and I saw too that this quarrel had been some time growing.

'The man's drunk,' said I, perhaps officiously; 'you'll do no good.'

Montgomery gave an ugly twist to his drooping lip.

'He's always drunk. Do you think that excuses his assaulting his passengers?'

'My ship,' began the captain, waving his hand unsteadily towards the cages, 'was a clean ship. Look at it now.' It was certainly anything but clean. 'Crew,' continued the captain, 'clean respectable crew.'

'You agreed to take the beasts.'

'I wish I'd never set eyes on your infernal island. What the devil . . . want beasts for on an island like that? Then that man of yours. . . . Understood he was a man. He's a lunatic. And he hadn't no business aft. Do you think the whole damned ship belongs to you?'

'Your sailors began to haze the poor devil as soon as he came aboard.'

'That's just what he is—he's a devil, an ugly devil. My men can't stand him. *I* can't stand him. None of us can't stand him. Nor *you* either.'

Montgomery turned away.

'*You* leave that man alone, anyhow,' he said, nodding his head as he spoke.

But the captain meant to quarrel now. He raised his voice:

'If he comes this end of the ship again I'll cut his insides out, I tell you. Cut out his blasted insides! Who are *you* to tell *me* what *I'm* to do. I tell you I'm captain of the ship—Captain and Owner. I'm the law here, I tell you—the law and the prophets. I bargained to take a man and his atttendant to and from Arica and bring back some animals. I never bargained to carry a mad devil and a silly Sawbones, a—'

Well, never mind what he called Montgomery. I saw the latter take a step forward, and interposed.

'He's drunk,' said I. The captain began some abuse even fouler than the last. 'Shut up,' I said, turning on him sharply, for I had seen danger in Montgomery's white face. With that I brought the downpour on myself.

However, I was glad to avert what was uncommonly near a scuffle, even at the price of the captain's drunken ill-will. I do not think I have ever heard quite so much vile language come in a continuous stream from any man's lips before, though I have frequented eccentric company enough. I found some of it hard to endure—though I am a mild-tempered man. But certainly when I told the captain to shut up I had forgotten I was merely a bit of human flotsam, cut off from my resources, and with my fare unpaid, a mere casual dependent on the bounty—or speculative enterprise—of the ship. He reminded me of it with considerable vigour. But at any rate I prevented a fight.

I V
At the Schooner's Rail

That night, land was sighted after sundown, and the schooner hove to. Montgomery intimated that was his destination. It was too far to see any details; it seemed to me then simply a low-lying patch of dim blue in the uncertain blue-grey sea. An almost vertical streak of smoke went up from it into the sky. *someone alive there*

The captain was not on deck when it was sighted. After he had vented his wrath on me he had staggered below, and I understand he went to sleep on the floor of his own cabin. The mate practically assumed the command. He was the gaunt, taciturn individual we had seen at the wheel. Apparently he too was in an evil temper with Montgomery. He took not the slightest notice of either of us. We dined with him in a sulky silence, after a few ineffectual efforts on my part to talk. It struck me, too, that the men regarded my companion and his animals in a singularly unfriendly manner. I found Montgomery very reticent about his purpose with these creatures, and about his destination, and though I was sensible of a growing curiosity I did not press him.

We remained talking on the quarter-deck until the sky was thick with stars. Except for an occasional sound in the yellow-lit forecastle, and a movement of the animals now and then, the night was very still. The puma lay crouched together, watching us with shining eyes, a black heap in the corner of its cage. The dogs seemed to be asleep. Montgomery produced some cigars.

He talked to me of London in a tone of half-painful reminiscence, asking all kinds of questions about changes that had taken place. He spoke like a man who had loved his life there, and had been suddenly and irrevocably cut off from it. I gossiped as well as I could of this and that. All the time the strangeness of him was shaping itself in my mind, and as I talked I peered at his odd pallid face in the dim light of the binnacle lantern behind me. Then I looked out at the darkling sea, where in the dimness his little island was hidden.

This man, it seemed to me, had come out of Immensity merely to save my life. To-morrow he would drop over the side and vanish again out of my existence. Even had it been under commonplace circumstances it would have made me a trifle thoughtful. But in the first place was the singularity of an educated man living on this unknown little island, and coupled with that, the extraordinary nature of his luggage. I found myself repeating the captain's question:

What did he want with the beasts? Why, too, had he pretended they were not his when I had remarked about them at first? Then again, in his personal attendant there was a bizarre quality that had impressed me profoundly. These circumstances threw a haze of mystery round the man. They laid hold of my imagination and hampered my tongue.

Towards midnight our talk of London died away, and we stood side by side leaning over the bulwarks, and staring dreamily over the silent starlit sea, each pursuing his own thoughts. It was the atmosphere for sentiment, and I began upon my gratitude.

'If I may say it,' said I, after a time, 'you have saved my life.'

'Chance,' he answered; 'just chance.'

'I prefer to make my thanks to the accessible agent.'

'Thank no one. You had the need, and I the knowledge, and I injected and fed you much as I might have collected a specimen. I was bored, and wanted something to do. If I'd been jaded that day, or hadn't liked your face, well —; it's a curious question where you would have been now.'

This damped my mood a little.

'At any rate —' I began.

'It's chance, I tell you,' he interrupted, 'as everything is in a man's life. Only the asses won't see it. Why am I here now—an outcast from civilisation—instead of being a happy man, enjoying all the pleasures of London? Simply because—eleven years ago—I lost my head for ten minutes on a foggy night.'

He stopped.

'Yes?' said I.

'That's all.'

We relapsed into silence. Presently he laughed.

'There's something in this starlight that loosens one's tongue. I'm an ass, and yet somehow I would like to tell you.'

'Whatever you tell me, you may rely upon my keeping to myself. . . . If that's it.'

He was on the point of beginning, and then shook his head doubtfully.

'Don't,' said I. 'It is all the same to me. After all, it is better to keep your secret. There's nothing gained but a little relief, if I respect your confidence. If I don't . . . well?'

He grunted undecidedly. I felt I had him at a disadvantage, had caught him in the mood of indiscretion; and, to tell the truth, I was not curious to learn what might have driven a young medical student out of London. I have an imagination.[11] I shrugged my shoulders, and turned away. Over the taffrail leant a silent black figure, watching the stars. It was Montgomery's strange attendant. It looked over its shoulder quickly with my movement, then looked away again.

It may seem a little thing to you, perhaps, but it came like a sudden blow to me. The only light near us was a lantern at the wheel. The creature's face was turned for one brief instant out of the dimness of the stern towards this illumination, and I saw that the eyes that glanced at me shone with a pale green light.

I did not know then that a reddish luminosity, at least, is not uncommon in human eyes. The thing came to me as stark inhumanity. That black figure, with its eyes of fire, struck down through all my adult thoughts and

---

[11] Montgomery's "secret" is never specified. With his lisp, hanging nether lip, fondness for Gower Street (currently called "pansy row" according to Stover [67]), and his mention early in Chapter 4 of a "shabby vice" that got him expelled from polite society and professional training because he lost his head "for ten minutes on a foggy night," he seems a possible figure for that particular type of "degeneracy" making headlines in the Oscar Wilde trial of 1895, the homosexual. In the preface to the Atlantic Edition of the novel, Wells said that *Moreau* was written partly in response to the Wilde trial, in which he saw "the graceless and pitiful downfall of a man of genius, a reminder that humanity is but animal rough-hewn to reasonable shape" (1924, I, ix). [Ed.]

Montgomery=gay

feelings, and for a moment the forgotten horrors of childhood came back to my mind. Then the effect passed as it had come. An uncouth black figure of a man, a figure of no particular import, hung over the taffrail, against the starlight, and I found Montgomery was speaking to me.

'I'm thinking of turning in, then,' said he; 'if you've had enough of this.'

I answered him incongruously. We went below, and he wished me good night at the door of my cabin.

That night I had some very unpleasant dreams. The waning moon rose late. Its light struck a ghostly faint white beam across my cabin, and made an ominous shape on the planking by my bunk. Then the staghounds woke, and began howling and baying, so that I dreamt fitfully, and scarcely slept until the approach of dawn.

V

The Man Who Had Nowhere to Go

In the early morning—it was the second morning after my recovery, and I believe the fourth after I was picked up—I awoke through an avenue of tumultuous dreams, dreams of guns and howling mobs, and became sensible of a hoarse shouting above me. I rubbed my eyes, and lay listening to the noise, doubtful for a little while of my whereabouts. Then came a sudden pattering of bare feet, the sound of heavy objects being thrown about, a violent creaking and rattling of chains. I heard the swish of the water as the ship was suddenly brought round, and a foamy yellow-green wave flew across the little round window and left it streaming. I jumped into my clothes and went on deck.

As I came up the ladder I saw against the flushed sky—for the sun was just rising—the broad back and red hair of the captain, and over his shoulder the puma spinning from a tackle rigged on to the mizzen spanker boom. The poor brute seemed horribly scared, and crouched in the bottom of its little cage.

'Overboard with 'em!' bawled the captain. 'Overboard with 'em! We'll have a clean ship soon of the whole bilin' of 'em.'

He stood in my way, so that I had perforce to tap his shoulder to come on deck. He came round with a start, and staggered back a few paces to stare at me. It needed no expert eye to tell that the man was still drunk.

'Hullo!' said he stupidly, and then with a light coming into his eyes, 'Why, it's Mister—Mister—?'

'Prendick,' said I.

'Prendick be damned!' said he. 'Shut Up—that's your name. Mister Shut Up.'

It was no good answering the brute. But I certainly did not expect his next move. He held out his hand to the gangway by which Montgomery stood talking to a massive white-haired man in dirty blue flannels, who had apparently just come aboard.

'That way, Mister Blasted Shut Up. That way,' roared the captain.

Montgomery and his companion turned as he spoke.

'What do you mean?' said I.

'That way, Mister Blasted Shut Up—that's what I mean. Overboard, Mister Shut Up—and sharp. We're clearing the ship out, cleaning the whole blessed ship out. And overboard you go.'

I stared at him dumbfounded. Then it occurred to me it was exactly the thing I wanted. The lost prospect of a journey as sole passenger with this quarrelsome sot was not one to mourn over. I turned towards Montgomery.

'Can't have you,' said Montgomery's companion concisely.

'You can't have me!' said I, aghast.

He had the squarest and most resolute face I ever set eyes upon.

'Look here,' I began, turning to the captain.

'Overboard,' said the captain. 'This ship ain't for beasts and cannibals, and worse than beasts, any more. Overboard you . . . Mr. Shut Up. If they can't have you, you goes adrift. But, anyhow, you go! With your friends. I've done with this blessed island for evermore amen! I've had enough of it.'

'But, Montgomery,' I appealed.

He distorted his lower lip, and nodded his head hopelessly at the grey-haired man beside him, to indicate his powerlessness to help me.

'I'll see to *you* presently,' said the captain.

Then began a curious three-cornered altercation. Alternately I appealed to one and another of the three men, first to the grey-haired man to let me land, and then to the drunken captain to keep me aboard. I even bawled entreaties to the sailors. Montgomery said never a word; only shook his head.

'You're going overboard, I tell you,' was the captain's refrain. . . . 'Law be damned! I'm king here.'

At last, I must confess, my voice suddenly broke in the middle of a vigorous threat. I felt a gust of hysterical petulance, and went aft, and stared dismally at nothing.

Meanwhile the sailors progressed rapidly with the task of unshipping the packages and caged animals. A large launch with two standing lugs[12] lay under the lee of the schooner, and into this the strange assortment of goods

---

[12] Lugsails. [Ed.]

were swung. I did not then see the hands from the island that were receiving the packages, for the hull of the launch was hidden from me by the side of the schooner. *foreshadowing*

Neither Montgomery nor his companion took the slightest notice of me, but busied themselves in assisting and directing the four or five sailors who were unloading the goods. The captain went forward, interfering rather than assisting. I was alternately despairful and desperate. Once or twice, as I stood waiting there for things to accomplish themselves, I could not resist an impulse to laugh at my miserable quandary. I felt all the wretcheder for the lack of a breakfast. Hunger and a lack of blood-corpuscles take all the manhood from a man. I perceived pretty clearly that I had not the stamina either to resist what the captain chose to do to expel me, or to force myself upon Montgomery and his companion. So I waited passively upon fate, and the work of transferring Montgomery's possessions to the launch went on as if I did not exist.

Presently that work was finished, and then came a struggle; I was hauled, resisting weakly enough, to the gangway. Even then I noticed the oddness of the brown faces of the men who were with Montgomery in the launch. But the launch was now fully laden, and was shoved off hastily. A broadening gap of green water appeared under me, and I pushed back with all my strength to avoid falling headlong.

The hands in the launch shouted derisively, and I heard Montgomery curse at them. And then the captain, the mate and one of the seamen helping him, ran me aft towards the stern. The dingey of the *Lady Vain* had been towing behind; it was half full of water, had no oars, and was quite unvictualled. I refused to go aboard her, and flung myself full-length on the deck. In the end they swung me into her by a rope—for they had no stern ladder—and then they cut me adrift.

I drifted slowly from the schooner. In a kind of stupor I watched all hands take to the rigging, and slowly but surely she came round to the wind. The sails fluttered, and then bellied out as the wind came into them. I stared at her weather-beaten side heeling steeply towards me. And then she passed out of my range of view.

I did not turn my head to follow her. At first I could scarcely believe what had happened. I crouched in the bottom of the dingey, stunned, and staring blankly at the vacant oily sea. Then I realised I was in that little hell of mine again, now half-swamped. Looking back over the gunwale I saw the schooner standing away from me, with the red-haired captain mocking at me over the taffrail; and, turning towards the island, saw the launch growing smaller as she approached the beach.

Abruptly the cruelty of this desertion became clear to me. I had no means of reaching the land unless I should chance to drift there. I was still weak, you must remember, from my exposure in the boat; I was empty and very faint, or I should have had more heart. But as it was I suddenly began to sob and weep as I had never done since I was a little child. The tears ran down my face. In a passion of despair I struck with my fists at the water in the bottom of the boat, and kicked savagely at the gunwale. I prayed aloud to God that he would let me die. *desolate* (D)

VI

The Evil-Looking Boatmen

But the islanders, seeing I was really adrift, took pity on me. I drifted very slowly to the eastward, approaching the island slantingly, and presently I saw with hysterical relief the launch come round and return towards me. She was heavily laden, and as she drew near I could make out Montgomery's white-haired broad-shouldered companion sitting cramped up with the dogs and several packing-cases in the stern sheets. This individual stared fixedly at me without moving or speaking. The black-faced cripple was glaring at me as fixedly in the bows near the puma. There were three other men besides, strange brutish-looking fellows, at whom the staghounds were snarling savagely. Montgomery, who was steering, brought the boat by me, and, rising, caught and fastened my painter to the tiller to tow me — for there was no room aboard.

I had recovered from my hysterical phase by this time, and answered his hail as he approached bravely enough. I told him the dingey was nearly swamped, and he reached me a piggin.[13] I was jerked back as the rope tightened between the boats. For some time I was busy bailing.

It was not until I had got the water under — for the water in the dingey had been shipped, the boat was perfectly sound — that I had leisure to look at the people in the launch again.

The white-haired man, I found, was still regarding me steadfastly, but with an expression, as I now fancied, of some perplexity. When my eyes met his he looked down at the staghound that sat between his knees. He was a powerfully built man, as I have said, with a fine forehead and rather heavy features; but his eyes had that odd drooping of the skin above the lids that often comes with advancing years, and the fall of his heavy mouth at the corners gave him an expression of pugnacious resolution. He talked to Montgomery in a tone too low for me to hear. From him my eyes travelled

---

[13] A small vessel usually used for drinking. [Ed.]

to his three men, and a strange crew they were. I saw only their faces, yet there was something in their faces—I knew not what—that gave me a queer spasm of disgust. I looked steadily at them, and the impression did not pass, though I failed to see what had occasioned it.

They seemed to me then to be brown men, but their limbs were oddly swathed in some thin dirty white stuff down even to the fingers and feet. I have never seen men so wrapped up before, and women so only in the East. They wore turbans too, and thereunder peered out their elfin faces at me, faces with protruding lower jaws and bright eyes. They had lank black hair, almost like horse-hair, and seemed, as they sat, to exceed in stature any race of men I have seen. The white-haired man, who I knew was a good six feet in height, sat a head below any one of the three.

I found afterwards that really none were taller than myself, but their bodies were abnormally long, and the thigh-part of the leg short and curiously twisted. At any rate they were an amazingly ugly gang, and over the heads of them, under the forward lug, peered the black face of the man whose eyes were luminous in the dark.

As I started at them they met my gaze, and then first one and then another turned away from my direct stare and looked at me in an odd furtive manner. It occurred to me that I was perhaps annoying them, and I turned my attention to the island we were approaching.

It was low, and covered with thick vegetation, chiefly a kind of palm that was new to me. From one point a thin white thread of vapour rose slantingly to an immense height, and then frayed out like a down feather. We were now within the embrace of a broad bay flanked on either hand by a low promontory. The beach was of dull grey sand, and sloped steeply up to a ridge, perhaps sixty or seventy feet above the sea-level, and irregularly set with trees and undergrowth. Half-way up was a square pie-bald stone enclosure that I found subsequently was built partly of coral and partly of pumiceous lava. Two thatched roofs peeped from within this enclosure.

A man stood awaiting us at the water's edge. I fancied, while we were still far off, that I saw some other and very grotesque-looking creatures scuttle into the bushes upon the slope, but I saw nothing of these as we drew nearer. This man was of a moderate size, and with a black negroid face. He had a large, almost lipless mouth, extraordinary lank arms, long thin feet and bow legs, and stood with his heavy face thrust forward staring at us. He was dressed like Montgomery and his white-haired companion, in jacket and trousers of blue serge.

As we came still nearer, this individual began to run to and fro on the beach, making the most grotesque movements. At a word of command from Montgomery the four men in the launch sprang up with singular awkward gestures and struck the lugs. Montgomery steered us round and into a narrow little dock excavated in the beach. Then the man on the beach hastened towards us. This dock, as I call it, was really a mere ditch just long enough at this phase of the tide to take the long-boat.

I heard the bows ground in the sand, staved the dingey off the rudder of the big boat with my piggin, and, freeing the painter, landed. The three muffled men, with the clumsiest movements, scrambled out upon the sand, and forthwith set to landing the cargo, assisted by the man on the beach. I was struck especially with the curious movements of the legs of the three swathed and bandaged boatmen—not stiff they were, but distorted in some odd way, almost as if they were jointed in the wrong place. The dogs were still snarling, and strained at their chains after these men, as the white-haired man landed with them.

The three big fellows spoke to one another in odd guttural tones, and the man, who had waited for us on the beach, began chattering to them excitedly—a foreign language, as I fancied—as they laid hands on some bales piled near the stern. Somewhere I had heard such a voice before, and I could not think where. The white-haired man stood holding in a tumult of six dogs, and bawling orders over their din. Montgomery, having unshipped the rudder, landed likewise, and all set to work at unloading. I was too faint, what with my long fast and the sun beating down on my bare head, to offer any assistance.

Presently the white-haired man seemed to recollect my presence, and came up to me.

'You look,' said he, 'as though you had scarcely breakfasted.'

His little eyes were a brilliant black under his heavy brows.

'I must apologise for that. Now you are our guest, we must make you comfortable—though you are uninvited, you know.'

He looked keenly into my face.

'Montgomery says you are an educated man, Mr. Prendick—says you know something of science. May I ask what that signifies?'

I told him I had spent some years at the Royal College of Science, and had done some research in biology under Huxley.[14] He raised his eyebrows slightly at that.

'That alters the case a little, Mr. Prendick,' he said, with a trifle more respect in his manner. 'As it happens, we are biologists here. This is a biological station—of a sort.' His eye rested on the men in white, who were busily hauling the puma, on rollers, towards the walled yard. 'I and Montgomery, at least,' he added.

---

[14] Wells attended the Royal College of Science, then called the Normal School of Science, in 1884 and studied for a year under Thomas Henry Huxley. See the Introduction. [Ed.]

Then:

'When you will be able to get away, I can't say. We're off the track to anywhere. We see a ship once in a twelvemonth or so.'

He left me abruptly and went up the beach past this group, and, I think,
entered the enclosure. The other two men were with Montgomery erecting
a pile of smaller packages on a low wheeled truck. The llama was still on the
launch with the rabbit-hutches; the staghounds still lashed to the thwarts.
The pile of things completed, all three men laid hold of the truck and began shoving the ton-weight or so upon it after the puma. Presently Montgomery left them, and coming back to me, held out his hand.

'I'm glad,' said he, 'for my own part. That captain was a silly ass. He'd
have made things lively for you.'

'It was you,' said I, 'that saved me again.'

'That depends. You'll find this island an infernally rum place, I promise
you. I'd watch my goings carefully if I were you. *He—*' He hesitated, and
seemed to alter his mind about what was on his lips. 'I wish you'd help me
with these rabbits,' he said.

His procedure with the rabbits was singular. I waded in with him and
helped him lug one of the hutches ashore. No sooner was that done than
he opened the door of it, and tilting the thing on one end, turned its living
contents out on the ground. They fell in a struggling heap one on the top
of the other. He clapped his hands, and forthwith they went off with that
hopping run of theirs, fifteen or twenty of them, I should think, up the
beach. 'Increase and multiply, my friends,' said Montgomery. 'Replenish
the island. Hitherto we've had a certain lack of meat here.' *cruel*

As I watched them disappearing, the white-haired man returned with a
brandy flask and some biscuits. 'Something to go on with, Prendick,' said
he in a far more familiar tone than before.

I made no ado, but set to work on the biscuits at once, while the white-
haired man helped Montgomery to release about a score more of the rabbits. Three big hutches, however, went up to the house with the puma. The
brandy I did not touch, for I have been an abstainer from my birth.

credible

VII
The Locked Door

The reader will perhaps understand that at first everything was so strange
about me, and my position was the outcome of such unexpected adventures,
that I had no discernment of the relative strangeness of this or that thing

about me. I followed the llama up the beach, and was overtaken by Montgomery, who asked me not to enter the stone enclosure. I noticed then that the puma in its cage and the pile of packages, had been placed outside the entrance to this quadrangle.

I turned and saw that the launch had now been unloaded, run out again, and was being beached, and the white-haired man was walking towards us. He addressed Montgomery.

'And now comes the problem of this uninvited guest. What are we to do with him?'

'He knows something of science,' said Montgomery.

'I'm itching to get to work again—with this new stuff,' said the grey-haired man, nodding towards the enclosure. His eyes grew brighter.

'I daresay you are,' said Montgomery, in anything but a cordial tone.

'We can't send him over there, and we can't spare the time to build him a new shanty. And we certainly can't take him into our confidence just yet.'

'I'm in your hands,' said I. I had no idea of what he meant by 'over there.'

'I've been thinking of the same things,' Montgomery answered. 'There's my room with the outer door—'

'That's it,' said the elder man promptly, looking at Montgomery, and all three of us went towards the enclosure. 'I'm sorry to make a mystery, Mr. Prendick—but you'll remember you're uninvited. Our little establishment here contains a secret or so, is a kind of Bluebeard's Chamber, in fact. Nothing very dreadful really—to a sane man. But just now—as we don't know you—'

'Decidedly,' said I; 'I should be a fool to take offence at any want of confidence.'

He twisted his heavy mouth into a faint smile—he was one of those saturnine people who smile with the corners of the mouth down,—and bowed his acknowledgment of my complaisance. The main entrance to the enclosure we passed; it was a heavy wooden gate, framed in iron and locked, with the cargo of the launch piled outside it; and at the corner we came to a small doorway I had not previously observed. The grey-haired man produced a bundle of keys from the pocket of his greasy blue jacket, opened this door, and entered. His keys and the elaborate locking up of the place, even while it was still under his eye, struck me as peculiar.

I followed him, and found myself in a small apartment, plainly but not uncomfortably furnished, and with its inner door, which was slightly ajar, opening into a paved courtyard. This inner door Montgomery at once closed. A hammock was slung across the darker corner of the room, and a small unglazed window, defended by an iron bar, looked out towards the sea.

This, the grey-haired man told me, was to be my apartment, and the inner door, which, 'for fear of accidents,' he said, he would lock on the other side, was my limit inward. He called my attention to a convenient deck-chair before the window, and to an array of old books, chiefly I found, surgical works and editions of the Latin and Greek classics—languages I cannot read with any comfort—on a shelf near the hammock. He left the room by the outer door, as if to avoid opening the inner one again.

'We usually have our meals in here,' said Montgomery, and then, as if in doubt, went out after the other. 'Moreau,' I heard him call, and for the moment I do not think I noticed. Then as I handled the books on the shelf it came up in consciousness: where had I heard the name of Moreau before?

I sat down before the window, took out the biscuits that still remained to me, and ate them with an excellent appetite.

'Moreau?'

Through the window I saw one of those unaccountable men in white lugging a packing-case along the beach. Presently the window-frame hid him. Then I heard a key inserted and turned in the lock behind me. After a little while I heard, through the locked door, the noise of the staghounds, which had now been brought up from the beach. They were not barking, but sniffing and growling in a curious fashion. I could hear the rapid patter of their feet, and Montgomery's voice soothing them.

I was very much impressed by the elaborate secrecy of these two men regarding the contents of the place, and for some time I was thinking of that, and of the unaccountable familiarity of the name of Moreau. But so odd is the human memory, that I could not then recall that well-known name in its proper connection. From that my thoughts went to the indefinable queerness of the deformed and white-swathed man on the beach.

I never saw such a gait, such odd motions, as he pulled at the box. I recalled that none of these men had spoken to me, though most of them I had found looking at me at one time or another in a peculiar furtive manner, quite unlike the frank stare of your unsophisticated savage. I wondered what language they spoke. They had all seemed remarkably taciturn, and when they did speak, endowed with very uncanny voices. What was wrong with them? Then I recalled the eyes of Montgomery's ungainly attendant.

Just as I was thinking of him, he came in. He was now dressed in white, and carried a little tray with some coffee and boiled vegetables thereon. I could hardly repress a shuddering recoil as he came, bending amiably, and placed the tray before me on the table.

Then astonishment paralysed me. Under his stringy black locks I saw his ear! It jumped upon me suddenly, close to my face. The man had pointed ears, covered with a fine brown fur! [15]

'Your breakfast, sair,' he said.

I stared at his face without attempting to answer him. He turned and went towards the door, regarding me oddly over his shoulder.

I followed him out with my eyes, and as I did so, by some trick of unconscious cerebration, there came surging into my head the phrase: 'The Moreau — Hollows' was it? 'The Moreau —?' Ah! it sent my memory back ten years. 'The Moreau Horrors.' The phrase drifted loose in my mind for a moment, and then I saw it in red lettering on a little buff-coloured pamphlet, that to read made one shiver and creep. Then I remembered distinctly all about it. That long-forgotten pamphlet came back with startling vividness to my mind. I had been a mere lad then, and Moreau was, I suppose, about fifty; a prominent and masterful physiologist, well known in scientific circles for his extraordinary imagination and his brutal directness in discussion.

Was this the same Moreau? He had published some very astonishing facts in connection with the transfusion of blood, and, in addition, was known to be doing valuable work on morbid growths. Then suddenly his career was closed. He had to leave England. A journalist obtained access to his laboratory in the capacity of laboratory assistant, with the deliberate intention of making sensational exposures; and by the help of a shocking accident — if it was an accident — his gruesome pamphlet became notorious. On the day of its publication, a wretched dog, flayed and otherwise mutilated, escaped from Moreau's house. [16]

It was in the silly season, and a prominent editor, a cousin of the temporary laboratory assistant, appealed to the conscience of the nation. It

---

[15] In the first chapter of *The Descent of Man* the "little blunt point projecting from the inwardly folding margin or helix" of the human ear forms one of the illustrations of Darwin's opening argument, that "the bodily structure of man shows traces, more or less plain, of his descent from lower forms" of mammals with pointed ears (*Descent,* 15, 6). [Ed.]

[16] The Cruelty to Animals Act passed in England in 1876 was, at the time of Wells's novel, the only legal restriction in the world against the experimental use of animals. The man behind the figure of the "archvivisector" treated in several English novels of the 1880s and 1890s, including *The Island of Doctor Moreau,* was the French physiologist Claude Bernard, whose *Introduction to the Study of Experimental Medicine* (1865) included the self-satisfied simile for physiological experimentation much quoted in antivivisection literature: "it was [like] a superb hall, glittering with light, to which the only entrance is through a long and horrible kitchen" (quoted in Lansbury, 160; see Part Three, Contemporary Views). [Ed.]

was not the first time that conscience has turned against the methods of research. The doctor was simply howled out of the country. It may be he deserved to be, but I still think the tepid support of his fellow-investigators,
and his desertion by the great body of scientific workers, was a shameful
thing. Yet some of his experiments, by the journalist's account, were wantonly cruel. He might perhaps have purchased his social peace by aban-
doning his investigations, but he apparently preferred the latter, as most
men would who have once fallen under the overmastering spell of research. He was unmarried, and had indeed nothing but his own interests
to consider. . . .

I felt convinced that this must be the same man. Everything pointed to
it. It dawned upon me to what end the puma and the other animals, which
had now been brought with other luggage into the enclosure behind the
house, were destined; and a curious faint odour, the halitus of something
familiar, an odour that had been in the background of my consciousness hither-to, suddenly came forward into the forefront of my thoughts.
It was the antiseptic odour of the operating-room. I heard the puma growling through the wall, and one of the dogs yelped as though it had been
struck.

Yet surely, and especially to another scientific man, there was nothing so
horrible in vivisection as to account for this secrecy. And by some odd leap
in my thoughts the pointed ears and luminous eyes of Montgomery's attendant came back again before me with the sharpest definition. I stared
before me out at the green sea, frothing under a freshening breeze, and let
these and other strange memories of the last few days chase each other
through my mind.

What could it mean? A locked enclosure on a lonely island, a notorious
vivisector, and these crippled and distorted men? . . .

VIII
The Crying of the Puma

Montgomery interrupted my tangle of mystification and suspicion about
one, and his grotesque attendant followed him with a tray bearing bread,
some herbs, and other eatables, a flask of whisky, a jug of water, and three
glasses and knives. I glanced askance at this strange creature, and found
him watching me with his queer restless eyes. Montgomery said he would
lunch with me, but that Moreau was too pre-occupied with some work
to come.

'Moreau!' said I, 'I know that name.'

'The devil you do!' said he. 'What an ass I was to mention it to you. I might have thought. Anyhow, it will give you an inkling of our—mysteries. Whisky?'

'No thanks—I'm an abstainer.'

'I wish I'd been. But it's no use locking the door after the steed is stolen. It was that infernal stuff led to my coming here. That and a foggy night. I thought myself in luck at the time when Moreau offered to get me off. It's queer. . . .'

'Montgomery,' said I suddenly, as the outer door closed; 'why has your man pointed ears?'

'Damn!' he said, over his first mouthful of food. He stared at me for a moment, and then repeated, 'Pointed ears?'

'Little points to them,' said I, as calmly as possible, with a catch in my breath; 'and a fine black fur at the edges.'

He helped himself to whisky and water with great deliberation.

'I was under the impression . . . that his hair covered his ears.'

'I saw them as he stooped by me to put that coffee you sent to me on the table. And his eyes shine in the dark.'

By this time Montgomery had recovered from the surprise of my question.

'I always thought,' he said deliberately, with a certain accentuation of his flavouring of lisp; 'that there *was* something the matter with his ears. From the way he covered them. . . . What were they like?'

I was persuaded from his manner that this ignorance was a pretence. Still I could hardly tell the man I thought him a liar.

'Pointed,' I said; 'rather small and furry—distinctly furry. But the whole man is one of the strangest beings I ever set eyes on.'

A sharp, hoarse cry of animal pain came from the enclosure behind us. Its depth and volume testified to the puma. I saw Montgomery wince.

'Yes?' he said.

'Where did you pick the creature up?'

'Er—San Francisco. . . . He's an ugly brute, I admit. Half-witted, you know. Can't remember where he came from. But I'm used to him, you know. We both are. How does he strike you?'

'He's unnatural,' I said, 'There's something about him. . . . Don't think me fanciful, but it gives me a nasty little sensation, a tightening of my muscles, when he comes near me. It's a touch . . . of the diabolical, in fact.'

Montgomery had stopped eating while I told him this.

'Rum,' he said. '*I* can't see it.'

He resumed his meal.

'I had no idea of it,' he said, and masticated. 'The crew of the schooner ... must have felt it the same. . . . Made a dead set at the poor devil. . . . You saw the captain?'

Suddenly the puma howled again, this time more painfully. Montgomery swore under his breath. I had half a mind to attack him about the men on the beach. Then the poor brute within gave vent to a series of short, sharp screams.

'Your men on the beach,' said I; 'what race are they?'

'Excellent fellows, aren't they?' said he absent-mindedly, knitting his brows as the animal yelled out sharply.

I said no more. There was another outcry worse than the former. He looked at me with his dull grey eyes, and then took some more whisky. He tried to draw me into a discussion about alcohol, professing to have saved my life with it. He seemed anxious to lay stress on the fact that I owed my life to him. I answered him distractedly.

Presently our meal came to an end, the misshapen monster with the pointed ears cleared away, and Montgomery left me alone in the room again. All the time he was in a state of ill-concealed irritation at the noise of the vivisected puma. He spoke of his odd want of nerve, and left me to the obvious application.

I found myself that the cries were singularly irritating, and they grew in depth and intensity as the afternoon wore on. They were painful at first, but their constant resurgence at last altogether upset my balance. I flung aside a crib of Horace[17] I had been reading, and began to clench my fist, to bite my lips, and pace the room.

Presently I got to stopping my ears with my fingers.

The emotional appeal of those yells grew upon me steadily, grew at last to such an exquisite expression of suffering that I could stand it in that confined room no longer. I stepped out of the door into the slumberous heat of the late afternoon, and walking past the main entrance—locked again I noticed—turned the corner of the wall.

The crying sounded even louder out of doors. It was as if all the pain in the world had found a voice. Yet had I known such pain was in the next room, and had it been dumb, I believe—I have thought since—I could have stood it well enough. It is when suffering finds a voice and sets our nerves quivering that this pity comes troubling us. But in spite of the brilliant sunlight and the green fans of the trees waving in the soothing sea-breeze, the world was a confusion, blurred with drifting black and red phantasms, until I was out of earshot of the house in the chequered wall.

---

[17] Horace (65–68 BC), Roman poet of a stoic philosophy. [Ed.]

IX

The Thing in the Forest

I strode through the undergrowth that clothed the ridge behind the house, scarcely heeding whither I went, passing on through the shadow of a thick cluster of straight-stemmed trees beyond it, and so presently found myself some way on the other side of the ridge, and descending towards a stream-let that ran through a narrow valley. I paused and listened. The distance I had come, or the intervening masses of thicket, deadened any sound that might be coming from the enclosure. The air was still. Then with a rustle a rabbit emerged, and went scampering up the slope before me. I hesitated, and sat down in the edge of the shade.

The place was a pleasant one. The rivulet was hidden by the luxuriant vegetation of the banks, save at one point, where I caught a triangular patch of its glittering water. On the farther side I saw, through a bluish haze, a tangle of trees and creepers, and above these again the luminous blue of the sky. Here and there a splash of white or crimson marked the blooming of some trailing epiphyte.[18] I let my eyes wander over this scene for a while, and then began to turn over in my mind again the strange peculiarities of Montgomery's man. But it was too hot to think elaborately, and presently I fell into a tranquil state midway between dozing and waking.

From this I was aroused, after I know not how long, by a rustling amidst the greenery on the other side of the stream. For a moment I could see nothing but the waving summits of the ferns and reeds. Then suddenly upon the bank of the stream appeared something—at first I could not distinguish what it was. It bowed its head to the water and began to drink. Then I saw it was a man, going on all-fours like a beast!

He was clothed in bluish cloth, and was of a copper-coloured hue, with black hair. It seemed that grotesque ugliness was an invariable character of these islanders. I could hear the suck of the water at his lips as he drank.

I leant forward to see him better, and a piece of lava, detached by my hand, went pattering down the slope. He looked up guiltily, and his eyes met mine. Forthwith he scrambled to his feet and stood wiping his clumsy hand across his mouth and regarding me. His legs were scarcely half the length of his body. So, staring one another out of countenance, we remained for

---

[18]According to Stover, nature offers more than a splash of color here. In the Indo-European color code, blue represents subjected labor; red, naked force; and white, not surprisingly, rule. The island folk will be dressed accordingly (Stover 96). An epiphyte is a plant supported physically on another plant but taking its nourishment directly from the air. [Ed.]

perhaps the space of a minute. Then, stopping to look back once or twice, he slunk off among the bushes to the right of me, and I heard the swish of the fronds grow faint in the distance and die away. Every now and then he regarded me with a steadfast stare. Long after he had disappeared I remained sitting up staring in the direction of his retreat. My drowsy tranquility had gone.

I was startled by a noise behind me, and, turning suddenly, saw the flapping white tail of a rabbit vanishing up the slope. I jumped to my feet.

The apparition of this grotesque half-bestial creature had suddenly populated the stillness of the afternoon for me. I looked around me rather nervously, and regretted that I was unarmed. Then I thought that the man I had just seen had been clothed in bluish cloth, had not been naked as a savage would have been, and I tried to persuade myself from that fact that he was after all probably a peaceful character, that the dull ferocity of his countenance belied him.

Yet I was greatly disturbed at the apparition. I walked to the left along the slope, turning my head about and peering this way and that among the straight stems of the trees. Why should a man go on all-fours and drink with his lips? Presently I heard an animal wailing again, and taking it to be the puma, I turned about and walked in a direction diametrically opposite to the sound. This led me down to the stream, across which I stepped and pushed my way up through the under-growth beyond.

I was startled by a great patch of vivid scarlet on the ground, and going up to it found it to be a peculiar fungus branched and corrugated like a foliaceous lichen, but deliquescing into slime at the touch. And then in the shadow of some luxuriant ferns I came upon an unpleasant thing, the dead body of a rabbit, covered with shining flies, but still warm, and with the head torn off. I stopped aghast at the sight of the scattered blood. Here at least was one visitor to the island disposed of!

There were no traces of other violence about it. It looked as though it had been suddenly snatched up and killed. And as I stared at the little furry body came the difficulty of how the thing had been done. The vague dread that had been in my mind since I had seen the inhuman face of the man at the stream grew distincter as I stood there. I began to realize the hardihood of my expedition among these unknown people. The thicket about me became altered to my imagination. Every shadow became something more than a shadow, became an ambush, every rustle became a threat. Invisible things seemed watching me. *Scared*

I resolved to go back to the enclosure on the beach. I suddenly turned away and thrust myself violently—possibly even frantically—through the bushes, anxious to get a clear space about me again.

I stopped just in time to prevent myself emerging upon an open space. It was a kind of glade in the forest made by a fall; seedlings were already starting up to struggle for the vacant space, and beyond, the dense growth of stems and twining vines and splashes of fungus and flowers closed in again. Before me, squatting together upon the fungoid ruins of a huge fallen tree, and still unaware of my approach, were three grotesque human figures. One was evidently a female. The other two were men. They were naked, save for swathings of scarlet cloth about the middles, and their skins were of a dull pinkish drab colour, such as I had seen in no savages before. They had fat heavy chinless faces, retreating foreheads, and a scant bristly hair upon their heads. Never before had I seen such bestial-looking creatures.

They were talking, or at least one of the men was talking to the other two, and all three had been too closely interested to heed the rustling of my approach. They swayed their heads and shoulders from side to side. The speaker's words came thick and sloppy, and though I could hear them distinctly I could not distinguish what he said. He seemed to me to be reciting some complicated gibberish. Presently his articulation became shriller, and spreading his hands he rose to his feet.

At that the others began to gibber in unison, also rising to their feet, spreading their hands, and swaying their bodies in rhythm with their chant. I noticed then the abnormal shortness of their legs and their lank clumsy feet. All three began slowly to circle round, raising and stamping their feet and waving their arms; a kind of tune crept into their rhythmic recitation, and a refrain—'Aloola' or 'Baloola' it sounded like.[19] Their eyes began to sparkle and their ugly faces to brighten with an expression of strange pleasure. Saliva dropped from their lipless mouths.

Suddenly, as I watched their grotesque and unaccountable gestures, I perceived clearly for the first time what it was that had offended me, what had given me the two inconsistent and conflicting impressions of utter strangeness and yet of the strangest familiarity. The three creatures engaged in this mysterious rite were human in shape, and yet human beings with the strangest air about them of some familiar animal. Each of these creatures, despite its human form, its rag of clothing, and the rough humanity of its bodily form, had woven into it, into its movements, into the expression of its countenance, into its whole presence, some now irresistible suggestion of a hog, a swinish taint, the unmistakable mark of the beast.

I stood overcome by this amazing realization, and then the most horrible questionings came rushing into my mind. They began leaping into the air,

---

[19] "Degenerated" vocalizing of the "alleluia" in a dim repetition of lessons in Christian hymn singing. [Ed.]

first one and then the other, whooping and grunting. Then one slipped, and for a moment was on all-fours, to recover indeed forthwith. But that transitory gleam of the true animalism of these monsters was enough.

I turned as noiselessly as possible, and becoming every now and then rigid with the fear of being discovered as a branch cracked or leaf rustled, I pushed back into the bushes. It was long before I grew bolder and dared to move freely.

My one idea for the moment was to get away from these foul beings, and I scarcely noticed that I had emerged upon a faint pathway amidst the trees. Then, suddenly traversing a little glade, I saw with an unpleasant start two clumsy legs among the trees, walking with noiseless footsteps parallel with my course, and perhaps thirty yards away from me. The head and upper part of the body were hidden by a tangle of creeper. I stopped abruptly, hoping the creature did not see me. The feet stopped as I did. So nervous was I that I controlled an impulse to headlong flight with the utmost difficulty.

Then, looking hard, I distinguished through the interlacing network the head and body of the brute I had seen drinking. He moved his head. There was an emerald flash in his eyes as he glanced at me from the shadow of the trees, a half-luminous colour, that vanished as he turned his head again. He was motionless for a moment, and then with noiseless tread began running through the green confusion. In another moment he had vanished behind some bushes. I could not see him, but I felt that he had stopped and was watching me again.

What on earth was he — man or animal? What did he want with me? I had no weapon, not even a stick. Flight would be madness. At any rate, the Thing, whatever it was, lacked the courage to attack me. Setting my teeth hard I walked straight towards him. I was anxious not to show the fear that seemed chilling my backbone. I pushed through a tangle of tall white-flowered bushes, and saw him twenty yards beyond, looking over his shoulder at me and hesitating. I advanced a step or two looking steadfastly into his eyes.

'Who are you?' said I.

He tried to meet my gaze.

'No!' he said suddenly, and, turning, went bounding away from me through the undergrowth. Then he turned and stared at me again. His eyes shone brightly out of the dusk under the trees.

My heart was in my mouth, but I felt my only chance was bluff, and walked steadily towards him. He turned again and vanished into the dusk. Once more I thought I caught the glint of his eyes, and that was all.

For the first time I realized how the lateness of the hour might affect me. The sun had set some minutes since, the swift dusk of the tropics was already fading out of the eastern sky, and a pioneer moth fluttered silently by my head. Unless I would spend the night among the unknown dangers of the mysterious forest, I must hasten back to the enclosure.

The thought of a return to that pain-haunted refuge was extremely disagreeable, but still more so was the idea of being overtaken in the open by darkness, and all that darkness might conceal. I gave one more look into the blue shadows that had swallowed up this odd creature, and then retraced my way down the slope towards the stream, going as I judged in the direction from which I had come.

I walked eagerly, perplexed by all these things, and presently found myself in a level place among scattered trees. The colourless clearness that comes after the sunset flush was darkling. The blue sky above grew momentarily deeper, and the little stars one by one pierced the attenuated light; the interspaces of the trees, the gaps in the farther vegetation, that had been hazy blue in the daylight, grew black and mysterious.

I pushed on. The colour vanished from the world, the tree-tops rose against the luminous blue sky in inky silhouette, and all below that outline melted into one formless blackness. Presently the trees grew thinner, and the shrubby undergrowth more abundant. Then there was a desolate space covered with white sand, and then another expanse of tangled bushes.

I was tormented by a faint rustling upon my right hand. I thought at first it was fancy, for whenever I stopped, there was silence, save for the evening breeze in the tree-tops. Then when I went on again there was an echo to my footsteps.

I moved away from the thickets, keeping to the more open ground, and endeavouring by sudden turns now and then to surprise this thing, if it existed, in the act of creeping upon me. I saw nothing, and nevertheless my sense of another presence grew steadily. I increased my pace, and after some time came to a slight ridge, crossed it and turned sharply, regarding it steadfastly from the farther side. It came out black and clear-cut against the darkling sky.

And presently a shapeless lump heaved up momentarily against the skyline and vanished again. I felt assured now that my tawny-faced antagonist was stalking me again. And coupled with that was another unpleasant realization that I had lost my way.

For a time I hurried on hopelessly perplexed, pursued by that stealthy approach. Whatever it was, the thing either lacked the courage to attack me, or it was waiting to take me at some disadvantage. I kept studiously to the open. At times I would turn and listen, and presently I half-persuaded myself that my pursuer had abandoned the chase, or was a mere creation of my disordered imagination. Then I heard the sound of the sea. I quickened my footsteps almost to a run, and immediately there was a stumble in my rear.

I turned suddenly and stared at the uncertain trees behind me. One black shadow seemed to leap into another. I listened rigid, and heard nothing but the creep of the blood in my ears. I thought that my nerves were unstrung, and that my imagination was tricking me, and turned resolutely towards the sound of the sea again.

In a minute or so the trees grew thinner, and I emerged upon a bare low headland running out into the somber water. The night was calm and clear, and the reflection of the growing multitude of the stars shivered in the tranquil heaving of the sea. Some way out, the wash upon an irregular band of reef shone with a pallid light of its own. Westward I saw the zodiacal light mingling with the yellow brilliance of the evening star. The coast fell away from me to the east, and westward it was hidden by the shoulder of the cape. Then I recalled the fact that Moreau's beach lay to the west.

A twig snapped behind me and there was a rustle. I turned and stood facing the dark trees. I could see nothing—or else I could see too much. Every dark form in the dimness had its ominous quality, its peculiar suggestion of alert watchfulness. So I stood for perhaps a minute, and then, with an eye to the trees still, turned westward to cross the headland. And as I moved, one among the lurking shadows moved to follow me.

My heart beat quickly. Presently the broad sweep of a bay to the westward became visible, and I halted again. The noiseless shadow halted a dozen yards from me. A little point of light shone on the further bend of the curve, and the grey sweep of the sandy beach lay faint under the starlight. Perhaps two miles away was that little point of light. To get to the beach I should have to go through the trees where the shadows lurked, and down a bushy slope.

I could see the thing rather more distinctly now. It was no animal, for it stood erect. At that I opened my mouth to speak, and found a hoarse phlegm choked my voice. I tried again, and shouted,

'Who is there?'

There was no answer. I advanced a step. The thing did not move; only gathered itself together. My foot struck a stone.

That gave me an idea. Without taking my eyes off the black form before me I stooped and picked up this lump of rock. But at my motion the thing turned abruptly as a dog might have done, and slunk obliquely into the farther darkness. Then I recalled a schoolboy expedient against big dogs, twisted the rock into my handkerchief, and gave this a turn round my wrist. I heard a movement farther off among the shadows as if the thing was in retreat. Then suddenly my tense excitement gave way; I broke into a profuse perspiration and fell a-trembling, with my adversary routed and this weapon in my hand.

It was some time before I could summon resolution to go down through the trees and bushes upon the flank of the headland to the beach. At last I did it at a run, and as I emerged from the thicket upon the sand I heard some other body come crashing after me.

At that I completely lost my head with fear, and began running along the sand. Forthwith there came the swift patter of soft feet in pursuit. I gave a wild cry and redoubled my pace. Some dim black things about three or four times the size of rabbits went running or hopping up from the beach towards the bushes as I passed. So long as I live I shall remember the terror of that chase. I ran near the water's edge, and heard every now and then the splash of the feet that gained upon me. Far away, hopelessly far, was the yellow light. All the night about us was black and still. Splash, splash came the pursuing feet nearer and nearer. I felt my breath going, for I was quite out of training; it whooped as I drew it, and I felt a pain like a knife at my side. I perceived the thing would come up with me long before I reached the enclosure, and, desperate and sobbing for breath, I wheeled round upon it and struck at it as it came up to me — struck with all my strength. The stone came out of the sling of the handkerchief as I did so.

As I turned, the thing, which had been running on all-fours, rose to its feet, and the missile fell fair on its left temple. The skull rang loud and the animal-man blundered into me, thrust me back with its hands, and went staggering past me to fall headlong upon the sand with its face in the water. And there it lay still.

I could not bring myself to approach that black heap. I left it there with the water rippling round it under the still stars, and, giving it a wide berth, pursued my way towards the yellow glow of the house. And presently, with a positive effect of relief, came the pitiful moaning of the puma, the sound that had originally driven me out to explore this mysterious island. At that, though I was faint and horribly fatigued, I gathered together all my strength, and began running again towards the light. It seemed to me a voice was calling me.

X
The Crying of the Man

As I drew near the house I saw that the light shone from the open door of my room; and then I heard, coming from out the darkness at the side of that orange oblong, the voice of Montgomery shouting 'Prendick.'

I continued running. Presently I heard him again. I replied by a feeble 'Hullo!' and in another moment had staggered up to him.

'Where have you been?' said he, holding me at arm's-length, so that the light from the door fell on my face. 'We have both been so busy that we forgot you until about half an hour ago.'

He led me into the room and sat me down in the deck chair. For a while I was blinded by the light.

'We did not think you would start to explore this island of ours without telling us,' he said. And then, 'I was afraid! But . . . what . . . Hullo!'

For my last remaining strength slipped from me, and my head fell forward on my chest. I think he found a certain satisfaction in giving me brandy.

'For God's sake,' said I, 'fasten that door.'

'You've been meeting some of our curiosities, eh?' said he.

He locked the door and turned to me again. He asked me no questions, but gave me some more brandy and water, and pressed me to eat. I was in a state of collapse. He said something vague about his forgetting to warn me, and asked me briefly when I left the house and what I had seen. I answered him as briefly in fragmentary sentences.

'Tell me what it all means,' said I, in a state bordering on hysterics.

'It's nothing so very dreadful,' said he. 'But I think you have had about enough for one day.' The puma suddenly gave a sharp yell of pain. At that he swore under his breath. 'I'm damned,' said he, 'if this place is not as bad as Gower Street—with its cats.'

'Montgomery,' said I, 'what was that thing that came after me. Was it a beast, or was it a man?'

'If you don't sleep to-night,' he said, 'you'll be off your head to-morrow.'

I stood up in front of him.

'What was that thing that came after me?' I asked.

He looked me squarely in the eyes and twisted his mouth askew. His eyes, which had seemed animated a minute before, went dull.

'From your account,' said he, 'I'm thinking it was a bogle.'[20]

I felt a gust of intense irritation that passed as quickly as it came. I flung myself into the chair again and pressed my hands on my forehead. The puma began again.

Montgomery came round behind me and put his hand on my shoulder.

'Look here, Prendick,' he said, 'I had no business to let you drift out into this silly island of ours. But it's not so bad as you feel, man. Your nerves are worked to rags. Let me give you something that will make you sleep. *That* . . . will keep on for hours yet. You must simply get to sleep, or I won't answer for it.'

---

[20] Northern British dialect for a "ghost" or "goblin." [Ed.]

I did not reply. I bowed forward and covered my face with my hands. Presently he returned with a small measure containing a dark liquid. This he gave me. I took it unresistingly, and he helped me into the hammock.

When I awoke it was broad day. For a little while I lay flat, staring at the roof above me. The rafters, I observed, were made out of the timbers of a ship. Then I turned my head and saw a meal prepared for me on the table. I perceived that I was hungry, and prepared to clamber out of the hammock, which, very politely, anticipating my intention, twisted round and deposited me upon all-fours on the floor.

I got up and sat down before the food. I had a heavy feeling in my head, and only the vaguest memory at first of the things that had happened overnight. The morning breeze blew very pleasantly through the unglazed window, and that and the food contributed to the sense of animal comfort I experienced. Presently the door behind me, the door inward towards the yard of the enclosure, opened. I turned and saw Montgomery's face.

'All right?' said he. 'I'm frightfully busy.' And he shut the door. Afterwards I discovered that he forgot to relock it.

Then I recalled the expression of his face the previous night, and with that the memory of all I had experienced reconstructed itself before me. Even as that fear returned to me came a cry from within. But this time it was not the cry of a puma.

I put down the mouthful that hesitated upon my lips, and listened. Silence, save for the whisper of the morning breeze. I began to think my ears had deceived me.

After a long pause I resumed my meal, but with my ears still vigilant. Presently I heard something else very faint and low. I sat as if frozen in my attitude. Though it was faint and low, it moved me more profoundly than all that I had hitherto heard of the abominations behind the wall. There was no mistake this time in the quality of the dim broken sounds, no doubt at all of their source; for it was groaning, broken by sobs and gasps of anguish. It was no brute this time. It was a human being in torment!

And as I realised this I rose, and in three steps had crossed the room, seized the handle of the door into the yard, and flung it open before me.

'Prendick, man! Stop!' cried Montgomery, intervening.

A startled deerhound yelped and snarled. There was blood, I saw, in the sink, brown, and some scarlet, and I smelt the peculiar smell of carbolic acid. Then through an open doorway beyond, in the dim light of the shadow, I saw something bound painfully upon a framework, scarred, red, and bandaged. And then blotting this out appeared the face of old Moreau, white and terrible.

In a moment he had gripped me by the shoulder with a hand that was smeared red, had twisted me off my feet, and flung me headlong back into my own room. He lifted me as though I was a little child. I fell at full length upon the floor, and the door slammed and shut out the passionate intensity of his face. Then I heard the key turn in the lock, and Montgomery's voice in expostulation.

'Ruin the work of a lifetime!' I heard Moreau say.

'He does not understand,' said Montgomery, and other things that were inaudible.

'I can't spare the time yet,' said Moreau.

The rest I did not hear. I picked myself up and stood trembling, my mind a chaos of the most horrible misgivings. Could it be possible, I thought, that such a thing as the vivisection of men was possible? The question shot like lightning across a tumultuous sky. And suddenly the clouded horror of my mind condensed into a vivid realisation of my danger.

XI
The Hunting of the Man

It came before my mind with an unreasonable hope of escape, that the outer door of my room was still open to me. I was convinced now, absolutely assured, that Moreau had been vivisecting a human being. All the time since I had heard his name I had been trying to link in my mind in some way the grotesque animalism of the islanders with his abominations; and now I thought I saw it all. The memory of his works in the transfusion of blood recurred to me. These creatures I had seen were the victims of some hideous experiment!

These sickening scoundrels had merely intended to keep me back, to fool me with their display of confidence, and presently to fall upon me with a fate more horrible than death, with torture, and after torture the most hideous degradation it was possible to conceive—to send me off, a lost soul, a beast, to the rest of their Comus rout.[21] I looked round for some weapon. Nothing. Then, with an inspiration, I turned over the deck chair, put my foot on the side of it, and tore away the side rail. It happened that a nail came away with the wood, and, projecting, gave a touch of danger to an otherwise petty weapon. I heard a step outside, incontinently flung open the door, and found Montgomery within a yard of it. He meant to lock the outer door.

---

[21] John Milton's masque *Comus* (1634) builds on Greek and Roman figurings of human-animal transformation and metamorphosis. [Ed.]

I raised this nailed stick of mine and cut at his face, but he sprang back. I hesitated a moment, then turned and fled round the corner of the house. 'Prendick, man!' I heard his astonished cry. 'Don't be a silly ass, man!'

Another minute, thought I, and he would have had me locked in, and as ready as a hospital rabbit for my fate. He emerged behind the corner, for I heard him shout:

'Prendick!'

Then he began to run after me, shouting things as he ran.

This time, running blindly, I went north-eastward, in a direction at right angles to my previous expedition. Once, as I went running headlong up the beach, I glanced over my shoulder and saw his attendant with him. I ran furiously up the slope, over it, then turned eastward along a rocky valley, fringed on either side with jungle. I ran for perhaps a mile altogether, my chest straining, my heart beating in my ears, and then, hearing nothing of Montgomery or his man, and feeling upon the verge of exhaustion, I doubled sharply back towards the beach, as I judged, and lay down in the shelter of a cane brake.

There I remained for a long time, too fearful to move, and indeed too fearful even to plan a course of action. The wild scene about me lay sleeping silently under the sun, and the only sound near me was the thin hum of some small gnats that had discovered me. Presently I became aware of a drowsy breathing sound—the soughing of the sea upon the beach.

After about an hour I heard Montgomery shouting my name far away to the north. That set me thinking of my plan of action. As I interpreted it then, this island was inhabited only by these two vivisectors and their animalised victims. Some of these, no doubt, they could press into their service against me, if need arose. I knew both Moreau and Montgomery carried revolvers; and, save for a feeble bar of deal, spiked with a small nail, the merest mockery of a mace, I was unarmed.

So I lay still where I was until I began to think of food and drink. And at that moment the real hopelessness of my position came home to me. I knew no way of getting anything to eat; I was too ignorant of botany to discover any resort of root or fruit that might lie about me; I had no means of trapping the few rabbits upon the island. It grew blanker the more I turned the prospect over.

At last, in the desperation of my position, my mind turned to the animal men I had encountered. I tried to find some hope in what I remembered of them. In turn I recalled each one I had seen, and tried to draw some augury of assistance from my memory.

Then suddenly I heard a staghound bay, and at that realised a new danger. I took little time to think, or they would have caught me then, but, snatching up my nailed stick, rushed headlong from my hiding-place towards the sound of the sea. I remember a growth of thorny plants with spines that stabbed like penknives. I emerged, bleeding, and with torn clothes, upon the lip of a long creek opening northward.

I went straight into the waves without a minute's hesitation, wading up the creek, and presently finding myself knee-deep in a little stream. I scrambled out at last on the westward bank, and, with my heart beating loudly in my ears, crept into a tangle of ferns to await the issue. I heard the dog—it was only one—draw nearer, and yelp when it came to the thorns. Then I heard no more, and presently began to think I had escaped.

The minutes passed, the silence lengthened out, and at last, after an hour of security, my courage began to return to me.

By this time I was no longer very terrified or very miserable. For I had, as it were, passed the limit of terror and despair. I felt now that my life was practically lost, and that persuasion made me capable of daring anything. I had even a certain wish to encounter Moreau face to face. And, as I had waded into the water, I remembered that if I were too hard pressed at least one path of escape from torment still lay open to me—they could not very well prevent my drowning myself. I had half a mind to drown myself then, but an odd wish to see the whole adventure out, a queer impersonal spectacular interest in myself, restrained me. I stretched my limbs, sore and painful from the pricks of the spiny plants, and stared around me at the trees; and, so suddenly that it seemed to jump out of the green tracery about it, my eyes lit upon a black face watching me.

I saw that it was the simian creature who had met the launch upon the beach. He was clinging to the oblique stem of a palm-tree. I gripped my stick, and stood up facing him. He began chattering. 'You, you, you,' was all I could distinguish at first. Suddenly he dropped from the tree, and in another moment was holding the fronds apart, and staring curiously at me.

I did not feel the same repugnance towards this creature that I had experienced in my encounters with the other Beast Men. 'You,' he said, 'in the boat.' He was a man, then—at least, as much of a man as Montgomery's attendant—for he could talk.

'Yes,' I said, 'I came in the boat. From the ship.'

'Oh!' he said, and his bright restless eyes travelled over me, to my hands, to the stick I carried, to my feet, to the tattered places in my coat, and the cuts and scratches I had received from the thorns. He seemed puzzled at something. His eyes came back to my hands. He held his own hand out, and counted his digits slowly, 'One, Two, Three, Four, Five—eh?'

I did not grasp his meaning then. Afterwards I was to find that a great proportion of these Beast People had malformed hands, lacking sometimes even three digits. But guessing this was in some way a greeting, I did the same thing by way of reply. He grinned with immense satisfaction. Then his quick roving glance went round again. He made a swift movement and vanished. The fern fronds he had stood between came swishing together.

I pushed out of the brake after him, and was astonished to find him swinging cheerfully by one lank arm from a rope of creepers that looped down from the foliage overhead. His back was to me.

'Hullo!' said I.

He came down with a twisting jump, and stood facing me.

'I say,' said I, 'where can I get something to eat?'

'Eat!' he said. 'Eat man's food now.' And his eyes went back to the swing of ropes. 'At the huts.'

'But where are the huts?'

'Oh!'

'I'm new, you know.'

At that he swung round, and set off at a quick walk. All his motions were curiously rapid. 'Come along,' said he. I went with him to see the adventure out. I guessed the huts were some rough shelter, where he and some more of these Beast People lived. I might perhaps find them friendly, find some handle in their minds to take hold of. I did not know yet how far they had forgotten the human heritage I ascribed them.

My ape-like companion trotted along by my side, with his hands hanging down and his jaw thrust forward. I wondered what memory he might have in him.

'How long have you been on this island?' said I.

'How long?' he asked. And, after having the question repeated, he held up three fingers. The creature was little better than an idiot. I tried to make out what he meant by that, and it seems I bored him. After another question or two, he suddenly left my side and sprang at some fruit that hung from a tree. He pulled down a handful of prickly husks, and went on eating the contents. I noted this with satisfaction, for here, at least, was a hint for feeding. I tried him with some other questions, but his chattering prompt responses were, as often as not, quite at cross-purposes with my question. Some few were appropriate, others quite parrot-like.

I was so intent upon these peculiarities that I scarcely noticed the path we followed. Presently we came to trees, all charred and brown, and so to a bare place covered with a yellow-white incrustation, across which a drifting smoke, pungent in whiffs to nose and eyes, went drifting. On our right, over a shoulder of bare rock, I saw the level blue of the sea. The path coiled down abruptly into a narrow ravine between two tumbled and knotty masses of blackish scoriæ.[22] Into this we plunged.

---

[22] Cinder-like lava. [Ed.]

It was extremely dark, this passage, after the blinding sunlight reflected from the sulphurous ground. Its walls grew steep, and approached one another. Blotches of green and crimson drifted across my eyes. My conductor stopped suddenly. 'Home,' said he, and I stood on a floor of a chasm that was at first absolutely dark to me. I heard some strange noises, and thrust the knuckles of my left hand into my eyes. I became aware of a disagreeable odour like that of a monkey's cage ill cleaned. Beyond, the rock opened again upon a gradual slope of sunlit greenery, and on either hand the light smote down through a narrow channel into the central gloom.

XII
The Sayers of the Law

Then something cold touched my hand. I started violently, and saw close to me a dim pinkish thing, looking more like a flayed child than anything else in the world. The creature had exactly the mild but repulsive features of a sloth, the same low forehead and slow gestures. As the first shock of the change of light passed, I saw about me more distinctly. The little sloth-like creature was standing and staring at me. My conductor had vanished.

The place was a narrow passage between high walls of lava, a crack in its knotted flow, and on either side interwoven heaps of sea-mat, palm fans and reeds leaning against the rock, formed rough and impenetrably dark dens. The winding way up the ravine between these was scarcely three yards wide, and was disfigured by lumps of decaying fruit-pulp and other refuse, which accounted for the disagreeable stench of the place.

The little pink sloth creature was still blinking at me when my Ape Man reappeared at the aperture of the nearest of these dens, and beckoned me in. As he did so a slouching monster wriggled out of one of the places further up this strange street, and stood up in featureless silhouette against the bright green beyond, staring at me. I hesitated—had half a mind to bolt the way I had come—and then, determined to go through with the adventure, gripped my nailed stick about the middle, and crawled into the little evil-smelling lean-to after my conductor.

It was a semicircular space, shaped like the half of a bee-hive, and against the rocky wall that formed the inner side of it was a pile of variegated fruits, coco-nuts and others. Some rough vessels of lava and wood stood about the floor, and one on a rough stool. There was no fire. In the darkest corner of the hut sat a shapeless mass of darkness that grunted 'Hey!' as I came in, and my Ape Man stood in the dim light of the doorway and held out a split coco-nut to me as I crawled into the other corner and squatted down. I took it and began gnawing it, as serenely as possible, in spite of my tense trepidation, and the nearly intolerable closeness of the den. The little pink sloth creature stood in the aperture of the hut, and something else with a drab face and bright eyes came staring over its shoulder.

'Hey,' came out of the lump of mystery opposite. 'It is a man! It is a man!' gabbled my conductor—'a man, a man, a live man, like me.'

'Shut up!' said the voice from the dark, and grunted. I gnawed my coco-nut amid an impressive silence. I peered hard into the blackness, but could distinguish nothing. 'It is a man,' the voice repeated. 'He comes to live with us?'

It was a thick voice with something in it, a kind of whistling overtone, that struck me as peculiar, but the English accent was strangely good.

The Ape Man looked at me as though he expected something. I perceived the pause was interrogative.

'He comes to live with you,' I said.

'It is a man. He must learn the Law.'

I began to distinguish now a deeper blackness in the black, a vague outline of a hunched-up figure. Then I noticed the opening of the place was darkened by two more heads. My hand tightened on my stick. The thing in the dark repeated in a louder tone, 'Say the words.' I had missed its last remark. 'Not to go on all-Fours; that is the Law'—it repeated in a kind of sing-song.

I was puzzled. 'Say the words,' said the Ape Man, repeating, and the figures in the doorway echoed this with a threat in the tone of their voices. I realized I had to repeat this idiotic formula. And then began the insanest ceremony.

The voice in the dark began intoning a made litany, line by line, and I and the rest to repeat it. As they did so, they swayed from side to side, and beat their hands upon their knees, and I followed their example. I could have imagined I was already dead and in another world. The dark hut, these grotesque dim figures, just flecked here and there by a glimmer of light, and all of them swaying in unison and chanting:

'Not to go on all-Fours; *that* is the Law. Are we not Men?'

'Not to suck up Drink; *that* is the Law. Are we not Men?'

'Not to eat Flesh nor Fish; *that* is the Law. Are we not Men?'

'Not to claw Bark of Trees; *that* is the Law. Are we not Men?'

'Not to chase other Men; *that* is the Law. Are we not Men?' [23]

---

[23] The rituals in the hut of the Sayer of the Law are a satire of the Ten Commandments, the Anglican Liturgies, and other rote-learned rules and praises. They satirize also the

And so from the prohibition of these acts of folly, on to the prohibition of what I thought then were the maddest, most impossible, and most indecent things one could well imagine.

A kind of rhythmic fervour fell on all of us; we gabbled and swayed faster and faster, repeating this amazing law. Superficially the contagion of these brute men was upon me, but deep down within me laughter and disgust struggled together.

We ran through a long list of prohibitions, and then the chant swung round to a new formula:

'*His* is the House of Pain.'

'*His* is the Hand that makes.'

'*His* is the Hand that wounds.'

'*His* is the Hand that heals.'

And so on for another long series, mostly quite incomprehensible gibberish to me, about *Him*, whoever he might be. I could have fancied it was a dream, but never before have I heard chanting in a dream.

'*His* is the lightning-flash,' we sang, '*His* is the deep salt sea.'

A horrible fancy came into my head that Moreau, after animalising these men, had infected their dwarfed brains with a kind of deification of himself. However, I was too keenly aware of white teeth and strong claws about me to stop my chanting on that account. '*His* are the stars in the sky.'

At last that song ended. I saw the Ape Man's face shining with perspiration, and my eyes being now accustomed to the darkness, I saw more distinctly the figure in the corner from which the voice came. It was the size of a man, but it seemed covered with a dull grey hair almost like a Skye terrier. What was it? What were they all? Imagine yourself surrounded by all the most horrible cripples and maniacs it is possible to conceive, and you may understand a little of my feelings with these grotesque caricatures of humanity about me.

'He is a five-man, a five-man, a five-man . . . like me,' said the Ape Man.

I held out my hands. The grey creature in the corner leant forward. 'Not to run on all-Fours; that is the Law. Are we not Men?' he said. He put out a strangely distorted talon, and gripped my fingers. The thing was almost like the hoof of a deer produced into claws. I could have yelled with surprise and pain. His face came forward and peered at my nails, came forward into the light of the opening of the hut, and I saw with a quivering dis-

---

"Laws of the Jungle" sing-songed by Baloo the Brown Bear in Rudyard Kipling's *Second Jungle Book* (1895); for instance, "Ye may kill for yourselves and your mates, and your cubs as they need, and ye can; / But kill not for pleasure of killing, and *seven times never kill Man*" (18). [Ed.]

gust that it was like the face of neither man or beast, but a mere shock of grey hair, with three shadowy over-archings to mark the eyes and mouth.

'He has little nails,' said this grisly creature in his hairy beard. 'It is well.'

He threw my hand down, and instinctively I gripped my stick.

'Eat roots and herbs — it is His will,' said the Ape Man.

"I am the Sayer of the Law,' said the grey figure. 'Here come all that be new, to learn the Law. I sit in the darkness and say the Law.'

'It is even so,' said one of the beasts in the doorway.

'Evil are the punishments of those who break the Law. None escape.'

'None escape,' said the Beast Folk, glancing furtively at each other.

'None, none,' said the Ape Man. 'None escape. See! I did a little thing, a wrong thing, once. I jabbered, jabbered, stopped talking. None could understand. I am burnt, branded in the hand. He is great, he is good!'

'None escape,' said the grey creature in the corner.

'None escape,' said the Beast People, looking askance at one another.

'For every one the want that is bad,' said the grey Sayer of the Law. 'What you will want, we do not know. We shall know. Some want to follow things that move, to watch and slink and wait and spring, to kill and bite, bite deep and rich, sucking the blood. . . . It is bad. "Not to chase other Men; that is the Law. *Are we not Men?* Not to eat Flesh nor Fish; that is the Law. *Are we not Men?*"'

'None escape,' said a dappled brute standing in the doorway.

'For every one the want that is bad,' said the grey Sayer of the Law. 'Some want to go tearing with teeth and hands into the roots of things, snuffing into the earth. . . . It is bad.'

'None escape,' said the men in the door.

'Some go clawing trees, some go scratching at the graves of the dead; some go fighting with foreheads or feet or claws; some bite suddenly, none giving occasion; some love uncleanness.'

'None escape,' said the Ape Man, scratching his calf.

'None escape,' said the little pink sloth creature.

'Punishment is sharp and sure. Therefore learn the Law. Say the words,' and incontinently he began again the strange litany of the Law, and again I and all these creatures began singing and swaying. My head reeled with this jabbering and the close stench of the place, but I kept on, trusting to find presently some chance of a new development. 'Not to go on all-Fours; that is the Law. *Are we not Men?*'

We were making such a noise that I noticed nothing of the tumult outside, until some one, who, I think, was one of the two Swine Men I had seen, thrust his head over the little pink sloth creature and shouted something excitedly, something that I did not catch. Incontinently those at the opening of the hut vanished, my Ape Man rushed out, the thing that had sat in the dark followed him—I only observed it was big and clumsy, and covered with silvery hair,—and I was left alone.

Then before I reached the aperture I heard the yelp of a staghound.

In another moment I was standing outside the hovel, my chair-rail in my hand, every muscle of me quivering. Before me were the clumsy backs of perhaps a score of these Beast People, their misshapen heads half-hidden by their shoulder-blades. They were gesticulating excitedly. Other half-animal faces glared interrogation out of the hovels. Looking in the direction in which they faced I saw coming through the haze under the trees beyond the end of the passage of dens the dark figure and awful white face of Moreau. He was holding the leaping staghound back, and close behind him came Montgomery, revolver in hand.

For a moment I stood horror-struck.

I turned and saw the passages behind me blocked by another heavy brute with a huge grey face and twinkling little eyes, advancing towards me. I looked round and saw to the right of me, and half a dozen yards in front of me, a narrow gap in the wall of rock through which a ray of light slanted into the shadows.

'Stop!' cried Moreau, as I strode towards this, and then, 'Hold him!' At that, first one face turned towards me, and then others. Their bestial minds were happily slow.

I dashed my shoulder into a clumsy monster who was turning to see what Moreau meant, and flung him forward into another. I felt his hands fly round, clutching at me and missing me. The little pink sloth creature dashed at me and I cut it over, gashed down its ugly face with the nail in my stick, and in another minute I was scrambling up a steep side pathway, a kind of sloping chimney out of the ravine. I heard a howl behind me, and cries of 'Catch him!' 'Hold him!' and the grey-faced creature appeared behind me and jammed his huge bulk into the cleft. 'Go on, go on!' they howled. I clambered up the narrow cleft in the rock, and came out upon the sulphur on the westward side of the village of the Beast Men.

That gap was altogether fortunate for me, for the narrow way slanting obliquely upward must have impeded the nearer pursuers. I ran over the white space and down a steep slope through a scattered growth of trees, and came to a low-lying stretch of tall reeds. Through this I pushed into a dark thick undergrowth that was black and succulent under foot. As I plunged into the reeds my foremost pursuers emerged from the gap. I broke my way through this undergrowth for some minutes. The air behind me and about me was soon full of threatening cries.

I heard the tumult of my pursuers in the gap up the slope, then the crashing of the reeds, and every now and then the crackling crash of a branch.

Some of the creatures roared like excited beasts of prey. The staghound yelped to the left. I heard Moreau and Montgomery shouting in the same direction. I turned sharply to the right. It seemed to me even then that I heard Montgomery shouting for me to run for my life.

Presently the ground gave, rich and oozy, under my feet; but I was desperate, and went headlong into it, struggled through knee-deep, and so came to a winding path among tall canes. The noise of my pursuers passed away to my left. In one place three strange pink hopping animals, about the size of cats, bolted before my footsteps. This pathway ran uphill, across another open space covered with white incrustation, and plunged into a cane brake again.

Then suddenly it turned parallel with the edge of a steep walled gap which came without warning like the ha-ha [24] of an English park—turned with unexpected abruptness. I was still running with all my might, and I never saw this drop until I was flying headlong through the air.

I fell on my forearms and head, among thorns, and rose with a torn ear and bleeding face. I had fallen into a precipitous ravine, rocky and thorny, full of a hazy mist that drifted about me in wisps, and with a narrow streamlet, from which this mist came, meandering down the centre. I was astonished at this thin fog in the full blaze of daylight, but I had not time to stand wondering then. I turned to my right down stream, hoping to come to the sea in that direction, and so have my way open to drown myself. It was only later I found that I had dropped my nailed stick in my fall.

Presently the ravine grew narrower for a space, and carelessly I stepped into the stream. I jumped out again pretty quickly, for the water was almost boiling. I noticed too there was a thin sulphurous scum drifting upon its coiling water. Almost immediately came a turn in the ravine and the indistinct blue horizon. The nearer sea was flashing the sun from a myriad facets. I saw my death before me. But I was hot and panting, with the warm blood oozing out of my face and running pleasantly through my veins. I felt more than a touch of exultation, too, at having distanced my pursuers. It was not in me then to go out and drown myself. I stared back the way I had come.

I listened. Save for the hum of the gnats and the chirp of some small insects that hopped among the thorns, the air was absolutely still. Then came the yelp of a dog, very faint, and a chattering and gibbering, the snap of a whip and voices. They grew louder, then fainter again. The noise receded up the stream and faded away. For a while the chase was over.

But I knew now how much hope of help for me lay in the Beast People.

---

[24] A sunken fence or barrier set in a trench to preserve the view. [Ed.]

XIII

A Parley

I turned again and went on down towards the sea. I found the hot stream broadened out to a shallow weedy sand, in which an abundance of crabs, and long-bodied, many-legged creatures started from my footfall. I walked to the very edge of the salt water, and then I felt I was safe. I turned and stared—arms akimbo—at the thick green behind me, into which the steamy ravine cut like a smoking gash. But as I say, I was too full of excitement, and—a true saying, though those who have never known danger may doubt it—too desperate to die.

Then it came into my head that there was one chance before me yet. While Moreau and Montgomery and their bestial rabble chased me through the island, might I not go round the beach until I came to their enclosure?— make a flank march upon them, in fact, and then with a rock lugged out of their loosely built wall perhaps, smash in the lock of the smaller door and see what I could find—knife, pistol, or what not—to fight them with when they returned? It was at any rate a chance of getting a price for my life.

So I turned to the westward and walked along by the water's edge. The setting sun flashed his blinding heat into my eyes. The slight Pacific tide was running in with a gentle ripple.

Presently the shore fell away southward and the sun came round upon my right hand. Then suddenly, far in front of me, I saw first one and then several figures emerging from the bushes,—Moreau with his grey staghound, then Montgomery, and two others. At that I stopped.

They saw me and began gesticulating and advancing. I stood watching them approach. The two Beast Men came running forward to cut me off from the undergrowth inland. Montgomery came running also, but straight towards me. Moreau followed slower with the dog.

At last I roused myself from inaction, and turning seaward walked straight into the water. The water was very shallow at first. I was thirty yards out before the waves reached to my waist. Dimly I could see the intertidal creatures darting away from my feet.

'What are you doing, man?' cried Montgomery.

I turned, standing waist-deep, and stared at them.

Montgomery stood panting at the margin of the water. His face was bright red with exertion, his long flaxen hair blown about his head, and his dropping nether lip showed his irregular teeth. Moreau was just coming up, his face pale and firm, and the dog at his hand barked at me. Both men had heavy whips. Further up the beach stared the Beast Men.

'What am I doing?—I am going to drown myself,' said I.

Montgomery and Moreau looked at one another.

'Why?' asked Moreau.

'Because that is better than being tortured by you.'

'I told you so,' said Montgomery, and Moreau said something in a low tone.

'What makes you think I shall torture you?' asked Moreau.

'What I saw,' I said. 'And those—yonder.'

'Hush!' said Moreau, and held up his hand.

'I will not,' said I; 'they were men: what are they now? I at least will not be like them.'

I looked past my interlocutors. Up the beach were M'ling, Montgomery's attendant, and one of the white swathed brutes from the boat. Further up, in the shadow of the trees, I saw my little Ape Man, and behind him some other dim figures.

'Who are these creatures?' said I, pointing to them, and raising my voice more and more that it might reach them. 'They were men—men like yourselves, whom you have infected with some bestial taint, men whom you have enslaved, and whom you still fear.—You who listen,' I cried, pointing now to Moreau, and shouting past him to the Beast Men, 'You who listen! Do you not see these men still fear you, go in dread of you? Why then do you fear them? You are many—' *slave uprising*

'For God's sake,' cried Montgomery, 'stop that, Prendick!'

'Prendick!' cried Moreau.

They both shouted together as if to drown my voice. And behind them lowered the staring faces of the Beast Men, wondering, their deformed hands hanging down, their shoulders hunched up. They seemed, as I fancied then, to be trying to understand me, to remember something of their human past.

I went on shouting, I scarcely remember what. That Moreau and Montgomery could be killed; that they were not to be feared: that was the burthen of what I put into the heads of the Beast People to my own ultimate undoing. I saw the green-eyed man in the dark rags, who had met me on the evening of my arrival, come out from among the trees, and others followed him to hear me better.

At last for want of breath I paused.

'Listen to me for a moment,' said the steady voice of Moreau, 'and then say what you will.'

'Well?' said I.

He coughed, thought, then shouted:

'Latin, Prendick! Bad Latin! Schoolboy Latin! But try and understand. *Hi non sunt homines, sunt animalia qui nos habemus* . . . vivisected. A humanising process. I will explain. Come ashore.'

I laughed. 'A pretty story,' said I. 'They talk, build houses, cook. They were men. It's likely I'll come ashore.'

'The water just beyond where you stand is deep . . . and full of sharks.'

'That's my way,' said I. 'Short and sharp. Presently.'

'Wait a minute.' He took something out of his pocket that flashed back the sun, and dropped the object at his feet. 'That's a loaded revolver,' said he. 'Montgomery here will do the same. Now we are going up the beach until you are satisfied the distance is safe. Then come and take the revolvers.'

'Not I. You have a third between you.'

'I want you to think over things, Prendick. In the first place, I never asked you to come upon this island. In the next, we had you drugged last night, had we wanted to work you any mischief; and in the next, now your first panic is over, and you can think a little—is Montgomery here quite up to the character you give him? We have chased you for your good. Because this island is full of . . . inimical phenomena. Why should we want to shoot you when you have just offered to drown yourself?'

'Why did you set . . . your people on to me when I was in the hut?'

'We felt sure of catching you and bringing you out of danger. Afterwards we drew away from the scent—for your good.'

I mused. It seemed just possible. Then I remembered something again. 'But I saw,' said I, 'in the enclosure—'

'That was the puma.'

'Look here, Prendick,' said Montgomery. 'You're a silly ass. Come out of the water and take these revolvers, and talk. We can't do anything more then than we could do now.'

I will confess that then, and indeed always, I distrusted and dreaded Moreau. But Montgomery was a man I felt I understood.

'Go up the beach,' said I, after thinking, and added, 'holding your hands up.'

'Can't do that,' said Montgomery, with an explanatory nod over his shoulder. 'Undignified.'

'Go up to the trees, then,' said I, 'as you please.'

'It's a damned silly ceremony,' said Montgomery.

Both turned and faced the six or seven grotesque creatures, who stood there in the sunlight, solid, casting shadows, moving, and yet so incredibly unreal. Montgomery cracked his whip at them, and forthwith they all turned and fled helter-skelter into the trees. And when Montgomery and Moreau were at a distance I judged sufficient, I waded ashore, and picked up and examined the revolvers. To satisfy myself against the subtlest trickery I discharged one at a rounded lump of lava, and had the satisfaction of seeing the stone pulverised and the beach splashed with lead.

Still I hesitated for a moment.

'I'll take the risk,' said I, at last, and with a revolver in each hand I walked up the beach towards them.

'That's better,' said Moreau, without affectation. 'As it is, you have wasted the best part of my day with your confounded imagination.'

And with a touch of contempt that humiliated me he and Montgomery turned and went on in silence before me.

The knot of Beast Men, still wondering, stood back among the trees. I passed them as serenely as possible. One started to follow me, but retreated again when Montgomery cracked his whip. The rest stood silent — watching. They may once have been animals. But I never before saw an animal trying to think.

XIV

Doctor Moreau Explains [25]

'And now, Prendick, I will explain,' said Doctor Moreau, so soon as we had eaten and drunk. 'I must confess you are the most dictatorial guest I ever entertained. I warn you that this is the last I do to oblige you. The next thing you threaten to commit suicide about I shan't do — even at some personal inconvenience.'

He sat in my deck chair, a cigar half consumed in his white dexterous-looking fingers. The light of the swinging lamp fell on his white hair; he stared through the little window out at the starlight. I sat as far away from him as possible, the table between us and the revolvers to hand. Montgomery was not present. I did not care to be with the two of them in such a little room.

'You admit that vivisected human being, as you called it, is, after all, only the puma?' said Moreau. He had made me visit that horror in the inner room to assure myself of its inhumanity.

'It is the puma,' I said, 'still alive, but so cut and mutilated as I pray I may never see living flesh again. Of all vile —'

---

[25] Wells developed his thought simultaneously as a writer of fiction and a contributor to popular newspapers and journals. Three of his essays have particular bearing on the ideas expressed in this key chapter: "The Province of Pain," published in *Science and Art* in February 1884; "The Limits of Individual Plasticity," written during his early conception of the story, published in the January 19, 1885, issue of the *Saturday Review;* and "Human Evolution, an Artificial Process," published in the October 1896 *Fortnightly Review* just a few months after *The Island of Doctor Moreau*. [Ed.]

'Never mind that,' said Moreau. 'At least spare me those youthful horrors. Montgomery used to be just the same. You admit it is the puma. Now be quiet while I reel off my physiological lecture to you.'

And forthwith, beginning in the tone of a man supremely bored, but presently warming a little, he explained his work to me. He was very simple and convincing. Now and then there was a touch of sarcasm in his voice. Presently I found myself hot with shame at our mutual positions.

The creatures I had seen were not men, had never been men. They were animals—humanised animals—triumphs of vivisection.

'You forget all that a skilled vivisector can do with living things,' said Moreau. 'For my own part I'm puzzled why the things I have done here have not been done before. Small efforts of course have been made—amputation, tongue-cutting, excisions. Of course you know a squint may be induced or cured by surgery? Then in the case of excisions you have all kinds of secondary changes, pigmentary disturbances, modifications of the passions, alterations in the modifications of the passions, alterations in the secretion of fatty tissue. I have no doubt you have heard of these things?'

'Of course,' said I. 'But these foul creatures of yours—'

'All in good time,' said he, waving his hand at me; 'I am only beginning. Those are trivial cases of alteration. Surgery can do better things than that. There is building up as well as breaking down and changing. You have heard, perhaps, of a common surgical operation resorted to in cases where the nose has been destroyed. A flap of skin is cut from the forehead, turned down on the nose, and heals in the new position. This is a kind of grafting a new position of part of an animal upon itself. Grafting of freshly obtained material from another animal is also possible—the case of teeth, for example. The grafting of skin and bone is done to facilitate healing. The surgeon places in the middle of the wound pieces of skin snipped from another animal, or fragments of bone from a victim freshly killed. Hunter's cockspur [26]—possibly you have heard of that—flourished on the bull's neck. And the rhinoceros rats of the Algerian zouaves are also to be thought of,—monsters manufactured by transferring a slip from the tail of an ordinary rat to its snout, and allowing it to heal in that position.'

'Monsters manufactured!' said I. 'Then you mean to tell me—'

'Yes. These creatures you have seen are animals carven and wrought into new shapes. To that—to the study of the plasticity of living forms—my life has been devoted. I have studied for years, gaining in knowledge as I go. I see you look horrified, and yet I am telling you nothing new. It all lay in the

---

[26] The English surgeon John Hunter (1728–93) experimented with these kinds of transplants. [Ed.]

surface of practical anatomy years ago, but no one had the temerity to touch it. It's not simply the outward form of an animal I can change. The physiology, the chemical rhythm of the creature, may also be made to undergo an enduring modification, of which vaccination and other methods of inoculation with living or dead matter are examples that will, no doubt, be familiar to you.

'A similar operation is the transfusion of blood, with which subject indeed I began. These are all familiar cases. Less so, and probably far more extensive, were the operations of those mediæval practitioners who made dwarfs and beggar cripples and show-monsters; some vestiges of whose art still remain in the preliminary manipulation of the young mountebank or contortionist. Victor Hugo gives an account of them in *L'Homme qui Rit.*[27] . . . But perhaps my meaning grows plain now. You begin to see that it is a possible thing to transplant tissue from one part of an animal to another, or from one animal to another, to alter its chemical reactions and methods of growth, to modify the articulations of its limbs, and indeed to change it in its most intimate structure?

'And yet this extraordinary branch of knowledge has never been sought as an end, and systematically, by modern investigators, until I took it up! Some such things have been hit upon in the last resort of surgery; most of the kindred evidence that will recur to your mind has been demonstrated, as it were, by accident—by tyrants, by criminals, by the breeders of horses and dogs, by all kinds of untrained clumsy-handed men working for their own immediate ends. I was the first man to take up this question armed with antiseptic surgery, and with a really scientific knowledge of the laws of growth.

'Yet one would imagine it must have been practised in secret before. Such creatures as the Siamese Twins. . . . And in the vaults of the Inquisition. No doubt their chief aim was artistic torture, but some, at least, of the inquisitors must have had a touch of scientific curiosity. . . .'

'But,' said I. 'These things—these animals *talk!*'

He said that was so, and proceeded to point out that the possibilities of vivisection do not stop at a mere physical metamorphosis. A pig may be educated. The mental structure is even less determinate than the bodily. In our growing science of hypnotism we find the promise of a possibility of replacing old inherent instincts by new suggestions, grafting upon or replacing the inherited fixed ideas. Very much, indeed, of what we call moral education is such an artificial modification and perversion of instinct;

---

[27] Victor Hugo's novel *The Man Who Laughed* (1869) speaks of rumored Chinese techniques for bringing up reshaped humans confined in differently shaped jars. [Ed.]

pugnacity is trained into courageous self-sacrifice, and suppressed sexuality into religious emotion.[28] And the great difference between man and monkey is in the larynx, he said, in the incapacity to frame delicately different sound-symbols by which thought could be sustained. In this I failed to agree with him, but with a certain incivility he declined to notice my objection. He repeated that the thing was so, and continued his account of his work.

But I asked him why he had taken the human form as a model. There seemed to me then, and there still seems to me now, a strange wickedness in that choice.

He confessed that he had chosen that form by chance.

'I might just as well have worked to form sheep into llamas, and llamas into sheep. I suppose there is something in the human form that appeals to the artistic turn of mind more powerfully than any animal shape can. But I've not confined myself to man-making. Once or twice. . . .' He was silent, for a minute perhaps. 'These years! How they have slipped by! And here I have wasted a day saving your life, and am now wasting an hour explaining myself!'

'But,' said I, 'I still do not understand. Where is your justification for inflicting all this pain? The only thing that could excuse vivisection to me would be some application—'

'Precisely,' said he. 'But you see I am differently constituted. We are on different platforms. You are a materialist.'

'I am *not* a materialist,' I began hotly.

'In my view—in my view. For it is just this question of pain that parts us. So long as visible or audible pain turns you sick, so long as your own pains drive you, so long as pain underlies your propositions about sin, so long, I tell you, you are an animal, thinking a little less obscurely what an animal feels. This pain—'

I gave an impatient shrug at such sophistry.

'Oh! but it is such a little thing. A mind truly opened to what science has to teach must see that it is a little thing. It may be that, save in this little planet, this speck of cosmic dust, invisible long before the nearest star could be attained—it may be, I say, that nowhere else does this thing called pain occur. But the laws we feel our way towards. . . . Why, even on this earth, even among living things, what pain is there?'

---

[28] The provocative juxtaposition of religion and sexuality permeated late nineteenth-century thought, but Moreau's scientific analysis of "suppression" predates Freud's formulation of his theory of "sublimation" and anticipates Freud's argument on this point in *The Future of an Illusion* (1927). [Ed.]

He drew a little penknife as he spoke from his pocket, opened the smaller blade and moved his chair so that I could see his thigh. Then, choosing the place deliberately, he drove the blade into his leg and withdrew it.

'No doubt you have seen that before. It does not hurt a pin-prick. But what does it show? The capacity for pain is not needed in the muscle, and it is not placed there; it is but little needed in the skin, and only here and there over the thigh is a spot capable of feeling pain. Pain is simply our intrinsic medical adviser to warn us and stimulate us. All living flesh is not painful, nor is all nerve, nor even all sensory nerve. There's no taint of pain, real pain, in the sensations of the optic nerve. If you wound the optic nerve you merely see flashes of light, just as disease of the auditory nerve merely means a humming in our ears. Plants do not feel pain; the lower animals — it's possible that such animals as the starfish and crayfish do not feel pain. Then with men, the more intelligent they become the more intelligently they will see after their own welfare, and the less they will need the goad to keep them out of danger. I never yet heard of a useless thing that was not ground out of existence by evolution sooner or later. Did you? And pain gets needless.

'Then I am a religious man, Prendick, as every sane man must be. It may be I fancy I have seen more of the ways of this world's Maker than you — for I have sought His laws, in *my* way, all my life, while you, I understand, have been collecting butterflies. And I tell you, pleasure and pain have nothing to do with heaven or hell. Pleasure and pain — Bah! What is your theologian's ecstasy but Mahomet's houri in the dark? This store men and women set on pleasure and pain, Prendick, is the mark of the beast upon them, the mark of the beast from which they came. Pain! Pain and pleasure — they are for us, only so long as we wriggle in the dust. . . .

'You see, I went on with this research just the way it led me. That is the only way I ever heard of research going. I asked a question, devised some method of getting an answer, and got — a fresh question. Was this possible, or that possible? You cannot imagine what this means to an investigator, what an intellectual passion grows upon him. You cannot imagine the strange colourless delight of these intellectual desires. The thing before you is no longer an animal, a fellow-creature, but a problem. Sympathetic pain — all I know of it I remember as a thing I used to suffer from years ago. I wanted — it was the only thing I wanted — to find out the extreme limit of plasticity in a living shape.'

'But,' said I, 'the thing is an abomination —'

'To this day I have never troubled about the ethics of the matter. The study of Nature makes a man at last as remorseless as Nature. I have gone on, not heeding anything but the question I was pursuing, and the material has

... dripped into the huts yonder. ... It is nearly eleven years since we came here, I and Montgomery and six Kanakas.[29] I remember the green stillness of the island and the empty ocean about us as though it was yesterday. The place seemed waiting for me.

'The stores were landed and the house was built. The Kanakas founded some huts near the ravine. I went to work here upon what I had brought with me. There were some disagreeable things happened at first. I began with a sheep, and killed it after a day and a half by a slip of the scalpel; I took another sheep and made a thing of pain and fear, and left it bound up to heal. It looked quite human to me when I had finished it, but when I went to it I was discontented with it; it remembered me, and was terrified beyond imagination, and it had no more than the wits of a sheep. The more I looked at it the clumsier it seemed, until at last I put the monster out of its misery. These animals without courage, these fear-haunted, pain-driven things, without a spark of pugnacious energy to face torment—they are no good for man-making.

'Then I took a gorilla I had, and upon that, working with infinite care, and mastering difficulty after difficulty, I made my first man. All the week, night and day, I moulded him. With him it was chiefly the brain that needed moulding; much had to be added, much changed. I thought him a fair specimen of the negroid type when I had done him, and he lay, bandaged, bound, and motionless before me. It was only when his life was assured that I left him, and came into the room again and found Montgomery much as you are. He had heard some of the cries as the thing grew human, cries like those that disturbed you so. I didn't take him completely into my confidence at first.

'And the Kanakas, too, had realised something of it. They were scared out of their wits by the sight of me. I got Montgomery over to me—in a way, but I and he had the hardest job to prevent the Kanakas deserting. Finally they did, and so we lost the yacht. I spent many days educating the brute—altogether I had him for three or four months. I taught him the rudiments of English, gave him ideas of counting, even made the thing read the alphabet. But at that he was slow—though I've met with idiots slower. He began with a clean sheet, mentally; had no memories left in his mind of what he had been. When his scars were quite healed, and he was no longer anything but painful and stiff, and able to converse a little, I took him yonder and introduced him to the Kanakas as an interesting stowaway.

'They were horribly afraid of him at first, somehow—which offended me rather, for I was conceited about him,—but his ways seemed so mild,

---

[29] Hawaiian for "person." [Ed.]

and he was so abject, that after a time they received him and took his education in hand. He was quick to learn, very imitative and adaptive, and built himself a hovel rather better, it seemed to me, than their own shanties. There was one among the boys, a bit of a missionary, and he taught the thing to read, or at least to pick out letters, and gave him some rudimentary ideas of morality, but it seems the beast's habits were not all that is desirable.

'I rested from work for some days, and was in a mind to write an account of the whole affair to wake up English physiology. Then I came upon the creature squatting up in a tree gibbering at two of the Kanakas who had been teasing him. I threatened him, told him the inhumanity of such a proceeding, aroused his sense of shame, and came here resolved to do better before I took my work back to England. I have been doing better; but somehow the things drift back again, the stubborn beast flesh grows, day by day, back again. . . . I mean to do better things still. I mean to conquer that. This puma . . .

'But that's the story. All the Kanaka boys are dead now. One fell overboard of the launch, and one died of a wounded heel that he poisoned in some way with plant-juice. Three went away in the yacht, and I suppose, and hope, were drowned. The other one . . . was killed. Well—I have replaced them. Montgomery went on much as you are disposed to do at first, and then . . .'

'What became of the other one?' said I sharply, — 'the other Kanaka who was killed?'

'The fact is, after I had made a number of human creatures I made a thing—' He hesitated.

'Yes?' said I.

'It was killed.'

'I don't understand,' said I; 'do you mean to say . . .'

'It killed the Kanaka—yes. It killed several other things that it caught. We chased it for a couple of days. It only got loose by accident—I never meant it to get away. It wasn't finished. It was purely an experiment. It was a limbless thing with a horrible face that writhed along the ground in a serpentine fashion. It was immensely strong and in infuriating pain, and it travelled in a rollicking way like a porpoise swimming. It lurked in the woods for some days, doing mischief to all it came across, until we hunted it, and then it wriggled into the northern part of the island, and we divided the party to close in upon it. Montgomery insisted upon coming with me. The man had a rifle, and when his body was found one of the barrels was curved into the shape of an S, and very nearly bitten through. . . . Montgomery shot the thing. . . . After that I stuck to the ideal of humanity—except for little things.'

He became silent. I sat in silence watching his face.

'So for twenty years altogether—counting nine years in England—I have been going on, and there is still something in everything I do that defeats me, makes me dissatisfied, challenges me to further effort. Sometimes I rise above my level, sometimes I fall below it, but always I fall short of the things I dream. The human shape I can get now, almost with ease, so that it is lithe and graceful, or thick and strong; but often there is trouble with the hands and claws—painful things that I dare not shape too freely. But it is in the subtle grafting and re-shaping one must needs do to the brain that my trouble lies. The intelligence is often oddly low, with unaccountable blank ends, unexpected gaps. And least satisfactory of all is something that I cannot touch, somewhere—I cannot determine where—in the seat of the emotions. Cravings, instincts, desires that harm humanity, a strange hidden reservoir to burst suddenly and inundate the whole being of the creature with anger, hate, or fear.

'These creatures of mine seemed strange and uncanny to you as soon as you began to observe them, but to me, just after I make them, they seem to be indisputable human beings. It's afterwards as I observe them that the persuasion fades. First one animal trait, then another, creeps to the surface and stares out at me. . . . But I will conquer yet. Each time I dip a living creature into the bath of burning pain, I say, This time I will burn out all the animal, this time I will make a rational creature of my own. After all, what is ten years? Man has been a hundred thousand in the making.'

He thought darkly.

'But I am drawing near the fastness. This puma of mine . . .'

After a silence:

'And they revert. As soon as my hand is taken from them the beast begins to creep back, begins to creep back, begins to assert itself again. . . .'

Another long silence.

'Then you take the things you make into those dens?' said I.

'They go. I turn them out when I begin to feel the beast in them, and presently they wander there. They all dread this house and me. There is a kind of travesty of humanity over there. Montgomery knows about it, for he interferes in their affairs. He has trained one or two of them to our service. He's ashamed of it, but I believe he half-likes some of these beasts. It's his business, not mine. They only sicken me with a sense of failure. I take no interest in them. I fancy they follow in the lines the Kanaka missionary marked out, and have a kind of mockery of a rational life—poor beasts! There's something they call the Law. Sing hymns about 'all thine.' They build themselves their dens, gather fruit and pull herbs—marry even. But I can see through it all, see into their very souls, and see there nothing but the souls of beasts, beasts that perish—anger, and the lusts to live and gratify themselves. . . . Yet they're odd. Complex, like everything else alive. There is a kind of upward striving in them, part vanity, part waste sexual emotion, part waste curiosity. It only mocks me. . . . I have some hope of that puma; I have worked hard at her head and brain. . . .[30]

'And now,' said he, standing up after a long gap of silence, during which we had each pursued our own thoughts; 'what do you think? Are you in fear of me still?'

I looked at him, and saw but a white-faced white-haired man, with calm eyes. Save for his serenity, the touch almost of beauty that resulted from his set tranquillity, and from his magnificent build, he might have passed muster among a hundred other comfortable old gentlemen. Then I shivered. By way of answer to his second question, I handed him a revolver with either hand.

'Keep them,' he said, and snatched at a yawn. He stood up, stared at me for a moment, and smiled. 'You have had two eventful days,' said he. 'I should advise some sleep. I'm glad it's all clear. Goodnight.'

He thought me over for a moment, then went out by the inner door. I immediately turned the key in the outer one.

I sat down again, sat for a time in a kind of stagnant mood, so weary, emotionally, mentally, and physically, that I could not think beyond the point at which he had left me. The black window stared at me like an eye. At last with an effort I put out the lamp, and got into the hammock. Very soon I was asleep.

X V
Concerning the Beast Folk

I woke early. Moreau's explanation stood before my mind, clear and definite, from the moment of my awakening. I got out of the hammock and went to the door to assure myself that the key was turned. Then I tried the window-bar, and found it firmly fixed. That these man-like creatures were in truth only bestial monsters, mere grotesque travesties of men, filled me with a vague uncertainty of their possibilities that was far worse than any definite fear. A tapping came at the door, and I heard the glutinous accents

---

[30] The puma has been "it" until it acquires female gender here. In the first draft of the story, Moreau's first try was a mermaid, which he left incomplete to take up the frenzied pursuit of the full-scale (male) human shape (see Philmus, Appendix I, "The First Moreau," 132). [Ed.]

of M'ling speaking. I pocketed one of the revolvers (keeping one hand upon it), and opened to him.

'Good morning, sair,' he said, bringing, in addition to the customary herb breakfast, an ill-cooked rabbit. Montgomery followed him. His roving eye caught the position of my arm, and he smiled askew.

The puma was resting to heal that day; but Moreau, who was singularly solitary in his habits, did not join us. I talked with Montgomery to clear my ideas of the way in which the Beast Folk lived. In particular, I was urgent to know how these inhuman monsters were kept from falling upon Moreau and Montgomery, and from rending one another.

He explained to me that the comparative safety of Moreau and himself was due to the limited mental scope of these monsters. In spite of their increased intelligence, and the tendency of their animal instincts to re-waken, they had certain Fixed Ideas implanted by Moreau in their minds, which absolutely bounded their imaginations. They were really hypnotised, had been told certain things were impossible, and certain things were not to be done, and these prohibitions were woven into the texture of their minds beyond any possibility of disobedience or dispute.

Certain matters, however, in which old instinct was at war with Moreau's convenience, were in a less stable condition. A series of propositions called the Law—I had already heard them recited—battled in their minds with the deep-seated, ever rebellious cravings of their animal natures. This Law they were ever repeating, I found, and—ever breaking. Both Montgomery and Moreau displayed particular solicitude to keep them ignorant of the taste of blood. They feared the inevitable suggestions of that flavour.

Montgomery told me that the Law, especially among the feline Beast People, became oddly weakened about nightfall; that then the animal was at its strongest; a spirit of adventure sprang up in them at the dusk; they would dare things they never seemed to dream about by day. To that I owed my stalking by the Leopard Man on the night of my arrival. But during these earlier days of my stay they broke the Law only furtively, and after dark; in the daylight there was a general atmosphere of respect for its multifarious prohibitions.

And here perhaps I may give a few general facts about the island and the Beast People. The island, which was of irregular outline, and lay low upon the wide sea, had a total area, I suppose, of seven or eight square miles.[31] It was volcanic in origin, and was now fringed on three sides by coral reefs. Some fumarolles to the northward, and a hot spring were the only vestiges

---

[31] This description corresponds in every respect to Noble's Isle. — C. E. P. [Wells's only note, supplied by Charles Edward Prendick, writer of the Introduction. Ed.]

of the forces that had long since originated it. Now and then a faint quiver of earthquake would be sensible, and sometimes the ascent of the spire of smoke would be rendered tumultuous by gusts of steam. But that was all. The population of the island, Montgomery informed me, now numbered rather more than sixty of these strange creations of Moreau's art, not counting the smaller monstrosities which lived in the undergrowth and were without human form.

Altogether, he had made nearly a hundred and twenty, but many had died; and others, like the writhing Footless Thing of which he had told me, had come by violent ends. In answer to my question, Montgomery said that they actually bore offspring, but that these generally died. There was no evidence of the inheritance of the acquired human characteristics. When they lived, Moreau took them and stamped the human form upon them. The females were less numerous than the males, and liable to much furtive persecution in spite of the monogamy the Law enjoined. *sexuality*

It would be impossible for me to describe these Beast People in detail — my eye has had no training in details — and unhappily I cannot sketch. Most striking perhaps in their general appearance was the disproportion between the legs of these creatures and the length of their bodies; and yet — so relative is our idea of grace — my eye became habituated to their forms, and at last I even fell in with their persuasion that my own long thighs were ungainly. Another point was the forward carriage of the head, and the clumsy and inhuman curvature of the spine. Even the Ape Man lacked that inward sinuous curve of the back that makes the human figure so graceful. Most had their shoulders hunched clumsily, and their short forearms hung weakly at their sides. Few of them were conspicuously hairy — at least, until the end of my time upon the island.

The next most obvious deformity was in their faces, almost all of which were prognathous, malformed about the ears, with large and protuberant noses, very furry or very bristly hair, and often strangely coloured or strangely placed eyes. None could laugh, though the Ape Man had a chattering titter. Beyond these general characters their heads had little in common; each preserved the quality of its particular species: the human mark distorted but did not hide the leopard, the ox, or the sow, or other animal or animals, from which the creature had been moulded. The voices, too, varied exceedingly. The hands were always malformed; and though some surprised me by their unexpected humanity, almost all were deficient in the number of the digits, clumsy about the finger-nails, and lacking any tactile sensibility.

The two most formidable animal-men were my Leopard Man and a creature made of Hyæna and Swine. Larger than these were the three bull creatures who pulled in the boat. Then came the Silvery Hairy Man who was also the Sayer of the Law, M'ling, and a satyr-like creature of Ape and Goat. There were three Swine Men and a Swine Woman, a Mare-Rhinoceros creature, and several other females whose sources I did not ascertain. There were several Wolf creatures, a Bear-Bull, and a Saint Bernard Dog Man. I have already described the Ape Man, and there was a particularly hateful (and evil-smelling) old woman made of Vixen and Bear, whom I hated from the beginning. She was said to be a passionate votary of the Law. Smaller creatures were certain dappled youths and my little sloth creature. But enough of this catalogue!

At first I had a shivering horror of the brutes, felt all too keenly that they were still brutes, but insensibly I became a little habituated to the idea of them, and, moreover, I was affected by Montgomery's attitude towards them. He had been with them so long that he had come to regard them as almost normal human beings—his London days seemed a glorious impossible past to him. Only once in a year or so did he go to Arica to deal with Moreau's agent, a trader in animals there. He hardly met the finest type of mankind in that seafaring village of Spanish mongrels. The men aboard ship, he told me, seemed at first just as strange to him as the Beast Men seemed to me,—unnaturally long in the leg, flat in the face, prominent in the forehead, suspicious, dangerous, and cold-hearted. In fact, he did not like men. His heart had warmed to me, he thought, because he had saved my life.

I fancied even then that he had a sneaking kindness for some of these metamorphosed brutes, a vicious sympathy with some of their ways, but that he attempted to veil from me at first.

M'ling, the black-faced man, his attendant, the first of the Beast Folk I had encountered, did not live with the others across the island, but in a small kennel at the back of the enclosure. The creature was scarcely so intelligent as the Ape Man, but far more docile, and the most human-looking of all the Beast Folk, and Montgomery had trained it to prepare food, and indeed to discharge all the trivial domestic offices that were required. It was a complex trophy of Moreau's horrible skill, a bear, tainted with dog and ox, and one of the most elaborately made of all his creatures. It treated Montgomery with a strange tenderness and devotion; sometimes he would notice it, pat it, call it half-mocking, half-jocular names, and so make it caper with extraordinary delight; sometimes he would ill-treat it, especially after he had been at the whisky, kicking it, beating it, pelting it with stones or lighted fusees.[32] But whether he treated it well or ill, it loved nothing so much as to be near him. *Little a pet*

---

[32] Large matchsticks. [Ed.]

I say I became habituated to the Beast People, that a thousand things that had seemed unnatural and repulsive speedily became natural and ordinary to me. I suppose everything in existence takes its colour from the average hue of our surroundings: Montgomery and Moreau were too peculiar and individual to keep my general impressions of humanity well defined. I would see one of the clumsy bovine creatures who worked the launch treading heavily through the undergrowth, and find myself asking, trying hard to recall, how he differed from some really human yokel trudging home from his mechanical labours; or I would meet the Fox-Bear Woman's vulpine, shifty face, strangely human in its speculative cunning, and even imagine I had met it before in some city byway.

Yet every now and then the beast would flash out upon me beyond doubt or denial. An ugly-looking man, a hunchbacked human savage to all appearance, squatting in the aperture of one of the dens, would stretch his arms and yawn, showing with startling suddenness scissor-edge incisors and sabre-like canines, keen and brilliant as knives. Or in some narrow pathway, glancing with a transitory daring into the eyes of some lithe white-swathed female figure, I would suddenly see (with a spasmodic revulsion) that they had slit-like pupils or, glancing down, note the curving nail with which she held her shapeless wrap about her. It is a curious thing, by the by, for which I am quite unable to account, that these weird creatures—the females I mean—had in the earlier days of my stay an instinctive sense of their own repulsive clumsiness, and displayed, in consequence, a more than human regard for the decencies and decorum of external costume.

females

XVI

How the Beast Folk Tasted Blood

But my inexperience as a writer betrays me, and I wander from the thread of my story. After I had breakfasted with Montgomery he took me across the island to see the fumarolle and the source of the hot spring, into whose scalding waters I had blundered on the previous day. Both of us carried whips and loaded revolvers. While going through a leafy jungle on our road thither we heard a rabbit squealing. We stopped and listened, but we heard no more, and presently we went on our way, and the incident dropped out of our minds. Montgomery called my attention to certain little pink animals with long hind-legs, that went leaping through the undergrowth. He told me they were creatures made of the offspring of the Beast People, that Moreau had invented. He had fancied they might serve for meat, but a rabbit-like habit of devouring their young had defeated this intention. I had already encountered some of these creatures, once during my moonlight flight from the Leopard Man, and once during my pursuit by Moreau on the previous day. By chance, one hopping to avoid us leapt into the hole caused by the uprooting of a wind-blown tree. Before it could extricate itself we managed to catch it. It spat like a cat, scratched and kicked vigorously with its hind-legs, and made an attempt to bite, but its teeth were too feeble to inflict more than a painless pinch. It seemed to me rather a pretty little creature, and as Montgomery stated that it never destroyed the turf by burrowing, and was very cleanly in its habits, I should imagine it might prove a convenient substitute for the common rabbit in gentlemen's parks.

We also saw on our way the trunk of a tree barked in long strips and splintered deeply. Montgomery called my attention to this. 'Not to claw Bark of Trees; *that* is the Law,' he said. 'Much some of them care for it!' It was after this, I think, that we met the Satyr and the Ape Man. The Satyr was a gleam of classical memory on the part of Moreau, his face ovine in expression—like the coarser Hebrew type—his voice a harsh bleat, his nether extremities Satanic.[33] He was gnawing the husk of a podlike fruit as he passed us. Both of them saluted Montgomery.

'Hail,' said they, 'to the Other with the whip!'

'There's a third with a whip now,' said Montgomery. 'So you'd better mind!'

'Was he not made?' said the Ape Man. 'He said—he said he was made.'

The Satyr Man looked curiously at me.

'The Third with the whip, he that walks weeping into the sea, has a thin white face.'

'He has a thin long whip,' said Montgomery.

'Yesterday he bled and wept,' said the Satyr.

'You never bleed nor weep. The Master does not bleed nor weep.'

'Ollendorffian[34] beggar!' said Montgomery. 'You'll bleed and weep if you don't look out.'

'He has five fingers; he is a five-man like me,' said the Ape Man.

'Come along, Prendick,' said Montgomery, taking my arm, and I went on with him.

The Satyr and the Ape Man stood watching us and making other remarks to each other.

---

[33] Darwinian science lent dangerous authority to racial typing. See Stover's long note on Wells and "the so-called 'Jewish problem'" (157–58). [Ed.]

[34] Heinrich Ollendorff (1803–65), author of numerous books on language acquisition. [Ed.]

'He says nothing,' said the Satyr. 'Men have voices.'

'Yesterday he asked me of things to eat,' said the Ape Man. 'He did not know.' Then they spoke inaudible things, and I heard the Satyr laughing.

It was on our way back that we came upon the dead rabbit. The red body of the wretched little beast was rent to pieces, many of the ribs stripped white, and the backbone indisputably gnawed.

At that Montgomery stopped.

'Good God!' said he, stooping down and picking up some of the crushed vertebræ to examine them more closely. 'Good God!' he repeated, 'what can this mean?'

'Some carnivore of yours has remembered its old habits,' I said, after a pause. 'This backbone has been bitten through.'

He stood staring, with his face white and his lip pulled askew.

'I don't like this,' he said slowly.

'I saw something of the same kind,' said I, 'the first day I came here.'

'The devil you did! What was it?'

'A rabbit with its head twisted off.'

'The day you came here?'

'The day I came here. In the undergrowth, at the back of the enclosure, when I came out in the evening. The head was completely wrung off.'

He gave a long low whistle.

'And what is more, I have an idea which of your brutes did the thing. It's only a suspicion, you know. Before I came on the rabbit I saw one of your monsters drinking in the stream.'

'Sucking his drink?'

'Yes.'

'Not to suck your Drink; *that* is the Law. Much the brutes care for the Law, eh—when Moreau's not about?'

'It was the brute who chased me.'

'Of course,' said Montgomery; 'it's just the way with carnivores. After a kill they drink. It's the taste of blood, you know.

'What was the brute like?' he asked. 'Would you know him again?' He glanced about us, standing astride over the mess of dead rabbit, his eyes roving among the shadows and screens of greenery, the lurking-places and ambuscade of the forest, that bounded us in. 'The taste of blood,' he said again.

He took out his revolver, examined the cartridges in it, and replaced it. Then he began to pull at his dropping lip.

'I think I should know the brute again. I stunned him. He ought to have a handsome bruise on the forehead of him.'

'But then we have to *prove* he killed the rabbit,' said Montgomery. 'I wish I'd never brought the things here.'

I should have gone on, but he stayed there thinking over the mangled rabbit in a puzzle-headed way. As it was, I went to such a distance that the rabbit's remains were hidden.

'Come on!' I said.

Presently he woke up and came towards me.

'You see,' he said, almost in a whisper, 'they are all supposed to have a fixed idea against eating anything that runs on land. If some brute has by accident tasted blood . . .'

We went on some way in silence.

'I wonder what can have happened,' he said to himself. Then, after a pause, again: 'I did a foolish thing the other day. That servant of mine . . . I showed him how to skin and cook a rabbit. It's odd . . . I saw him licking his hands . . . It never occurred to me.'

Then: 'We must put a stop to this. I must tell Moreau.'

He could think of nothing else on our homeward journey.

Moreau took the matter even more seriously than Montgomery, and I need scarcely say I was infected by their evident consternation.

'We must make an example,' said Moreau. 'I've no doubt in my mind that the Leopard Man was the sinner. But how can we prove it? I wish, Montgomery, you had kept your taste for meat in hand, and gone without these exciting novelties. We may find ourselves in a mess yet through it.'

'I was a silly ass,' said Montgomery. 'But the thing's done now. And you said I might have them, you know.'

'We must see to the thing at once,' said Moreau. 'I suppose, if anything should turn up, M'ling can take care of himself.'

'I'm not so sure of M'ling,' said Montgomery, 'I think I ought to know him.'

In the afternoon, Moreau, Montgomery, myself, and M'ling went across the island to the huts in the ravine. We three were armed. M'ling carried the little hatchet he used in chopping firewood, and some coils of wire. Moreau had a huge cowherd's horn slung over his shoulder.

'You will see a gathering of the Beast People,' said Montgomery. 'It's a pretty sight.' Moreau said not a word on the way but his heavy white-fringed face was grimly set.

We crossed the ravine, down which smoked the stream of hot water, and followed the winding pathway through the cane brakes until we reached a wide area covered over with a thick powdery yellow substance, which I believe was sulphur. Above the shoulder of a weedy bank the sea glittered. We came to a kind of shallow natural amphitheatre, and here the four of us halted. Then Moreau sounded the horn and broke the sleeping stillness of the tropical afternoon. He must have had strong lungs. The hooting note rose and rose amidst its echoes to at last an ear-penetrating intensity. 'Ah!' said Moreau, letting the curved instrument fall to his side again.

Immediately there was a crashing through the yellow canes, and a sound of voices from the dense green jungle that marked the morass through which I had run on the previous day. Then at three or four points on the edge of the sulphurous area appeared the grotesque forms of the Beast People, hurrying towards us. I could not help a creeping horror as I perceived first one and then another trot out from the trees or reeds, and come shambling along over the hot dust. But Moreau and Montgomery stood calmly enough, and, perforce, I stuck beside them. First to arrive was the Satyr, strangely unreal, for all that he cast a shadow, and tossed the dust with his hoofs; after him, from the brake, came a monstrous lout, a thing of horse and rhinoceros, chewing a straw as it came; and then appeared the Swine Woman and two Wolf Women; then the Fox-Bear Witch with her red eyes in her peaked red face, and then others—all hurrying eagerly. As they came forward they began to cringe towards Moreau and chant, quite regardless of one another, fragments of the latter half of the litany of the Law: '*His* is the Hand that wounds, *His* is the Hand that heals,' and so forth.

As soon as they had approached within a distance of perhaps thirty yards they halted, and bowing on knees and elbows, began flinging the white dust upon their heads. Imagine the scene if you can. We three blue-clad men, with our misshapen black-faced attendant, standing in a wide expanse of sunlit yellow dust under the blazing blue sky, and surrounded by this circle of crouching and gesticulating monstrosities, some almost human, save in their subtle expression and gestures, some like cripples, some so strangely distorted as to resemble nothing but the denizens of our wildest dreams. And beyond, the ready lines of a cane brake in one direction, a dense tangle of palm trees on the other, separating us from the ravine with the huts, and to the north the hazy horizon of the Pacific Ocean.

'Sixty-two, sixty-three,' counted Moreau.

'There are four more.'

'I do not see the Leopard Man,' said I.

Presently Moreau sounded the great horn again, and at the sound of it all the Beast People writhed and grovelled in the dust. Then, slinking out of the cane brake, stooping near the ground, and trying to join the dust-throwing circle behind Moreau's back, came the Leopard Man. And I saw that his forehead was bruised. The last of the Beast People to arrive was the little Ape Man. The earlier animals, hot and weary with their grovelling, shot vicious glances at him.

'Cease,' said Moreau, in his firm loud voice, and the Beast People sat back upon their hams and rested from their worshipping.

'Where is the Sayer of the Law?' said Moreau, and the hairy grey monster bowed his face in the dust.

'Say the words,' said Moreau, and forthwith all in the kneeling assembly, swaying from side to side and dashing up the sulphur with their hands, first the right hand and a puff of dust, and then the left, began once more to chant their strange litany.

When they reached 'Not to eat Flesh or Fish; that is the Law,' Moreau held up his lank white hand.

'*Stop!*' he cried, and there fell absolute silence upon them all.

I think they all knew and dreaded what was coming. I looked round at their strange faces. When I saw their wincing attitudes and the furtive dread in their bright eyes, I wondered that I had ever believed them to be men.

'That Law has been broken,' said Moreau.

'None escape,' from the faceless creature with the Silvery Hair. 'None escape,' repeated the kneeling circle of Beast People.

'Who is he?' cried Moreau, and looked round at their faces, cracking his whip. I fancied the Hyæna-Swine looked dejected, so too did the Leopard Man. Moreau stopped, facing this creature, who cringed towards him with the memory and dread of infinite torment. 'Who is he?' repeated Moreau, in a voice of thunder.

'Evil is he who breaks the Law,' chanted the Sayer of the Law.

Moreau looked into the eyes of the Leopard Man, and seemed to be dragging the very soul out of the creature.

'Who breaks the Law—' said Moreau, taking his eyes off his victim and turning towards us. It seemed to me there was a touch of exultation in his voice.

'—goes back to the House of Pain,' they all clamoured;—'goes back to the House of Pain, O Master!'

'Back to the House of Pain—back to the House of Pain,' gabbled the Ape Man, as though the idea was sweet to him.

'Do you hear?' said Moreau, turning back to the criminal, 'my frien . . . Hullo!'

For the Leopard Man, released from Moreau's eye, had risen straight from his knees, and now, with eyes aflame and his huge feline tusks flashing out from under his curling lips, leapt towards his tormentor. I am convinced that only the madness of unendurable fear could have prompted this attack. The whole circle of three-score monsters seemed to rise about us. I drew my revolver. The two figures collided. I saw Moreau reeling back from the Leopard Man's blow. There was a furious yelling and howling all about us. Everyone was moving rapidly. For a moment I thought it was a general revolt.

The furious face of the Leopard Man flashed by mine, with M'ling close in pursuit. I saw the yellow eyes of the Hyæna-Swine blazing with excitement, his attitude as if he were half-resolved to attack me. The Satyr, too, glared at me over the Hyæna-Swine's hunched shoulders. I heard the crack of Moreau's pistol, and saw the pink flash dart across the tumult. The whole crowd seemed to swing round in the direction of the glint of fire, and I, too, was swung round by the magnetism of the movement. In another second I was running, one of a tumultuous shouting crowd, in pursuit of the escaping Leopard Man.

That is all that I can tell definitely. I saw the Leopard Man strike Moreau, and then everything spun about me, until I was running headlong.

M'ling was ahead, close in pursuit of the fugitive. Behind, their tongues already lolling out, ran the Wolf-Women in great leaping strides. The Swine-Folk followed, squealing with excitement, and the two Bull Men in their swathings of white. Then came Moreau in a cluster of the Beast People, his wide-brimmed straw hat blown off, his revolver in hand, and his lank white hair streaming out. The Hyæna-Swine ran beside me, keeping pace with me, and glancing furtively at me out of his feline eyes, and the others came pattering and shouting behind us.

The Leopard Man went bursting his way through the long canes, which sprang back as he passed and rattled in M'ling's face. We others in the rear found a trampled path for us when we reached the brake. The chase lay through the brake for perhaps a quarter of a mile, and then plunged into a dense thicket, that retarded our movements exceedingly, though we went through it in a crowd together—fronds flicking into our faces, ropy creepers catching us under the chin, or gripping our ankles, thorny plants hooking into and tearing cloth and flesh together.

'He has gone on all-fours through this,' panted Moreau, now just ahead of me.

'None escape,' said the Wolf-Bear, laughing into my face with the exultation of hunting.

We burst out again among rocks, and saw the quarry ahead, running lightly on all-fours, and snarling at us over his shoulder. At that the Wolf-Folk howled with delight. The thing was still clothed, and, at a distance, its face still seemed human, but the carriage of its four limbs was feline, and the furtive droop of its shoulder was distinctly that of a hunted animal. It leapt over some thorny yellow-flowering bushes and was hidden. M'ling was half-way across the space.

Most of us now had lost the first speed of the chase, and had fallen into a longer and steadier stride. I saw, as we traversed the open, that the pursuit was now spreading from a column into a line. The Hyæna-Swine still ran close to me, watching me as it ran, every now and then puckering its muzzle with a snarling laugh.

At the edge of the rocks, the Leopard Man, realising he was making for the projecting cape upon which he had stalked me on the night of my arrival, had doubled in the undergrowth. But Montgomery had seen the manœuvre, and turned him again.

So, panting, tumbling against rocks, torn by brambles, impeded by ferns and reeds, I helped to pursue the Leopard Man, who had broken the Law, and the Hyæna-Swine ran, laughing savagely, by my side. I staggered on, my head reeling, and my heart beating against my ribs, tired almost to death, and yet not daring to lose sight of the chase, least I should be left alone with this horrible companion. I staggered on in spite of infinite fatigue and the dense heat of the tropical afternoon.

And at last the fury of the hunt slackened. We had pinned the wretched brute into a corner of the island. Moreau, whip in hand, marshalled us all into an irregular line, and we advanced, now slowly, shouting to one another as we advanced, and tightening the cordon about our victim. He lurked, noiseless and invisible, in the bushes through which I had run from him during that midnight pursuit.

'Steady!' cried Moreau; 'steady!' as the ends of the line crept round the tangle of undergrowth, and hemmed the brute in.

''Ware a rush!' came the voice of Montgomery from beyond the thicket.

I was on the slope above the bushes. Montgomery and Moreau beat along the beach beneath. Slowly we pushed in among the fretted network of branches and leaves. The quarry was silent.

'Back to the House of Pain, the House of Pain, the House of Pain!' yelped the voice of the Ape Man, some twenty yards to the right.

When I heard that I forgave the poor wretch all the fear he had inspired in me.

I heard the twigs snap and the boughs swish aside before the heavy tread of the Horse-Rhinoceros upon my right. Then suddenly, through a polygon of green, in the half-darkness under the luxuriant growth, I saw the creature we were hunting. I halted. He was crouched together into the smallest possible compass, his luminous green eyes turned over his shoulder regarding me.

It may seem a strange contradiction in me—I cannot explain the fact—but now, seeing the creature there in a perfectly animal attitude, with the light gleaming in its eyes, and its imperfectly human face distorted with terror, I realised again the fact of its humanity. In another moment other of its pursuers would see it, and it would be overpowered and captured, to experience once more the horrible tortures of the enclosure. Abruptly I slipped out my revolver, aimed between its terror-struck eyes, and fired.

As I did so the Hyæna-Swine saw the thing, and flung itself upon it with an eager cry, thrusting thirsty teeth into its neck. All about me the green masses of the thicket were swaying and cracking as the Beast People came rushing together. One face and then another appeared.

'Don't kill it, Prendick,' cried Moreau. 'Don't kill it!' And I saw him stooping as he pushed through under the fronds of the big ferns.

In another moment he had beaten off the Hyæna-Swine with the handle of his whip, and he and Montgomery were keeping away the excited carnivorous Beast People, and particularly M'ling, from the still quivering body. The Hairy Grey Thing came sniffing at the corpse under my arm. The other animals, in their animal ardour, jostled me to get a nearer view.

'Confound you, Prendick!' said Moreau. 'I wanted him.'

'I'm sorry,' said I, though I was not. 'It was the impulse of the moment.'

I felt sick with exertion and excitement. Turning, I pushed my way out of the crowding Beast People, and went on alone up the slope towards the higher part of the headland. Under the shouted instructions of Moreau, I heard the three white-swathed Bull Men begin dragging the victim down towards the water.

It was easy now for me to be alone. The Beast People manifested a quite human curiosity about the dead body, and followed it in a thick knot, sniffing and growling at it, as the Bull Men dragged it down the beach. I went to the headland, and watched the Bull Men, black against the evening sky, as they carried the weighted dead body out to sea, and, like a wave across my mind, came the realisation of the unspeakable aimlessness of things upon the island.

Upon the beach, among the rocks beneath me, was the Ape Man, the Hyæna-Swine, and several other of the Beast People, standing about Montgomery and Moreau. They were all still intensely excited, and all overflowing with noisy expressions of their loyalty to the Law. Yet I felt an absolute assurance in my own mind that the Hyæna-Swine was implicated in the rabbit-killing. A strange persuasion came upon me that, save for the grossness of the line, the grotesqueness of the forms, I had here before me the whole balance of human life in miniature, the whole interplay of instinct, reason, and fate, in its simplest form. The Leopard Man had happened to go under. That was all the difference.

Poor brutes! I began to see the viler aspect of Moreau's cruelty. I had not thought before of the pain and trouble that came to these poor victims after they had passed from Moreau's hands. I had shivered only at the days of actual torment in the enclosure. But now that seemed to be the lesser part. Before they had been beasts, their instincts fitly adapted to their surroundings, and happy as living things may be. Now they stumbled in the shackles of humanity, lived in a fear that never died, fretted by a law they could not understand; their mock-human existence began in an agony, was one long internal struggle, one long dread of Moreau—and for what? It was the wantonness that stirred me.

Had Moreau had any intelligible object I could have sympathised at least a little with him. I am not so squeamish about pain as that. I could have forgiven him a little even had his motive been hate. But he was so irresponsible, so utterly careless. His curiosity, his mad, aimless investigations, drove him on, and the things were thrown out to live a year or so, to struggle, and blunder, and suffer; at last to die painfully. They were wretched in themselves, the old animal hate moved them to trouble one another, the Law held them back from a brief hot struggle and a decisive end to their natural animosities.

In those days my fear of the Beast People went the way of my personal fear for Moreau. I fell indeed into a morbid state, deep and enduring, alien to fear, which has left permanent scars upon my mind. I must confess I lost faith in the sanity of the world when I saw it suffering the painful disorder of this island.

A blind fate, a vast pitiless mechanism, seemed to cut and shape the fabric of existence, and I, Moreau (by his passion for research), Montgomery (by his passion for drink), the Beast People, with their instincts and mental restrictions, were torn and crushed, ruthlessly, inevitably, amid the infinite complexity of its incessant wheels. But this condition did not come all at once. . . . I think indeed that I anticipate a little in speaking of it now.

XVII
A Catastrophe

Scarcely six weeks passed before I had lost every feeling but dislike and abhorrence for these infamous experiments of Moreau's. My one idea was to get away from these horrible caricatures of my Maker's image, back to the sweet and wholesome intercourse of men. My fellow-creatures, from whom I was thus separated, began to assume idyllic virtue and beauty in my memory. My first friendship with Montgomery did not increase. His long separation from humanity, his secret vice of drunkenness, his evident sympathy with the Beast People, tainted him to me. Several times I let him go alone among them. I avoided intercourse with them in every possible way.

I spent an increasing proportion of my time upon the beach, looking for some liberating sail that never appeared, until one day there fell upon us an appalling disaster, that put an altogether different aspect upon my strange surroundings.

It was about seven or eight weeks after my landing — rather more, I think, though I had not troubled to keep account of the time — when this catastrophe occurred. It happened in the early morning — I should think about six. I had risen and breakfasted early, having been aroused by the noise of three Beast Men carrying wood into the enclosure.

After breakfast I went to the open gateway of the enclosure and stood there smoking a cigarette and enjoying the freshness of the early morning. Moreau presently came round the corner of the enclosure and greeted me.

He passed by me, and I heard him behind me unlock and enter his laboratory. So indurated was I at that time to the abomination of the place, that I heard without a touch of emotion the puma victim begin another day of torture. It met its persecutor with a shriek almost exactly like that of an angry virago.

Then something happened. I do not know what it was exactly to this day. I heard a sharp cry behind me, a fall, and, turning, saw an awful face rushing upon me, not human, not animal, but hellish, brown, seamed with red branching scars, red drops starting out upon it, and the lidless eyes ablaze. I flung up my arm to defend myself from the blow that flung me headlong with a broken forearm, and the great monster, swathed in lint and with red-stained bandages fluttering about it, leapt over me and passed.

I rolled over and over down the beach, tried to sit up, and collapsed upon my broken arm. Then Moreau appeared, his massive white face all the more terrible for the blood that trickled from his forehead. He carried a revolver in one hand. He scarcely glanced at me, but rushed off at once in pursuit of the puma.

I tried the other arm and sat up. The muffled figure in front ran in great striding leaps along the beach, and Moreau followed her. She turned her head and saw him, then, doubling abruptly, made for the bushes. She gained upon him at every stride. I saw her plunge into them, and Moreau, running slantingly to intercept her, fired and missed as she disappeared. Then he too vanished in the green confusion.

I stared after them, and then the pain in my arm flamed up, and with a groan I staggered to my feet. Montgomery appeared in the doorway dressed, and with his revolver in his hand.

'Great God, Prendick!' he said, not noticing that I was hurt. 'That brute's loose! Tore the fetter out of the wall. Have you seen them?' Then sharply, seeing I gripped my arm, 'What's the matter?'

'I was standing in the doorway,' said I.

He came forward and took my arm.

'Blood on the sleeve,' said he, and rolled back the flannel. He pocketed the weapon, felt my arm about painfully, and led me inside. 'Your arm is broken,' he said; and then, 'Tell me exactly how it happened—what happened.'

I told him what I had seen, told him in broken sentences, with gasps of pain between them, and very dexterously and swiftly he bound my arm meanwhile. He slung it from my shoulder, stood back, and looked at me.

'You'll do,' he said. 'And now?' He thought. Then he went out and locked the gates of the enclosure. He was absent some time.

I was chiefly concerned about my arm. The incident seemed merely one more of many horrible things. I sat down in the deck chair and, I must admit, swore heartily at the island.

The first dull feeling of injury in my arm had already given way to a burning pain when Montgomery reappeared.

His face was rather pale, and he showed more of his lower gums than ever.

'I can neither see nor hear anything of him,' he said. 'I've been thinking he may want my help.' He stared at me with his expressionless eyes. 'That was a strong brute,' he said. 'It simply wrenched its fetter out of the wall.'

He went to the window, then to the door, and there turned to me.

'I shall go after him,' he said. 'There's another revolver I can leave with you. To tell you the truth, I feel anxious somehow.'

He obtained the weapon, and put it ready to my hand on the table, then went out, leaving a restless contagion in the air. I did not sit long after he left. I took the revolver in hand and went to the doorway.

The morning was as still as death. Not a whisper of wind was stirring, the sea was like polished glass, the sky empty, the beach desolate. In my half-excited, half-feverish state this stillness of things oppressed me.

I tried to whistle, and the tune died away. I swore again—the second time that morning. Then I went to the corner of the enclosure and stared inland at the green bush that had swallowed up Moreau and Montgomery. When would they return. And how?

Then far away up the beach a little grey Beast Man appeared, ran down to the water's edge, and began splashing about. I strolled back to the doorway, then to the corner again, and so began pacing to and fro like a sentinel upon duty. Once I was arrested by the distant voice of Montgomery bawling.

'Coo-ee . . . Mor-eau!'

My arm became less painful, but very hot. I got feverish and thirsty. My shadow grew shorter. I watched the distant figure until it went away again.

Would Moreau and Montgomery never return?

Three sea-birds began fighting for some stranded treasure.

Then from far away behind the enclosure I heard a pistol-shot. A long silence, and then came another. Then a yelling cry nearer, and another dismal gap of silence. My unfortunate imagination set to work to torment me. Then suddenly a shot close by.

I went to the corner, startled, and saw Montgomery, his face scarlet, his hair disordered, and the knee of his trousers torn. His face expressed profound consternation. Behind him slouched the Beast Man M'ling, and round M'ling's jaws were some ominous brown stains.

'Has he come?' he said.

'Moreau?' said I. 'No.'

'My God!' The man was panting, almost sobbing for breath. 'Go back in,' he said, taking my arm. 'They're mad. They're all rushing about mad. What can have happened? I don't know. I'll tell you when my breath comes. Where's some brandy?'

He limped before me into the room and sat down in the deck chair. M'ling flung himself down just outside the doorway, and began panting like a dog. I got Montgomery some brandy and water. He sat staring blankly in front of him, recovering his breath. After some minutes he began to tell me what had happened.

He had followed their track for some way. It was plain enough at first on account of the crushed and broken bushes, white rags torn from the puma's bandages, and occasional smears of blood on the leaves of the shrubs and undergrowth.

He lost the track, however, on the stony ground beyond the stream where I had seen the Beast Man drinking, and went wandering aimlessly westward shouting Moreau's name.

Then M'ling had come to him carrying a light hatchet. M'ling had seen nothing of the puma affair, had been felling wood and heard him calling. They went on shouting together. Two Beast Men came crouching and peering at them through the undergrowth, with gestures and a furtive carriage that alarmed Montgomery by their strangeness. He hailed them, and they fled guiltily. He stopped shouting after that, and after wandering some time further in an undecided way, determined to visit the huts.

He found the ravine deserted.

Growing more alarmed every minute, he began to retrace his steps. Then it was he encountered the two Swine Men I had seen dancing on the night of my arrival; blood-stained they were about the mouth, and intensely excited. They came crashing through the ferns, and stopped with fierce faces when they saw him.

He cracked his whip in some trepidation, and forthwith they rushed at him. Never before had a Beast Man dared to do that. One he shot through the head, M'ling flung himself upon the other, and the two rolled grappling.

M'ling got his brute under and with his teeth in its throat, and Montgomery shot that too as it struggled in M'ling's grip. He had some difficulty in inducing M'ling to come on with him.

Thence they had hurried back to me. On the way M'ling had suddenly rushed into a thicket and driven out an under-sized Ocelot Man, also blood-stained, and lame through a wound in the foot. This brute had run a little way and then turned savagely at bay, and Montgomery—with a certain wantonness I thought—had shot him.

'What does it all mean?' said I.

He shook his head and turned once more to the brandy.

XVIII
The Finding of Moreau

When I saw Montgomery swallow a third dose of brandy I took it upon myself to interfere. He was already more than half-fuddled. I told him that some serious thing must have happened to Moreau by this time, or he would have returned, and that it behoved us to ascertain what that catastrophe was. Montgomery raised some feeble objections, and at last agreed. We had some food, and then all three of us started.

It is possibly due to the tension of my mind at the time, but even now that start into the hot stillness of the tropical afternoon is a singularly vivid impression. M'ling went first, his shoulders hunched, his strange black head moving with quick starts as he peered first on this side of the way and then on that. He was unarmed. His axe he had dropped when he encountered the Swine Men. Teeth were *his* weapons when it came to fighting. Montgomery followed with stumbling footsteps, his hands in his pockets, his face downcast; he was in a state of muddled sullenness with me on account of the brandy. My left arm was in a sling—it was lucky it was my left—and I carried my revolver in my right.

We took a narrow path through the wild luxuriance of the island, going north-westward. And presently M'ling stopped and became rigid with watchfulness. Montgomery almost staggered into him, and then stopped too. Then, listening intently, we heard, coming through the trees, the sound of voices, and footsteps approaching us.

'He is dead,' said a deep vibrating voice.

'He is not dead, he is not dead,' jabbered another.

'We saw, we saw,' said several voices.

'*Hul*-lo!' suddenly shouted Montgomery. 'Hullo there!'

'Confound you!' said I, and gripped my pistol.

There was a silence, then a crashing among the interlacing vegetation, first here, then there, and then half a dozen faces appeared, strange faces, lit by a strange light. M'ling made a growling noise in his throat. I recognised the Ape Man—I had, indeed, already identified his voice—and two of the white-swathed brown-featured creatures I had seen in Montgomery's boat. With them were the two dappled brutes, and that grey horribly crooked creature who said the Law, with grey hair streaming down its cheeks, heavy grey eyebrows, and grey locks pouring off from a central parting upon its sloping forehead, a heavy faceless thing, with strange red eyes, looking at us curiously from amidst the green.

For a space no one spoke. Then Montgomery hiccoughed:

'Who . . . said he was dead?'

The Monkey Man looked guiltily at the Hairy Grey Thing.

'He is dead,' said this monster. 'They saw.'

There was nothing threatening about this detachment at any rate. They seemed awestricken and puzzled.

'Where is he?' said Montgomery.

'Beyond,' and the grey creature pointed.

'Is there a Law now?' asked the Monkey Man. 'Is it still to be this and that? Is he dead indeed?'

'Is there a Law?' repeated the man in white.

'Is there a Law, thou Other with the whip? He is dead,' said the Hairy Grey Thing.

And they all stood watching us.

'Prendick,' said Montgomery, turning his dull eyes to me. 'He's dead—evidently.'

I had been standing behind him during this colloquy. I began to see how things lay with them. I suddenly stepped in front of him and lifted up my voice:

'Children of the Law,' I said, 'he is *not* dead.'

M'ling turned his sharp eyes on me.

'He has changed his shape—he has changed his body,' I went on. 'For a time you will not see him. He is . . . there'—I pointed upward—'where he can watch you. You cannot see him. But he can see you. Fear the Law.'

I looked at them squarely. They flinched.

'He is great, he is good,' said the Ape Man, peering fearfully upward among the dense trees.

'And the other Thing?' I demanded.

'The Thing that bled and ran screaming and sobbing—that is dead too,' said the Grey Thing, still regarding me.

'That's well,' grunted Montgomery.

'The Other with the whip,' began the Grey Thing.

'Well?' said I.

'Said he was dead.'

But Montgomery was still sober enough to understand my motive in denying Moreau's death.

'He is not dead,' he said slowly. 'Not dead at all. No more dead than me.'

'Some,' said I, 'have broken the Law. They will die. Some have died. Show us now where his old body lies. The body he cast away because he had no more need of it.'

'It is this way, Man who walked in the Sea,' said the Grey Thing.

And with these six creatures guiding us, we went through the tumult of ferns and creepers and tree-stems towards the north-west. Then came a yelling, a crashing among the branches, and a little pink homunculus rushed by us shrieking. Immediately after appeared a feral monster in headlong pursuit, blood-bedabbled, who was amongst us almost before he could stop his career.

The Grey Thing leapt aside; M'ling with a snarl flew at it, and was struck aside; Montgomery fired and missed, bowed his head, threw up his arm, and turned to run. I fired, and the thing still came on; fired again point-blank into its ugly face. I saw its features vanish in a flash. Its face was driven in. Yet it passed me, gripped Montgomery, and holding him, fell headlong beside him, and pulled him sprawling upon itself—in its death agony.

I found myself alone with M'ling, the dead brute, and the prostrate man. Montgomery raised himself slowly and stared in a muddled way at the shattered Beast Man beside him. It more than half-sobered him. He scrambled to his feet. Then I saw the Grey Thing returning cautiously through the trees.

'See,' said I, pointing to the dead brute. 'Is the Law not alive? This came of breaking the Law.'

He peered at the body.

'He sends the Fire that kills,' said he in his deep voice, repeating part of the ritual.

The others gathered round and stared for a space.

At last we drew near the westward extremity of the island. We came upon the gnawed and mutilated body of the puma, its shoulder-bone smashed by a bullet, and perhaps twenty yards further found at last what we sought. He lay face downward in a trampled space in a cane brake.

One hand was almost severed at the wrist, and his silvery hair was dabbled in blood. His head had been battered in by the fetters of the puma. The broken canes beneath him were smeared with blood. His revolver we could not find. *F: Creation v. Creator*
Montgomery turned him over.

* * * *

Resting at intervals, and with the help of the seven Beast People — for he was a heavy man, — we carried him back to the enclosure. The night was darkling. Twice we heard unseen creatures howling and shrieking past our little band, and once the little pink sloth creature appeared and stared at us, and vanished again. But we were not attacked again. At the gates of the enclosure our company of Beast People left us — M'ling going with the rest. We locked ourselves in, and then took Moreau's mangled body into the yard, and laid it upon a pile of brushwood.

Then we went into the laboratory and put an end to all we found living there.

XIX
Montgomery's 'Bank Holiday' [35]

When this was accomplished, and we had washed and eaten, Montgomery and I went into my little room and seriously discussed our position for the first time. It was then near midnight. He was almost sober, but greatly disturbed in his mind. He had been strangely under the influence of Moreau's personality. I do not think it had ever occurred to him that Moreau could die. This disaster was the sudden collapse of the habits that had become *God* part of his nature in the ten or more monotonous years he had spent on the island. He talked vaguely, answered my questions crookedly, wandered into general questions.

'This silly ass of a world,' he said. 'What a muddle it all is! I haven't had any life. I wonder when it's going to begin. Sixteen years being bullied by nurses and school-masters at their own sweet will, five in London

---

[35] A working-day holiday, created in 1871 for bank employees and soon extended to the general public. Wells may be thinking here of George Gissing's 1889 novel *The Nether World*, whose Chapter 12, "Io Saturnalia!" depicts an August Bank Holiday full of explicitly "bestial" drunkenness and violence among the working classes. [Ed.]

grinding hard at medicine—bad food, shabby lodgings, shabby clothes, shabby vice—a blunder—*I* didn't know any better—and hustled off to this beastly island. Ten years here! What's it all for, Prendick? Are we bubbles blown by a baby?'

It was hard to deal with such ravings.

'The thing we have to think of now,' said I, 'is how to get away from this island.'

'What's the good of getting away? I'm an outcast. Where am *I* to join on? It's all very well for *you*, Prendick. Poor old Moreau! We can't leave him here to have his bones picked. As it is . . . And besides, what will become of the decent part of the Breast Folk?'

'Well,' said I. 'That will do to-morrow. I've been thinking we might make the brushwood into a pyre and burn his body—and those other things . . . Then what will happen with the Beast Folk?'

'*I* don't know. I suppose those that were made of beasts of prey will make silly assess of themselves sooner or later. We can't massacre the lot. Can we? I suppose that's what *your* humanity would suggest? . . . But they'll change. They are sure to change.'

He talked thus inconclusively until at last I felt my temper going.

'Damnation!' he exclaimed, at some petulance of mine. 'Can't you see I'm in a worse hole than you are?' And he got up and went for the brandy. 'Drink,' he said, returning. 'You logic-chopping, chalky-faced saint of an atheist, drink.'

'Not I,' said I, and sat grimly watching his face under the yellow paraffin flare as he drank himself into a garrulous misery. I have a memory of infinite tedium. He wandered into a maudlin defence of the Beast People and of M'ling.

M'ling, he said, was the only thing that had ever really cared for him. And suddenly an idea came to him.

'I'm damned,' said he, staggering to his feet, and clutching the brandy-bottle. By some flash of intuition I knew what it was he intended.

'You don't give drink to that beast!' I said, rising and facing him.

'Beast!' said he. 'You're the beast. He takes his liquor like a Christian. Come out of the way, Prendick.'

'For God's sake,' said I.

'*Get* . . . out of the way,' he roared, and suddenly whipped out his revolver.

'Very well,' said I, and stood aside, half-minded to fall upon him as he put his hand upon the latch, but deterred by the thought of my useless arm. 'You've made a beast of yourself. To the beasts you may go.'

He flung the doorway open and stood, half-facing me, between the yellow lamp-light and the pallid glare of the moon; his eye-sockets were blotches of black under his stubbly eyebrows.

'You're a solemn prig, Prendick, a silly ass! You're always fearing and fancying. We're on the edge of things. I'm bound to cut my throat to-morrow. I'm going to have a damned good bank holiday to-night.'

He turned and went out into the moonlight.

'M'ling,' he cried; 'M'ling, old friend!'

Three dim creatures in the silvery light came along the edge of the wan beach, one a white-wrapped creature, the other two blotches of blackness following it.

They halted, staring. Then I saw M'ling's hunched shoulders as he came round the corner of the house.

'Drink,' cried Montgomery; 'drink, ye brutes! Drink, and be men. Dammy, I'm the cleverest! Moreau forgot this. This is the last touch. Drink, I tell you.' And waving the bottle in his hand, he started off at a kind of quick trot to the westward, M'ling ranging himself between him and the three dim creatures who followed.

I went to the doorway. They were already indistinct in the mist of the moonlight before Montgomery halted. I saw him administer a dose of the raw brandy to M'ling, and saw the five figures melt into one vague patch.

'Sing,' I heard Montgomery shout: 'sing all together, "Confound old Prendick." . . . That's right, Now, again: "Confound old Prendick."'

The black group broke up into five separate figures and wound slowly away from me along the band of shining beach. Each went howling at his own sweet will, yelping insult at me, or giving what ever other vent this new inspiration of brandy demanded.

Presently I heard Montgomery's remote voice shouting, 'Right turn!' and they passed with their shouts and howls into the blackness of the land-ward trees. Slowly, very slowly, they receded into silence.

The peaceful splendour of the night healed again. The moon was now past the meridian and travelling down the west. It was at its full, and very bright, riding through the empty blue sky.

The shadow of the wall lay, a yard wide, and of inky blackness, at my feet. The eastward sea was a featureless grey, dark and mysterious, and between the sea and the shadow, the grey sands (of volcanic glass and crystals) flashed and shone like a beach of diamonds. Behind me the paraffin lamp flared hot and ruddy.

Then I shut the door, locked it, and went into the enclosure where Moreau lay beside his latest victims—the staghounds and the llama, and some other wretched brutes—his massive face, calm even after his terrible death, and with the hard eyes open, staring at the dead white moon above. I sat down upon the edge of the sink, and, with my eyes upon that ghastly pile of silvery light and ominous shadows, began to turn over my plans in my mind.

In the morning I would gather some provisions in the dingey, and after setting fire to the pyre before me, push out into the desolation of the high sea once more. I felt that for Montgomery there was no help; that he was in truth half akin to these Beast Folk, unfitted for human kindred.

I do not know how long I sat there scheming. It must have been an hour or so. Then my planning was interrupted by the return of Montgomery to my neighbourhood. I heard a yelling from many throats, a tumult of exultant cries, passing down towards the beach, whooping and howling and excited shrieks, that seemed to come to a stop near the water's edge. The riot rose and fell; I heard heavy blows and the splintering smash of wood, but it did not trouble me then.

A discordant chanting began.

My thoughts went back to my means of escape. I got up, brought the lamp, and went into a shed to look at some kegs I had seen there.

Then I became interested in the contents of some biscuit tins, and opened one. I saw something out of the tail of my eye, a red figure, and turned sharply.

Behind me lay the yard, vividly black and white in the moonlight, and the pile of wood and faggots on which Moreau and his mutilated victims lay, one on another. They seemed to be gripping one another in one last revengeful grapple. His wounds gaped black as night, and the blood that had dripped lay in black patches upon the sand. Then I saw, without understanding, the cause of the phantom, a ruddy glow that came and danced and went upon the wall opposite. I misinterpreted this, fancied it was a reflection of my flickering lamp, and turned again to the stores in the shed.

I went on rummaging among them as well as a one-armed man could, finding this convenient thing and that, and putting them aside for tomorrow's launch. My movements were slow, and the time passed quickly. Presently the daylight crept upon me.

The chanting died down, gave place to a clamour, then began again, and suddenly broke into a tumult. I heard cries of 'More, more!' a sound like quarrelling, and a sudden wild shriek. The quality of the sounds changed so greatly that it arrested my attention. I went out into the yard and listened. Then, cutting like a knife across the confusion, came the crack of a revolver.

I rushed at once through my room to the little doorway. As I did so I heard some of the packing-cases behind me go sliding down and smash together, with a clatter of glass on the floor of the shed. But I did not heed these. I flung the door open and looked out.

Up the beach by the boathouse a bonfire was burning, raining up sparks into the indistinctness of the dawn. Around this struggled a mass of black figures. I heard Montgomery call my name. I began to run at once towards this fire, revolver in hand. I saw the pink tongue of Montgomery's pistol lick out once, close to the ground. He was down. I shouted with all my strength and fired into the air.

I heard some one cry 'The Master!' The knotted black struggle broke into scattering units, the fire leapt and sank down. The crowd of Beast People fled in sudden panic before me up the beach. In my excitement I fired at their retreating backs as they disappeared among the bushes. Then I turned to the black heaps upon the ground.

Montgomery lay on his back with the hairy grey Beast Man sprawling across his body. The brute was dead, but still gripping Montgomery's throat with its curving claws. Near by lay M'ling on his face, and quite still, his neck bitten open, and the upper part of the smashed brandy-bottle in his hand. Two other figures lay near the fire, the one motionless, the other groaning fitfully, every now and then raising its head slowly, then dropping it again.

I caught hold of the Grey Man and pulled him off Montgomery's body; his claws drew down the torn coat reluctantly as I dragged him away.

Montgomery was dark in the face and scarcely breathing. I splashed sea-water on his face, and pillowed his head on my rolled-up coat. M'ling was dead. The wounded creature by the fire—it was a Wolf Brute with a bearded grey face—lay, I found, with the fore part of its body upon the still glowing timber. The wretched thing was injured so dreadfully that in mercy I blew its brains out at once. The other brute was one of the Bull Men swathed in white. He too was dead.

The rest of the Beast People had vanished from the beach. I went to Montgomery again and knelt beside him, cursing my ignorance of medicine.

The fire beside me had sunk down, and only charred beams of timber glowing at the central ends, and mixed with a grey ash of brushwood, remained. I wondered casually where Montgomery had got his wood. Then I saw that the dawn was upon us. The sky had grown brighter, the setting moon was growing pale and opaque in the luminous blue of the day. The sky to the eastward was rimmed with red.

Then I heard a thud and a hissing behind me, and, looking round, sprang to my feet with a cry of horror. Against the warm dawn great tumultuous masses of black smoke were boiling up out of the enclosure, and through their stormy darkness shot flickering threads of blood-red flame. Then the thatched roof caught. I saw the curving charge of the flames across the sloping straw. A spurt of fire jetted from the window of my room.

I knew at once what had happened. I remembered the crash I had heard. When I had rushed out to Montgomery's assistance I had overturned the lamp.

The hopelessness of saving any of the contents of the enclosure stared me in the face. My mind came back to my plan of flight, and turning swiftly I looked to see where the two boats lay upon the beach. They were gone!

Two axes lay upon the sands beside me, chips and splinters were scattered broadcast, and the ashes of the bonfire were blackening and smoking under the dawn. He had burnt the boats to revenge himself upon me and prevent our return to mankind.

A sudden convulsion of rage shook me. I was almost moved to batter his foolish head in as he lay there helpless at my feet. Then suddenly his hand moved, so feebly, so pitifully, that my wrath vanished. He groaned and opened his eyes for a minute.

I knelt down beside him and raised his head. He opened his eyes again, staring silently at the dawn, and then they met mine. The lids fell.

'Sorry,' he said presently, with an effort. He seemed trying to think. 'The last,' he murmured, 'the last of this silly universe. What a mess —'

I listened. His head fell helplessly to one side. I thought some drink might revive him, but there was neither drink nor vessel in which to bring drink at hand. He seemed suddenly heavier. My heart went cold.

I bent down to his face, put my hand through the rent in his blouse. He was dead; and even as he died a line of white heat, the limb of the sun, rose eastward beyond the projection of the bay, splashing its radiance across the sky, and turning the dark sea into a weltering tumult of dazzling light. It fell like a glory upon his death-shrunken face.

I let his head fall gently upon the rough pillow I had made for him, and stood up. Before me was the glittering desolation of the sea, the awful solitude upon which I had already suffered so much; behind me the island, hushed under the dawn, its Beast People silent and unseen. The enclosure with all its provisions and ammunition burnt noisily, with sudden gusts of flame, a fitful crackling, and now and then a crash. The heavy smoke drove up the beach away from me, rolling low over the distant tree-tops towards the huts in the ravine. Beside me were the charred vestiges of the boats and these five dead bodies.

Then out of the bushes came three Beast People, with hunched shoulders, protruding heads, misshapen hands awkwardly held, and inquisitive unfriendly eyes, and advanced towards me with hesitating gestures.

XX
Alone with the Beast Folk

I faced these people, facing my fate in them, single-handed — now literally single-handed, for I had a broken arm. In my pocket was a revolver with two empty chambers. Among the chips scattered about the beach lay the two axes that had been used to chop up the boats. The tide was creeping in behind me.

There was nothing for it but courage. I looked squarely into the faces of the advancing monsters. They avoided my eyes, and their quivering nostrils investigated the bodies that lay beyond me on the beach. I took half a dozen steps, picked up the blood-stained whip that lay beneath the body of the Wolf Man, and cracked it.

They stopped and stared at me.

'Salute,' said I. 'Bow down!'

They hesitated. One bent his knees. I repeated my command, with my heart in my mouth, and advanced upon them. One knelt, then the other two.

I turned and walked towards the dead bodies, keeping my face towards the three kneeling Beast Men, very much as an actor passing up the stage faces his audience.

'They broke the Law,' said I, putting my foot on the Sayer of the Law. 'They have been slain. Even the Sayer of the Law. Even the Other with the whip. Great is the Law! Come and see.'

'None escape,' said one of them, advancing and peering.

'None escape,' said I. 'Therefore hear and do as I command.'

They stood up, looking questioningly at one another.

'Stand there,' said I.

I picked up the hatchets and swung them by their heads from the sling of my arm, turned Montgomery over, picked up his revolver, still loaded in two chambers, and bending down to rummage, found half a dozen cartridges in his pocket.

'Take him,' said I, standing up again and pointing with the whip; 'take him and carry him out, and cast him into the sea.'

They came forward, evidently still afraid of Montgomery, but still more afraid of my cracking red whiplash, and, after some fumbling and hesitation, some whip-cracking and shouting, lifted him gingerly, carried him down to the beach, and went splashing into the dazzling welter of the sea.

'On,' said I, 'on! — carry him far.'

They went in up to their armpits and stood regarding me. 'Let go,' said I, and the body of Montgomery vanished with a splash. Something seemed to tighten across my chest. 'Good!' said I, with a break in my voice, and they came back, hurrying and fearful, to the margin of the water, leaving long wakes of black in the silver. At the water's edge they stopped, turning and glaring into the sea as though they presently expected Montgomery to arise thencefrom and exact vengeance.

'Now these,' said I, pointing to the other bodies.

They took care not to approach the place where they had thrown Montgomery into the water, but, instead, carried the four dead Beast People slantingly along the beach for perhaps a hundred yards before they waded out and cast them away.

As I watched them disposing of the mangled remains of M'ling I heard a light footfall behind me, and turning quickly saw the big Hyæna-Swine perhaps a dozen yards away. His head was bent down, his bright eyes were fixed upon me, his stumpy hands clenched and held close by his side. He stopped in this crouching attitude when I turned, his eyes a little averted.

For a moment we stood eye to eye. I dropped the whip and snatched at the pistol in my pocket. For I meant to kill this brute—the most formidable of any left now upon the island—at the first excuse. It may seem treacherous, but so I was resolved. I was far more afraid of him than of any other two of the Beast Folk. His continued life was, I knew, a threat against mine.

I was perhaps a dozen seconds collecting myself. Then I cried:

'Salute! Bow down!'

His teeth flashed upon me in a snarl.

'Who are *you*, that I should. . . .'

Perhaps a little too spasmodically, I drew my revolver, aimed, and quickly fired. I heard him yelp, saw him run sideways and turn, knew I had missed, and clicked back the cock with my thumb for the next shot. But he was already running headlong, jumping from side to side, and I dared not risk another miss. Every now and then he looked back at me over his shoulder. He went slanting along the beach, and vanished beneath the driving masses of dense smoke that were still pouring out from the burning enclosure. For some time I stood staring after him. I turned to my three obedient Beast Folk again, and signalled them to drop the body they still carried. Then I went back to the place by the fire where the bodies had fallen, and kicked the sand until all the brown blood-stains were absorbed and hidden.

I dismissed my three serfs with a wave of the hand, and went up the beach into the thickets. I carried my pistol in my hand, my whip thrust, with the hatchets, in the sling of my arm. I was anxious to be alone, to think out the position in which I was now placed.

A dreadful thing, that I was only beginning to realise, was that over all this island there was now no safe place where I could be alone, and secure to rest or sleep. I had recovered strength amazingly since my landing, but I was still inclined to be nervous, and to break down under any great stress. I felt I ought to cross the island, and establish myself with the Beast People, making myself secure in their confidence. And my heart failed me. I went back to the beach, and, turning eastward past the burning enclosure, made for a point where a shallow spit of coral sand ran out towards the reef. Here I could sit down and think, my back to the sea, and my face against any surprise. And there I sat, chin on knees, the sun beating down upon my head, and a growing dread in my mind, plotting how I could live on against the hour of my rescue (if ever rescue came). I tried to review the whole situation as calmly as I could, but it was impossible to clear the thing of emotion.

I began turning over in my mind the reason of Montgomery's desire. 'They will change,' he said. 'They are sure to change.' And Moreau — what was it that Moreau had said? 'The stubborn beast flesh grows day by day back again. . . .' Then I came round to the Hyæna-Swine. I felt assured that if I did not kill that brute he would kill me. . . . The Sayer of the Law was dead — worse luck! . . . They knew now that we of the Whips could be killed, even as they themselves were killed. . . .

Were they peering at me already out of the green masses of ferns and palms over yonder — watching until I came within their spring? Were they plotting against me? What was the Hyæna-Swine telling them? My imagination was running away with me into a morass of unsubstantial fears.

My thoughts were disturbed by a crying of sea-birds, hurrying towards some black object that had been stranded by the waves on the beach near the enclosure. I knew what that object was, but I had not the heart to go back and drive them off. I began walking along the beach in the opposite direction, designing to come round the eastward corner of the island, and so approach the ravine of the huts, without traversing the possible ambuscades of the thickets.

Perhaps half a mile along the beach I became aware of one of my three Beast Folk advancing out of the landward bushes towards me. I was now so nervous with my own imaginings that I immediately drew my revolver.

Even the propitiatory gestures of the creature failed to disarm me.

He hesitated as he approached.

'Go away,' cried I.

There was something very suggestive of a dog in the cringing attitude of the creature. It retreated a little way, very like a dog being sent home, and stopped, looking at me imploringly with canine brown eyes.

'Go away,' said I. 'Do not come near me.'

'May I not come near you?' it said.

'No. Go away,' I insisted, and snapped my whip. Then, putting my whip in my teeth, I stopped for a stone, and with that threat drove the creature away.

So, in solitude, I came round by the ravine of the Beast People, and, hiding among the weeds and reeds that separated this crevice from the sea, I watched such of them as appeared, trying to judge from their gestures and appearance how the death of Moreau and Montgomery and the destruction of the House of Pain had affected them. I know now the folly of my cowardice. Had I kept my courage up to the level of the dawn, had I not allowed it to ebb away in solitary thought, I might have grasped the vacant sceptre of Moreau, and ruled over the Beast People. As it was, I lost the opportunity, and sank to the position of a mere leader among my fellows.

Towards noon certain of them came and squatted basking in the hot sand. The imperious voices of hunger and thirst prevailed over my dread. I came out of the bushes, and, revolver in hand, walked down towards these seated figures. One, a Wolf Woman, turned her head and stared at me, and then the others. None attempted to rise or salute me. I felt too faint and weary to insist against so many, and I let the moment pass.

'I want food,' said I, almost apologetically, and drawing near.

'There is food in the huts,' said an Ox-Boar Man drowsily, and looking away from me.

I passed them, and went down into the shadow and odours of the almost deserted ravine. In an empty hut I feasted on some fruit, and then, after I had propped some specked and half-decayed branches and sticks about the opening, and placed myself with my face towards it, and my hand upon my revolver, the exhaustion of the last thirty hours claimed its own, and I let myself fall into a light slumber, trusting that the flimsy barricade I had erected would cause sufficient noise in its removal to save me from surprise.

XXI
The Reversion of the Beast Folk

In this way I became one among the Beast People in the Island of Doctor Moreau. When I awoke it was dark about me. My arm ached in its bandages. I sat up, wondering at first where I might be. I heard coarse voices talking outside. Then I saw that my barricade had gone, and that the opening of the hut stood clear. My revolver was still in my hand.

I heard something breathing, saw something crouched together close beside me. I held my breath, trying to see what it was. It began to move slowly, interminably. Then something soft and warm and moist passed across my hand.

All my muscles contracted. I snatched my hand away. A cry of alarm began, and was stifled in my throat. Then I just realised what had happened sufficiently to stay my fingers on the revolver.

'Who is that?' I said in a hoarse whisper, the revolver still pointed.

'I, Master.'

'Who are you?'

'They say there is no Master now. But I know, I know. I carried the bodies into the sea, O Walker in the Sea, the bodies of those you slew. I am your slave, Master.'

'Are you the one I met on the beach?' I asked.

'The same, Master.'

The thing was evidently faithful enough, for it might have fallen upon me as I slept.

'It is well,' I said, extending my hand for another licking kiss. I began to realise what its presence meant, and the tide of my courage flowed. 'Where are the others?' I asked.

'They are mad. They are fools,' said the Dog Man. 'Even now they talk together beyond there. They say, "The Master is dead; the Other with the Whip is dead. That Other who walked in the Sea is — as we are. We have no Master, no Whips, no House of Pain any more. There is an end. We love the Law, and will keep it; but there is no pain, no Master, no Whips for ever again." So they say. But I know, Master, I know.'

I felt in the darkness and patted the Dog Man's head.

'It is well,' I said again.

'Presently you will slay them all,' said the Dog Man.

'Presently,' I answered, 'I will slay them all — after certain days and certain things have come to pass. Every one of them save those you spare, every one of them shall be slain.'

'What the Master wishes to kill the Master kills,' said the Dog Man with a certain satisfaction in his voice.

'And that their sins may grow,' I said; 'let them live in their folly until their time is ripe. Let them not know that I am the Master.'

'The Master's will is sweet,' said the Dog Man, with the ready tact of his canine blood.

'But one has sinned,' said I. 'Him I will kill, whenever I may meet him. When I say to you, '*That is he*,' see that you fall upon him. — And now I will go to the men and women who are assembled together.'

For a moment the opening of the hut was blackened by the exit of the Dog Man. Then I followed and stood up, almost in the exact spot where I had been when I had heard Moreau and his staghound pursuing me. But now it was night, and all the miasmatic ravine about me was black, and beyond, instead of a green sunlit slope, I saw a red fire before which hunched grotesque figures moved to and fro. Further were the thick trees, a bank of black fringed above with the black lace of the upper branches. The moon was just riding up on the edge of the ravine, and like a bar across its face drove the spire of vapour that was for ever streaming from the fumarolles of the island.

'Walk by me,' said I, nerving myself, and side by side we walked down the narrow way, taking little heed of the dim things that peered at us out of the huts.

None about the fire attempted to salute me. Most of them disregarded me — ostentatiously. I looked round for the Hyæna-Swine, but he was not there. Altogether, perhaps, twenty of the Beast Folk squatted, staring into the fire or talking to one another.

'He is dead, he is dead, the Master is dead,' said the voice of the Ape Man to the right of me. 'The House of Pain—there *is* no House of Pain.'

'He is not dead,' said I, in a loud voice. 'Even now he watches us.'

This startled them. Twenty pairs of eyes regarded me.

'The House of Pain is gone,' said I. 'It will come again. The Master you cannot see. Yet even now he listens above you.'

'True, true!' said the Dog Man.

They were staggered at my assurance. An animal may be ferocious and cunning enough, but it takes a real man to tell a lie.

'The Man with the Bandaged Arm speaks a strange thing,' said one of the Beast Folk.

'I tell you it is so,' I said. 'The Master and the House of Pain will come again. Woe be to him who breaks the Law!'

They looked curiously at one another. With an affectation of indifference I began to chop idly at the ground in front of me with my hatchet. They looked, I noticed, at the deep cuts I made in the turf.

Then the Satyr raised a doubt; I answered him, and then one of the dappled things objected, and an animated discussion sprang up round the fire. Every moment I began to feel more convinced of my present security. I talked now without the catching in my breath, due to the intensity of my excitement, that had troubled me at first. In the course of about an hour I had really convinced several of the Beast Folk of the truth of my assertions, and talked most of the others into a dubious state.

I kept a sharp eye for my enemy the Hyæna-Swine, but he never appeared. Every now and then a suspicious movement would startle me, but my confidence grew rapidly. Then as the moon crept down from the zenith, one by one the listeners began to yawn (showing the oddest teeth in the light of the sinking fire), and first one, and then another, retired towards the dens in the ravine. And I, dreading the silence and darkness, went with them, knowing I was safer with several of them than with one alone.

In this manner began the longer part of my sojourn upon this Island of Doctor Moreau. But from that night until the end came there was but one thing happened to tell, save a series of innumerable small unpleasant details and the fretting of an incessant uneasiness. So that I prefer to make no chronicle for that gap of time, to tell only one cardinal incident of the ten months I spent as an intimate of these half-humanised brutes. There is much that sticks in my memory that I could write, things that I would cheerfully give my right hand to forget. But they do not help the telling of the story. In the retrospect it is strange to remember how soon I fell in with these monsters' ways and gained my confidence again. I had my quarrels, of course, and could show some teeth-marks still, but they soon gained a wholesome respect for my trick of throwing stones and the bite of my hatchet. And my St. Bernard Dog Man's loyalty was of infinite service to me. I found their simple scale of honour was based mainly on the capacity for inflicting trenchant wounds. Indeed I may say—without vanity, I hope—that I held something like a pre-eminence among them. One or two whom, in various disputes, I had scarred rather badly, bore me a grudge, but it vented itself, chiefly behind my back, and at a safe distance from my missiles, in grimaces.

The Hyæna-Swine avoided me, and I was always on the alert for him. My inseparable Dog Man hated and dreaded him intensely. I really believe that was at the root of the brute's attachment to me. It was soon evident to me that the former monster had tasted blood, and gone the way of the Leopard Man. He formed a lair somewhere in the forest, and became solitary. Once I tried to induce the Beast Folk to hunt him, but I lacked the authority to make them co-operate for one end. Again and again I tried to approach his den and come upon him unawares, but always he was too acute for me, and saw or winded me and got away. He too made every forest pathway dangerous to me and my allies with his lurking ambuscades. The Dog Man scarcely dared to leave my side.

In the first month or so the Beast Folk, compared with their latter condition, were human enough, and for one or two besides my canine friend I even conceived a friendly tolerance. The little pink sloth creature displayed an odd affection for me, and took to following me about. The Monkey Man bored me, however. He assumed, on the strength of his five digits, that he was my equal, and was for ever jabbering at me, jabbering the most arrant nonsense. One thing about him entertained me a little: he had a fantastic trick of coining new words. He had an idea, I believe, that to gabble about names that meant nothing was the proper use of speech. He called it 'big thinks,' to distinguish it from 'little thinks'—the sane everyday interests of life. If ever I made a remark he did not understand, he would praise it very much, ask me to say it again, learn it by heart, and go off repeating it, with a word wrong here or there, to all the milder of the Beast People. He thought nothing of what was plain and comprehensible. I invented some very curious 'big thinks' for his especial use. I think now that he was the silliest creature I ever met; he had developed in the most wonderful way the distinctive silliness of man without losing one jot of the natural folly of a monkey.

This, I say, was in the earlier weeks of my solitude among these brutes. During that time they respected the usage established by the Law, and behaved with general decorum. Once I found another rabbit torn to pieces—by the Hyæna-Swine, I am assured—but that was all. It was about May when I first distinctly perceived a growing difference in their speech and carriage, a growing coarseness of articulation, a growing disinclination to talk. My Monkey Man's jabber multiplied in volume, but grew less and less comprehensible, more and more simian. Some of the others seemed altogether slipping their hold upon speech, though they still understood what I said to them at that time. Can you imagine language, once clear-cut and exact, softening and guttering, losing shape and import, becoming mere lumps of sound again? And they walked erect with an increasing difficulty. Though they evidently felt ashamed of themselves, every now and then I would come upon one or other running on toes and finger-tips, and quite unable to recover the vertical attitude. They held things more clumsily; drinking by suction, feeding by gnawing; grew commoner every day. I realised more keenly than ever what Moreau had told me about the 'stubborn beast flesh.' They were reverting, and reverting very rapidly.

Some of them—the pioneers, I noticed with some surprise, were all females—began to disregard the injunction of decency—deliberately for the most part. Others even attempted public outrages upon the institution of monogamy. The tradition of the Law was clearly losing its force. I cannot pursue this disagreeable subject. My Dog Man imperceptibly slipped back to the dog again; day by day he became dumb, quadrupedal, hairy. I scarcely noticed the transition from the companion on my right hand to the lurching dog at my side. As the carelessness and disorganisation increased from day to day, the lane of dwelling-places, at no time very sweet, became so loathsome that I left it, and going across the island made myself a hovel of boughs amid the black ruins of Moreau's enclosure. Some memory of pain, I found, still made that place the safest from the Beast Folk.

It would be impossible to detail every step of the lapsing of these monsters; to tell how, day by day, the human semblance left them; how they gave up bandagings and wrappings, abandoned at last every stitch of clothing; how the hair began to spread over the exposed limbs; how their foreheads fell away and their faces projected; how the quasi-human intimacy I had permitted myself with some of them in the first month of my loneliness became a horror to recall.

The change was slow and inevitable. For them and for me it came without any definite shock. I still went among them in safety, because no jolt in the downward glide had released the increasing charge of explosive animalism that ousted the human day by day. But I began to fear that soon now that shock must come. My St. Bernard brute followed me to the enclosure, and his vigilance enabled me to sleep at times in something like peace. The little pink sloth thing became shy and left me, to crawl back to its natural life once more among the tree-branches. We were in just the state of equilibrium that would remain in one of those 'Happy Family' cages that animal-tamers exhibit, if the tamer were to leave it for ever.

Of course these creatures did not decline into such beasts as the reader has seen in zoological gardens—into ordinary bears, wolves, tigers, oxen, swine, and apes. There was still something strange about each; in each Moreau had blended this animal with that; one perhaps was ursine chiefly, another feline chiefly, another bovine chiefly, but each was tainted with other creatures—a kind of generalised animalism appeared through the specific dispositions. And the dwindling shreds of the humanity still startled me every now and then, a momentary recrudescence of speech perhaps, an unexpected dexterity of the forefeet, a pitiful attempt to walk erect.

I too must have undergone strange changes. My clothes hung about me as yellow rags, through whose rents glowed the tanned skin. My hair grew long, and became matted together. I am told that even now my eyes have a strange brightness, a swift alertness of movement.

At first I spent the daylight hours on the southward beach watching for a ship, hoping and praying for a ship. I counted on the *Ipecacuanha* returning as the year wore on, but she never came. Five times I saw sails, and thrice smoke, but nothing ever touched the island. I always had a bonfire ready, but no doubt the volcanic reputation of the island was taken to account for that.

It was only about September or October that I began to think of making a raft. By that time my arm had healed, and both my hands were at my service again. At first I found my helplessness appalling. I had never done any carpentry or suchlike work in my life, and I spent day after day in experimental chopping and binding among the trees. I had no ropes, and could hit on nothing wherewith to make ropes; none of the abundant creepers seemed limber or strong enough, and with all my litter of scientific education I could not devise any way of making them so. I spent more than a fortnight grubbing among the black ruins of the enclosure and on the beach where the boats had been burnt, looking for nails and other stray pieces of metal that might prove of service. Now and then some Beast creature would watch me, and go leaping off when I called to it. Then came a season of thunderstorms and heavy rain that greatly retarded my work, but at last the raft was completed.

I was delighted with it. But with a certain lack of practical sense that has always been my bane I had made it a mile or more from the sea, and before I had dragged it down to the beach the thing had fallen to pieces. Perhaps it is as well that I was saved from launching it. But at the time my misery at my failure was so acute, that for some days I simply moped on the beach and stared at the water and thought of death.

But I did not mean to die, and an incident occurred that warned me unmistakably of the folly of letting the days pass so—for each fresh day was fraught with increasing danger from the Beast Monsters. I was lying in the shade of the enclosure wall staring out to sea, when I was startled by something cold touching the skin of my heel, and starting round found the little pink sloth creature blinking into my face. He had long since lost speech and active movement, and the lank hair of the little brute grew thicker every day, and his stumpy claws more askew. He made a moaning noise when he saw he had attracted my attention, went a little way towards the bushes, and looked back at me.

At first I did not understand, but presently it occurred to me that he wished me to follow him, and this I did at last, slowly—for the day was hot. When he reached the trees he clambered into them, for he could travel better among their swinging creepers than on the ground.

And suddenly in a trampled space I came upon a ghastly group. My St. Bernard creature lay on the ground dead, and near his body crouched the Hyæna-Swine, gripping the quivering flesh with misshapen claws, gnawing at it and snarling with delight. As I approached the monster lifted its glaring eyes to mine, its lips went trembling back from its red-stained teeth, and it growled menacingly. It was not afraid and not ashamed; the last vestige of the human taint had vanished. I advanced a step further, stopped, pulled out my revolver. At last I had him face to face.

The brute made no sign of retreat. But its ears went back, its hair bristled, and its body crouched together. I aimed between the eyes and fired. As I did so the thing rose straight at me in a leap, and I was knocked over like a ninepin. It clutched at me with its crippled hand, and struck me in the face. Its spring carried it over me. I fell under the hind part of its body, but luckily I had hit as I meant, and it had died even as it leapt. I crawled out from under its unclean weight and stood up trembling, staring at its quivering body. That danger at least was over. But this, I knew, was only the first of the series of relapses that must come.

I burnt both the bodies on a pyre of brushwood. Now, indeed, I saw clearly that unless I left the island my death was only a question of time. The Beasts by that time had, with one or two exceptions, left the ravine, and made themselves lairs, according to their tastes, among the thickets of the island. Few prowled by day; most of them slept, and the island might have seemed deserted to a newcomer; but at night the air was hideous with their calls and howling. I had half a mind to make a massacre of them—to build traps or fight them with my knife. Had I possessed sufficient cartridges, I should not have hesitated to begin the killing. There could now be scarcely a score left of the dangerous carnivores; the braver of these were already dead. After the death of this poor dog of mine, my last friend, I too adopted to some extent the practice of slumbering in the daytime, in order to be on my guard at night. I rebuilt my den in the walls of the enclosure with such a narrow opening that anything attempting to enter must necessarily make a considerable noise. The creatures had lost the art of fire, too, and recovered their fear of it. I turned once more, almost passionately now, to hammering together stakes and branches to form a raft for my escape.

I found a thousand difficulties. I am an extremely unhandy man — my schooling was over before the days of Slöjd[36] — but most of the requirements of a raft I met at last in some clumsy circuitous way or other, and this time I took care of the strength. The only insurmountable obstacle was, that I had no vessel to contain the water I should need if I floated forth upon these untravelled seas. I would have even tried pottery, but the island contained no clay. I used to go moping about the island, trying with all my might to solve this one last difficulty. Sometimes I would give way to wild outbursts of rage, and hack and splinter some unlucky tree in my intolerable vexation. But I could think of nothing.

And then came a day, a wonderful day, that I spent in ecstasy. I saw a sail to the south-west, a small sail like that of a little schooner, and forthwith I lit a great pile of brushwood and stood by it in the heat of it and the heat of the midday sun, watching. All day I watched that sail, eating or drinking nothing, so that my head reeled; and the Beasts came and glared at me, and seemed to wonder and went away. The boat was still distant when night came and swallowed it up, and all night I toiled to keep my blaze bright and high, and the eyes of the Beasts shone out of the darkness, marvelling. In the dawn it was nearer, and I saw it was the dirty lug-sail of a small boat. My eyes were weary with watching, and I peered and could not believe them. Two men were in the boat, sitting low down, one by the bows and the other at the rudder. But the boat sailed strangely. The head was not kept to the wind; it yawed and fell away.

As the day grew brighter I began waving the last rag of my jacket to them; but they did not notice me, and sat still facing one another. I went to the lowest point of the low headland and gesticulated and shouted. There was no response, and the boat kept on her aimless course, making slowly, very slowly, for the bay. Suddenly a great white bird flew up out of the boat, and neither of the men stirred nor noticed it. It circled round, and then came sweeping overhead with its strong wings out-spread. *albatross*

Then I stopped shouting, and sat down on the headland and rested my chin on my hands and stared. Slowly, slowly, the boat drove past towards the west. I would have swum out to it, but something, a cold vague fear, kept me back. In the afternoon the tide stranded it, and left it a hundred yards or so to the westward of the ruins of the enclosure.

---

[36] A system of manual instruction in handiwork originally developed in Sweden. [Ed.]

The men in it were dead, had been dead so long that they fell to pieces when I tilted the boat on its side and dragged them out. One had a shock of red hair like the captain of the *Ipecacuanha,* and a dirty white cap lay in the bottom of the boat. As I stood beside the boat, three of the Beasts came slinking out of the bushes and sniffing towards me. One of my spasms of disgust came upon me. I thrust the little boat down the beach and clambered on board her. Two of the brutes were Wolf Beasts, and came forward with quivering nostrils and glittering eyes; the third was the horrible nondescript of bear and bull.

When I saw them approaching those wretched remains, heard them snarling at one another, and caught the gleam of their teeth, a frantic horror succeeded my repulsion. I turned my back upon them, struck the lug, and began paddling out to sea. I could not bring myself to look behind me.

But I lay between the reef and the island that night, and the next morning went round to the stream and filled the empty keg aboard with water. Then, with such patience as I could command, I collected a quantity of fruit, and waylaid and killed two rabbits with my last three cartridges. While I was doing this I left the boat moored to an inward projection of the reef, for fear of the Beast Monsters.

XXII

The Man Alone

In the evening I started and drove out to sea before a gentle wind from the south-west, slowly and steadily, and the island grew smaller and smaller, and the lank spire of smoke dwindled to a finer and finer line against the hot sunset. The ocean rose up around me, hiding that low dark patch from my eyes. The daylight, the trailing glory of the sun, went streaming out of the sky, was drawn aside like some luminous curtain, and at last I looked into that blue gulf of immensity that the sunshine hides, and saw the floating hosts of the stars. The sea was silent, the sky was silent; I was alone with the night and silence.

So I drifted for three days, eating and drinking sparingly, and meditating upon all that happened to me, nor desiring very greatly then to see men again. One unclean rag was about me, my hair was a black tangle. No doubt my discoverers thought me a madman. It is strange, but I felt no desire to return to mankind. I was only glad to be quit of the foulness of the Beast Monsters. And on the third day I was picked up by a brig from Apia[37] to San

---

[37] The seaport capital of western Samoa. [Ed.]

Francisco. Neither the captain nor the mate would believe my story, judging that solitude and danger had made me mad. And fearing their opinion might be that of others, I refrained from telling my adventure further, and professed to recall nothing that had happened to me between the loss of the *Lady Vain* and the time when I was picked up again—the space of a year.

I had to act with the utmost circumspection to save myself from the suspicion of insanity. My memory of the Law, of the two dead sailors, of the ambuscades of the darkness, of the body in the cane brake, haunted me. And, unnatural as it seems, with my return to mankind came, instead of that confidence and sympathy I had expected, a strange enhancement of the uncertainty and dread I had experienced during my stay upon the island. No one would believe me, I was almost as queer to men as I had been to the Beast People. I may have caught something of the natural wildness of my companions.

They say that terror is a disease, and anyhow, I can witness that, for several years now, a restless fear has dwelt in my mind, such a restless fear as a half-tamed lion cub may feel. My trouble took the strangest form. I could not persuade myself that the men and women I met were not also another, still passably human, Beast People, animals half-wrought into the outward image of human souls, and that they would presently begin to revert, to show first this bestial mark and then that. But I have confided my case to a strangely able man, a man who had known Moreau, and seemed half to credit my story, a mental specialist—and he has helped me mightily.

Though I do not expect that the terror of that island will ever altogether leave me, at most times it lies far in the back of my mind, a mere distant cloud, a memory and a faint distrust; but there are times when the little cloud spreads until it obscures the whole sky. Then I look about me at my fellow-men. And I go in fear. I see faces keen and bright, others dull or dangerous, others unsteady, insincere; none that have the calm authority of a reasonable soul. I feel as though the animal was surging up through them; that presently the degradation of the Islanders will be played over again on a larger scale.[38] I know this is an illusion, that these seeming men and women about me are indeed men and women, men and women for ever, perfectly reasonable creatures, full of human desires and tender solicitude, emancipated from instinct, and the slaves of no fantastic Law—being altogether different from the Beast Folk. Yet I shrink from them, from their curious glances, their inquiries and assistance, and long to be away from them and alone.

---

[38] Wells described this form of degeneration in his essay "Zoological Regression" (1891). See also the opening section of Greenslade's second chapter, "Biological Poetics." [Ed.]

For that reason I live near the broad free downland, and can escape thither when this shadow is over my soul; and very sweet is the empty downland then, under the wind-swept sky. When I lived in London the horror was wellnigh insupportable. I could not get away from men; their voices came through windows; locked doors were flimsy safeguards. I would go out into the streets to fight with my delusion, and prowling women would mew after me, furtive craving men glance jealously at me, weary pale workers go coughing by me, with tired eyes and eager paces like wounded deer dripping blood, old people, bent and dull, pass murmuring to themselves, and all unheeding a ragged tail of gibing children. Then I would turn aside into some chapel, and even there, such was my disturbance, it seemed that the preacher gibbered Big Thinks even as the Ape Man had done; or into some library, and there the intent faces over the books seemed but patient creatures waiting for prey. Particularly nauseous were the blank expressionless faces of people in trains and omnibuses; they seemed no more my fellow-creatures than dead bodies would be, so that I did not dare to travel unless I was assured of being alone. And even it seemed that I, too, was not a reasonable creature, but only an animal tormented with some strange disorder in its brain, that sent it to wander alone, like a sheep stricken with the gid.[39]

But this is a mood that comes to me now — I thank God — more rarely. I have withdrawn myself from the confusion of cities and multitudes, and spend my days surrounded by wise books, bright windows, in this life of ours lit by the shining souls of men. I see few strangers, and have but a small household. My days I devote to reading and to experiments in chemistry, and I spend many of the clear nights in the study of astronomy. There is, though I do not know how there is or why there is, a sense of infinite peace and protection in the glittering hosts of heaven. There it must be, I think, in the vast and eternal laws of matter, and not in the daily cares and sins and troubles of men, that whatever is more than animal within us must find its solace and its hope. I hope, or I could not live. And so, in hope and solitude, my story ends.

EDWARD PRENDICK.

---

[39] A brain disease in sheep. [Ed.]

Part Two

CONTEXTS: SCIENCE AND LITERATURE
IN THE NINETEENTH CENTURY

Author's Introduction
to the Standard Novels Edition
(1831)

Mary Shelley

In 1831, the unknown naturalist Charles Darwin set off on his world-changing journey on the *Beagle,* and the ambitious Charles Dickens began a writing career transcribing, in newspaper journalist's short-hand, the first parliamentary debates on the Reform Bill. At the same time, the widowed author of *Frankenstein* received 50 pounds to write an introduction to a new edition of the novel in Richard Colburn and Henry Bentley's series of inexpensive one-volume reprints de-signed, like the Reform Bill, to reach a wider audience. Here, Mary Shelley makes the story of the conception and writing of the novel a gothic tale of its own, and the past of her girlhood with distinguished parents and young married life with the chief poets of the age is res-urrected. For contemporary scholars' cautions about her claim to have "changed no portion of the story," see A Note on the Texts.

The publishers of the Standard Novels, in selecting *Frankenstein* for one of their series, expressed a wish that I should furnish them with some account of the origin of the story. I am the more willing to comply, because I shall thus give a general answer to the question, so very frequently asked me — 'How I, then a young girl, came to think of and to dilate upon so very hideous an idea?' It is true that I am very averse to bringing myself forward in print; but as my account will only appear as an appendage to a former produc-tion, and as it will be confined to such topics as have connexion with my authorship alone, I can scarcely accuse myself of a personal intrusion.

From *Frankenstein: or, The Modern Prometheus.* London: Henry Colburn and Richard Bentley, 1831. (All notes are by the present editor.)

It is not singular that, as the daughter of two persons of distinguished literary celebrity, I should very early in life have thought of writing. As a child I scribbled; and my favourite pastime during the hours given me for recreation was to 'write stories'. Still, I had a dearer pleasure than this, which was the formation of castles in the air—the indulging in waking dreams—the following up trains of thought, which had for their subject the formation of a succession of imaginary incidents. My dreams were at once more fantastic and agreeable than my writings. In the latter I was a close imitator—rather doing as others had done than putting down the suggestions of my own mind. What I wrote was intended at least for one other eye—my childhood's companion and friend,[1] but my dreams were all my own; I accounted for them to nobody; they were my refuge when annoyed—my dearest pleasure when free.

I lived principally in the country as a girl, and passed a considerable time in Scotland. I made occasional visits to the more picturesque parts; but my habitual residence was on the blank and dreary northern shores of the Tay, near Dundee. Blank and dreary on retrospection I call them; they were not so to me then. They were the eyry of freedom, and the pleasant region where unheeded I could commune with the creatures of my fancy. I wrote then—but in a most common-place style. It was beneath the trees of the grounds belonging to our house, or on the bleak sides of the woodless mountains near, that my true compositions, the airy flights of my imagination, were born and fostered. I did not make myself the heroine of my tales. Life appeared to me too common-place an affair as regarded myself. I could not figure to myself that romantic woes or wonderful events would ever be my lot; but I was not confined to my own identity, and I could people the hours with creations far more interesting to me at that age than my own sensations.

After this my life became busier, and reality stood in place of fiction. My husband, however, was from the first, very anxious that I should prove myself worthy of my parentage, and enrol myself on the page of fame. He was for ever inciting me to obtain literary reputation, which even on my own part I cared for then, though since I have become infinitely indifferent to it. At this time he desired that I should write, not so much with the idea that I could produce any thing worthy of notice, but, that he might himself judge how far I possessed the promise of better things hereafter. Still I did nothing. Travelling, and the cares of a family, occupied my time; and study, in the way of reading or improving my ideas in communication with his

---

[1] The teenage Mary Godwin spent nearly a year and a half in two long visits to the Baxter family in Dundee in 1812–14. The companionship of the daughters, Christina and Isabella, was as important as the rambles around Loch Lomond and the valley of the Tay.

far more cultivated mind, was all of literary employment that engaged my attention.

In the summer of 1816, we visited Switzerland, and became the neighbours of Lord Byron. At first we spent our pleasant hours on the lake, or wandering on its shores; and Lord Byron, who was writing the third canto of *Childe Harold,* was the only one among us who put his thoughts upon paper. These, as he brought them successively to us, clothed in all the light and harmony of poetry, seemed to stamp as divine the glories of heaven and earth, whose influences we partook with him.

But it proved a wet, ungenial summer, and incessant rain often confined us for days to the house. Some volumes of ghost stories, translated from the German into French, fell into our hands. There was the *History of the Inconstant Lover,* who, when he thought to clasp the bride to whom he had pledged his vows, found himself in the arms of the pale ghost of her whom he had deserted. There was the tale of the sinful founder of his race whose miserable doom it was to bestow the kiss of death on all the younger sons of his fated house, just when they reached the age of promise. His gigantic, shadowy form, clothed like the ghost in *Hamlet,* in complete armour, but with the beaver up, was seen at midnight, by the moon's fitful beams, to advance slowly along the gloomy avenue. The shape was lost beneath the shadow of the castle walls; but soon a gate swung back, a step was heard, the door of the chamber opened, and he advanced to the couch of the blooming youths, cradled in healthy sleep. Eternal sorrow sat upon his face as he bent down and kissed the forehead of the boys, who from that hour withered like flowers snapt upon the stalk. I have not seen these stories since then; but their incidents are as fresh in my mind as if I had read them yesterday.

'We will each write a ghost story', said Lord Byron; and his proposition was acceded to. There were four of us. The noble author began a tale, a fragment of which he printed at the end of his poem of *Mazeppa.* Shelley, more apt to embody ideas and sentiments in the radiance of brilliant imagery, and in the music of the most melodious verse that adorns our language, than to invent the machinery of a story, commenced one founded on the experiences of his early life. Poor Polidori had some terrible idea about a skull-headed lady who was so punished for peeping through a keyhole—what to see I forget—something very shocking and wrong of course; but when she was reduced to a worse condition than the renowned Tom of Coventry,[2] he did not know what to do with her and was obliged to

---

[2] Refers to the folktale about the boy Tom who spied on Lady Godiva and was blinded for his peeping.

dispatch her to the tomb of the Capulets, the only place for which she was fitted. The illustrious poets also, annoyed by the platitude of prose, speedily relinquished their uncongenial task.

I busied myself *to think of a story,*—a story to rival those which had excited us to this task. One which would speak to the mysterious fears of our nature and awaken thrilling horror—one to make the reader dread to look round, to curdle the blood, and quicken the beatings of the heart. If I did not accomplish these things, my ghost story would be unworthy of its name. I thought and pondered—vainly. I felt that blank incapability of invention which is the greatest misery of authorship, when dull Nothing replies to our anxious invocations. 'Have you thought of a story?' I was asked each morning, and each morning I was forced to reply with a mortifying negative.

Every thing must have a beginning, to speak in Sanchean phrase;[3] and that beginning must be linked to something that went before. The Hindoos give the world an elephant to support it, but they make the elephant stand upon a tortoise. Invention, it must be humbly admitted, does not consist in creating out of void, but out of chaos; the materials must, in the first place, be afforded: it can give form to dark, shapeless substances, but cannot bring into being the substance itself. In all matters of discovery and invention, even of those that appertain to the imagination, we are continually reminded of the story of Columbus and his egg.[4] Invention consists in the capacity of seizing on the capabilities of a subject: and in the power of moulding and fashioning ideas suggested to it.

Many and long were the conversations between Lord Byron and Shelley, to which I was a devout but nearly silent listener. During one of these, various philosophical doctrines were discussed, and among others the nature of the principle of life, and whether there was any probability of its ever being discovered and communicated. They talked of the experiments of Dr Darwin (I speak not of what the Doctor really did, or said that he did, but, as more to my purpose, of what was then spoken of as having been done by him), who preserved a piece of vermicelli in a glass case, till by some extraordinary means it began to move with voluntary motion.[5] Not thus, after all, would life be given. Perhaps a corpse would be reanimated; galvanism

---

[3] The country wisdom of *Don Quixote*'s Sancho Panza.

[4] Told by a nobleman that his discovery was only an accidental deed that might have been done by anyone, Columbus, the tale goes, challenged the company to stand an egg on end. When everyone failed, he did it himself by crushing one end: the planet was round, but the egg needed a flattened end.

[5] For Mary's consideration of Erasmus Darwin's ideas, see the Introduction, pp. 4–5.

had given token of such things: perhaps the component parts of a creature might be manufactured, brought together, and endued with vital warmth.

Night waned upon this talk, and even the witching hour had gone by, before we retired to rest. When I placed my head on my pillow, I did not sleep, nor could I be said to think. My imagination, unbidden, possessed and guided me, gifting the successive images that arose in my mind with a vividness far beyond the usual bounds of reverie. I saw—with shut eyes, but acute mental vision—I saw the pale student of unhallowed arts kneeling beside the thing he had put together. I saw the hideous phantasm of a man stretched out, and then, on the working of some powerful engine, show signs of life, and stir with an uneasy, half-vital motion. Frightful must it be; for supremely frightful would be the effect of any human endeavour to mock the stupendous mechanism of the Creator of the world. His success would terrify the artist; he would rush away from his odious handywork, horror-stricken. He would hope that, left to itself, the slight spark of life which he had communicated would fade; that this thing, which had received such imperfect animation would subside into dead matter; and he might sleep in the belief that the silence of the grave would quench forever the transient existence of the hideous corpse which he had looked upon as the cradle of life. He sleeps; but he is awakened; he opens his eyes; behold, the horrid thing stands at his bedside, opening his curtains and looking on him with yellow, watery, but speculative eyes.

I opened mine in terror. The idea so possessed my mind, that a thrill of fear ran through me, and I wished to exchange the ghastly image of my fancy for the realities around. I see them still; the very room, the dark *parquet*, the closed shutters, with the moonlight struggling through, and the sense I had that the glassy lake and white high Alps were beyond. I could not so easily get rid of my hideous phantom; still it haunted me. I must try to think of something else. I recurred to my ghost story—my tiresome, unlucky ghost story! O! if I could only contrive one which would frighten my reader as I myself had been frightened that night!

Swift as light and as cheering was the idea that broke in upon me. 'I have found it! What terrified me will terrify others; and I need only describe the spectre which had haunted my midnight pillow.' On the morrow I announced that I had *thought of a story*. I began that day with the words, 'It was on a dreary night of November,' making only a transcript of the grim terrors of my waking dream.

At first I thought but a few pages—of a short tale; but Shelley urged me to develop the idea at greater length. I certainly did not owe the suggestion of one incident, nor scarcely of one train of feeling, to my husband, and yet but for his incitement it would never have taken the form in which it was presented to the world. From this declaration I must except the preface. As far as I can recollect, it was entirely written by him.

And now, once again, I bid my hideous progeny go forth and prosper. I have affection for it, for it was the offspring of happy days, when death and grief were but words, which found no true echo in my heart. Its several pages speak of many a walk, many a drive, and many a conversation, when I was not alone; and my companion was one who, in this world, I shall never see more. But this is for myself; my readers have nothing to do with these associations.

I will add but one word as to the alterations I have made. They are principally those of style. I have changed no portion of the story nor introduced any new ideas or circumstances. I have mended the language where it was so bald as to interfere with the interest of the narrative; and these changes occur almost exclusively in the beginning of the first volume. Throughout they are entirely confined to such parts as are mere adjuncts to the story, leaving the core and substance of it untouched.

> *M.W.S.*
> *London,*
> *October 15th, 1831.*

From *The Botanic Garden Part II,* Containing the Loves of the Plants: A Poem (1789)

Erasmus Darwin

INTERLUDE. II.

Erasmus Darwin (1731–1802) might well have supplied Mary Shelley with some of the aesthetic and visual as well as the scientific cues that produced *Frankenstein*. Well known as a physician and inventor, poet and scientist, he was a member of several societies that brought together thinkers prominent in the industrial, political, artistic, and intellectual ferment of his time, including William Godwin and Mary Wollstonecraft. Among the work familiar to their household while Mary was growing up would have been the publication most famous

---

From *The Loves of the Plants 1789*. Oxford: Woodstock Books, 1991.

in his time, a long poem with prose "interludes" published in 1789 as the "second" volume of *The Botanic Garden,* titled "The Loves of the Plants." In the second interlude, "bookseller" and "poet" discuss the differences between the tragic and "the horrid." In the canto that follows, Darwin included a description of the disturbing and by then much reproduced painting "The Nightmare." The artist, J. H. Fuseli, was the object of an intense but unactualized passion in Mary Wollstonecraft. Godwin's 1798 memoir of his dead wife made this passion the stuff of international scandal, and probably of Mary's nightmares. Darwin's 1794–96 *Zoönomia* combines a naturalist's observation, a physician's interest in healing, and a philosopher's insistence on the qualities that connect the behavior of fecund "matter" across the categories of vegetable, animal, and human. The posthumously published *The Temple of Nature* (1803) celebrates likewise the creative and imaginative centrality of human sexuality and offers a benignly imagined theory of evolution.

Bookseller. THE monsters of your Botanic Garden are as surprising as the bulls with brazen feet, and the fire-breathing dragons, which guarded the Hesperian fruit; yet are they not disgusting, nor mischievous: and in the manner you have chained them together in your exhibition, they succeed each other amusingly enough, like prints of the London Cries, wraped upon rollers, with a glass before them. In this at least they resemble the monsters in Ovid's Metamorphoses [. . .].[1] May not the reverie of the reader be dissipated or disturbed by disagreeable images being presented to his imagination, as well as by improbable or incongruous ones?

[*Poet.*] Certainly, he will endeavour to rouse himself from a disagreeable reverie, as from the night-mare. And from this may be discovered the line of boundary between the Tragic and the Horrid: which line however will veer a little this way or that according to the prevailing manners of the age or country, and the peculiar associations of ideas, or idiosyncrasy of mind, of individuals. For instance, if an artist should represent the death of an officer in battle by shewing a little blood on the bosom of his shirt, as if a bullet had there penetrated, the dying figure would affect the beholder with pity; and if fortitude was at the same time expressed in his countenance,

---

[1] *Metamorphoses,* by the influential Roman poet Ovid (43 BC–AD 17), was a multibook poem featuring mythological and legendary stories mostly of humans turned by the gods into animal or vegetable forms, an appropriate reference for Darwin's "humanizing" story of plant and animal nature. [Ed.]

admiration would be added to our pity. On the contrary, if the artist should chuse to represent his thigh as shot away by a cannon ball, and should exhibit the bleeding flesh and shattered bone of the stump, the picture would introduce into our minds ideas from a butcher's shop, or a surgeon's operation-room, and we should turn from it with disgust. [. . .]

B. By what definition would you distinguish the Horrid from the Tragic?

P. I suppose the latter consists of Distress attended with Pity, which is said to be allied to Love, the most agreeable of all our passions: and the former in Distress accompanied with Disgust, which is allied to Hate, and is one of our most disagreeable sensations. Hence when horrid scenes of cruelty are represented in pictures, we wish to disbelieve their existence, and voluntarily exert ourselves to escape from the deception: whereas the bitter cup of true Tragedy is mingled with some sweet consolatory drops, which endear our tears, and we continue to contemplate the interesting delusion with a delight, which it is not easy to explain. [. . .]

[FROM CANTO III, "THE LOVES OF THE PLANTS"]

So on his NIGHTMARE through the evening fog
Flits the squab Fiend o'er fen, and lake, and bog;
Seeks some love-wilder'd Maid with sleep oppress'd,
Alights, and grinning sits upon her breast.
55 — Such as of late amid the murky sky
Was mark'd by FUSSELI's poetic eye;
Whose daring tints, with SHAKESPEAR's happiest grace,
Gave to the airy phantom form and place. —
Back o'er her pillow sinks her blushing head,
60 Her snow-white limbs hang helpless from the bed;
While with quick sighs, and suffocative breath,
Her interrupted heart-pulse swims in death.
— Then shrieks of captured towns, and widow's tears,
Pale lovers stretch'd upon their blood-stain'd biers,
65 The headlong precipice that thwarts her flight,
The trackless desert, the cold starless night,
And stern-eye'd Murderer with his knife behind,
In dread succession agonize her mind.
O'er her fair limbs convulsive tremors fleet,
70 Start in her hands, and struggle in her feet;
In vain to scream with quivering lips she tries,
And strains in palsy'd lids her tremulous eyes;

J. H. Fuseli's *The Nightmare* (1782–1791). Erasmus Darwin describes this famous painting, no doubt familiar to Mary Shelley and likely an influence on *Frankenstein*, in Canto III of "The Loves of the Plants."

> In vain she *wills* to walk, swim, run, fly, leap;
> The WILL presides not in the bower of SLEEP.
> 75 —On her fair bosom sits the Demon-Ape
> Erect, and ballances his boated shape;
> Rolls in their marble orbs his Gorgon-eyes,
> And drinks with leathern ears her tender cries. [. . .]

From *Zoönomia*
(1794 – 6)
Erasmus Darwin

PREFACE.

The purport of the following pages is an endeavour to reduce the facts belonging to ANIMAL LIFE into classes, orders, genera, and species; and, by comparing them with each other, to unravel the theory of diseases. It happened, perhaps unfortunately for the inquirers into the knowledge of diseases, that other sciences had received improvement previous to their own; whence, instead of comparing the properties belonging to animated nature with each other, they, idly ingenious, busied themselves in attempting to explain the laws of life by those of mechanism and chemistry; they considered the body as an hydraulic machine, and the fluids as passing through a series of chemical changes, forgetting that animation was its essential characteristic.

The great CREATOR of all things has infinitely diversified the works of his hands, but has at the same time stamped a certain similitude on the features of nature, that demonstrates to us, that *the whole is one family of one parent.* On this similitude is founded all rational analogy; which, so long as it is concerned in comparing the essential properties of bodies, leads us to many and important discoveries; but when with licentious activity it links together objects, otherwise discordant, by some fanciful similitude; it may indeed collect ornaments for wit and poetry, but philosophy and truth recoil from its combinations.

The want of a theory, deduced from such strict analogy, to conduct the practice of medicine is lamented by its professors; for, as a great number of unconnected facts are difficult to be acquired, and to be reasoned from, the art of medicine is in many instances less efficacious under the direction of its wisest practitioners; and by that busy crowd, who either boldly wade in darkness, or are led into endless error by the glare of false theory, it is daily practised to the destruction of thousands; add to this the unceasing injury which accrues to the public by the perpetual advertisements of pretended nostrums; the minds of the indolent become superstitiously fearful of diseases, which they do not labour under; and thus become the daily prey of some crafty empyric.

Zoönomia. Language, Man, and Society Ser. AMS Press: New York, 1974. (All notes are by the present editor.)

A theory founded upon nature, that should bind together the scattered facts of medical knowledge, and converge into one point of view the laws of organic life, would thus on many accounts contribute to the interest of society. It would capacitate men of moderate abilities to practise the art of healing with real advantage to the public; it would enable every one of literary acquirements to distinguish the genuine disciples of medicine from those of boastful effrontery, or of wily address; and would teach mankind in some important situations the *knowledge of themselves.* [. . .]

[. . .] I ask, by what means are the anthers in many flowers, and stigmas in other flowers, directed to find their paramours? How do either of them know, that the other exists in their vicinity? Is this curious kind of storge[1] produced by mechanic attraction, or by the sensation of love? The latter opinion is supported by the strongest analogy, because a reproduction of the species is the consequence; and then another organ of sense must be wanted to direct these vegetable amourettes to find each other, one probably analogous to our sense of smell, which in the animal world directs the new-born infant to its source of nourishment, and they may thus possess a faculty of perceiving as well as of producing odours.

Thus, besides a kind of taste at the extremities of their roots, similar to that of the extremities of our lacteal vessels, for the purpose of selecting their proper food; and besides different kinds of irritability residing in the various glands, which separate honey, wax, resin, and other juices from their blood; vegetable life seems to possess an organ of sense to distinguish the variations of heat, another to distinguish the varying degrees of moisture, another of light, another of touch, and probably another analogous to our sense of smell. To these must be added the indubitable evidence of their passion of love, and I think we may truly conclude, that they are furnished with a common sensorium belonging to each bud, and that they must occasionally repeat those perceptions either in their dreams or waking hours, and consequently possess ideas of so many of the properties of the external world, and of their own existence.

PRODUCTION OF IDEAS.

[. . .] I. PHILOSOPHERS have been much perplexed to understand, in what manner we become acquainted with the external world; insomuch that Dr. Berkly even doubted its existence, from having observed (as he

---

[1] From the Greek word for "innate or natural affection." Throughout *Zoönomia* and *The Temple of Nature,* Darwin imagines this as a material substance midway between a fluid and a fiber. The OED's early references call this substance "parental"; nineteenth-century references assume it is "maternal."

thought) that none of our ideas resemble their correspondent objects. Mr. Hume asserts, that our belief depends on the greater distinctness or energy of our ideas from perception; and Mr. Reid has lately contended, that our belief of external objects is an innate principle necessarily joined with our perceptions.

So true is the observation of the famous Malbranch, "that our senses are not given us to discover the essences of things, but to acquaint us with the means of preserving our existence," (L. I. ch. v.) a melancholy reflection to philosophers![2]

Some philosophers have divided all created beings into material and immaterial: the former including all that part of being, which obeys the mechanic laws of action and reaction, but which can begin no motion of itself; the other is the cause of all motion, and is either termed the power of gravity, or of specific attraction, or the spirit of animation. This immaterial agent is supposed to exist in or with matter, but to be quite distinct from it, and to be equally capable of existence, after the matter, which now possesses it, is decomposed.

Nor is this theory ill supported by analogy, since heat, electricity, and magnetism, can be given to or taken from a piece of iron; and must therefore exist, whether separated from the metal, or combined with it. From a parity of reasoning, the spirit of animation would appear to be capable of existing as well separately from the body as with it.

I beg to be understood, that I do not wish to dispute about words, and am ready to allow, that the powers of gravity, specific attraction, electricity, magnetism, and even the spirit of animation, may consist of matter of a finer kind; and to believe, with St. Paul and Malbranch, that the ultimate cause only of all motion is immaterial, that is God. St. Paul says, "in him we live and move, and have our being;" and, in the 15th chapter to the Corinthians, distinguishes between the psyche or living spirit, and the pneuma or reviving spirit. By the words spirit of animation or sensorial power, I mean only that animal life, which mankind possesses in common with brutes, and in some degree even with vegetables, and leave the consideration of the immortal part of us, which is the object of religion, to those who treat of revelation. [. . .]

---

[2] Bishop George Berkeley (1685–1753), Anglican theologian and philosopher, and David Hume (1711–76), Scottish historian, economist and skeptic, were Enlightenment empiricists, students of the process of knowledge as sensory perception. Scottish philosopher John Reid (1710–1796) defended nationalistic ethics against a current of subjectivism. Nicolas Malebranche (1638–1715), French priest and student of Descartes, emphasized the action of God in enabling perception and knowledge.

CLASSES OF IDEAS.

3. Invention is an operation of the sensorium, by which we voluntarily continue to excite one train of ideas, suppose the design of raising water by a machine; and at the same time attend to all other ideas, which are connected with this by every kind of catenation; and combine or separate them voluntarily for the purpose of obtaining some end.

For we can create nothing new, we can ónly combine or separate the ideas, which we have already received by our perceptions: thus if I wish to represent a monster, I call to my mind the ideas of every thing disagreeable and horrible, and combine the nastiness and gluttony of a hog, the stupidity and obstinacy of an ass, with the fur and awkwardness of a bear, and call the new combination Caliban.[3] Yet such a monster may exist in nature, as all his attributes are parts of nature. So when I wish to represent every thing, that is excellent and amiable; when I combine benevolence with cheerfulness, wisdom, knowledge, taste, wit, beauty of person, and elegance of manners, and associate them in one lady as a pattern to the world, it is called invention; yet such a person may exist, — such a person does exist! — It is —— ——, who is as much a monster as Caliban. [. . .]

GENERATION.

[. . .] 3. I conclude, that the imagination of the male at the time of copulation, or at the time of the secretion of the semen, may so affect this secretion by irritative or sensitive association, [. . .] as to cause the production of similarity of form and of features, with the distinction of sex; as the motions of the chissel of the turner imitate or correspond with those of the ideas of the artist. It is not here to be understood, that the first living fibre, which is to form an animal, is produced with any similarity of form to the future animal; but with propensities, or appetencies, which shall produce by accretion of parts the similarity of form, feature, or sex, corresponding to the imagination of the father.

Our ideas are movements of the nerves of sense, as of the optic nerve in recollecting visible ideas, suppose of a triangular piece of ivory. The fine moving fibres of the retina act in a manner to which I give the name of white; and this action is confined to a defined part of it; to which figure I give the name of triangle. And it is a preceding pleasurable sensation existing in my mind, which occasions me to produce this particular motion of the retina,

---

[3] Shakespeare's humanized monster from *The Tempest.*

when no triangle is present. Now it is probable, that the acting fibres of the ultimate terminations of the secreting apertures of the vessels of the testes, are as fine as those of the retina; and that they are liable to be thrown into that peculiar action, which marks the sex of the secreted embryo, by sympathy with the pleasurable motions of the nerves of vision, or of touch; that is, with certain ideas of imagination. From hence it would appear, that the world has long been mistaken in ascribing great power to the imagination of the female, whereas from this account of it, the real power of imagination, in the act of generation, belongs solely to the male. [. . .]

It may be objected to this theory, that a man may be supposed to have in his mind, the idea of the form and features of the female, rather than his own, and therefore there should be a greater number of female births. On the contrary, the general idea of our own form occurs to every one almost perpetually, and is termed consciousness of our existence, and thus may effect, that the number of males surpasses that of females. [. . .] And what further confirms this idea is, that the male children most frequently resemble the father in form, or feature, as well as in sex; and the female most frequently resemble the mother, in feature, and form, as well as in sex.

It may again be objected, if a female child sometimes resembles the father, and a male child the mother, the ideas of the father, at the time of procreation, must suddenly change from himself to the mother, at the very instant, when the embryon is secreted or formed. This difficulty ceases when we consider, that it is as easy to form an idea of feminine features with male organs of reproduction, or of male features with female ones, as the contrary; as we conceive the idea of a sphinx or mermaid, as easily and as distinctly as of a woman. Add to this, that at the time of procreation the idea of the male organs, and of the female features, are often both excited at the same time, by contact, or by vision. [. . .]

From *The Temple of Nature,* Canto II (1803)

Erasmus Darwin

[. . .] "In these lone births no tender mothers blend
Their genial powers to nourish or defend;
No nutrient streams from Beauty's orbs improve

The Temple of Nature. Scholar Press Limited: London, 1973.

These orphan babes of solitary love;
Birth after birth the line unchanging runs,
And fathers live transmitted in their sons;
Each passing year beholds the unvarying kinds,
110 The same their manners, and the same their minds.
Till, as erelong successive buds decay,
And insect shoals successive pass away,
Increasing wants the pregnant parents vex
With the fond wish to form a softer sex;
Whose milky rills with pure ambrosial food
Might charm and cherish their expected brood.
The potent wish in the productive hour
Calls to its aid Imagination's power,
O'er embryon throngs with mystic charm presides,
120 And sex from sex the nascent world divides,
With soft affections warms the callow trains,
And gives to laughing Love his nymphs and swains;
Whose mingling virtues interweave at length
The mother's beauty with the father's strength.[1]

"So tulip-bulbs emerging from the seed,
Year after year unknown to sex proceed;
Erewhile the stamens and the styles display
Their petal-curtains, and adorn the day;
The beaux and beauties in each blossom glow
130 With wedded joy, or amatorial woe."

---

[1] It has been supposed by some, that mankind were formerly quadrupeds as well as hermaphrodites; and that some parts of the body are not yet so convenient to an erect attitude as to a horizontal one; as the fundus of the bladder in an erect posture is not exactly over the insertion of the urethra; whence it is seldom completely evacuated, and thus renders mankind more subject to the stone, than if he had preserved his horizontality: these philosophers, with Buffon and Helvetius, seem to imagine, that mankind arose from one family of monkeys on the banks of the Mediterranean; who accidentally had learned to use the adductor pollicis, or that strong muscle which constitutes the ball of the thumb, and draws the point of it to meet the points of the fingers; which common monkeys do not; and that this muscle gradually increased in size, strength, and activity, in successive generations; and by this improved use of the sense of touch, that monkeys acquired clear ideas, and gradually became men.

Perhaps all the productions of nature are in their progress to greater perfection! an idea countenanced by modern discoveries and deductions concerning the progressive formation of the solid parts of the terraqueous globe, and consonant to the dignity of the Creator of all things. [Erasmus Darwin's note]

From *In Memoriam*
(1850)
Alfred Lord Tennyson

Alfred Lord Tennyson (1809–92) dramatized, perhaps better than any other English poet, the century's struggle to hold in focus the active and "humanist" nature bequeathed by Erasmus Darwin and the poets of the Romantic age, while absorbing the information from geology, biology, and physics that posited a mechanistic or random cosmos indifferent or even inimical to humankind. *In Memoriam* (1850) recalls the poet's grief over the death of his college friend and mentor Arthur Hallam, and his recovery from the scientific and philosophical skepticism that grief imposes.

III

O Sorrow, cruel fellowship,
    O Priestess in the vaults of Death,
    O sweet and bitter in a breath,
80 What whispers from thy lying lip?

"The stars," she whispers, "blindly run;
    A web is wov'n across the sky;
    From out waste places comes a cry,
And murmurs from the dying sun:

"And all the phantom, Nature, stands—
    With all the music in her tone,
    A hollow echo of my own,—
A hollow form with empty hands."

And shall I take a thing so blind,
    Embrace her as my natural good;
    Or crush her, like a vice of blood,
90 Upon the threshold of the mind?

From *Victorian Literature: Poetry.* Ed. Donald J. Gray and G. B. Tennyson. New York, Macmillan, 1976.

LV

The wish, that of the living whole
No life may fail beyond the grave,
Derives it not from what we have
The likest God within the soul? [1]

Are God and Nature then at strife,
That Nature lends such evil dreams?
So careful of the type she seems,
1060   So careless of the single life;

That I, considering everywhere
Her secret meaning in her deeds,
And finding that of fifty seeds [2]
She often brings but one to bear,

I falter where I firmly trod,
And falling with my weight of cares
Upon the great world's altar-stairs
That slope thro' darkness up to God,

I stretch lame hands of faith, and grope,
1070   And gather dust and chaff, and call
To what I feel is Lord of all,
And faintly trust the larger hope.

LVI

"So careful of the type?" but no.
From scarped cliff and quarried stone
She cries, "A thousand types are gone:
I care for nothing, all shall go.

"Thou makest thine appeal to me:
I bring to life, I bring to death:
The spirit does but mean the breath:
1080   I know no more." And he, shall he,

Man, her last work, who seem'd so fair,
Such splendid purpose in his eyes,

---

[1] "The inner consciousness—the divine in man." [Tennyson's note]
[2] "'Fifty' should be 'myriad'." [Tennyson's note]

Who roll'd the psalm to wintry skies,
Who built him fanes[3] of fruitless prayer,

Who trusted God was love indeed
And love Creation's final law—
Tho' Nature, red in tooth and claw
With ravine, shriek'd against his creed—

Who loved, who suffer'd countless ills,
1090   Who battled for the True, the Just,
Be blown about the desert dust,
Or seal'd within the iron hills?

No more? A monster then, a dream,
A discord. Dragons of the prime,[4]
That tare each other in their slime,
Were mellow music match'd with him.

O life as futile, then, as frail!
O for thy voice to soothe and bless!
What hope of answer, or redress?
1100 Behind the veil, behind the veil.

CXVIII

Contemplate all this work of Time,
The giant labouring in his youth;
Nor dream of human love and truth,
As dying Nature's earth and lime;

But trust that those we call the dead
Are breathers of an ampler day
For ever nobler ends. They say,
2520 The solid earth whereon we tread

In tracts of fluent heat began,
And grew to seeming-random forms,
The seeming prey of cyclic storms,
Till at the last arose the man;

---

[3] Fanes: temples. [Orig. ed.]
[4] Prime: dawn of time. [Orig. ed.]

Who throve and branch'd from clime to clime,
> The herald of a higher race,
> And of himself in higher place,
If so he type this work of time

Within himself, from more to more;
2530   Or, crown'd with attributes of woe
> Like glories, move his course, and show
That life is not as idle ore,

But iron dug from central gloom,
> And heated hot with burning fears,
> And dipt in baths of hissing tears,
And batter'd with the shocks of doom

To shape and use. Arise and fly
> The reeling Faun, the sensual feast;
> Move upward, working out the beast,
2540 And let the ape and tiger die.

From *The Descent of Man*
(1874)
Charles Darwin

Charles Darwin (1809–82), the son of a physician and the grandson of Erasmus Darwin, first studied for the ministry but turned scientist during a five-year voyage of exploration (1831–6) through the southern hemisphere as ship's naturalist for the H.M.S. *Beagle*. Twenty years' further reading and thinking became the foundation for the groundbreaking *On the Origin of Species by Natural Selection* (1859), which summarized and crystallized a half-century of evolutionary speculation. Darwin's own writing is a stream of precise observations in the service of overarching ideas. Some of these, like "survival of the fittest," the "struggle for existence," and evolution through "sexual selection," became the foundation for post-*Origin* thinking about the social, intellectual, even moral development of humankind itself. Darwin did not contribute to this stage, however, until he published *The Descent of Man* in 1871, arguing from the evi-

From *The Descent of Man, and Selection in Relation to Sex.* Rev. ed. New York: Merrill and Baker, 1874. (All notes are Charles Darwin's.)

dence of "human" modes of intellection and emotion in animals for humankind's intimate immersion in, and emergence from, the natural world. The text below is from Darwin's 1874 revised edition and omits some parts of Darwin's notes.

[FROM CHAPTER III:] COMPARISON OF THE MENTAL POWERS OF MAN AND THE LOWER ANIMALS.

[. . .] We have seen in the last two chapters that man bears in his bodily structure clear traces of his descent from some lower form; but it may be urged that, as man differs so greatly in his mental power from all other animals, there must be some error in this conclusion. No doubt the difference in this respect is enormous, even if we compare the mind of one of the lowest savages, who has no words to express any number higher than four, and who uses hardly any abstract terms for common objects or for the affections with that of the most highly organized ape. The difference would, no doubt, still remain immense, even if one of the higher apes had been improved or civilized as much as a dog has been in comparison with its parent-form, the wolf or jackal. The Fuegians rank amongst the lowest barbarians, but I was continually struck with surprise how closely the three natives on board H.M.S. "Beagle," who had lived some years in England and could talk a little English, resembled us in disposition and in most of our mental faculties. If no organic being excepting man had possessed any mental power, or if his powers had been of a wholly different nature from those of the lower animals, then we should never have been able to convince ourselves that our high faculties had been gradually developed. But it can be shown that there is no fundamental difference of this kind. We must also admit that there is a much wider interval in mental power between one of the lowest fishes, as a lamprey or lancelet, and one of the higher apes, than between an ape and man; yet this interval is filled up by numberless gradations.

Nor is the difference slight in moral disposition between a barbarian, such as the man described by the old navigator Byron, who dashed his child on the rocks for dropping a basket of sea-urchins, and a Howard or Clarkson; and in intellect between a savage who uses hardly any abstract terms, and a Newton or Shakespeare. Differences of this kind between the highest men of the highest races and the lowest savages, are connected by the finest gradations. Therefore it is possible that they might pass and be developed into each other. [. . .]

[. . . W]e may easily underrate the mental powers of the higher animals, and especially of man, when we compare their actions founded on the memory of past events, on foresight, reason, and imagination, with exactly similar actions instinctively performed by the lower animals; in this latter case the capacity of performing such actions has been gained, step by step, through the variability of the mental organs and natural selection, without any conscious intelligence on the part of the animal during each successive generation. No doubt, as Mr. Wallace has argued,[1] much of the intelligent work done by man is due to imitation and not to reason; but there is this great difference between his actions and many of those performed by the lower animals, namely, that man cannot, on his first trial, make, for instance, a stone hatchet or a canoe, through his power of imitation. He has to learn his work by practice; a beaver, on the other hand, can make its dam or canal, and a bird its nest, as well, or nearly as well, and a spider its wonderful web, quite as well, the first time it tries, as when old and experienced. [. . .]

[FROM CHAPTER IV]

Summary of the last two Chapters. — There can be no doubt that the difference between the mind of the lowest man and that of the highest animal is immense. An anthropomorphous ape, if he could take a dispassionate view of his own case, would admit that though he could form an artful plan to plunder a garden — though he could use stones for fighting or for breaking open nuts, yet that the thought of fashioning a stone into a tool was quite beyond his scope. Still less, as he would admit, could he follow out a train of metaphysical reasoning, or solve a mathematical problem, or reflect on God, or admire a grand natural scene. Some apes, however, would probably declare that they could and did admire the beauty of the colored skin and fur of their partners in marriage. They would admit, that though they could make other apes understand by cries some of their perceptions and simpler wants, the notion of expressing definite ideas by definite sounds had never crossed their minds. They might insist that they were ready to aid their fellow-apes of the same troop in many ways, to risk their lives for them,

---

[1] "Contributions to the Theory of Natural Selection" (1870). [Alfred Russel Wallace (1823–1913) was a famous naturalist-colleague whose readiness to publish similar ideas on evolution finally pushed Darwin to publish *The Origin of Species*. — Ed.]

and to take charge of their orphans; but they would be forced to acknowledge that disinterested love for all living creatures, the most noble attribute
of man, was quite beyond their comprehension.

Nevertheless the difference in mind between man and the higher animals, great as it is, certainly is one of degree and not of kind. We have seen
that the senses and intuitions, the various emotions and faculties, such
as love, memory, attention, curiosity, imitation, reason, &c., of which man
boasts, may be found in an incipient, or even sometimes in a well developed
condition, in the lower animals. They are also capable of some inherited
improvement, as we see in the domestic dog compared with the wolf or
jackal. If it could be proved that certain high mental powers, such as the
formation of general concepts, self-consciousness, &c., were absolutely peculiar to man, which seems extremely doubtful, it is not improbable that
these qualities are merely the incidental results of other highly-advanced
intellectual faculties; and these again mainly the result of the continued use
of a perfect language. At what age does the new-born infant possess the
power of abstraction, or become self-conscious, and reflect on its own existence? We cannot answer; nor can we answer in regard to the ascending
organic scale. The half-art, half-instinct of language still bears the stamp of
its gradual evolution. The ennobling belief in God is not universal with
man; and the belief in spiritual agencies naturally follows from other mental powers. The moral sense perhaps affords the best and highest distinction between man and the lower animals; but I need say nothing on this
head, as I have so lately endeavored to show that the social instincts, — the
prime principle of man's moral constitution — with the aid of active intellectual powers and the effects of habit, naturally lead to the golden rule, "As
ye would that men should do to you, do ye to them likewise;" and this lies
at the foundation of morality. [. . .]

[FROM CHAPTER VI]

[. . .] If the various checks [to population growth] specified in the two last
paragraphs, and perhaps others as yet unknown, do not prevent the reckless, the vicious and otherwise inferior members of society from increasing
at a quicker rate than the better class of men, the nation will retrograde, as
has too often occurred in the history of the world. We must remember that
progress is no invariable rule. It is very difficult to say why one civilized nation rises, becomes more powerful, and spreads more widely, than another; or why the same nation progresses more quickly at one time than at
another. We can only say that it depends on an increase in the actual number of the population on the number of the men endowed with high intel-

lectual and moral faculties, as well as on their standard of excellence. Corporeal structure appears to have little influence, except so far as vigor of body leads to vigor of mind.

It has been urged by several writers that as high intellectual powers are advantageous to a nation, the old Greeks, who stood some grades higher in intellect than any race that has ever existed, ought, if the power of natural selection were real, to have risen still higher in the scale, increased in number, and stocked the whole of Europe. Here we have the tacit assumption, so often made with respect to corporeal structures, that there is some innate tendency towards continued development in mind and body. But development of all kinds depends on many concurrent favorable circumstances. Natural selection acts only tentatively. Individuals and races may have acquired certain indisputable advantages, and yet have perished from failing in other characters. The Greeks may have retrograded from a want of coherence between the many small states, from the small size of their whole country, from the practice of slavery, or from extreme sensuality; for they did not succumb until "they were enervated and corrupt to the very core."[2] The western nations of Europe, who now so immeasurably surpass their former savage progenitors, and stand at the summit of civilization, owe little or none of their superiority to direct inheritance from the old Greeks, though they owe much to the written works of that wonderful people.

Who can positively say why the Spanish nation, so dominant at one time, has been distanced in the race. The awakening of the nations of Europe from the dark ages is a still more perplexing problem. At that early period, as Mr. Galton has remarked, almost all the men of a gentle nature, those given to meditation or culture of the mind, had no refuge except in the bosom of a Church which demanded celibacy;[3] and this could hardly fail to have had a deteriorating influence on each successive generation. During this same period the Holy Inquisition selected with extreme care the freest and boldest men in order to burn or imprison them. In Spain alone some of the best men — those who doubted and questioned, and without doubting there can be no progress — were eliminated during three centuries at the rate of a thousand a year. The evil which the Catholic Church has thus effected is incalculable, though no doubt counterbalanced to a certain, perhaps to a large, extent in other ways; nevertheless, Europe has progressed at an unparalleled rate. [. . .]

---

[2] Mr. Greg, 'Fraser's Magazine,' Sept. 1868. [This is William Rathbone Greg, Manchester essayist and political economist. —Ed.]

[3] "Hereditary Genius," 1870, pp. 357–9. [Francis Galton (1822–1911), anthropologist and explorer, was a cousin of Darwin's. —Ed.]

Natural selection follows from the struggle for existence; and this from a rapid rate of increase. It is impossible not to regret bitterly, but whether wisely is another question, the rate at which man tends to increase; for this leads in barbarous tribes to infanticide and many other evils, and in civilized nations to abject poverty, celibacy, and to the late marriages of the prudent. But as man suffers from the same physical evils as the lower animals, he has no right to expect an immunity from the evils consequent on the struggle for existence. Had he not been subjected during primeval times to natural selection, assuredly he would never have attained to his present rank. Since we see in many parts of the world enormous areas of the most fertile land capable of supporting numerous happy homes, but peopled only by a few wandering savages, it might be argued that the struggle for existence had not been sufficiently severe to force man upwards to his highest standard. Judging from all that we know of man and the lower animals, there has always been sufficient variability in their intellectual and moral faculties, for a steady advance through natural selection. No doubt such advance demands many favorable concurrent circumstances; but it may be well doubted whether the most favorable would have sufficed, had not the rate of increase been rapid, and the consequent struggle for existence extremely severe. It even appears from what we see, for instance, in parts of S. America, that a people which may be called civilized, such as the Spanish settlers, is liable to become indolent and to retrograde, when the conditions of life are very easy. With highly civilized nations continued progress depends in a subordinate degree on natural selection; for such nations do not supplant and exterminate one another as do savage tribes. Nevertheless the more intelligent members within the same community will succeed better in the long run than the inferior, and leave a more numerous progeny, and this is a form of natural selection. [. . .]

[FROM CHAPTER XX:]
SECONDARY SEXUAL CHARACTERS OF MAN

[. . .] We have seen in the last chapter that with all barbarous races ornaments, dress, and external appearance are highly valued; and that the men judge of the beauty of their women by widely different standards. We must next inquire whether this preference and the consequent selection during many generations of those women, which appear to the men of each race the most attractive, has altered the character either of the females alone, or of both sexes. With mammals the general rule appears to be that characters of all kinds are inherited equally by the males and females; we might therefore expect that with mankind any characters gained by the females or by the males through sexual selection, would commonly be transferred to the offspring of both sexes. If any change has thus been effected, it is almost certain that the different races would be differently modified, as each has its own standard of beauty.

With mankind, especially with savages, many causes interfere with the action of sexual selection as far as the bodily frame is concerned. Civilized men are largely attracted by the mental charms of women, by their wealth, and especially by their social position; for men rarely marry into a much lower rank. The men who succeed in obtaining the more beautiful women, will not have a better chance of leaving a long line of descendants than other men with plainer wives, save the few who bequeath their fortunes according to primogeniture. With respect to the opposite form of selection, namely of the more attractive men by the women, although in civilized nations women have free or almost free choice, which is not the case with barbarous races, yet their choice is largely influenced by the social position and wealth of the men; and the success of the latter in life depends much on their intellectual powers and energy, or on the fruits of these same powers in their forefathers. [. . .]

[FROM CHAPTER XXI]

[. . .] Man scans with scrupulous care the character and pedigree of his horses, cattle and dogs before he matches them; but when he comes to his own marriage he rarely, or never, takes any such care. He is impelled by nearly the same motives as the lower animals, when they are left to their own free choice, though he is in so far superior to them that he highly values mental charms and virtues. On the other hand he is strongly attracted by mere wealth or rank. Yet he might by selection do something not only for the bodily constitution and frame of his offspring, but for their intellectual and moral qualities. Both sexes ought to refrain from marriage if they are in any marked degree inferior in body or mind; but such hopes are Utopian and will never be even partially realized until the laws of inheritance are thoroughly known. Everyone does good service, who aids towards this end. When the principles of breeding and inheritance are better understood, we shall not hear ignorant members of our legislature rejecting with scorn a plan for ascertaining whether or not consanguineous marriages are injurious to man.

The advancement of the welfare of mankind is a most intricate problem: all ought to refrain from marriage who cannot avoid abject poverty for their children; for poverty is not only a great evil, but tends to its own increase by leading to recklessness in marriage. On the other hand, as

Mr. Galton has remarked, if the prudent avoid marriage, whilst the reckless marry, the inferior members tend to supplant the better members of society. Man, like every other animal, has no doubt advanced to his present high condition through a struggle for existence consequent on his rapid multiplication; and if he is to advance still higher, it is to be feared that he must remain subject to a severe struggle. Otherwise he would sink into indolence, and the more gifted men would not be more successful in the battle of life than the less gifted. Hence our natural rate of increase, though leading to many and obvious evils, must not be greatly diminished by any means. There should be open competition for all men; and the most able should not be prevented by laws or customs from succeeding best and rearing the largest number of offspring. Important as the struggle for existence has been and even still is, yet as far as the highest part of man's nature is concerned there are other agencies more important. For the moral qualities are advanced, either directly or indirectly, much more through the effects of habit, the reasoning powers, instruction, religion, &c., than through natural selection; though to this latter agency may be safely attributed the social instincts, which afforded the basis for the development of the moral sense.

The main conclusion arrived at in this work, namely that man is descended from some lowly organized form, will, I regret to think, be highly distasteful to many. But there can hardly be a doubt that we are descended from barbarians. The astonishment which I felt on first seeing a party of Fuegians on a wild and broken shore will never be forgotten by me, for the reflection at once rushed into my mind—such were our ancestors. These men were absolutely naked and bedaubed with paint, their long hair was tangled, their mouths frothed with excitement, and their expression was wild, startled, and distrustful. They possessed hardly any arts, and like wild animals lived on what they could catch; they had no government, and were merciless to every one not of their own small tribe. He who has seen a savage in his native land will not feel much shame, if forced to acknowledge that the blood of some more humble creature flows in his veins. For my own part I would as soon be descended from that heroic little monkey, who braved his dreaded enemy in order to save the life of his keeper, or from that old baboon, who descending from the mountains, carried away in triumph his young comrade from a crowd of astonished dogs—as from a savage who delights to torture his enemies, offers up bloody sacrifices, practices infanticide without remorse, treats his wives like slaves, knows no decency, and is haunted by the grossest superstitions.

Man may be excused for feeling some pride at having risen, though not through his own exertions, to the very summit of the organic scale; and the fact of his having thus risen, instead of having been aboriginally placed there, may give him hope for a still higher destiny in the distant future. But we are not here concerned with hopes or fears, only with the truth as far as our reason permits us to discover it; and I have given the evidence to the best of my ability. We must, however, acknowledge, as it seems to me, that man with all his noble qualities, with sympathy which feels for the most debased, with benevolence which extends not only to other men but to the humblest living creature, with his god-like intellect which has penetrated into the movements and constitution of the solar system — with all these exalted powers — Man still bears in his bodily frame the indelible stamp of his lowly origin.

From "Evolution and Ethics" (1893)

Thomas Henry Huxley

Thomas Henry Huxley (1825–95), physician, naturalist, educator, and controversialist, was H. G. Wells's teacher and perhaps the foremost writer about science in late Victorian England. He coined the term *agnosticism* in 1870 and wrote about religion and science from this perspective. The essay "Evolution and Ethics" began as a public lecture at Oxford in 1893 and was published the next year with a prolegomenon. The text below omits part of Huxley's notes.

———

[. . .] We have climbed our bean-stalk and have reached a wonderland in which the common and the familiar become things new and strange. In the exploration of the cosmic process thus typified, the highest intelligence of man finds inexhaustible employment; giants are subdued to our service; and the spiritual affections of the contemplative philosopher are engaged by beauties worthy of eternal constancy.

But there is another aspect of the cosmic process, so perfect as a mechanism, so beautiful as a work of art. Where the cosmopoietic energy works through sentient beings, there arises, among its other manifestations, that which we call pain or suffering. This baleful product of evolution increases in quantity and in intensity, with advancing grades of animal organization, until it attains its highest level in man. Further, the consummation is not

From *The Major Prose of Thomas Henry Huxley*. Ed. Alan P. Barr. Athens, GA: U of Georgia P, 1997.

reached in man, the mere animal; nor in man, the whole or half savage; but only in man, the member of an organized polity. And it is a necessary consequence of his attempt to live in this way; that is, under those conditions which are essential to the full development of his noblest powers.

Man, the animal, in fact, has worked his way to the headship of the sentient world, and has become the superb animal which he is, in virtue of his success in the struggle for existence. The conditions having been of a certain order, man's organization has adjusted itself to them better than that of his competitors in the cosmic strife. In the case of mankind, the self-assertion, the unscrupulous seizing upon all that can be grasped, the tenacious holding of all that can be kept, which constitute the essence of the struggle for existence, have answered. For his successful progress, throughout the savage state, man has been largely indebted to those qualities which he shares with the ape and the tiger; his exceptional physical organization; his cunning, his sociability, his curiosity, and his imitativeness; his ruthless and ferocious destructiveness when his anger is roused by opposition.

But, in proportion as men have passed from anarchy to social organization, and in proportion as civilization has grown in worth, these deeply ingrained serviceable qualities have become defects. After the manner of successful persons, civilized man would gladly kick down the ladder by which he has climbed. He would be only too pleased to see "the ape and tiger die." [1] But they decline to suit his convenience; and the unwelcome intrusion of these boon companions of his hot youth into the ranged existence of civil life adds pains and griefs, innumerable and immeasurably great, to those which the cosmic process necessarily brings on the mere animal. In fact, civilized man brands all these ape and tiger promptings with the name of sins; he punishes many of the acts which flow from them as crimes; and, in extreme cases, he does his best to put an end to survival of the fittest of former days by axe and rope.

I have said that civilized man has reached this point; the assertion is perhaps too broad and general; I had better put it that ethical man has attained thereto. The science of ethics professes to furnish us with a reasoned rule of life; to tell us what is right action and why it is so. Whatever differences of opinion may exist among experts there is a general consensus that the ape and tiger methods of the struggle for existence are not reconcilable with sound ethical principles.

The hero of our story descended the bean-stalk, and came back to the common world, where fare and work were alike hard; where ugly com-

---

[1] From Tennyson's *In Memoriam*, CXVIII, 1, 2540. [Ed.]

petitors were much commoner than beautiful princesses; and where the everlasting battle with self was much less sure to be crowned with victory than a turn-to with a giant. We have done the like. Thousands upon thousands of our fellows, thousands of years ago, have preceded us in finding themselves face to face with the same dread problem of evil. They also have seen that the cosmic process is evolution; that it is full of wonder, full of beauty, and, at the same time, full of pain. They have sought to discover the bearing of these great facts on ethics; to find out whether there is, or is not, a sanction for morality in the ways of the cosmos.

Theories of the universe, in which the conception of evolution plays a leading part, were extant at least six centuries before our era. Certain knowledge of them, in the fifth century, reaches us from localities as distant as the valley of the Ganges and the Asiatic coasts of the Aegean. To the early philosophers of Hindostan, no less than to those of Ionia, the salient and characteristic feature of the phenomenal world was its changefulness; the unresting flow of all things, through birth to visible being and thence to not being, in which they could discern no sign of a beginning and for which they saw no prospect of an ending. It was no less plain to some of these antique forerunners of modern philosophy that suffering is the badge of all the tribe of sentient things; that it is no accidental accompaniment, but an essential constituent of the cosmic process. The energetic Greek might find fierce joys in a world in which "strife is father and king"; but the old Aryan spirit was subdued to quietism in the Indian sage; the mist of suffering which spread over humanity hid everything else from his view; to him life was one with suffering and suffering with life. [. . .]

Hence the pressing interest of the question, to what extent modern progress in natural knowledge, and, more especially, the general outcome of that progress in the doctrine of evolution, is competent to help us in the great work of helping one another?

The propounders of what are called the "ethics of evolution," when the "evolution of ethics" would usually better express the object of their speculations, adduce a number of more or less interesting facts and more or less sound arguments in favour of the origin of the moral sentiments, in the same way as other natural phenomena, by a process of evolution. I have little doubt, for my own part, that they are on the right track; but as the immoral sentiments have no less been evolved, there is, so far, as much natural sanction for the one as the other. The thief and the murderer follow nature just as much as the philanthropist. Cosmic evolution may teach us how the good and the evil tendencies of man may have come about; but, in itself, it is incompetent to furnish any better reason why what we call good is preferable to what we call evil than we had before. Some day, I doubt not, we shall arrive at an understanding of the evolution of the aesthetic faculty; but all the understanding in the world will neither increase nor diminish the force of the intuition that this is beautiful and that is ugly.

There is another fallacy which appears to me to pervade the so-called "ethics of evolution." It is the notion that because, on the whole, animals and plants have advanced in perfection of organization by means of the struggle for existence and the consequent "survival of the fittest"; therefore men in society, men as ethical beings, must look to the same process to help them towards perfection. I suspect that this fallacy has arisen out of the unfortunate ambiguity of the phrase "survival of the fittest." "Fittest" has a connotation of "best"; and about "best" there hangs a moral flavour. In cosmic nature, however, what is "fittest" depends upon the conditions. Long since, I ventured to point out that if our hemisphere were to cool again, the survival of the fittest might bring about, in the vegetable kingdom, a population of more and more stunted and humbler and humbler organisms, until the "fittest" that survived might be nothing but lichens, diatoms, and such microscopic organisms as those which give red snow its colour; while, if it became hotter, the pleasant valleys of the Thames and Isis might be uninhabitable by any animated beings save those that flourish in a tropical jungle. They, as the fittest, the best adapted to the changed conditions, would survive.

Men in society are undoubtedly subject to the cosmic process. As among other animals, multiplication goes on without cessation, and involves severe competition for the means of support. The struggle for existence tends to eliminate those less fitted to adapt themselves to the circumstances of their existence. The strongest, the most self-assertive, tend to tread down the weaker. But the influence of the cosmic process on the evolution of society is the greater the more rudimentary its civilization. Social progress means a checking of the cosmic process at every step and the substitution for it of another, which may be called the ethical process; the end of which is not the survival of those who may happen to be the fittest, in respect of the whole of the conditions which obtain, but of those who are ethically the best.

As I have already urged, the practice of that which is ethically best — what we call goodness or virtue — involves a course of conduct which, in all respects, is opposed to that which leads to success in the cosmic struggle for existence. In place of ruthless self-assertion it demands self-restraint; in place of thrusting aside, or treading down, all competitors, it requires that the individual shall not merely respect, but shall help his fellows; its influence is directed, not so much to the survival of the fittest, as to the fitting of as many as possible to survive. It repudiates the gladiatorial theory of existence. It demands that each man who enters into the enjoyment of the advantages of a polity shall be mindful of his debt to those who have laboriously constructed it; and shall take heed that no act of his weakens the fabric on which he has been permitted to live. Laws and moral precepts are directed to the end of curbing the cosmic process and reminding the individual of his duty to the community, to the protection and influence of which he owes, if not existence itself, at least the life of something better than a brutal savage.

It is from neglect of these plain considerations that the fanatical individualism of our time attempts to apply the analogy of cosmic nature to society. Once more we have a misapplication of the stoical injunction follow nature; the duties of the individual to the state are forgotten, and his tendencies to self-assertion are dignified by the name of rights. It is seriously debated whether the members of a community are justified in using their combined strength to constrain one of their number to contribute his share to the maintenance of it; or even to prevent him from doing his best to destroy it. The struggle for existence which has done such admirable work in cosmic nature, must, it appears, be equally beneficent in the ethical sphere. Yet if that which I have insisted upon is true; if the cosmic process has no sort of relation to moral ends; if the imitation of it by man is inconsistent with the first principles of ethics; what becomes of this surprising theory?

Let us understand, once for all, that the ethical progress of society depends, not on imitating the cosmic process, still less in running away from it, but in combating it. It may seem an audacious proposal thus to pit the microcosm against the macrocosm and to set man to subdue nature to his higher ends; but I venture to think that the great intellectual difference between the ancient times with which we have been occupied and our day, lies in the solid foundation we have acquired for the hope that such an enterprise may meet with a certain measure of success.

The history of civilization details the steps by which men have succeeded in building up an artificial world within the cosmos. Fragile reed as he may be, man, as Pascal says, is a thinking reed:[2] there lies within him a fund of energy operating intelligently and so far akin to that which pervades the universe, that it is competent to influence and modify the cosmic process. In virtue of his intelligence, the dwarf bends the Titan to his will. In every family, in every polity that has been established, the cosmic process

---

[2] Here Huxley quoted (in French) a famous passage from the *Pensées* of Blaise Pascal (1623–62), French mathematician, physicist, and religious philosopher: "Man is but a reed, the most feeble thing in nature; but he is a thinking reed. The entire universe need not arm itself to crush him. A vapor, a drop of water, suffices to kill him. But if the universe were to crush him, man would still be more noble than that which killed him, because he knows that he dies and the advantage which the universe has over him; the universe knows nothing of this." [Ed.]

in man has been restrained and otherwise modified by law and custom; in surrounding nature, it has been similarly influenced by the art of the shepherd, the agriculturist, the artisan. As civilization has advanced, so has the extent of this interference increased; until the organized and highly developed sciences and arts of the present day have endowed man with a command over the course of non-human nature greater than that once attributed to the magicians. The most impressive, I might say startling, of these changes have been brought about in the course of the last two centuries; while a right comprehension of the process of life and of the means of influencing its manifestations is only just dawning upon us. We do not yet see our way beyond generalities; and we are befogged by the obtrusion of false analogies and crude anticipations. But Astronomy, Physics, Chemistry, have all had to pass through similar phases, before they reached the stage at which their influence became an important factor in human affairs. Physiology, Psychology, Ethics, Political Science, must submit to the same ordeal. Yet it seems to me irrational to doubt that, at no distant period, they will work as great a revolution in the sphere of practice.

The theory of evolution encourages no millennial anticipations. If, for millions of years, our globe has taken the upward road, yet, some time, the summit will be reached and the downward route will be commenced. The most daring imagination will hardly venture upon the suggestion that the power and the intelligence of man can ever arrest the procession of the great year.

Moreover, the cosmic nature born with us and, to a large extent, necessary for our maintenance, is the outcome of millions of years of severe training, and it would be folly to imagine that a few centuries will suffice to subdue its masterfulness to purely ethical ends. Ethical nature may count upon having to reckon with a tenacious and powerful enemy as long as the world lasts. But, on the other hand, I see no limit to the extent to which intelligence and will, guided by sound principles of investigation, and organized in common effort, may modify the conditions of existence, for a period longer than that now covered by history. And much may be done to change the nature of man himself.[3] The intelligence which has converted the brother of the wolf into the faithful guardian of the flock ought to be able to do something towards curbing the instincts of savagery in civilized men.

---

[3] The use of the word "Nature" here may be criticised. Yet the manifestation of the natural tendencies of men is so profoundly modified by training that it is hardly too strong. Consider the suppression of the sexual instinct between near relations. [Thomas Henry Huxley's note]

But if we may permit ourselves a larger hope of abatement of the essential evil of the world than was possible to those who, in the infancy of exact knowledge, faced the problem of existence more than a score of centuries ago, I deem it an essential condition of the realization of that hope that we should cast aside the notion that the escape from pain and sorrow is the proper object of life.

We have long since emerged from the heroic childhood of our race, when good and evil could be met with the same "frolic welcome"; the attempts to escape from evil, whether Indian or Greek, have ended in flight from the battle-field; it remains to us to throw aside the youthful over-confidence and the no less youthful discouragement of nonage. We are grown men, and must play the man

> strong in will
> To strive, to seek, to find, and not to yield,

cherishing the good that falls in our way, and bearing the evil, in and around us, with stout hearts set on diminishing it. So far, we all may strive in one faith towards one hope:

> It may be that the gulfs will wash us down,
> It may be we shall touch the Happy Isles,
>
> . . . . but something ere the end,
> Some work of noble note may yet be done.[4]

---

[4]A great proportion of poetry is addressed by the young to the young; only the great masters of the art are capable of divining, or think it worth while to enter into, the feelings of retrospective age. The two great poets whom we have so lately lost, Tennyson and Browning, have done this, each in his own inimitable way; the one in the *Ulysses*, from which I have borrowed; the other in that wonderful fragment "Childe Roland to the dark Tower came." [Thomas Henry Huxley's note]

Part Three

———◆———

CONTEMPORARY VIEWS

Frankenstein and Radical Science
(1993)
Marilyn Butler

Mary Shelley's *Frankenstein* is famously reinterpretable. It can be a late version of the Faust myth, or an early version of the modern myth of the mad scientist; the id on the rampage, the proletariat running amok, or what happens when a man tries to have a baby without a woman.[1] Mary Shelley invites speculation, and in the last generation has been rewarded with a great deal of it.

From professionals, that is. Since 1823, the year when the novel's title, characters and plot first became public property, the general public has seemed remarkably little divided about what the action signifies. A Californian researcher recently employed to find out what the public thinks of scientists was able to summarise his findings wordlessly, with a quick sketch of Frankenstein's Monster. Readers, filmgoers, people who are neither, take the very word Frankenstein to convey an awful warning: don't usurp God's prerogative in the Creation-game, or don't get too clever with technology.

Yet this is by no means what knowledgeable first readers in 1818 were likely to think, or on the evidence of early press comment did think. All three serious reviews in 1818 mention that the novel is topical. No-one appears to discern, as some modern critics do, an allegory of revolution or popular unrest; instead they suspect it of covertly promoting 'favourite projects and passions of the times'. By 'projects' must be meant the novel's network of allusions to contemporary science—not science as formally taught, but current scientific activity as represented to the British public in the 1810s by lectures, newspapers, a few accessible books, above all the serious Reviews.

From *Times Literary Supplement*, 1 April 1993. (All notes are Marilyn Butler's.)

[1] See Lowry Nelson Jr., 'Night Thoughts on the Gothic Novel', *Yale Review* 52 (1963), 236–57; Franco Moretti, *Signs Taken for Wonders* (London: Verso, 1983), 83–108; Anne Mellor, *Mary Shelley: Her Life, Her Fiction, Her Monsters* (London: Routledge, 1988), 40.

The idea Mary Shelley famously hit upon in a house rented by Byron beside the shores of Lake Geneva between 16 and 20 June 1816 almost certainly does draw on a scientific dispute, conducted in lectures afterwards published as books, the first of which was the subject of an article in the *Edinburgh Review* the previous year.[2] The novel which grew from this anecdotal beginning introduces a range of scientific *news*, reported as such, particularly in the *Quarterly Review*, in the years 1816 –18: topics such as electricity and magnetism, vivisection and Polar exploration — and the spectre of new radical French work in what became evolutionism.[3]

After a long, costly European war, these were years of recession, social unrest, and much frantic comment, in moods ranging between outrageous and outraged, in media that included popular papers calling themselves black, red and yellow. From early 1817 the pro-government press, including the leading cultural journal, the Anglican and Tory *Quarterly Review*, published articles calling for press censorship, especially of radical materials intended for a popular readership.[4] From 1818 the *Quarterly* several times called for the revival of the long-neglected charge of blasphemy against irreverent writings.[5] In 1819 it for the first time directed this call against a serious book on evolution science — with which, as I shall show, *Frankenstein* itself is directly implicated.[6]

The 1818 *Frankenstein*, which had drawn nourishment, energy, importance from lectures and journals, had lived by the media, and after 1819 might well have died by the media. The public controversy concerning some of the kinds of science represented in *Frankenstein* endangered the book's future, for it read differently after readers became more knowing. It is not so much because of what Mary Shelley thought, but because of what readers thought, that *Frankenstein* became a substantially different and less contentious novel when reissued in popular form in 1831.

However unalike their approaches, modern critics are likely to be looking at the same text of *Frankenstein*. It will be a reprint of this very third edition of 1831, which Mary Shelley not only changed but, in a new Preface,

---

[2] *Edinburgh Review* 23 (1814), 384 –98.

[3] See e.g. [John Barrow], 'Capt. Burney, *Memoir . . . on the Question whether Asia and America are Contiguous*', *Quarterly Review* 18 (1818), 457–58 and [G, D'Oyley], review of eight works on the vitalist issue, *Quarterly Review* 22 (1820), 1–34.

[4] See especially [R. Southey], *Quarterly Review* 16 (1816), 225–78.

[5] E.g. article on John Bellamy's translation of the New Testament, *Quarterly Review* 19 (1818), 250–81.

[6] Key evidence for this connection appears in the article on vitalism in the *Quarterly* (1820), for which see n. 3 above. That article is reprinted as Appendix C to my edition, *Frankenstein; Or, The Modern Prometheus: The 1818 Text* (London: William Pickering, 1993); reprinted as a World's Classics paperback (Oxford, 1994), 229–51.

interpreted—as the story of a 'human endeavour to mock the stupendous mechanism of the Creator of the world'.[7] That is not an impression easily left by the novel in its 1818 form. But in 1831 Mary Shelley added long passages in which her main narrator, Frankenstein, expresses religious remorse for making a creature, and it is on such passages of reflection and analysis that the empathetic modern reader is encouraged to dwell. Our current understanding of *Frankenstein* is disproportionately impressed by passages introduced in what might be called the composite *Frankenstein,* the product of a decade and a half of religious-scientific controversy.

It is of course standard practice for an editor to select the last version the author revised, on the grounds that no-one has a better right to determine its final form. But, like all rules, this one exists to be challenged. Wordsworth's early versions of 1799 and 1805 of his great poem *The Prelude,* first published posthumously in 1850, are now widely preferred to the much-revised text of 1850. Last year, Simon Gatrell for Oxford's Worlds Classics passed over the standard 1895 text of *The Return of the Native* in favour of the first edition (1878), neatly summarising the historical reasons why the two differed, and the imaginative reasons why the first was to be preferred. The case for *Frankenstein* (1818) resembles these two precedents, since an urgent, unusual, brilliantly-imagined earlier book has been neutered or at best overfreighted with inessential additions. In one respect the case for the early *Frankenstein* is the strongest of the three. The newsworthiness of this novel meant that after publication text and author were subjected to outside pressures which have little to do with aesthetics, and make it hard to say that it was she who changed her mind.

Within the last two decades the 1818 text has become available again. The first scholarly edition by James Rieger (1974, reprinted 1982) remains in print, and since 1990 two new editions based on 1818 have come on the market. The more helpful versions of either text now give some account of the variations between the two. But it requires an external, circumstantial perspective to show how the first *Frankenstein* arose, and why the second is almost a new book.

The single most striking new fact to emerge is the link between *Frankenstein* and the celebrated, publicly-staged debate of 1814–19 between the two professors at London's Royal College of Surgeons on the origins and nature of life, now known as the vitalist debate. The issue was raised in a lecture of 1814 by the senior of the surgeons, John Abernethy, who apparently sought to unite religious and secular opinion with a formula acceptable to both. Materialist science, concentrating on the organisation and

---

[7] Mary Shelley, Preface to 1931 ed., Betty T. Bennett and Charles E. Robinson (eds.), *Mary Shelley Reader* (N.Y.: Oxford University Press, 1990), p. 170.

function of living bodies, could not, Abernethy acknowledged, adequately explain life itself. A mysterious 'superadded' force was needed, some 'subtile, mobile, invisible substance', analogous on the one hand to soul and on the other to electricity.[8]

Coleridge scholars are aware of Abernethy because Coleridge approved of him, and built on his arguments in an essay, 'The Theory of Life', which remained unpublished in the poet's lifetime. Some modern Shelleyans have recognized that Abernethy's antagonist William Lawrence was Percy Shelley's physician (and in the very years of the vitalist row, 1814–19).[9] But in fact no critic has examined Lawrence's boldly sceptical lectures in relation to the writings of the intellectually close-knit Shelley group, which at this time included Percy and Mary Shelley, Peacock, Hunt and Byron.

Unimpeded by being Abernethy's colleague and former protégé, Lawrence took care to make the materialist position sound like the professional position. A more brilliant, cogent writer than Abernethy, he was also a charismatic lecturer and a formidable adversary. Historians of science make claims, if often cautious ones, for Lawrence's contribution to the long-running evolution controversy. But his major book, *Lectures on Physiology, Zoology and the Natural History of Man* (1819), shows that he can be sceptical and discriminating over new evolutionist positions as over everything else. What seems more certain is that his succinct briefings on current Continental work, the French doctor Bichat's research into the nerves and connecting tissue, or the German J. F. Blumenberg's ethnography, must have opened up the way anatomy and physiology were taught to London medical students in the second decade of the century.

Their friendship with Lawrence probably ensured that both Shelleys wrote more accurately and less speculatively on scientific matters than they otherwise might. But he also had a strong imaginative appeal for their disaffected group: after the defeat of the French Revolution, his style of science offered an alternative way of envisaging progress, free of the old discredited political vocabulary. This was above all *natural* history—the early evolutionists' non-scriptural and for some minds anti-scriptural narrative of the life of animal species. Mankind, the other animals, even plants now appeared capable, in response to their environment, driven by mechanisms of their own, of adaptation or what 1790s progressives had called perfectibil-

---

[8] John Abernethy, *An Enquiry into the Probability and Rationality of Mr Hunter's 'Theory of Life'* (London: Longman, etc., 1814), pp. 48, 52.

[9] For pathbreaking work on P. B. Shelley's education and scientific contacts, especially William Lawrence, see Hugh J. Luke Jr., 'Sir William Lawrence, Physician to Shelley and Mary', *Papers on English Language and Literature* i (1965), 141–52, and N. Crook and D. Guiton, *Shelley's Venomed Melody* (Cambridge: C.U.P., 1986).

ity. The writers in turn showed Lawrence an alternative career route: a literary platform from which to address the general public over the heads of cautious colleagues.

It would be possible to treat Lawrence's role in *Frankenstein* as a standard case of influence; some ideas from Erasmus Darwin and Humphry Davy also figure here and there in the novel. But the coincidences between Lawrence's best book and Mary Shelley's are so different in scale that they need following through as, in effect, a single intermeshing story. Both books were associated with aggressive materialism, and this seems to be the main reason why both became *causes célèbres*. It was because each writer took on characteristics of the other's work that Lawrence came to read like a satirist as well as a medical professional, and Mary Shelley could be deemed to have attacked Christianity. In fact it is only when their stories are considered together that we see the extent of the cultural challenge offered by this striking episode in Romantic literary experiment and in the social history of science.

Lawrence was appointed a second Professor at the Royal College of Surgeons in 1815, and in March 1816 gave the two lectures which opened his campaign against Abernethy. The first is a wide-ranging survey of recent Continental work in the physical sciences, while the second, 'On Life', focuses rigorously on the issue raised by Abernethy as physiology and anatomy can properly handle it. For biologists (a word Lawrence allegedly introduced to Britain), life is the 'assemblage of all the functions' a living body can perform. We have done what we can, Lawrence says, to find origins and 'to observe living bodies in the moment of their formation . . . when matter may be supposed to receive the stamp of life. . . . Hitherto, however, we have not been able to catch nature in the fact.' On the contrary, what we can observe of animals is that 'all have participated in the existence of other living beings . . . the motion proper to living bodies, or in one word, life, has its origin in that of their parents.'[10] The materialist thinker sees no means of abstracting the animating power from the animal.

By the time of his 1817 lectures, Lawrence was willing to identify Abernethy as his opponent, and openly to ridicule the argument that electricity, or 'something analogous' to it, could do duty for the soul — 'For subtle matter is still matter; and if this fine stuff can possess vital properties, surely they may reside in a fabric which differs only in being a little coarser.'[11] But even in the more guarded 1816 lectures there was an offensive tone of

---

[10] William Lawrence, *An Introduction to Comparative Anatomy, being two introductory lectures delivered at the Royal College of Surgeons* (London, 1816), 140–42.

[11] Lawrence, *Lectures on Physiology, Zoology and the Natural History of Man* (London: Callow, 1819), Lecture 3 [1817], p. 84.

superiority in the demand that the Life question should be left to the real professionals. In this case that meant excluding chemists, including presumably Davy, whom Abernethy had recruited: 'Organized bodies must be treated differently from . . . inorganic. . . . The reference to gravity, to attraction, to chemical affinity, to electricity and galvanism, can only serve to perpetuate false notes in philosophy.' The great John Hunter, after whom his and Abernethy's lectures were named, would have been on his, Lawrence's, side when it came to method: 'He did not attempt to explain life by . . . *a priori* speculations, or by the illusory analogies of other sciences; . . . [but] by a patient examination of the fabric, and close observation of the actions of living creatures.'[12]

Mary and Percy Shelley, Lawrence's friends, were living near London in that March of 1816, when Lawrence first put the materialist case against spiritualised vitalism. On June 15 1816, at Geneva, Byron's doctor Polidori recorded in his diary that he and P. B. Shelley had a conversation 'about principles—whether man was to be thought merely an instrument'.[13] Fifteen years later Mary Shelley remembered several conversations on subsequent days, with Byron participating, she silently auditing, on 'the nature of the principle of life, and whether there was any probability of its ever being discovered and communicated.' On 16 June, most members of the party agreed to take part in a ghost-story contest.

There surely cannot be much doubt that the group were speaking of the vitalist debate, and presumably of Lawrence's lectures, which were on sale by June 1816 in book form. In fact, Mary's contribution to the ghost-story competition to some degree acts out the debate between Abernethy and Lawrence, in a form close enough for those who knew it to recognise. Frankenstein the blundering experimenter, still working with superseded notions, suggests the position of Abernethy, who proposes that the superadded life-element is analogous to electricity—particularly when he uses a machine, reminiscent of a battery, to impart the spark of life.[14] Frankenstein's other procedures are made unpleasantly anti-life, recalling Lawrence's unfavourable comparison of inorganic with organic methods.[15] The

---

[12] Ibid., *Introduction to Comparative Anatomy* (1816), pp. 161–63.

[13] (Ed.) W. M. Rossetti, *Diary of J. W. Polidori, 1816* (1911), quoted James Rieger (ed.), 'Introduction', *Frankenstein, or the Modern Prometheus: The 1818 Text* (Chicago: U. of Chicago Press, 1982), p. xvii.

[14] See opening sentences, *Frankenstein* (1818), ch. 4.

[15] Not only does he rob graves for the flesh of the dead (ch. 3); he performs vivisection ('tortures the living animal'). This, along with other forms of cruelty to animals, was particularly objectionable to humanitarians and principled vegetarians such as the Shelleys.

fact is that in 1818 Mary Shelley's portrayal of her hero is harsh, contemptuous, with a touch of Lawrence's sarcastic debating manner. Not so much a mythical Prometheus, more a humble Sorceror's Apprentice, Frankenstein as first devised seems to know too little science rather than too much.

Compared with the professional qualifications of the novel's first two narrators, Frankenstein and Walton, an inventor and an explorer, the Creature has few claims to act as the third. Just as he owes his existence to a unique and unnatural process, he defies all odds, as a parentless being, by learning language at all. Yet the voice in which he narrates the second of the three volumes is impressive, in a strange register appropriate to a witness brought back from the remote past — a phrase the scientific showman Georges Cuvier had recently used to describe the fossils he patiently reconstructed into lifelike animals.[16] He is more eloquent than Frankenstein in the conversations that introduce and end their meeting, and still more persuasive when relating his life-history, an exercise in self-observation, social observation, and retrospective analysis. By tracking his own maturation, from a solitary to a social animal, the Creature succeeds in the task Frankenstein abandons, that of scientifically following up Frankenstein's technological achievement.

He begins his narration on the night of the experiment, substituting his careful record for Frankenstein's excitable recollection of the same events. Still unable to focus his eyes, the Creature blundered round Frankenstein's lodgings in the big Ingolstadt rooming house, before finding himself, very cold, out in the woods near the town. His visual impressions were still unclear, but he now began to make the distinction between light and dark. He might have died of hunger and exposure had he not found berries he instinctively ate, water to drink, and a cloak to wrap himself in. He responded, pleasurably, to moonlight and birds when still unable to name them, let alone classify 'the little winged animals who had often intercepted the light from my eyes'.

In this chapter Mary Shelley employs language experimentally and imaginatively, in a way that anticipates the scenes in William Golding's novel *The Inheritors* where the Neanderthal narrator describes his first encounters with *homo sapiens*. But there are conventionally-written eighteenth-century precedents, in the literature on Wild Boys and Girls who had

---

[16]Georges Cuvier (1769–1832) popularised paleontology, in a triumphantly imaginative presentation of the remote past. 'My key, my principle, will enable us to restore the appearance of these long-vanished beasts and relate them to the life of the present' (Cuvier, *Essay on the Theory of the Earth*, Edinburgh, 1815). See also *Edinburgh Review* 20 (1812) 382, and Loren Eiseley, *Darwin's Century*, p. 84.

supposedly grown up among wild animals, or at any rate isolated from humanity. Already in his *System of Nature* (1735), Linnaeus speaks of *homo ferus* as a distinct human species, 'four-footed, mute and hairy', and lists ten recorded instances from 1544. The most famous case of Mary Shelley's day was the Wild Boy of Aveyron, whose discovery came to light in Paris in 1799. For what it reveals of early human physical and cognitive development, this remains a classic instance, thanks to the devoted teaching and careful reporting of Jean-Marc Gaspard Ikard, the young physician of the Paris institution for deaf-mutes, who cared for the boy and analysed his problems as the loss of nurture by human parents in infancy.[17]

Rousseau and Monboddo enthusiastically contributed to the wider debate, over whether the wild man is a sub-species, and if so how he relates both to advanced man and to the primates. Unlike both, but like J. F. Blumenbach, Lawrence in his *Natural History of Man* (1819) argues against generalising from such cases: the child concerned was likely to have been born an idiot, and had either strayed from home or been cast out. The lack of bodily coordination in a case such as that of Peter of Hamelin, an earlier wild boy brought in the 1720s to England, and the Aveyron boy's difficulty in learning language, had explanations less astonishing than Monboddo's supposition that such children represented a sub-species between mankind and the primates.[18]

A significant aspect of Mary Shelley's treatment of the Creature's rearing in isolation from humanity is its avoidance of idealised, sentimental or scientifically-bold claims. The Creature's life in the woods is neither superior, nor even natural; it raises no question of his belonging to a species other than the human. So firmly is that speculative historical narrative omitted that it seems as if Mary Shelley, like Lawrence, deliberately avoided committing herself to the evolutionist hypothesis both Erasmus Darwin and Lamarck espoused, that all forms of organic life had evolved from single cells. Yet the Creature's life-experience hardly seems scientifically ill-informed, since it bears out the careful physiology of Itard's leading contemporary Bichat, in *Traité sur les membranes* (1800), *Recherches physiologiques sur la vie et sur la mort* (1800), and *Anatomie Générale* (1801), works which explore the functions and connecting tissue of the nerves, senses and organs, and give the most accurate account yet of every creature's sensitive interactions with its environment.

---

[17] 'Cast upon this globe without physical strength or innate ideas . . . , it is only in the heart of society that man can attain the preeminent position which is his natural destiny.' Ikard, opening sentence of Preface to *The Wild Boy of Aveyron* [1807], (New York: Appleton-Century-Crofts, 1962), p. xxi.

[18] Lawrence, *Lectures on Physiology . . . and Natural History of Man*, pp. 134–40.

In fact, once it is considered in relation to fiction's established conventions, the Creature's career works on two levels, as a survival-story like Robinson Crusoe's, and as a story which does after all have historical implications, for it can be read as an allegorical account of the progress of mankind over aeons of time. That sidestep into allegory evades, yet for the knowing reader might also bring to mind, the evolutionist's long view of the ascent of the species.

For all the excellence and the intriguing suggestiveness of volume II as a Voltairean fable, most modern readers probably find volume III the most brilliantly imaginative and original part of the book, and this seems as true of its science as of its characterisation. There are signs by now of a rich literary interaction between the Shelleys and Lawrence, one that flows in both directions. In his polemical 1817 lecture on the Life question, Lawrence seems to stray into Mary Shelley's Gothicised rhythms and vocabulary— 'an immaterial and spiritual being could not have been discovered among the blood and filth of the dissecting room.'[19] In turn Mary Shelley seems to draw more in her later scenes on details from different writings by Lawrence, not necessarily contemporaneous. They include entries he contributed to Rees's *Cyclopaedia*, particularly one on Monsters, and an academic paper of 1815 on the case of a boy born without part of his brain, whom Lawrence had cared for in his own home.[20] That piece of fieldwork must surely have helped prompt Mary Shelley's 'hideous phantom', since *Frankenstein* must from the start have involved a scientist studying the relations of brain to physical functions, who fosters (or fails to foster) a monster. Even more clearly, the Lawrence case provided a plot for Peacock's satire *Melincourt* (1817), in which an intellectual called Forester (full form of the name Foster) adopts an orang-utan and tries to teach him to speak. Forester fails in his immediate objective, but a richly corrupt system enables him to secure his protégé a baronetcy and a seat in Parliament.

Lawrence's *Natural History of Man*, his one fullscale book, takes as its topic the human species, considered as a variety of animal. Lawrence states that his text is substantially based on lectures he gave in 1814, which no

---

[19] Ibid., p. 7.

[20] Lawrence also contributed entries on 'Cranium', 'Generation' and 'Man' for Rees's *Cyclopaedia* (individual volumes undated, edition complete by 1819). The *Quarterly*'s attack on radical science (1820) refers xenophobically in passing to the *Cyclopaedia* articles as borrowings from 'the school of modern French philosophy', naming Cuvier and Bichat, and from unnamed 'freethinking physiologists of Germany.' Percy Shelley had already unwarily drawn attention to the debt of *Frankenstein* to German physiologists, hardly as yet well-known to the English public, in the opening sentences of his anonymous Preface to the 1818 *Frankenstein*.

doubt explains why so much of it surveys the current state of knowledge in the appropriate field—ethnography, with inputs from anatomy and sociology. In his division of racial types into five, and his emphasis on physical differences between humans and primates, Lawrence largely repeats Blumenbach, with and without attribution. But in his freshest, most dynamic passages he works his own witty, distinctive variations on Blumenbach's memorable observation, 'man is the most perfect of domesticated animals'.[21] Most domesticated animals are smaller, weaker, less audacious than their wild-life ancestors. In an offensive, powerful passage, Lawrence develops a Swiftian put-down to humanity, by remarking on the tendency of the European upper orders to 'breed', by sexual selection, for physical beauty and elegance rather than strength or ability. But to judge by the ugly, stunted London Cockney, examples of degeneracy are plentiful among urban populations. Lawrence goes on to reflect that inbreeding within the European royal families has thrown up many recent cases of hereditary weakness and madness.[22] He need not remind his readers of the obvious example, England's George III.

Several topics Lawrence considers in his *Natural History* reappear, in yet more ingenious adaptations, in the third volume of *Frankenstein*. Mankind as a domesticated animal, pretentious but flawed, could also be the best way to summarise Mary Shelley's larger theme. Incidentally she touches on Lawrence's professional issues: heredity, fosterage and nurturance, sexual selection and the perverse adoption of choices which lead to extinction. She displays them by portraying the aristocratic Frankensteins as unhealthy, even incestuous, in their marriages; in the first edition Frankenstein's bride Elizabeth is his first cousin, who has been brought up like a sister. Frankenstein exhibits a neurotic resistance when asked to fix the date of their wedding. His excuse to himself and us is that he must first make a female Mon-

---

[21] See entry 'J. F. Blumenbach' (1752–1840), *Dictionary of Scientific Biography*. In a series of major articles, Timothy Lenoir has demonstrated that Blumenbach's 'materialist vitalism', which was sceptical, cautious and scrupulously environmental, contributed importantly to the scientific thought of his Gottingen colleague Kant in the 1780s and 1790s, and in helping generate a *philosophy of biology* had a key influence on the early nineteenth-century emergence of the subject (Lenoir, 'Kant, Blumenbach and Vital Materialism in German Biology', *Isis* 71 (1980), 77–108; 'The Development of Transcendental Naturphilosophile', *Studies in Historical Biology* (1981), 111–205). As a key English translator and follower of Blumenbach, Lawrence's intellectual role takes on enhanced significance; so does *Frankenstein,* once it can be seen to convey quite sophisticated biological concepts in a familiar form.

[22] *Lectures . . . and Natural History of Man,* pp. 459–60: 'Natural History of Man', Section II, ch. VI, subsections on 'Powerful Influence of Attention to Breed' and 'Inattention to This Point in the Human Race'.

ster for the Creature to mate with, thus helping to underline how much stronger and healthier are the Creature's instincts. Frankenstein indeed seems more aroused when making and dismembering the female Monster than at the prospect of joining Elizabeth on his own wedding night. It is, of course, the Creature who gets there first. This means that Frankenstein has a hand in his bride's death—because he brought the Creature to life, because his neglect of him afterwards indeed made a Monster, and because he neglects Elizabeth too. That hideously terminated marriage kills Frankenstein's father, and raises the prospect that the family will become extinct.

When it comes to parenting, Frankenstein is himself a monster. He will not acknowledge his only child, the Being he chooses to call Monster, Fiend and Demon, though no human father ever played so thoroughgoing a role in any birth. *Frankenstein* ironically illustrates Lawrence's scholarly observations about parenting—the medical mishaps to which the birth-process is subject; the one sure feature of any birth, which is the involvement of at least one parent of the same species. But, if this parent-child relationship after a fashion obeys the rules, the roles of those involved become perversely displaced. After Frankenstein vows to hunt down his 'progeny', the Creature nurtures Frankenstein to keep him alive, feeding him for example with a dead hare: it's only when killing for Frankenstein that the vegetarian Creature kills for food. He still tries in his way to live by the precept that the child is father to the man—and, anthropologically, primitive man *is* father to sophisticated man. But the Creature has slowly emerged as the dominant partner, though originally he was a dependent, a deformed huge child. Of the two antagonists, he is the stronger and better adapted when the chase ends in the Arctic, where natural conditions are at their most severe. He shares Frankenstein's fate of extinction, but goes to it voluntarily, with a consoling sense that even he now returns to nature.

The sequence of events after publication makes a story on its own, significant and intricate because it involves so many key institutions—the law, commercial publishers, the journals, the Royal College of Surgeons. The three reviews the novel received queried its attitudes,[23] and this is unsurprising since, though anonymous, it was dedicated to the 1790s radical William Godwin. Even so, Mary had a kindlier, larger press than her husband had in his lifetime—and better reviews than the Shelleys must have feared. But the next year the publication of Lawrence's *Lectures on Physiology, Zoology and the Natural History of Man* provoked the virulent and

[23] *Quarterly Review* 18 (1818), 378–85; *Edinburgh Magazine and Literary Miscellany* 2 (1818), 249–53; [Scott], *Blackwood's Edinburgh Magazine* 2 (1817–18), 613–26.

prominently placed denunciation in the *Quarterly Review* of November 1819. This unusually long opening article surveyed the vitalist controversy over five years, and itself constituted a major event in the public reception of evolution theory. Encouraged by his editor William Gifford, the author George D'Oyley devoted most space to Lawrence, denouncing him for taking the leading role on the materialist side in the vitalist issue. He included Lawrence's other published writings in the indictment, but surprisingly omitted his treatment of heredity and breeding, possibly out of regard for good taste. D'Oyley's tone is exceptionally harsh and personal: after dealing with six other works on either side, he abruptly returns to Lawrence, and calls on the Royal College of Surgeons to discipline him. On pain of dismissal he should be made to withdraw the offending passages, and to undertake not to write again in the same vein.

The Royal College of Surgeons did indeed suspend Lawrence, and, going a little further than asked, would not reinstate him till he withdrew the book entirely. He did so for fear of losing his appointment as Surgeon to some of the London hospitals. The result ironically was that during the next few years several publishers pirated the volume, under cover of a ruling of 1817 by the Lord Chancellor, Lord Eldon, that where a book was blasphemous, seditious or immoral the author should not be protected by the law of copyright.[24] In March 1822, under pressure again from the Royal College, Lawrence tried to claim his copyright, and initially obtained an injunction restraining the firm of J. and C. Smith from selling their edition of his book. The Smiths' lawyers argued that the work was not protected because of passages 'hostile to natural and revealed religion'. After reading both the book and its reviews, Lord Eldon upheld the publishers, even though the book would in consequence remain in circulation, in cheap popular formats. Lord Byron lost similar cases, also tried before Eldon, in February 1822 and in 1823, involving *Cain* and *Don Juan* respectively.

The great notoriety of Lawrence's volume between 1819 and 1822 becomes part of the post-publication history of *Frankenstein*. For the author, her circle, potential publishers, and a significant number of informed readers, whether their sympathies were theological or materialist, the plot of *Frankenstein* was either already associated with Lawrence's style of radical

---

[24] In addition to the first edition by J. Callow (1819), the British Library owns early pirated editions by W. Benbow (1822), Kaygill & Rice (1822) and J. and C. Smith (1823). There was a further edition in 1823 by Richard Carlile, the radical publisher jailed for reissuing Paine's critique of the Bible, *The Age of Reason* (1819). Carlile wrote an *Address to the Men of Science* (1821), singling out Lawrence for praise as a popular radical writer, and dedicated his edition of Lawrence's book ironically to Lord Eldon. See O. Temkin, 'Basic Science, Medicine and the Romantic Era', in *The Double Face of Janus* (Baltimore: Johns Hopkins U.P., 1977), p. 355.

science, or was imminently in danger of becoming so — until, that is, Mary Shelley removed most of the telltale signs.

For the 1831 edition Mary Shelley added remorseful passages which made Frankenstein a more sympathetic as well as a more religious character; she pared away details of his scientific education and, most interestingly, changed all those facts about the Frankenstein family's marriages that in the first edition touch on genetic concerns. Her alterations were acts of damage-limitation rather than a reassertion of authority. They perhaps seemed advisable when surgeons and their experiments became the objects of public hysteria because of the Burke and Hare murders in Edinburgh in the late 1820s. What made them inevitable was that conservatives everywhere now interpreted the plot of *Frankenstein* as they wished to, and expected most readers to agree. As a writer in *Fraser's Magazine* (November 1830) remarks in passing, 'A State without religion is like a human body without a soul, or rather like a human body of the species of the Frankenstein Monster, without a pure and vivifying principle.'[25] Before Mary Shelley made the novel fit this description, a journalist confidently claimed it for Abernethy's rather than Lawrence's side in the vitalist dispute.

From "Literate Species"
(2000)
Maureen N. McLane

[. . .] The peculiar dignity of these arts is said to lie in the fact that their cultivation and pursuit differentiates the activities distinctive of man from those of animals.

— R. S. Crane, *The Idea of The Humanities*

I believe that the monster's *bildung* makes explicit the problematic status of "human being" (a species category) and "the humanities" (the cultivation

From *Romanticism and the Human Sciences: Poetry, Population, and the Discourse of the Species*. Cambridge: Cambridge UP, 2000. (All notes are Maureen N. McLane's.)

[25] Lee Sterrenberg, 'Mary Shelley's Monster: Politics and Psyche in *Frankenstein*, in (eds.) Levine and Knocpfemacher, *The Endurance of Frankenstein* (Berkeley: U. of California Press, 1979), p. 166.

of the "good arts"—as R. S. Crane described it—whether considered as eloquence and reason, belles lettres, or the "liberal arts").[1] If the monster appears as the product of scientific experiment fueled by romantic ambition, his attempt to acquire know-how and fellowship through speech and writing represents another effort at producing himself, this time as a speaking and reasoning being. History and literature, supported by a basic literacy, figure as the most sophisticated techniques for the monster's experiment in his own humanization. He tells his maker that he happened upon a cache of books, "written in the language the elements of which I had acquired at the cottage." Among these books are *Paradise Lost*, a volume of *Plutarch's Lives*, and the *Sorrows of Werther*. How is it possible that all these books should be "written in the language" the monster has acquired? He never speaks of translation, although this is an obvious solution to the difficulty. He makes a point of telling old De Lacey that he "was educated by a French family, and understand[s] that language only." Perhaps I am stressing this point too much—yet we may also understand the monster's assimilation of Milton's English, Plutarch's Greek, and Goethe's German to be a typically "European"—or perhaps Romantically eclecticizing—gesture. The linguistic, historical, and cultural heterogeneity of the monster's canon is an intriguingly unthought aspect of the novel. And yet, as the monster's assertion of monolingual fluency suggests, the aspirant to human community must speak at least *one* particular language fluently, must be able to identify his language with a kind of national or at least regional seal—in this case, French.

Several critics have discussed the monster's reading course: the significance of Shelley's choices; the sequence in which the monster reads his books; their political, religious, and aesthetic valences.[2] When considering the anthropomorphic problematic of the *Frankenstein*, the content of and

---

[1] In "Shifting Definitions and Evaluations," R. S. Crane traces the historical emergence, development, and interpenetration of such concepts as "humanity" and "the humanities." The humanities have encompassed different subjects in different periods (Quintilian's rhetoric, the "good arts" commended by the grammarian Aulus Gellius, the medieval trivium and quadrivium, Matthew Arnold's "culture"). Regardless of subject content, however, it is the humanities, as Crane notes, which traditionally offered the means of cultivating "humanitas": educators in antiquity assumed that the men who pursued the "good arts" "are most humanized" (The Idea of the Humanities, U of Chicago P, 1967, p. 23).

[2] See Anne McWhir, "Teaching the Monster to Read: Mary Shelley, Education, and *Frankenstein*," *The Educational Legacy of Romanticism*, ed. John Willinsky (Waterloo, Ontario: Wilfrid Laurier U P, 1990), for a wonderful discussion of the monster as ideologically trapped by his education, which provides him "intellectual parents" and "a sense of self only to discover that he has no right to exist" (p. 74). See also Alan Richardson's "From *Emile* to *Frankenstein*; The Education of Monsters."

expectations generated by such material as *Paradise Lost* (Adamic sonship and prerogative, Satanic exile and heroic despair) seem less significant than the very literacy which such reading presupposes. What is most striking is not what the monster reads and speaks, or even that he reads and speaks, but rather what he thinks such accomplishments should signify: the precondition for his "becoming one among my fellows," as he puts it. Shelley repeatedly emphasizes the function of linguistic mediation in constituting communities. She takes care to provide her Europeans with a linguistic education, Elizabeth and Victor having learned English and Latin. Victor also familiarizes himself with "the easiest Greek" and German (this in addition to his native French). Thus the novel traces a linguistic range for her inhabitants and points to the colonial, commercial, and sexual extension of this range, as in Henry Clerval's orientalism and in the "Arabian" Safie's linguistic Europeanization. Given the novel's elision of "European" and "human," it is not at all surprising that the monster looks to language and to European history and literature as the media for his transformation into a member of the community.

The monster understands language to be a route to common human being; he also conceives of language not as an oral exchange but rather as literate (lettered) speech. In his hovel by the De Laceys, the monster discovers the "science of words or letters." Eventually he recognizes that the De Laceys communicate "by articulate sounds"—a "godlike science" he wishes to learn. There is a particular urgency to the monster's wish: he decides he will remain hidden until he has made himself "master of their language." He expects to use his articulate voice against their perception of his hideous form. His idiosyncratic schooling emphasizes the acquisition of speech and writing, a double linguistic fluency which he acquires almost simultaneously. He becomes both phoneticized and alphabeticized. In this he registers the nineteenth-century turn-to-language, in which scholars increasingly established the study of language as the basis of the human sciences (as in the proliferation of universal grammars, the birth of philology, the development of comparative linguistics). He understands human being to be constituted through a very particular "discourse network," in Friedrich Kittler's terms, in which the learning of language required a "naturalization of the alphabet" and as well as an "oralization" of the alphabet; in this way pedagogues attempted to obscure the arbitrariness of what the monster calls the "science of words or letters."[3] The monster's choice of "science" in this last phrase introduces an interesting ambiguity (as does his mention of the "godlike science" of language): he may well be using

---

[3] Friedrich A. Kittler, "The Mother's Mouth," *Discourse Networks, 1800/1900*, trans. Michael Metteer with Chris Cullens (Stanford U P, 1990), pp. 29, 32. See especially the

"science" in its full elasticity, as equivalent to a formal knowledge or method, but he may also register what Kittler describes as the "revolution of the European alphabet"—its oralization through syllabic and spelling methods around 1800 which contributed to "the epistemological shift from a general grammar to the science of language."[4] The problem of phonetics and the alphabet, posed by the monster to himself, suggests that language has been denaturalized, already broken into a particular *combinatoire*. The monster is unable to acquire French by purely oral means; he requires the intervention of a book, of transcription, whose words he then *hears* Felix reading to Safie. This oral method thus rests on a literate precondition. Whether considered as an art (for example, as part of rhetoric) or as a science (for example, as part of phonetics), language appears as the most basic medium for his humanization. [. . .]

It is striking that the monster's first murder appears as the climax of a pedagogical fantasy. The real question is not why little William responded so violently to this monster (who is consistently visually aversive to humans), but why the monster ever considered him educable—or more broadly, why the monster entertains educational fantasies at all. The monster persists in taking himself as an appropriate object of the liberal arts. He believes the methods and arts available to, for example, Safie, are equally available to him. As he says, relishing his language lessons, "I resolved to make use of the same instructions [given Safie] to the same end." The "end" for Safie is the learning of French in order to be assimilated linguistically and sexually into the Christian, republican, patriarchal domicile; so too the monster aspires, but his aspiration also bears the weight of his desire to humanize himself, to distinguish himself from the animals (as both R. S. Crane and Godwin describe the task of the humanities). In entertaining humanist fantasies, the monster forgets his corporeally and nominally indeterminate status: the community of letters presupposes a human community, and the humanities presuppose humans. The monster

---

section entitled, "Learning to Read in 1800." In my turn to Kittler I elide several differences, including Kittler's focus on German discourse networks, on the mother as the new state-created pedagogue, and on the role of the new grammars and the phonetic method circa 1800. Clearly the monster has no mediating mother (alas for him); moreover he learns not from grammars but from an auralized/oralized written history. Yet his encounter with the "science of letters" (p. 114) suggests that his experience of language is always already alphabeticized; the monster's labor (and Safie's) also highlights the differing and simultaneous functions of Felix's pedagogy—the monster seeks to enter human being by accessing what seems to the residents of the cabin a closed discourse network. That the monster succeeds in acquiring words, letters, eloquence, consciousness demonstrates the monstrous productivity of Felix's pedagogic machine.

[4]Kittler, *Discourse Networks*, p. 32.

presupposes his potential humanity; in this he succumbs to the ruse of the humanities.

Renouncing Human Being: Species Revising

It is only after the spectacular failure of the monster's education—both in his own training-into-language with the De Laceys, and in his wish to "educate" little William—that the monster admits the anthropological crisis he presents, both for himself and for humans. The monster's tale of his "progress" concludes with his request of Victor:

> I am alone and miserable; man will not associate with me; but one as deformed and horrible as myself would not deny herself to me. My companion must be of the same species, and have the same defects. This being you must create.

The creature's understanding of species takes up, and perhaps parodies, the conceptualization of that term throughout what Michel Foucault terms the Classical period (from the mid-seventeenth to the late eighteenth century in Western Europe). As both Foucault and François Jacob note, species was defined in this era according to the persistence of the visible structure.[5] For the creature, to be "of the same species" is to look alike, however "deformed and horrible" that might be. Species here seems to follow a logic of appearance. It seems less a scientific category denoting classes of beings which reproduce their like over time than a perceptual-social category which organizes the possibility of contact among beings. Creatures of different species will "not associate" together. Aesthetic revulsion precludes social interaction. This has been repeatedly demonstrated by the visual paranoia the monster induces and the semiological riddle he presents. Yet he is not merely a signifier: he is a body, a potentially reproductive body, as Victor comes to see.

Requesting a female "with whom I can live in the interchange of those sympathies necessary for my being," the monster links the problem of his "being" to the problem of sympathy. As David Marshall has argued, *Frankenstein* may be read as an inquiry into the specular and spectacular logic of sympathy: the monster appears as the very limit of the economy of sympathetic exchange. The monster is of course repeatedly presented as a

---

[5] In the section "Species" in the chapter "The Visible Structure," Jacob writes, "Throughout the Classical period, it was primarily by their visible structure that living beings were known and investigated" (*The Logic of Life: A History of Heredity*, trans. Betty E. Spillman [Princeton UP, 1973], p. 44). Foucault asserts, in his chapter called "Classifying": "Natural history is nothing more than the nomination of the visible." See *The Order of Things* [(New York: Random House, 1973)], p. 132.

specular problem; I have argued that the visual distress he induces may be read as well as a figure for the imaginal-conceptual breakdown he embodies. This leads us to the interesting question: is common species being a pre-requisite for sympathy, or is sympathy the precondition for what I am calling "common species being"? The question of theoretic priority is ultimately less important than the monster's analysis of the mutual implication of the discourse of sympathy and the construction of human being. The monster acquiesces in the proposition that only beings "of the same species" are capable of sympathizing with each other.[6] His request reflects his experience of sympathy as a specifically *human* specular logic: a body requires a human appearance to stimulate, elicit and participate in human sympathetic reactions. Of course, the monster shows himself capable of sympathizing with humans; yet sighted humans refuse that reciprocity. That blind De Lacey offers an alternative vision of the monster provides not an instance of superior insight (see, the monster really *is* like us) so much as another moment in which blindness calls forth insight. The monster's pleasant discussion with Old De Lacey promises an alternative discourse network, a community independent of visual affinity. The sympathetic blindness of Old De Lacey allows us to read normal human vision as ideologically blinkered; and yet the visual persists as the most powerful mode of understanding the world. Shelley shows us how humans experience sight as transparency; sympathy and its counter, revulsion, occur as if naturally to the sighted. Those with normal and normalizing sight will perceive the anomaly as a threat, as an invasion, and will, like Felix De Lacey, vigorously and righteously resist. She thus displays and critiques the anthropomorphic supports of sympathy. The monster marks the species limit of what Donna Haraway calls, in another context, "primate vision."[7] Both Victor and the monster come to agree: sympathy will not cross the species barrier.

---

[6] Marshall brilliantly conjoins the problem of species and the "failure of sympathy" [*The Surprising Effects of Sympathy: Marivaux, Diderut, Rousseau, and Mary Shelley* (U of Chicago P, 1988; p. 195)]; in many ways his reading of the monster's request and Victor's response anticipates and coincides with my own. He constellates Shelley's critique of the species-sympathy problem through Godwin, Wollstonecraft, and Rousseau. As he notes, Shelley's "story about the denial of sympathy, fellow feeling, and fellow creatures seems to draw upon Wollstonecraft's critique of the ideology of sexual difference" (p. 199).

[7] See Donna J. Haraway, *Primate Visions: Gender, Race, and Nature in the World of Modern Science* [Routledge, 1999]. Haraway's insistence that vision and perspective be embodied and theorized as such, as well as her call for "situated knowledges," has obvious implications for my reading of *Frankenstein*. See especially the section "The Persistence of Vision" in "Situated Knowledges: The Science Question in Feminism and the Privilege of Partial Perspective," *Simians, Cyborgs, and Women: The Reinvention of Nature*, [Routledge, 1991].

Recognizing the primarily specular logic of human sympathy, the monster arrives at a new self-conception. Requesting as he does a being "of the same species," a female who with the "same defects" will presumably violate "human nature" (that is, human appearance) as much as himself, the monster marks his formal and explicit renunciation of human being.

In his turn to Victor for a mate, the monster also marks the narrative convergence of two functions—the critique of the "human" and the critique of the "humanities." The discourse of species confronts the differential power of the disciplines. The well-read and eloquent monster lacks the tools he most needs—the instruments of speciation, the means of production. The monster makes clear the implicit hierarchy of knowledge: the science of "modern chemistry" which led Victor to his first creation stands as a more efficacious knowledge than what the monster hailed as the "science of words or letters." Victor has the solution, the means of production, technical and ideational—the "chemical apparatus," as he calls it, and the university training in natural philosophy. Natural science—not language, literature, or consciousness—will provide for the monster the community of two he desires. Implicitly acknowledging the failure of the humanities, of "literature—taken in all its bearings" (as Godwin wrote), the monster also acknowledges his acquiescence in the human—that is, the European—reading of him, which has featured such epithets as "savage," "ogre," and "demoniacal corpse." He defines difference as species difference and no longer looks to linguistic or cultural filiation as a means to override his problematic genealogy and form. Thus his request for another "of the same species."

What I read as the monster's understanding of the stakes of species and sympathy must be contrasted and complemented with Victor's reading of this same request. It is Victor who transforms and fixes the meaningful force of these terms. The category of "species," while obviously a multivalent and potentially vague term, requires a reproductive specificity, as Victor's deliberations illuminate. Just as the "idea" which governs the first making of a creature undergoes several ideational modifications (from creating human to giant to "new species"), so too Victor's conception of his second labor of creation undergoes a kind of imaginative transformation. What was originally latent in the monster's request—reproductive possibility—is made manifest in Victor's panicked thought. Sitting in his laboratory in the Orkney Isles, Victor considers how his new creature might turn out: "she might become ten thousand times more malignant than her mate," or she might find her fellow creature loathsome and desert him. Even more appalling to Victor is the following possibility:

> Even if they were to leave Europe, and inhabit the deserts of the new world, yet one of the first results of those sympathies for which the

demon thirsted would be children, and a race of devils would be propagated upon the earth, who would make the very existence of the species of man a condition precarious and full of terror. Had I a right, for my own benefit, to inflict this curse upon everlasting generations?

Is Victor right to envision an apocalyptic threat to the "very existence of the species of man"? Does Victor suffer from reproductive paranoia? How do we know the creature could reproduce? After all, he is a motley assemblage, and Mary Shelley has done nothing to specify his sexual capacity or organs. He may well be a kind of mule—composite, sterile.

Perhaps another way to phrase the problem of the monster's request is this: what does a monster really want? Victor thinks he knows. The monster's request indicates a refutation of Malthus, who in 1798 wrote that, "Life is, generally speaking, a blessing independent of a future state."[8] Victor comes to envision, quite anxiously, the monster's future state in reproductive terms. Victor materializes and sexualizes what the creature has presented in more ambiguous language: the "interchange of sympathies" the creature desires becomes in Victor's imaginings a primarily sexual intercourse. The creature had earlier predicted that, with a mate, his "virtues will necessarily arise when I live in communion with an equal. I shall feel the affections of a sensitive being, and become linked to the chain of existences and events, from which I am now excluded." Certainly this could be read as a series of sexual puns—the monster's phallic virtues rising. We, like Victor, may hear in this the creature's wish to become inserted in the reproductive chain of being, into the time of natural history and generation. In Victor's view, the monster demands a reproductive future, a phylogenetic future (to speak anachronistically) and not a mere ontogenetic existence. To use terms not yet formally defined in Mary Shelley's day, what the creature aspires to is existence *as* a reproductive species being. Only if he can beget like by like will this individual constitute a member of a species. Thus the creature's request for one "of the same species" ironically seeks to make good on Victor's long-dead aspiration, to "create a new species [which] would bless me as its creator and source."

In this second experiment Mary Shelley transforms the problem of monstrous life: Victor shows his Malthusian hand and gropes his way toward the principle of population, a principle through which he finally excuses his frenzied dismemberment of the half-finished female "thing."

---

[8]Thomas Robert Malthus, *An Essay on the Principle of Population* (1798), ed. Philip Appleman (New York: Norton, 1976), p. 128.

What the monster proposes as a solution—a species companion—becomes in Victor's prospectus the route to a further and more horrifying problem, that of species competition. The work of speciation, so troubling in the first experiment, now introduces the further threat of reproductive populations. The contest between Victor and monster, at first an agonistic doubling of individuals, becomes in this second experiment a world-historical contest between imagined populations—the "whole human race" versus "a race of devils." Victor's thought follows and parodies the inexorable logic of the principle of population. He cannot imagine his creatures *not* reproducing: this is the most striking thing about his reflection. In this second experiment and its truncation, Victor shows himself to be an adept not of Paracelsus nor even of Humphry Davy but rather of Malthus, who wrote, regarding progress in human society, that "in reasoning upon this subject, it is evident that we ought to consider chiefly the mass of mankind and not individual instances."[9] From the moment Victor imagines the children of his creatures—monsters as "mass" and not "individual instance"—he introduces a Malthusian calculus in which species "struggle for existence."[10] Whereas the monster newly conceives of himself as an other species being, Victor comes to conceive of him and his potential mate as Malthusian bodies, progenitors of a "mass." Victor is obviously not a doctrinal Malthusian; he does not dabble in the particulars of geometric versus arithmetic growth (increase of people versus increase in means of subsistence); he is a Malthusian inasmuch as he is a population theorist, an imaginer of mass bodies competitively peopling the globe.

In these last pages, Shelley makes clear what has been suspended throughout the novel: the self-cultivation of the problematic body, the assumption of consciousness by the monster—these achievements in the Godwinian "science of education" count for little when the monster is considered as a mass being, a specimen of a potential population. The introduction of the Malthusian problematic thus supports Victor in the contest over the meaning of species difference. That Shelley may be satirizing the Malthusian position—Victor is no reliable narrator, and his thoughts are frequently disordered—does not erode this point: thinking species difference in reproductive terms involves Victor in a Malthusian calculus, and this calculus leads to Victor's thwarting of the monster's aspirations.

---

[9] Malthus, *Essay*, p. 122.

[10] Malthus, *Essay*, p. 29. Malthus introduces the "struggle for existence" in his review of the "savage or hunter state." We should read Malthus as much as Rousseau as a theorist of primitive encounters.

Securing the World for Human Being:
Toward a Malthusian Humanitarianism

Victor is not just a Malthusian; he is a humanist Malthusian. The emergence of a Malthusian calculus in *Frankenstein* propels the final revaluation of the category "human." Both monster and Victor circulate the category "human" in this final contest. In his request for a mate, the monster convincingly presents his request for a partner as his last and greatest attempt at humanizing himself. Describing how he will live as a peaceful vegetarian with his mate in South America, the creature says, "The picture I present you is peaceful and human, and you must feel that you could deny it only in the wantonness of power and cruelty." At the very moment he renounces human being, the monster demonstrates his fluency in anthropologic: clearly his literary education has taught him how to speak human being if not to inhabit it. Indeed, the monster identifies the relentless anthropomorphic prejudice of Victor's thought; as he says to Victor, "you would not call it murder, if you could . . . destroy my frame, the work of your own hands." He is even willing to acquiesce in the naturalization of this lethal anthropomorphism: he wants his own mate precisely because he recognizes that "the human senses are insurmountable barriers to our union."

The monster shows himself to be a canny theorist of human being, a theorist from the outside; Victor persists in the muddy and ultimately murderous thought of the natively and naively human being. Even as the monster promises to "quit the neighborhood of man, and dwell, as it may chance, in the most savage of places," Victor questions whether he will truly be able to "fly from the habitations of man." "How can you," he asks the monster, "who long for the love and sympathy of man, persevere in this exile?" Victor persists in conjuring the romance of humanization, the appealing exchange of "sympathy" among men, precisely as the monster has imagined for himself and his mate a future as "monsters, cut off from all the world"—i.e. from Europe. Victor finally accedes to the request on one condition—that the monster promise "to quit Europe for ever, and every other place in the neighborhood of man, as soon as I shall deliver into your hands a female who will accompany you in your exile." It is striking that "the vast wilds of South America" do not register—for either Victor or the monster—as among the "neighborhood[s] of man." Both Victor and monster imagine this emigration to the New World as an exile from Europe (the ambiguous geographic territory) and from human being (the contested category of being). The monster's prospective exile from Europe thus defines his status as de-territorialized non-human body and reminds us of that early equation established in Walton's account of his first sighting: "Man" = European.

Victor's Malthusian deliberations lead him, then, to re-think not only the problem of anomaly (monstrous individual becomes monstrous population) but also to re-configure the humanly habitable world. Victor asks the monster "to quit Europe forever"—a dream of forced deportation and species isolation (and a bleak parody of forced emigration throughout Europe). He seeks to ensure that the savage within Europe will exile himself from Europe. Yet, as suggested earlier, the very idea of "Europe" appears as a linguistic and juridical phantom to which human citizens appeal only in a crisis of differentiation. The world no longer offers a secure place for the "exile" of undesirables. The world has contracted to a contest: as Victor foresees, the world is already potentially populated. The problem of exile and emigration—formerly described in terms of individual movement (e.g. Victor's exile from Geneva, the monster's "emigration" from the "native wood")—acquires world-historical importance when considered as a movement of potential populations. There is no safely policed or policeable border; the monster who invades Geneva cannot be confined to the "vast wilds of South America." Monsters will mate, monsters will people (as it were) the globe, monsters will eventually threaten the "existence of the species of man."

Now that the monster appears not as a local but rather as a global threat to humanity, Victor can no longer persist in his second experiment in speciation. His final deliberations suggest a transvaluation of the category human, since he is simultaneously capable of envisioning the female monster as a future "thinking and reasoning animal" and as a threat to the "whole human race." Victor clearly resolves the contradiction of the monster: he decisively dissociates literacy and rationality from human being. Contrary to Godwin's belief, thinking and reasoning will not, indeed must not, carry a creature across the border from animal (or "creature") to human. Confronted by the monstrous contradiction to human being, Victor must dissociate human being from certain capacities and sympathies thought native to it. The culmination of his work on the female shows the violence required to secure such a resolution. Victor looks on the work of his hands: "The remains of the half-finished creature, whom I had destroyed, lay scattered on the floor, and I almost felt as if I had mangled the living flesh of a human being." Almost as the monster had predicted, Victor "would not call it murder" if he destroyed "the work of [his] own hands."

Victor's aborting of the monster-mate becomes, as he reflects, an exercise in humanitarianism. His increasingly biological interpretation of "species" and of the monster's future state provides Victor with the humanist alibi:

> During these last days I have been occupied in examining my past conduct; nor do I find it blameable. In a fit of enthusiastic madness I created a rational creature, and was bound towards him, to assure, as far as was in my power, his happiness and well-being. This was my duty; but there was another still paramount to that. My duties towards my fellow creatures had greater claims to my attention, because they included a greater proportion of happiness or misery. Urged by this view, I refused, and I did right in refusing, to create a companion for the first creature.

Victor's declamation of human conscientiousness invokes and revises a utilitarian calculus: Godwinian concerns about "duty," "happiness," and universal benevolence confront the species barrier. The "duties towards [his] fellow creatures" trump the duties toward created living non-human beings. Indeed, by 1831 Shelley had revised the phrase "fellow creatures" to "beings of my own species," further reminding us that one's "own species" has come to stand, for Victor, as a reified category for human fellowship conceived over and against this monstrous alternative.

By tearing up the female, Victor begins to repair the rent in the humanly habitable world. His heightened species-consciousness allows him a partial recovery of natality, not as a native Genevese but as a "human." In "exile," having left Geneva to create the second monster, he comes to see himself as the species-being *par excellence*. To invoke Marx, "Man is a species being, not only because in practice and in theory he adopts the species as his object (his own as well as those of other things), but—and this is only another way of expressing it—also because he treats himself as the actual, living species."[11] Taking his species, "the whole human race," as his object, Victor acquires, or rather produces, a distinctive consciousness of human species being, which allows him to remember the destroyed female thing with a clear conscience. Victor's refusal to complete the monster-mate does, at least for him, mark his re-entry into the human social body, one which is now imagined as persisting through time, unto "everlasting generations." In a roundabout and perverse way, Victor does traffic in a human reproductive economy, if only in his capacity to imagine future human generations under threat. Indeed, the dismembered female—recollected in tranquillity—embodies the culmination of Victor's conscientious foresight,

---

[11] Karl Marx, *Economic and Philosophic Manuscripts of 1844*, in *The Marx-Engels Reader*, ed. Robert Tucker, 2nd edn. (New York: Norton, 1978), p. 75.

his carefully defended Malthusian humanitarianism. From a purely human perspective, Victor's violence appears as a true demonstration of Malthusian philanthropy.

What we might call ideological biologization of species difference—first by the monster (who wants one "of the same species") and then by Victor (who refers to "his [i.e. the monster's] own species")—fixes the asymmetry between monster and man. In Victor's turn to population he demonstrates the motivation of a discursive shift: he is no innocent, ingenuous, or disinterested speculator but rather a human being who imagines his "species" under threat and acts accordingly. Victor's Malthusian panic ensures that the conflict of monster and man will be imagined as a species or race conflict. Clearly this progression can be read as an allegory of the colonial enterprise, or of the racial consciousness of English Romanticism, or as a representation of the unruly proletariat. Yet, in a more localized reading, we can also see how biologization—the nominalization of a corporeal and social problem as a species *difference*—succeeds (that is, follows) and supports the failure both of humanism and the humanities. It is Victor— the human being, the natural philosopher, the population theorist—who emerges dominant, both in terms of species competition and in the utility of his education. The course of the novel suggests that the principle of population—of species competition in a world become suddenly too small— trumps the principle of benevolence. Considered as such, the novel undermines not only Godwin's faith in the "science of education" but in fact the anthropological foundations of *Political Justice*. One could say, in fact, that in *Frankenstein*, Malthus triumphs over Godwin: the "perfectibility of man" announced by Godwin and ridiculed by Malthus appears in the novel as a perfectibility for European species men only. In the ideological contest between "benevolence" (the Godwinian principle) and "misery" (the Malthusian check), benevolence extends only to the limits of one's own species being, a status represented in the novel as constituted through various local apparatuses—familial, political, educational, yet with a biological, anthropological determination in the last instance. The monster's misery is, in the end, no business of Victor's and indeed must be resisted with the newly discovered language of human-all-too-human fellowship. Victor's experiments have demonstrated, however ironically, the truth of Malthus's dictum: ". . . an experiment with the human race is not like an experiment upon inanimate objects."[12] Neither human nor inanimate, the monster persists as a challenge to those who would build communities of affinity, to those who wish to redeem the promise of the humanities.

---

[12]Malthus, *Essay*, p. 94.

Behold the Villain's dire disgrace!
Not Death itself can end.
He finds no peaceful Burial Place,
His breathless Corse, no friend.

Torn from the Root, that wicked Tongue,
Which daily swore and curst!
Those Eyeballs, from their Sockets wrung,
That glow'd with lawless Lust!

His Heart exposd to prying Eyes,
To Pity has no Claim:
But, dreadful! from his Bones shall rise,
His Monument of Shame.

"The Reward of Cruelty," the final and most gruesome panel in William Hogarth's "The Four Stages of Cruelty" (1751). Both Shelley and Wells would have been familiar with Hogarth's widely-distributed prints while they were exploring similar themes in their novels.

From *The Old Brown Dog* (1985)

Coral Lansbury

[FROM CHAPTER 3: IGNORING PREJUDICES]

[. . .] What roused Battersea in 1907 was not the plight of women but a fear that had its origins at Tyburn in the eighteenth century. Public hangings were undoubtedly the most popular of all bloodsports, and the "jingling antithesis between life and death," to use Thackeray's phrase, always roused the spectators to a frenzy. Brawls often broke out at the foot of the gallows between the friends of the dead and the servants of the Royal College of Physicians or Company of Barber-Surgeons, who had the right to claim ten corpses a year for dissection. Private surgeons too were ready to pay high prices for a fresh corpse, and in 1736 the grave-digger of St. Dunstan's, Stepney, felt the full fury of the law and the populace when he was convicted for having sold bodies to a private surgeon:

> Sentence was executed upon him very severely by John Hooper, the then common Executioner; and on the Day appointed for him to be whipped; there was, perhaps, the greatest Concourse of People that was ever known. A Mob of Sailors and Chimney Sweepers rendevouz'd in Stepney Church-yard, and when [the] poor Culprit was ty'd to the Cart, they led the Horses so slow, that he received some Hundreds of Lashes, the Hangman being encouraged by the Mob (who gave him a good deal of Money) not to favour the Delinquent, but to do his Duty.[1]

It was not only the corpses of convicted felons which provided subjects for anatomical research; the poor lived in constant fear that their dead would be taken and dissected on the surgeon's table. There were stories told of dead men suddenly reviving under the knife and meeting a death more painful than any received from the hangman's noose. Certainly, it is doubtful if the English working class went in dread of the pains of hell; what did concern many of them was the likelihood of some surgeon's hack

---

From *The Old Brown Dog: Women, Workers, and Vivisection in Edwardian England,* Madison, WI: U of Wisconsin P, 1985. (All notes are Coral Lansbury's.)

[1] Peter Lynebaugh, "The Tyburn Riot against the Surgeons," in *Albion's Fatal Tree,* ed. Douglas Hay et al. (New York: Pantheon, 1975), p. 71.

stealing their bodies before they were cold and then cutting them up like carcasses of meat.

The progress from cruelty to animals to the dissection table in Surgeons' Hall had been horrifyingly depicted by William Hogarth in his *Four Stages of Cruelty* (1751). The prints were "intentionally explicit . . . to grip the attention of the ignorant and brutal."[2] Here the most dreaded working-class fears were cast into the form of a cautionary tract—four pictures that expressed the terrors of vivisection in a sequence from Tom Nero's skewering of a dog, to his flogging of a horse, the murder of his mistress, and his eventual death by hanging, with his body given over to the dissectors. In Hogarth's plates the persecutor of animals was the murderer of women— and this became more than a narrative concept: it was to be an article of faith in popular opinion. It was Hogarth's genius to borrow his images from life, cast them into the form of narrative art and then impose them upon the world as reality.[3]

James Mill stated that "nothing is remembered but through its IDEA. The memory, however, of a thing, and the idea of it, are not the same. The idea may be without the memory; but the memory cannot be without the idea."[4] And for the nineteenth century it was Hogarth's idea that framed arguments and shaped the form of working-class belief even when his pictures were not held in the mind's eye. In the first plate Tom Nero is driving a stake into a dog; he is surrounded by emblems of cruelty as boys blind a sparrow, set cats fighting from a lamp post, or tie a bone to the tail of a dog. In the next plate Tom has graduated to hackney coachman, and he flogs a horse that has collapsed with fatigue while another man beats a lamb with a club. The third plate shows Tom arrested for having murdered his pregnant mistress; and in the fourth and final plate, the reward of cruelty, his corpse is laid out before the surgeons who scoop out the eyes, drag forth the entrails, and cut the tendons of the foot. All around the spectators gossip and gloat, and as the intestines and heart are cast to the floor, a famished dog seizes on Tom Nero's cruel heart and devours it. In drawing these pictures for "the lower orders of society," Hogarth had done more than provide a tract: he had taken the fears of Tyburn and the surgeons and made them a direct consequence of the wanton cruelty of children tortur-

---

[2] William Gaunt, *The World of William Hogarth* (London: Jonathan Cape, 1978), p. 93.

[3] Hogarth's art was increasingly popular in the latter years of the nineteenth century, and his works were reprinted in the three volumes entitled *Hogarth's Works* by John Ireland and John Nichols (London: Chatto and Windus, 1875). Austin Dobson published a study of Hogarth in 1879.

[4] James Mill, *Analysis of the Phenomena of the Human Mind*, ed. with additional notes by John Stuart Mill (London: Longmans, Green, Reader, and Dyer, 1869), 1:320.

ing animals for sport. The horror in Hogarth's last plate is concentrated in the face of the corpse, for Tom Nero does not seem dead; it is as if he is silently screaming for help and for mercy. The idea of cruelty to animals leading to a murdered wife or mistress and ending under the surgeon's knife was to remain a recurring figure and traditional belief, for as Mill also stated, "Belief is a matter of habit and accident, and not of reason."[5]

The last two etchings of *The Four Stages of Cruelty* were sold for sixpence in the form of John Bell's woodcuts, but all of Hogarth's prints were widely disseminated. Just as the temperance societies used *Gin Lane* in their publicity, the antivivisection societies made Tom Nero familiar in their publications and flyers. However, it was the popularity of Hogarth among the working class which made the progress from cruelty to animals to murder and dissection seem part of the natural order. Charles Mitchell has written of the way that "the prints were cast adrift on an open sea and might fetch up anywhere. They were pasted up in inns and taverns . . . country yokels pored over stray '*pickters* come from Lunnon;' and any sort of person might stop to join the crowds round the print-shop windows."[6] The colored print shaped the mind and imagination of the working class at this time just as television does today, and the recurring theme in many of these prints was body snatching and the disposition of the poor dead. [. . .]

[FROM CHAPTER 8: THE TRUTHS OF FICTION]

[. . .] When the curator of the Medical Museum of London University received a kidney in the post which was almost certainly removed from one of the murdered victims of Jack the Ripper, there were sporadic riots outside the hospital, and doctors were jostled. The working-class fear of vivisection was inflamed by rumors that the murderer was a surgeon taking out his revenge on prostitutes for having infected his son with venereal disease.[7] And there was a long working-class tradition for regarding doctors as enemies "who preyed, for personal profit and success, on their helplessness and destitution."[8] What could be found in these demonstrations was the feeling that the vivisector had links with sexuality and death, a point that Edward Berdoe stressed in his romans à clef, *St. Bernard's: The Romance of a Medical Student* (1887) and *Dying Scientifically: A Key to St. Bernard's* (1888).

---

[5] Ibid.

[6] Charles Mitchell, "Pictorial Satire," *Times Literary Supplement,* 20 Nov. 1948.

[7] Daniel Farson, *Jack the Ripper* (London: Michael Joseph, 1972), p. 11.

[8] Michael Durey, *The Return of the Plague* (London: Gill and Macmillan, 1979), p. 171.

Berdoe was a doctor with impeccable credentials: he was a Member of the Royal College of Surgeons, Licentiate of the Society of Apothecaries, Member of the British Medical Association, and a Gold Medallist in Medicine and Medical Scholar of the London Hospital—but he belonged to the old school which maintained that clinical observation was more important than animal research. In his later years Berdoe was to write that "in our great general hospitals to which medical schools are attached, the healing of the patients is made subordinate to the professional advantage of the medical staff and the students."[9] James Turner says that Berdoe "lived mentally in the first half of the century"; at best he was regarded by his younger colleagues as a blethering old idiot.[10] Nonetheless, Berdoe acquired a small reputation as a novelist with the popular St. Bernard's—and Berdoe's delination of that grisly institution became the prototype for all those hospitals where medicine serves doctors at the expense of the patients.[11]

Harrowby Elsworth, an idealistic young man, has distinguished himself at Oxford and becomes a medical student at St. Bernard's, a large metropolitan hospital. There he soon encounters the sinister Dr. Malthus Crowe, lecturer in physiology, who embodies Sir Astley Cooper's remark that "the art of medicine is founded on conjecture and improved by murder." His porters are accomplished dog stealers and no less malefic than their master: "They were scarred and furrered about the hands and arms with bites, cuts, and scratches, which had healed badly, and to the skilled observer sufficiently stamped them with the trade mark of the hospital." Crowe's assistant and demonstrator is Mr. Mole, a suspicious and ambitious young physiologist who yearns for the day when he will have Crowe's position.

The plot moves into an Hogarthian configuration that will be repeated in all the fictional studies of vivisection. It is not enough that Crowe tortures dogs and uses charity patients for experimental research; he is also, like Tom Nero, a murderer whose victim is his hapless but wealthy wife. Slowly Crowe distills a poison from toadstools (having first made sure of its lethal potency on some dogs and a couple of old patients) and then prescribes it as a tonic for his wife's "nerves." She dies in agony, but the crime does not go undetected, for Mole has made it his business to become friendly with the maid, Janet Sprigg, and from her he discovers the truth. He sets out the evidence before his master and blackmails him into retir-

[9]Edward Berdoe, Dying Scientifically: A Key to St. Bernard's (London: Swan, Sonnenschein, and Lowrey, 1888), p. 7.

[10]James Turner, Reckoning with the Beast (Baltimore: Johns Hopkins University Press, 1980), p. 119.

[11]Edward Berdoe, St. Bernard's: The Romance of a Medical Student (London: Swan, Sonnenschein, 1887).

ing after he has recommended Mole for the position of lecturer in physiology. Always it is the wife who is the vivisector's unsuspecting victim, a narrative progression which becomes an inevitable trope in works of this kind.
St. Bernard's enjoyed a tremendous success with its revelations of medical
malfeasance, and it was helped too by the publicity of Jack the Ripper and
the Whitechapel murders. Harrowby, of course, forsakes St. Bernard's and
founds a Nightingale hospital in Spain with a young nurse who has also left
London in despair of being able to change the way patients are treated at
St. Bernard's. So influential was Berdoe's novel and its sequel that a Society
for the Protection of Hospital Patients was founded in 1897.

Novel followed novel with a similar theme: the vivisector's wife is first
driven mad and then used for purposes of research. Barry Pain, a very pro-
lific author indeed, provided a slight variation in 1897 with *The Octave of
Claudius*. Dr. Lamb has already driven his wife, Hilda, insane when he proposes a particular experiment to Claudius Sandell: he will have eight days
with a thousand pounds a day to spend; then he must submit to an experiment which will cost him fifty seconds of pain and his life. With a lot of
luck and at the expense of a very fragile plot, Claudius manages to outwit
the fiendish vivisector, keeping both the money and his life.

Hogarth's progression from cruelty to animals to the murder of women
was consistently used as a theme by male novelists, however, there was a
significant difference when the writer was female. Marie Daal's *Anna, the
Professor's Daughter,* translated into English in 1885, included all the customary antivivisection themes, but Daal does not show her heroine suc-
cumbing to madness and death. The vivisector can be resisted: Anna helps
to reform the brutish Herman, and only when he has renounced his callous attitude to animals does she agree to marry him.[12] [...]

The Hogarthian association of vivisection and women was still explicit
in works like [Sarah Grand's] *The Beth Book,* but the relationship was different: the wife no longer became the victim of inevitable madness but instead
resisted her oppressor with intelligence and determination. John Galswor-
thy always saw the potential wife-beater in a vivisector and frequently described Irene Forsyte, Soames' wife, in *The Man of Property* (1906), as a
wounded animal. The marriage has broken, Irene is unfaithful, but Soames
cannot let her go: "Many people, no doubt, including the editor of the
'Ultra Vivisectionist', then in the bloom of its first youth, would say that
Soames was less than a man not to have removed the locks from his wife's
doors, and after beating her soundly resumed wedded happiness" (pt. 3,
chap. 1). Like Beth, Irene is prepared to risk poverty and disgrace rather

---

[12] Marie Daal, *Anna, the Professor's Daughter,* trans. from the Dutch by Colonel Charles
Mueller (London: Swan, Sonnenschein, 1885).

than endure a wretched marriage, and because she will not submit to Soames' authority, she succeeds. This was the response to the pornography of the riding master and his victims, and increasingly it was to challenge the male fantasies of aggression and power.

The New Woman did not go mad and refused to become a victim, but it was H. G. Wells who gave the icon of woman and vivisected animal its most terrifying accent. This was all the more remarkable since, although Wells was a feminist, he was not opposed to vivisection. Indeed, he was a member of the Research Defence Society, but in the latter years of the nineteenth century he had been troubled by the nature of so much physiological research: animals were being subjected to bizarre transplants, extra tails implanted on rats, a cat's leg sewn onto the stump of a dog's limb. Then too, he had heard Thomas Huxley's Romanes Lecture of 1894, "Evolution and Ethics," in which Huxley had spoken of suffering as "the badge of all the tribe of sentient things, attaining to its highest level in man." [13] In consequence, ethical progress could only be made, not through an imitation of the cosmic process, still less by evading it, but by combating it with all the strength of man's moral energy. [14] Nature had decreed that pain should be the law of the universe, but man's noblest creation, ethics, imposed justice and order upon life. From this contest between nature and ethics Wells created *The Island of Dr. Moreau* (1896), and the Hogarthian icon was dramatically and irrevocably changed.

When Edward Prendick is cast ashore on the strange island ruled by Dr. Moreau, he finds it inhabited by disturbing creatures which seem human and yet remind him of animals. Immediately his curiosity is aroused, for Prendick is not the ordinary traveller but a biologist who had studied for some years under Huxley. He suspects that Moreau is the notorious physiologist who had been driven out of England some years previously because of his research into morbid growths. A pamphlet had been published about his activities, and on "the day of its publication, a wretched dog, flayed and otherwise mutilated, escaped from Moreau's house" (chap. 7). Even Moreau's fellow investigators had denounced him from amidst the public outcry, and the vivisector suddenly vanished from England. Prendick now knew where Moreau had found refuge and a place to continue his research.

Montgomery, Moreau's assistant, has brought several animals to the island, including a puma, and now Prendick hears this animal shrieking in pain from the laboratory. Its cries are so terrible that Prendick takes refuge

---

[13] *Life and Letters of Thomas Henry Huxley*, 2:374–82.
[14] Lovat Dickson, *H. G. Wells: His Turbulent Life and Times* (New York: Athenaeum, 1969), pp. 66–69.

in the forest, where he finds the vivisector's creations, animals surgically transformed into the semblance of human beings. They have been taught to obey Moreau as a god, a god who presides over the antiseptic hell of his laboratory, the House of Pain. Several days pass, and the cries from the puma have begun to change; Prendick recognizes the voice of a human being:

> After a long pause I resumed my meal, but with my ears still vigilant. Presently I heard something else very faint and low. I sat as if frozen in my attitude. Though it was faint and low, it moved me more profoundly than all that I had hitherto heard of the abominations behind the wall. There was no mistake this time in the quality of the dim broken sounds, no doubt at all of their source; for it was groaning, broken by sobs and gasps of anguish. It was no brute this time. It was a human being in torment!
>
> And as I realized this I rose, and in three steps had crossed the room, seized the handle of the door into the yard, and flung it open before me.
>
> "Prendick, man! Stop!" cried Montgomery, intervening.
>
> A startled deerhound yelped and snarled. There was blood, I saw, in the sink, brown, and some scarlet, and I smelt the peculiar smell of carbolic acid. Then through an open doorway beyond, in the dim light of the shadow, I saw something bound painfully upon a framework, scarred, red, and bandaged. And then blotting this out appeared the face of old Moreau, white and terrible. (Chap. 10)

When Moreau sees fit to explain his research, it is as though he had taken Huxley's Romanes Lecture and turned it inside out, declaring that "to this day I have never troubled about the ethics of the matter. The study of Nature makes a man at last as remorseless as Nature. I have gone on, not heeding anything but the question I was pursuing" (chap. 14)

There is an insidious appeal to Moreau's reasoning that begins to affect Prendick, who finds that he is slowly accepting the research and its creations. Prendick is proof of all the antivivisectionist arguments that people who are forced to participate in acts of cruelty or who watch scenes of torture will lose all sense of compassion and pity, becoming dead to feeling. It has even become possible for him to endure the daily tormented shrieks of the puma:

> So indurated was I at that time to the abomination of the place, that I heard without a touch of emotion the puma victim begin another day of torture. It met its persecutor with a shriek almost exactly like that of an angry virago.
>
> Then something happened. I do not know to this day what it was exactly. I heard a sharp cry behind me, a fall, and, turning, saw an awful face rushing upon me, not human, not animal, but hellish, brown, seamed with red branching scars, red drops starting out upon it, and the lidless

eyes ablaze. I flung up my arm to defend myself from the blow that flung me headlong with a broken forearm, and the great monster, swathed in lint and with red-stained bandages fluttering about it, leapt over me and passed. (Chap. 17)

It is no ordinary woman who breaks her bonds and rages forth to destroy the vivisector, but a virago trailing bloody rags as proof of her sex. And the virago will not rest until she has killed the vivisector who has tortured and maimed her in the name of science. All the themes of women, vivisection, and animals are drawn together in this explosive and prophetic image of anger and revenge: in the realm of fiction, the victory clearly belonged to the woman and puma who destroyed Dr. Moreau. [. . .]

[FROM CHAPTER 9: THE NEW PRIESTHOOD]

[. . .] Sacrifice has always been at the heart of religion, and it was in a spirit of sacrifice that animals were vivisected. Nothing outraged a physiologist more than the accusation that he was a sadist who enjoyed an animal's suffering, and he would promptly invoke Claude Bernard's description of the vivisector as a man engaged in the dispassionate experiments of science, enduring the spectacle of pain for the benefit of humanity, a man "sublime and terrible in martyrdom," to use Davidson's phrase.[15] The antivivisectionists pointed to the human predilection for blood sports and wondered if the vivisector was indeed unlike his fellow men. Shaw spoke of "the psychology of credulity and cruelty," and told the surgeons that "you will soon prove that you are justified not only in vivisecting dogs and guinea-pigs, but in dissecting every human being you can get into your power."[16] He mocked medical pretensions, but he was always aware of the power of this new priesthood, and in an exchange with H. G. Wells over the issue of animal experimentation he freely admitted: "When a vivisector says in effect, 'I have a dread secret to wrest from Nature: so you must license me to sacrifice a guinea-pig', the Sambo in us assents; and the more hideously the guinea-pig is sacrificed the more we feel the importance of the secret. The vivisector can sell us anything as a cure next day."[17] To Shaw's sorrow the Sambos were now in a clear majority, and there was widespread acceptance for the necessity of animal sacrifice, provided that the detailed procedure of the sacrifice was not made known to disturb the sensibilities of the general public.

---

[15] John Davidson, *The Testament of a Vivisector* (London: Grant Richards, 1901), p. 24.

[16] *Shaw on Vivisection*, comp. and ed. G. H. Bowker, for the National Anti-Vivisection Society (London: G. Allen & Unwin, 1949), p. 23.

[17] Shaw's reply to Wells was published in the *Sunday Express*, 24 July 1927.

Antivivisectionists jeered when the Research Defence Society opened a shop alongside the British Union for the Abolition of Vivisection in Oxford Street in 1912. But the window of the Research Defence Society contained the icon that was to become an article of faith in people's lives, and one that would challenge and supersede Hogarth's progression of cruelty: a picture of a smiling woman with a baby on her knee and underneath it a question: "Which will you save—your child or a guinea-pig?" [18]

The only path to the glittering salon lay through a ghastly kitchen, and in that dark and terrible place there must of necessity be sacrifice and death. Here was a vision to win the heart of the most humane individual, who knew that heaven is never gained without bitter travail. Women and workers, many reluctantly, joined Claude Bernard's church and learned there to worship the new gods of science.[19]

From "Deforming Island Races" (1998)

Jennifer DeVere Brody

Throughout the nineteenth century, Thomas Atkins, a menagerist at the Liverpool Zoological Gardens, successfully bred lions and tigers. Advertisements for Atkins's ligers, tigons, or lion-tigers, to use the phrase purportedly coined by William IV, read: "The greatest phenomenon . . . in the history of these animals . . . once the most implacable enemies in the forest . . . [is that] the Proprietor of these Gardens [has proven], that under the dominion of man even the most savage spirits may be subdued." [1] Although Atkins effectively mastered his hybrid animals, many other Victorian men succumbed to the power of the beast. The perceived similarity of man and beast flourished in the wake of Darwinian ideology, and was viewed as a threat to and symptom of the dissolution of the boundaries that

---

From *Impossible Purities: Blackness, Femininity, and Victorian Culture* Durham, NC: Duke UP, 1998. (All notes are Jennifer DeVere Brody's.)

[18] *Abolitionist*, 1 Aug. 1912, p. 2.

[19] Paraphrasing the last line of "The Female Animal: Medical and Biological Views of Woman and Her Role in Nineteenth-Century America," by Carroll Smith-Rosenberg and Charles Rosenberg, *Journal of American History* 60 (1973): 356.

[1] Harriet Ritvo, *The Animal Estate: The English and Other Creatures in the Victorian Age* (Cambridge, Mass.: Harvard University Press, 1987), pp. 236–37.

distinguished not only the tame from the wild, but also one race, sex, and/or class from another.

This chapter examines attempts to subdue savage man-beast hybrids, and discusses ways in which many nineteenth-century critics conflated monstrous hybrids and their white, "middle-class" male creators. More specifically, this chapter explores ideas about hybridity, blackness, femininity, and monstrosity in H. G. Wells's novel, *The Island of Dr. Moreau*.[2] This late-nineteenth-century text reflects the pervasiveness of the hybrid anxiety documented as being an important aspect of much Victorian discourse.[3] *The Island of Dr. Moreau* registers as well as reinscribes the belief that the fate and status of the *English race* itself is in jeopardy of becoming monstrously hybrid, blackened, and feminized.

Wells claimed to see his work as a response to Oscar Wilde's infamous trial.

> There was a scandalous trial . . . the graceless and piteous downfall of a man of genius, and [my] story was the response of an imaginative mind to the reminder that humanity is but animal, rough-hewn to a reasonable shape and in perpetual internal conflict between instinct and injunction. The story embodies this ideal, but apart from this embodiment it has no allegorical quality. It was written just to give the utmost possible vividness to that conception of men as hewn and confused and tormented beasts.[4]

This statement shows how the "pure" English gentleman becomes bestial at the end of the century. What Wells was responding to may not only have been the trial, but also Wilde's *The Picture of Dorian Gray*, which mentions many "impossible" and "monstrous" things that "breed horrors," and has at least one "half-caste dressed in a ragged turban and shabby ulster grin[ning] a hideous greeting."[5] The fascination with unnatural hybrids

---

[2] H. G. Wells, *The Island of Dr. Moreau* (New York: Lanser Books, 1968). First published in 1896.

[3] John MacKenzie's reading of Victorian culture's shift from "domestic class conflict and towards racial and international conflict . . . [in which] the melodramatic villain became an externalised . . . barbarous 'fuzzy-wuzzy' or black, facing a cross-class brotherhood of heroism," informs this chapter. See John MacKenzie, ed., *Propaganda and Empire: The Manipulation of British Public Opinion* (Manchester: Manchester University Press, 1984), p. 45.

[4] Wells quoted in Elaine Showalter, *Sexual Anarchy: Gender and Culture in the Fin de Siècle* (London: Penguin Books, 1990), p. 178.

[5] Oscar Wilde, *The Picture of Dorian Gray*, in *The Portable Oscar Wilde*, ed. Richard Aldington and Stanley Weintraub (New York: Penguin Books, 1981), p. 352. First published in 1890.

reflects attitudes toward race, gender, and generation that were crucial in the age of imperialist trauma.

The degenerative transformations of the protagonist, Mr. Prendick, an upstanding Englishman, occur at the height of English imperial power and nationalistic supremacy. Indeed, many middle-class English*men* in this generation became newly aware of themselves as racialized beings. The representative Englishman questioned his ability to maintain the various boundaries (economic, geographic, gender, sexual, psychological) he created. In other words, as ideas about "little England" succumbed to Benjamin Disraeli's ideology of imperialism, and as England's geopolitical borders expanded, fears about maintaining English borders (both real and imagined) multiplied. Although in 1898 C. F. Adams asserted that imperialism "has saved the Anglo-Saxon stock from being a nation of half-breeds and miscengenates" (*OED*), as we have seen, the Anglo-Saxon race is always already a hybrid nation. Moreover, *The Island of Dr. Moreau* makes a black female puma, a defiant daughter, the source of the threatening downfall. The black female puma contrasts with the black tulip, the compliant daughter produced by Van Bearle.

Even though ideas about the invasion and influence of un-English "others" had always played a part in discussions of domestic policy and in definitions of English identity, the new economic and intellectual climate at the end of the century fueled and magnified these fears. Would the English nation be able to control its growing hybrid border-populations, such as the Irish Catholics, the Africans, and the Hindus? More important, would the strong Anglo-Saxon race survive the threats to its assumed racial purity when some of its own breed seemed to succumb to the power of the horrific hybridity "invading" England? Was man evolving or devolving? What role did his sexuality and heredity play in determining his position?

The magnitude of these queries results from the fact that ideas about "race" hardened as the nineteenth century "progressed." The Darwinian revolution made organizing disciplines such as taxonomy and other sciences available to a greater number of educated Victorians, who then disseminated and distorted, as well as reinforced, this Darwinian ideology. Wells is one of the major writers to elaborate corrupted versions of Darwinian thought, as his scientific fantasy, *The Island of Dr. Moreau*, demonstrates.

In order to discuss nineteenth-century reactions to "man-beast" hybrids, I present a brief overview of the relationship between man and animals in the British, Western tradition. That man himself was a unique being situated, by God's glory, halfway between the beasts and the angels was a common conception in early modern England. Indeed, this is the basic thesis of the Great Chain of Being. The Great Chain of Being dominated intellectual thought in the Renaissance and its imaginative power persisted throughout the nineteenth century.[6] Some scholars have argued that even Darwin only temporalized the theory, rendering it dynamic in our time rather than fixed.[7] Constructions (philosophical, economic, linguistic, and social) of the relationship between humans and animals throughout British culture concur with readings of the function of the hybrid in Victorian discourse. Various strategies of classification and categorization are an enduring part of the quest to define Englishness.

Before the nineteenth century, philosophers, members of the clergy, and other officials of nationally sanctioned bodies that produced dominant cultural ideology, attempted to "fix" ambiguous, nondiscrete categories into a stable, differentiated framework. This project went hand in hand with the Newtonian scientific revolution enterprise of stressing order, stability, and regularity. Earlier in the Renaissance, according to Harriet Ritvo, bestiaries "made no attempt to group animals that were physically similar . . . such as the lion and the tiger; nor in arranging their contents did they employ the anthropocentric binary distinctions, such as edible-inedible, useful-useless, wild-tame, and beautiful-ugly. . . ."[8] These oppositional definitions began to appear during the seventeenth century with the development of empirical science, natural history, and more analytic systems of classification.[9]

Many Puritan thinkers believed that it was dangerous to pretend to be an animal on the stage, as this might be read as a desecration of man's godly image.[10] As John Stuart Mill, among many other Victorians who argued for the Sanitation Acts, said, cleanliness is essential because its absence, "more than anything else renders man bestial."[11] Other practices that were thought to render humans bestial were overindulgence of the sexual appetite, vivisection, and vaccination. But it was the act of bestiality that was believed, until 1861 when it was no longer illegal, to "turn man into a very beast . . . and was seen as the sin of confusion . . . the immoral mix[ing of] categories,"

---

[6] See Arthur Lovejoy, *The Great Chain of Being: The Study of the History of an Idea* (Cambridge, Mass.: Harvard University Press, 1966).

[7] See Gillian Beer, *Darwin's Plots: Evolutionary Narrative in Darwin, George Eliot, and Nineteenth-Century Fiction* (London: Routledge, 1983), p. 28.

[8] Ritvo, *Animal Estate*, p. 13.

[9] See Michel Foucault, *The Order of Things: An Archeology of the Human Sciences* (New York: Vintage Books, 1973).

[10] William Prynne in Keith Thomas, *Man and the Natural World* (New York: Pantheon Books, 1983).

[11] John Stuart Mill, *Essays on Ethics, Religion, and Society*, ed. J. M. Robson (Toronto: University of Toronto, 1969). First published in 1864.

according to Keith Thomas.[12] The decision to allow bestiality seemed to confirm the clarity of the species and, in some sense, lent humanity to the animals.

The mutability of this previously fixed barrier drives many late-Victorian fantasies that discuss man-beast hybrids. As Michel Foucault notes,

> It is often said that the establishment of botanical gardens and zoological collections expressed a new curiosity about exotic plants and animals. In fact, these had already claimed men's interest. . . . What had changed was the space in which it was possible to describe them. To the Renaissance the strangeness of animals was spectacle: . . . the natural history room and the garden as created in the Classical period, replace the circular procession of the show with the arrangement of things in a table. What came surreptitiously into being between the age of the theatre and that of the catalogue was not the desire for knowledge, but a new way of connecting things both to the eye and to discourse. A new way of making history.[13]

The barriers become mutable as well through the loss of faith, changes in the economic structure of England that valued the symbolic cash nexus over more concrete material exchange, and increased imperial expansion. In *Past and Present,* Thomas Carlyle characterized his era as ". . . a great unintelligible PERHAPS."[14] The question of man, and especially the *English* man's place on the scale of human civilization, was vexed by conflicting social, scientific, and political theories.

The eighteenth-century naturalist Charles Bingley asserted, "How slender so ever it may appear . . . the barrier which separates men from brutes is fixed and immutable."[15] This assertion was challenged throughout the nineteenth century. The slender but assiduously maintained barrier that separated man from beast slowly eroded. New developments in the nineteenth century assailed the comparatively simple, dichotomous ordering so common in the seventeenth and eighteenth centuries. Although fears about man's place in the natural order predate Darwin, his science gave such anxieties new immediacy and legitimacy. Through the dissemination of Darwinian thought, the English gentleman had to work harder than ever to distinguish himself from his animal brethren (as well as "lower" beings — such as the Irish, black people, and women — and those associated

---

[12] Keith Thomas, *Man and the Natural World* (New York: Pantheon Books, 1983), p. 39.

[13] Foucault, *The Order of Things,* p. 131.

[14] Thomas Carlyle, *Past and Present,* ed. Richard Altick (New York: New York University Press, 1965), p. 139.

[15] Quoted in Thomas, *Man and the Natural World,* p. 35.

with them). How successful were Victorians at "mov[ing] upward/working out the beast," to use Alfred Tennyson's suggestive phrase?[16] [. . .]

[. . .] In *The Island of Dr. Moreau*, the mad scientist attempts to speed up this process through his vivisection experiments. Moreau's plan to "humanize" all the beasts seems to be a literal translation of Tennyson's utopic fantasy. Of course, Moreau fails — the ape and tiger stubbornly refuse to die or to be tamed, just as, it might be said, the Englishman fails to "[m]ove upward, working out the beast[ly]" aspects of his humanity.

What had changed from earlier in the century was man's control of science and technology. Indeed, by the end of the century, racial theories were aided by the predominance of imperialism and the birth of eugenics, which replaced "natural" (read random) selection with ideas about genetic transformation. The term *eugenics* was coined in 1883 by Darwin's cousin, Francis Galton, who defined it as "the study of agencies under social control that may improve or impair the racial qualities of future generations either physically or mentally."[17] The idea that racial populations could be controlled by human effort appealed to Victorian notions of progress and, although resisted by some, eugenic theory gained popularity. Certainly, it played a role in Wells's work.

Because evolutionary theorists had such an impact on Victorian cultural classifications, writers across a range of disciplines grappled with new representations of man's place in this endlessly transforming world. Wells, along with such other "empire boys" as Robert Louis Stevenson, Rider Haggard, and Rudyard Kipling, wrote in the aftermath of Darwin's astonishing assertions. As late-nineteenth-century intellectuals, these writers were interested in and influenced by scientific inquiry. Their work, almost as much as that of the evolutionary theorists, helped to seal the continuity between men and animals, and for many, even cemented the parallels between these (now more than ever) closely related species.[18] Their novels quite clearly reinterpret Darwinian ideas about man's relationship to animals. Wells's work, in particular, focuses on man's relationship to the animal within himself — in short, to the wild aspects of the tame English gentleman. References to and constructions of this "doubled" standard man are

---

[16] Alfred Tennyson, *In Memoriam*, ed. Robert Ross (New York: W. W. Norton, 1973). All subsequent references are from this edition. First published in 1842.

[17] Francis Galton quoted in Nancy Leys Stepan, *The Idea of Race in Science* (London: Macmillan Publishers, 1982), p. 111.

[18] Such works include *Kim, Dr. Jekyll and Mr. Hyde, The Picture of Dorian Gray*, and *She*. For a full explication, see Joseph Bristow, *Empire Boys: Adventures in a Man's World* (London: Unwin Hyman, 1991).

ubiquitous during the final decades of the century. Moreover, *The Island of Dr. Moreau* may be seen as a supreme example of "imperial gothic."[19]

The Island of Dr. Moreau describes the imagined rapid degeneration of the English race as a result of imperial expansion, scientific theories, and political and economic conflict. The birth of the hybrid (monstrous) middle-class Englishman in this book, and in late-Victorian culture in general, signals the breakdown of national boundaries. The heart of darkness invades what became known as "Darkest England."[20] This metaphoric contamination of Anglo-Irish and Anglo-Indian, as well as Anglo-Saxon, populations appears frequently in late-Victorian literature. As Patrick Brantlinger asserts:

> Not only do stereotypes of natives and savages degenerate toward the ignoble and the bestial in late Victorian thinking, however; so do the seemingly contrasting images of European explorers, traders, and colonizers. . . . Robinson Crusoe held out manfully against the cannibals. . . . [L]ate Victorian literature is filled with *backsliders* who like Conrad's Kurtz themselves become white savages. (italics added)[21]

In the nineteenth century, the classification of animals changed. During this period, animals, like women, were divided into two categories: domestic (owned) and wild. When, as was the case in Regent's Park beginning in 1840, animals were arranged taxonomically, the exhibits showed "nature not only confined and restrained, but interpreted and ordered."[22] Of course, as has been suggested earlier, the absolute division between wild and tame is logically inconsistent, and therefore, difficult to maintain. Thus, anxiety remained about the measure of control one had over other creatures.

The numerous injunctions against ill-bred dogs and the negative descriptions of animal hybrids were similar to injunctions against the creation of human hybrids at the end of the century. Darwin made these connections explicit when he wrote, "the dichotomy between domesticated

---

[19] Patrick Brantlinger quoted in Howard L. Malchow, *Gothic Images of Race in Nineteenth-Century Britain* (Palo Alto, Calif.: Stanford University Press, 1996).

[20] This refers to the many texts that employ the metaphor of an ominous dark cloud over England, including Dickens's *Bleak House*, Booth's *In Darkest England* (the title originally from Blake), Conrad's *Heart of Darkness*, and others too numerous to name.

[21] Patrick Brantlinger, *Rule of Darkness: British Literature and Imperialism, 1830–1914* (Ithaca, N.Y.: Cornell University Press, 1988), p. 39.

[22] Ritvo, *Animal Estate*, p. 218.

animals and wild animals is similar to that between the civilized and the savage human societies. The wildness often shown by hybrids of domestic species had the same cause as the wickedness that characterized human half-breeds."[23] Clarity of category and purity of breed were to be preserved, since that was one way of maintaining a distinctive, linear (if mythical) history of the English race.

The injunction against some kinds of hybridity and forms of hybridizing and the sanction of others raises the question of value. It seems that professional breeders, in response to patron's demands and market pressures (some of which they helped to foster), were rewarded, while natural hybridization led to the production of mongrels — especially in animals. Indeed, scientific hybridizers or eugenicists thought that their man-supervised hybridizing could be beneficial to society; they frowned, however, on "brute" miscegenation as evil, as untamed nature mixed too promiscuously. Only white Englishmen were able to strike the proportionate balance between variation and stability.

Responding to anxiety aroused by Darwin's *The Origins of Species by Means of Natural Selection, of the Preservation of Favoured Races in the Struggle for Life,*[24] "hybridizers" became obsessed with asserting man's dominance over lower animals and sought to prove their superiority by controlling the breeding of others. Eugenicists attempted to solidify stereotypical figures, thereby fixing forms forever. This desire is read most clearly in the development of dog pedigrees and the pervasiveness of dog shows, the purpose of which, as Harriet Ritvo explains, was to "improve various breeds, display model specimens, and to discourage the breeding of mongrels."[25] Nevertheless, she continues, "the desire to triumph over obstacles mounted by nature may also explain the Victorian fascination with hybrids, which explicitly violated natural categories." The differences between these two reactions to hybrid mongrels become sharper when the division between man and animal is more distinct. That is, hybrid animals produced under man's control could be fascinating, whereas randomly produced or indiscriminate hybrid humans were usually read as threatening to the social order.

When monkey hides were displayed in a booth at the Great Exhibition of 1851, viewers noted that "it was painful to think of the suffering the poor

---

[23] Charles Darwin, *The Variation of Animals and Plants under Domestication* (London: J. Murray, 1868).

[24] Charles Darwin, *The Origins of Species by Means of Natural Selection, of the Preservation of Favoured Races in the Struggle for Life* (London: Penguin, 1859).

[25] Ritvo, *Animal Estate*, p. 101. Subsequent reference is noted in the text.

beasts must have undergone [yet some good was also shown since] the work of catching these animals civilizes the Africans."[26] This remark unwittingly provides evidence of the English propensity to equate civilized value with conquest. Some fifty years later, the 1908 Franco-British exhibit displayed "primitive" people of the British empire (including the Irish) as "savage spirits subdued."[27] [. . .]

For many in the nineteenth century, black people of African descent were imperfect, enslaved, animalistic creatures equated with Irish and other "low" species. In the growing field of racial science, Africa and Africans played key roles in England's economic, political, and cultural life. As England's empire expanded, the question posed by Matthew Arnold in his lectures on Celtic literature, "And We, What Are We? What is England?" became more difficult to answer, since it now included a host of others both culturally and geopolitically distant. For the Victorians, explains George Watson,

> race is more often a matter of cultural affinity and allegiance. . . . The Victorian interest in race is vastly in excess of that of any previous generation of Englishman, and it is the culminating of a long-developing interest that owes its beginnings to a fascination with regions and nations.[28]

We recall that Edward Dicey said, "in fact the instinct for self-preservation revolts at hybridism."[29] This negative view of "hybridity," understood here as a synonym for miscegenation, dominates future discussions about this phenomenon. If, as many feminist analyses of Victorian culture have argued, white women were demonized when they performed what were traditionally thought to be "manly projects," an obverse if similar process occurred when black men attended Royal College in the 1870s. In *Moreau*, Prendick damns the doctor by defining the beast people as "men whom you have infected with some bestial taint, men whom you have enslaved, and whom you still fear."[30] This statement reminds us of the nineteenth-century debates about the humanity of black people, who were thought to be both sickly and superior. [. . .]

---

[26] Thomas, *Man and the Natural World*, p. 30.

[27] Ibid. p. 30.

[28] George Watson, *The English Ideology: Studies in the Language of Victorian Politics* (London: Allen Lane, 1973), p. 200.

[29] Edward Dicey, *Egypt and England* (London: Darf, 1986), p. 208. First published 1881.

[30] Wells, *Dr. Moreau*, p. 92. Subsequent references are noted in the text.

The slavery debates, or more accurately, the debates about the humanity and civility of black people, continued throughout the century. When Prendick observes a "misshapen man, short, broad, clumsy, with crooked back, hairy neck, and a head sunk beneath his shoulders . . . [who] turned with animal swiftness," he is quick to point out that "the black face . . . was a singularly deformed one. The facial part projected, forming something dimly suggestive of a muzzle, and the huge half-open mouth as big white teeth as I had ever seen in a human mouth. His eyes were bloodshot at the edges." This creature is known most often as "the black-faced man." For example, when Prendick pauses "halfway up the ladder, [he] looks back . . . at the grotesque ugliness of this black-faced creature." This creature is called "it" or the "black." Its external features are its most relevant attribute. Its loss of gendered humanity transforms it into "stark inhumanity."

Chapter 11, "The Hunting of the Man," makes explicit Prendick's implicit racialist perspective, for it is in this section that he encounters the simian creature he names "Ape-Man." This encounter with another creature who "walks upright and possesses language"—whose English accent was strangely good—is nonetheless labeled "far from human heritage." The metaphoric use of temporal and spatial distance invokes the great chain of being, or the hierarchical scale of gradation that clearly delineated the different (and distinct) relation of each "type." Since "nature made no leaps," each creature was said to have a fixed place on the scale. Prendick is able to confront his past ancestry when he meets the ape-man. This affront from the past causes confusion because the separation is eerily indistinct; and yet, Prendick sees his own essential character in these confrontations. [. . .]

The ape-man calls himself "a five man," in reference to his digits, and persistently compares himself to Prendick by pointing out their physical similarities. Yet Moreau's monkey man with five digits merely mimes speech as opposed to being fully articulate. We remember that Prendick's own speech becomes broken when he is on the island. The distinction between "broken beast speech" and pure English prose, or the division between hybrid (substandard) and proper (standard) English grammar, appears in this text as the contested site of language.

Dr. Moreau tells Prendick that the first man he made was from a gorilla. He "thought the gorilla-brain was a fair specimen of the negroid type. I made the thing read the alphabet and taught him the rudiments of English." The emphasis on the brain and on negroid types is a direct paraphrase of racialist, nineteenth-century scientific naturalism that, as Peter Bowler describes, "popularized the view that a person's character was determined by the physical structure of his or her brain—not by a spiritual entity."[31] The various spurious investigations conducted by phrenologists, craneologists, and other nineteenth-century scientists resulted in added "evidence" for the vast chasm that divided human races by promoting the polygenetic origins of the world.

Among the most sophisticated of these theorists was Houston Chamberlain. Chamberlain had no problems with humankind's animalistic nature. Indeed, he rejected the notion that humans were completely unrelated to animals purely by virtue of "reason." Rather, he believed that people's ability to create "symbolic truths" placed them above other animals on a graded scale. Martin Woodroffe notes that, "For Chamberlain, in contrast to Darwin, the most striking characteristic of Nature was the permanency of form; [he believed] that the natural rule was conformity to type. [For him] race was a gestalt; miscegenation led to loss of gestalt, hence loss of life."[32]

The composer Samuel Coleridge-Taylor, himself racially mixed, held a different opinion:

> It is amazing that grown-up, and presumably educated, people can listen to such primitive and ignorant nonsense-mongers. . . . An arrogant white man . . . dared to say to the great Dumas: "And I hear you actually have negro blood in you!" Yes, said the witty writer; my father was a mulatto, his father a negro, and his father a monkey. My ancestry began where yours ends![33]

This clever reversal of the descent of humankind was an exception to the dominant beliefs recorded elsewhere. As we have seen, a majority of Victorians popularly accepted the belief that hybridity was one of the worst aspects of modern England. Even Karl Marx adhered to this conservative view when he described his intellectual rival, Ferdinand Lassalle, as follows:

> It is now perfectly clear to me that, as the shape of his head and the growth of his hair indicate, he is descended from the negroes who joined the flight of Moses from Egypt, unless his mother or grandmother on the father's side were crossed with a nigger. This union of Jew and German on

[31] Peter Bowler, *The Mendelian Revolution: The Emergence of Hereditarian Concepts in Modern Science and Society* (Baltimore, Md.: Johns Hopkins University Press, 1989), p. 153.

[32] Martin Woodroffe, "Racial Theories of History and Politics: The Example of H. S. Chamberlain," in *Nationalist and Racialist Movements in Britain and Germany Before 1914*, eds. Paul Kennedy and Anthony Nicolls (London: Macmillan Publishers, 1981), p. 146–47.

[33] Samuel Coleridge-Taylor quoted in Jane Beckett and Deborah Cherry, eds., *The Edwardian Era* (London: Phaidon Press and Barbican Art Gallery, 1987), p. 49.

a negro basis was bound to produce an extraordinary hybrid. The importunity of the fellow is also negroid.[34]

In the first volume of his socialist utopian trilogy, entitled *Anticipations,* Wells imagined that Jews would intermarry and "cease to be a physically distinct element in human affairs in a century or so."[35] Along with his or her physical traits, the Jew would also lose his or her characteristic usury. The belief that both distinct physical and social traits were specifically *racial* traits grew out of the polygenesist view of humankind. Here, Wells scapegoats the Jews for their propensity to interbreed, in direct contrast to Disraeli's or George Eliot's earlier assertions that the Hebrews were "that unmixed race of unsullied idiosyncrasy."[36]

Anticipations exemplifies the worst of the racist attitudes propounded in the late-nineteenth century. As Wells writes:

those swarms of black, and brown, and dirty-white and yellow people, who do not come into the new needs of efficiency? Well, the world is a world, not a charitable institution, and I take it they will have to go. The whole tenor and meaning of the world as I see it, is that they will have to go. So far as they fail to develop sane, vigorous and distinctive personalities for the great world of the future, it is their portion to die out and disappear.[37]

Wells sees the "dirty-white" beings as an insane swarm, as weak and undifferentiated personalities who will not have a place in the world of the future. A similar sentiment is expressed by this pronouncement: "Negroes in the Soudan are as black as ebony, not at all like the sickly hybrids one sees on Oxford Street" (*OED*). This statement echoes the ideology of the "pure" primitive advanced by *Dr. Jekyll and Mr. Hyde, The Picture of Dorian Gray,* and *The Island of Dr. Moreau.* The visible markers of race are kept inviolate in these texts as a means of keeping confusion, deception, and hypocrisy at bay. [...]

---

[34] Karl Marx in an 1862 letter to Friedrich Engels quoted in Watson, *The English Ideology,* p. 211. Engels agreed with Marx's description of their rival, Lassalle, that the latter's "thirst to push his way into polite society, *de parvenir,* to smear over the dirty Breslau Jew, for appearance's sake, with grease and paint, was always revolting" (ibid.). Engels's comments here reconstitute the discussion about the parvenue players and actresses who were allied with "painted ladies."

[35] H. G. Wells, *Anticipations of the Reaction of Mechanical and Scientific Progress Upon Human Life and Thought* (London: Chapman and Hill, 1901) p. 317.

[36] Benjamin Disraeli, *Coningsby, or the New Generation* (London: Penguin Books, 1983), p. 12.

[37] Wells, *Anticipations,* p. 317.

CHRONOLOGY

Science, Scientists, and Novelists

1794   Erasmus Darwin publishes the first volume of *Zoönomia; or, The Laws of Organic Life.*

1797   Mary Shelley born to feminist writer Mary Wollstonecraft and political theorist and novelist William Godwin; mother dies shortly after from complications of childbirth; father remarries four years later.

1802   Humphry Davy becomes professor of chemistry at London's Royal Institution; begins series of public experiments in electricity and chemistry.

1808   Goethe publishes *Faust* Part I, foundation text for Western warnings about "overreaching" in the search for knowledge.

1814   Mary Godwin and Percy Bysshe Shelley elope to Switzerland.

1816   Mary Shelley bears a son, William; travels with Percy to Geneva; reads Davy's publications; begins in June to write *Frankenstein*. After the suicide of Shelley's wife, Mary and Percy marry.

1818   First edition of *Frankenstein* published.

1822   Percy Shelley drowns, leaving Mary with four children.

1826   Mary Shelley publishes *The Last Man*, which is both a roman à clef still struggling with the loss (and flaws) of Shelley and Byron, and a key early text in the nineteenth century's fantasies about "degeneration."

1830   Charles Lyell publishes first volume of *Principles of Geology*, assembling evidence for the "uniformitarian" position that presently observable forces acting over huge expanses of time are sufficient to account for all phenomena.

1831 Revised (third) edition of *Frankenstein* published.

Michael Faraday begins the experiments serialized in *Experimental Researches* that establish him as the century's central figure in the analysis of electricity.

Darwin sets sail on *The Beagle;* observations on that voyage form the theoretical basis of his future work.

1844 Robert Chambers publishes *Vestiges of the Natural History of Creation.*

1850 Tennyson publishes *In Memoriam,* which makes the struggle between faith and doubt, insights from religion and science, a central concern of art.

1851 Mary Shelley dies in London at age 53, after writing six novels and numerous journals, stories, and biographies.

1859 After twenty years of study and rewriting, Darwin publishes *The Origin of Species.*

1860 Thomas Henry Huxley debates Bishop Wilberforce at Oxford on *The Origin of Species.*

1866 Herbert George Wells born in Bromley Village near London to lower-middle-class shopkeeping parents.

1871 Darwin publishes *The Descent of Man and Selection in Relation to Sex.*

1873 James Clerk Maxwell's *Treatise on Electricity and Magnetism* formulates unified theory of forces.

1884 After a series of apprenticeships and clerkships, the education-hungry Wells wins a scholarship to the Normal School of Science in London; studies with Thomas Henry Huxley.

1893 Thomas Henry Huxley's Romanes lecture, published as "Evolution and Ethics."

1895 Max Nordau publishes *Degeneration.*

Sigmund Freud's *Studies in Hysteria,* the first of a series of pathbreaking attempts to document the materialist and physiological basis of the psyche.

Wells's first novel, *The Time Machine,* published.

1896 First edition of *The Island of Doctor Moreau* published.

1901 Death of Queen Victoria.

1905 Wells publishes *Kipps*, a novel of the plight of the late Victorian genteel poor, as well as *A Modern Utopia*, a fable about a world created on the doctrine of the "Rise of Man."

Albert Einstein writes three papers, reflecting on the theories of Faraday and Maxwell, that establish the theory of relativity and the quantum theory of radiation.

1914 World War I begins.

1924 Wells revises and writes preface for *The Island of Doctor Moreau* as part of the "Atlantic Edition" of his Collected Works.

1938 Orson Welles's radio broadcast of Wells's 1898 novel *War of the Worlds* causes wave of panic in the United States. Wells contributes to English artistic community's efforts to aid refugee writers and intellectuals from Germany and Eastern Europe.

1945 Explosion of atomic bomb ends World War II.

1946 H. G. Wells dies just before his eightieth birthday, author of more than one hundred books of fiction, history, polemic and education.

WORKS CITED

Baudrillard, Jean. *Simulacra and Simulation*. 1981. Trans. Sheila Faria Glaser. Ann Arbor, MI: U of Michigan P, 1994.

Burke, Edmund. *A Philosophical Enquiry into the Origin of our Ideas of the Sublime and Beautiful*. 1757. Ed. James T. Boulton. Notre Dame, IN: U of Notre Dame P, 1968.

Gilbert, Sandra, and Susan Gubar. *The Madwoman in the Attic: The Woman Writer and the Nineteenth-Century Literary Imagination*. New Haven, CT: Yale UP, 1979.

Gissing, George. *The Nether World*. 1889. New York: Oxford UP, 1992.

Greenslade, William. *Degeneration, Culture and the Novel 1880 – 1940*. New York: Cambridge UP, 1994.

Hardy, Thomas. *Jude the Obscure*. 1895. New York: W. W. Norton & Co, 1978.

Kipling, Rudyard. *The Second Jungle Book*. 1895. New York: Oxford UP, 1987.

Levine, George. *The Realistic Imagination: English Fiction from Frankenstein to Lady Chatterley*. Chicago, IL: U of Chicago P, 1981.

MacKenzie, Norman and Jeanne. *The Time Traveller: The Life of H. G. Wells*. London: Weidenfeld and Nicolson, 1973.

Mellor, Anne K. "Choosing a Text of *Frankenstein* to Teach." *Approaches to Teaching Shelley's "Frankenstein"*. Ed. Stephen C. Behrendt. New York: MLA, 1990.

———. *Mary Shelley: Her Life, Her Fiction, Her Monsters*. New York: Methuen, 1988.

Moretti, Franco. *Signs Taken for Wonders: Essays in the Sociology of Literary Forms*. Trans. Susan Fischer, David Forgacs, and David Miller. New York: Verso, 1988.

Morus, Iwan Rhys. *Frankenstein's Children: Electricity, Exhibition, and Experiment in Early-Nineteenth-Century London*. Princeton, NJ: Princeton UP, 1998.

Nordau, Max. *Degeneration*. 1895. Trans. George L. Mosse. New York: Howard Fertig, 1968.

Parrinder, Patrick, and Robert Philmus, eds. *H. G. Wells's Literary Criticism*. Totowa, NJ: Barnes and Noble, 1980.

Philmus, Robert. *The Island of Doctor Moreau: A Variorum Text*. Athens, GA: U of Georgia P, 1993.

Roszak, Theodore. *The Memoirs of Elizabeth Frankenstein*. New York: Random House, 1995.

Shattuck, Roger. *The Forbidden Experiment: The Story of the Wild Boy of Aveyron*. New York: Farrar Straus Giroux, 1980.

Spivak, Gayatri Chakravorty. "Three Women's Texts and a Critique of Imperialism." *"Race," Writing, and Difference*. Ed. Henry Louis Gates, Jr. Chicago, IL: U of Chicago P, 1986.

Stewart, Garrett. *Dear Reader: The Conscripted Audience in Nineteenth-Century British Fiction*. Baltimore, MD: The Johns Hopkins UP, 1996.

Stover, Leon, ed. *The Island of Doctor Moreau: A Critical Text of the 1896 London First Edition, with an Introduction and Appendices*. Jefferson, NC: McFarland & Company, Inc., 1996.

Wells, H. G. *H. G. Wells's Literary Criticism*. Ed. Patrick Parrinder and Robert Philmus. Totowa, NJ: Barnes & Noble Books, 1980.

Young, G. M. *Victorian England: Portrait of an Age*. New York: Oxford UP, 1964.

FOR FURTHER READING

Baldick, Chris. *In Frankenstein's Shadow: Myth, Monstrosity, and Nineteenth Century Writing*. Oxford: Clarendon P, 1987.

Botting, Fred. *Making Monstrous: Frankenstein, Criticism, Theory*. Manchester: Manchester UP, 1991.

Forry, Steven Earl. *Hideous Progenies: Dramatizations of "Frankenstein" from Mary Shelley to the Present*. Philadelphia, PA: U of Pennsylvania P, 1990.

Fried, Michael. "Impressionist Monsters: H. G. Wells's 'The Island of Dr Moreau.'" *Frankenstein: Creation and Monstrosity*. Ed. Stephen Bann. London: ReaktionBooks Ltd., 1994.

Hassler, Donald M. *The Comedian as the Letter D: Erasmus Darwin's Comic Materialism*. The Hague: Martinus Hijhoff, 1973.

Huntington, John. *The Logic of Fantasy: H. G. Wells and Science Fiction*. New York: Columbia UP, 1982.

Parrinder, Patrick. *Shadows of the Future: H. G. Wells, Science Fiction and Prophecy*. Liverpool: Liverpool UP, 1995.

Reed, John. "The Vanity of Law in *The Island of Doctor Moreau*." *H. G. Wells Under Revision*, Ed. Patrick Parrinder and Christopher Rolfe. London: Associated UP, 1990.

CREDITS